Reframing
Theology and Film

Reframing
Theology and Film

New Focus
for an Emerging Discipline

Robert K. Johnston, editor

B
Baker Academic
Grand Rapids, Michigan

Published by Baker Academic
a division of Baker Publishing Group
P.O. Box 6287, Grand Rapids, MI 49516-6287
www.bakeracademic.com

Printed in the United States of America

Library of Congress Cataloging-in-Publication Data
Reframing theology and film : new focus for an emerging discipline cultural exegesis /
    Robert K. Johnston, editor.
        p.   cm.
    Includes bibliographical references and index.
    ISBN 10: 0-8010-3240-7 (pbk.)
    ISBN 978-0-8010-3240-0 (pbk.)
    1. Motion pictures—Religious aspects. I. Johnston, Robert K., 1945– II. Title.
PN1995.5.R43 2007
261.5′7—dc22   2007026890

Method is not a set of rules to be followed meticulously by a dolt. It is a framework for collaborative creativity.

Bernard Lonergan, *Method in Theology*

The surface meaning lies open before us and charms beginners. Yet the depth is amazing, my God, the depth is amazing. To concentrate on it is to experience awe.

Augustine, *Confessions*

Contents

Section 4: Engaging the Experience of the Viewer

Section 5: Reconsidering the Normative

Section 6: Making Better Use of Our Theological Traditions

Acknowledgments

This book is the outgrowth of a three-year consultation on theology and film sponsored by the Reel Spirituality Institute at Fuller Theological Seminary and funded by the Henry Luce Foundation, Michael Gilligan, president. The generous provision from the Luce Foundation allowed fifteen scholars, church leaders, and filmmakers from Europe and the United States to come together to share ideas and to strategize on the discipline of theology and film. These gatherings, which were held on the campus of Fuller Seminary in Pasadena, California, allowed for a unique community of discourse to be formed. We, as contributors to this volume, wish to thank the Luce Foundation for this contribution to an important emerging discipline.

Collections of essays by disparate scholars often suffer from a lack of cohesion. However, the opportunity to discuss together the future of the discipline before beginning our research and writing, and then to hear the results of one another's reflection and research in draft form, allowed the participants to truly be engaged in a common project. It even allowed us to identify several additional areas of research that extended beyond the expertise of the initial group and to enfold the work of other senior scholars into the final project while maintaining a collective voice.

This book would also not have been possible without the support of the Brehm Center for Worship, Theology, and the Arts at Fuller Theological Seminary, J. Frederick Davison, executive director. Its community on campus of several hundred graduate students, faculty, and staff, all committed to theology and the arts, is perhaps singular in size and scope among graduate institutions in English-speaking countries. The center provides a rich resource for dialogue and reflection. Nick Connell and Matt Webb, two students in the program, as well as staff members at Fuller, provided invaluable logistical support for the on-campus consultations. Catherine Barsotti, my partner in teaching, writing, and marriage, was the coordinator for the consultations as well as an active participant in the dialogue. Three of my doctoral students—Tim Basselin, Nelleke Bosshardt, and Tony Mills—provided helpful backup and recorded the sessions. And Brian Pounds, my graduate research assistant, provided valuable editorial assistance as the various essays were brought together and put into a standard form. To all of these I give my thanks.

Notes on the Contributors

Mitch Avila is associate professor of philosophy at California State University, Fullerton, where he teaches political philosophy and aesthetics. His research focuses primarily on theories of global justice, including tolerance for nondemocratic societies and rights for religious minorities. Avila's interest in film derives from both its pedagogical value and its potential to reveal—and sometimes to obscure—the manifold abundance of reality.

Catherine M. Barsotti is a regular instructor at Centro Hispano de Estudios Teológicos in Bell Gardens, California, in the areas of theology, ethics, and spirituality. She is also an adjunct professor for Fuller Theological Seminary in Pasadena, California, in the Hispanic church ministries and online education departments. Together with Rob Johnston, she has been writing movie reviews for "The Covenant Companion" and "Faith@Work" for the last ten years. They also coauthored the book *Finding God in the Movies: 33 Films of Reel Faith* (2004), which won the Spiritus Award for best writing in theology and film.

Christopher Deacy is head of religious studies at the University of Kent (United Kingdom) and a member of the UK Theology, Religion and Popular Culture Network Group. A member of Interfilm, he has sat on the Ecumenical Jury of international film festivals at Locarno and Karlovy Vary. His publications include *Screen Christologies: Redemption and the Medium of Film* (2001), *Faith in Film: Religious Themes in Contemporary Cinema* (2005), and *Theology and Film: Challenging the Sacred/Secular Divide* (coauthored with Gaye Ortiz, 2007).

Craig Detweiler codirects the Reel Spirituality Institute at Fuller Theological Seminary, where he also teaches. Craig is a working screenwriter and documentarian and the former chair of Biola University's film and television program. He is the coauthor with Barry Taylor of *A Matrix of Meanings: Finding God in Pop Culture* (2003). As a cultural commentator, Craig has been featured in the *New York Times*, on CNN, and on National Public Radio.

Robert K. Johnston is professor of theology and culture at Fuller Theological Seminary, where he codirects the Reel Spirituality Institute and serves on the board of the City of Angels Film Festival. His publications include *Reel Spirituality: Theology and Film in Dialogue*, 2nd ed. (2006), which won the Spiritus Award for best writing in theology and film; *Useless Beauty: Ecclesiastes through the Lens of Contemporary Film* (2004); and *Finding God in the Movies: 33 Films of Reel Faith* (with Catherine Barsotti, 2004).

Terry Lindvall holds the C. S. Lewis Chair of Communication and Christian Thought at Virginia Wesleyan College. Formerly Mason Chair of Religious Studies at the College of William and Mary and visiting professor in film and theology at Duke University School of Divinity, he is the author of *The Silents of God* (2001) and *Sanctuary Cinema* (2007), as well as executive producer of "Cradle of Genius" and "Lost Letters of Faith."

Gerard Loughlin is professor of theology and religion at the University of Durham (United Kingdom), where he teaches systematic theology as well as religion and film. He is the author of *Alien Sex: The Body and Desire in Cinema and Theology* (2004), as well as "Cinéma Divinité: A Theological Introduction," in *Cinéma Divinité: Religion, Theology and the Bible in Film* (2005). Among his current projects is a theological study on the films of Andrei Tarkovsky.

John Lyden is professor and chair of religion at Dana College in Blair, Nebraska. He is the author of *Film as Religion: Myths, Morals, and Rituals* (2003), as well as numerous articles about film and religion. He is currently cochair of the Religion, Film, and Visual Culture Group of the American Academy of Religion.

Gordon Lynch is professor of sociology of religion at Birkbeck University of London and the author of *Understanding Theology and Popular Culture* (2005) and *The New Spirituality: An Introduction to Progressive Belief in the Twenty-first Century* (2007). He is co-chair of the Religion, Media, and Culture Group of the American Academy of Religion and lead convenor of the UK research network for Theology, Religion, and Popular Culture.

Clive Marsh is principal of the East Midlands Ministry Training Course and lectures in the school of education and the department of theology and religious studies at the University of Nottingham (United Kingdom). He coedited, with Gaye Ortiz, *Explorations in Theology and Film* (1997), and his more recent writings include *Cinema and Sentiment: Film's Challenge to Theology* (2004), *Christ in Focus: Radical Christocentrism in Christian Theology* (2005), *Christ in Practice: A Christology of Everyday Life* (2006), and *Theology Goes to the Movies* (2007).

Gaye Williams Ortiz teaches communication studies at Augusta State University in Georgia. She is the coeditor of two volumes: *Explorations in Theology and Film* (with Clive Marsh, 1997) and *Theology and Literature: Rethinking Reader Responsibility* (with Clara Joseph, 2006). Her latest book, *Theology and Film: Challenging the Sacred/Secular Divide*, is coauthored with Christopher Deacy and will be published in 2007.

Rose Pacatte, FSP, is director of the Pauline Center for Media Studies in Culver City, California, where she also teaches media literacy. A film/television columnist for *St. Anthony Messenger* and media editor for *Homiletics,* Sister Rose is the coauthor with Peter Malone, MSC, of the award-winning series of books on Scripture and film *Lights, Camera . . . Faith! A Movie Lectionary.* In 2006 she both edited *The Nativity Story: Contemplating Mary's Journeys of Faith* and wrote *The Nativity Story: A Film Study Guide for Catholics.* Her newest book, with coauthor Gretchen Hailer, RSHM, is *Media Mindfulness: Educating Teens about Faith and Media.*

Barry Taylor lives and works in Los Angeles. He wears many hats, teaching on the intersections between theology and popular culture at Fuller Theological Seminary and on advertising and creativity at Art Center College of Design in Pasadena, California. Taylor also writes music, composing film scores for movies, as well as writing pop songs for his own band. He is the coauthor of *A Matrix of Meanings: Finding God in Pop Culture* (with Craig Detweiler, 2003). As a Brit living in Los Angeles, he is constantly on the search for the perfect cup of tea.

Sara Anson Vaux, formerly adjunct professor of theology and film at Garrett-Evangelical Seminary, currently teaches religion and film at Northwestern University. Her courses, ranging from Kieślowski to French cinema to Dreyer to Eastwood, draw students from film, theater, journalism, philosophy, and religion departments. She speaks widely about movies, ethics, and spirituality, has authored *Finding Meaning at the Movies* (1999) and articles on international films, and promotes the need for critical analysis of film texts.

Rebecca Ver Straten-McSparran is director of the L.A. Film Studies Center, director of the City of Angels Film Festival, as well as a member of the planning committee of the Reel Spirituality Conference. She speaks on film and theological issues at conferences, seminars, and college campuses. She is also the pastor of an emerging church, Tribe of Los Angeles, and was previously pastor at First Congregational Church of Los Angeles.

Introduction:
Reframing the Discussion

ROBERT K. JOHNSTON

Theology and film as a field of inquiry is still in its infancy, less than three decades old—at least in its contemporary expression. Although there was theological reflection on film as early as Herbert Jump's 1910 pamphlet "The Religious Possibilities of the Motion Picture," and although in the late 1960s and early 1970s a few books were published that sought to establish a conversation between film and the church (e.g., Robert Konzelman's *Marquee Ministry: The Movie Theater as Church and Community Forum* [1971], William Jones's *Sunday Night at the Movies* [1967], Neil Hurley's *Theology through Film* [1970], and James Wall's *Church and Cinema* [1971]), there was no sustained interest in the topic prior to the 1980s. At the time, the unavailability of most movies after their initial screening was perhaps reason enough for film to be largely ignored as an ongoing conversation partner for theology. But caution and even skepticism by some in the church no doubt also played a role.

We can perhaps date the new era for theology and film studies as beginning in 1979. In that year George Atkinson revolutionized how one saw Hollywood movies by opening the first video rental store, making the ongoing viewing and re-viewing of movies a possibility. Although studios had for a few years been selling feature-length films on videocassette, their steep price meant that few bothered to buy them. Atkinson, however, saw a business opportunity, and with fifty films that he had purchased—*The Sound of Music* and *Butch Cassidy and the Sundance Kid* were two of them—he began renting films to eager customers. Technological and marketing advances followed at an escalating pace: the DVD with its extra features, Netflix, and the advent of movie downloads are three of the more significant.

The results have been staggering. Customers in the United States alone spent $45.7 billion on movies in 2005 and averaged seeing forty-five films. We in the West are a movie culture, and religious bodies and their theologians have necessarily taken note. As I argued in *Reel Spirituality*,

> movies function as a primary source of power and meaning for people throughout the world. Along with the church, the synagogue, the mosque, and the temple, they often provide people stories through which they can understand their lives. . . . There are, of course, places of worship that are vibrant and meaningful. But people both within the church and outside it recognize that movies are also providing primary stories around which we shape our lives. . . . Presenting aspects of their daily lives both intimate and profound [real and imagined], movies exercise our moral and religious imagination.[1]

Film has become our Western culture's major storytelling and myth-producing medium. As such it has begun to invite the best (and worst!) of our theological reflection.

As those in the field of theology and film began their work, they were spurred on by "readings" of a significant number of film "texts" (the terms perhaps betray an overly dependent use of literary models in these early stages of theology and film analysis, as Joseph Kickasola helpfully points out[2]). These movies might give expression to theological themes found in their own faith tradition or sacred texts, or perhaps even more radically, might be the occasion for an experience with the divine itself. As movies give expression to questions of meaning or portray possible answers, they have been perceived as being of interest to those in biblical and/or theological studies, as well as in religious studies more broadly.

The fact that theology and film studies is still in a developmental phase must also be seen in relation to other realities within the academy, particularly with regard to film itself. We forget that the granting of the first PhD in film studies is a recent event: it was probably the University of Southern California that, in the early 1960s, offered the first doctorate. According to the National Research Council, film studies itself is still considered an emerging discipline, with one observer labeling it a discipline of "ambiguous provenance" (i.e., study in cinema takes place in departments of modern language, theater, and communication, as well as in programs in comparative literature and cinema and media studies).[3]

When a focus on theology is added to the emerging field of film studies, making for an interdisciplinary study, matters become further complicated in the academy. Interdisciplinary study in theology and any of the arts has consistently struggled to find its place. The Divinity School of the University of Chicago pioneered an area of study in religion and literature in the 1950s, seeking to explore the reciprocal relations between the two. A few other institutions have followed its lead. Yet programs in theology/religion and the arts still remain at the margins of academic life in most institutions today. Thus, it is hardly a surprise that the field of theology and film remains within the academy of "ambiguous provenance," class offerings being found in a variety of departments—English, communication, religious studies, American studies, foreign language, and occasionally, film studies itself. There is no home base in the academy at present, even though the number of colleges and universities that include such studies somewhere in their curriculum continues to grow.

Despite its recent beginnings and disparate academic locations, the study of theology and film is attracting widespread interest. Books and Web sites are proliferating. Terry Lindvall's recent bibliography on religion/theology and film (2004–5) stretched to almost eighty pages, and at present there are fifty Christian Web sites and a dozen blogs that review films and offer resources for study and reflection. David Ford has now included a chapter titled "Theology and Film" (written by Jolyon Mitchell) in his recently published third edition of *The Modern Theologians*,[4] and sessions on the topic at the annual meetings of both the American Academy of Religion and the Society of Biblical Literature are regularly held. Despite its present limitations, few still question the importance of the discipline.

Yet problems remain. Have those in the field simply (and mistakenly) taken literature's understanding of narrative and applied it to film, reading the "text" of a film as we might a novel? Is the discipline of theology and film at present unduly influenced by popular culture, failing to take note of the excellence of less commercially viable movies and/or world cinema? Why have other cognate disciplines too often been ignored in the discussion? What about history, sociology, and philosophy, not to mention film studies itself? What is the theological value in focusing our reflection on the viewer of a film, and what happens affectively to the viewer as meaning is constructed? What place does "normative" analysis hold in the public arena? Is theology's normativity an impediment to film viewing and analysis? How might theologians escape the tendency to reduce film to an illustration of truth independently arrived at? And how might our interdisciplinary conversation be deepened by using the resources of theology and its rich tradition? Questions are easily multiplied, as one would expect of any new enterprise.

It is this situation of burgeoning interest in a significant new field, combined with the recognition of present limitations and inadequacies as to how the discipline is being practiced, that was the catalyst for bringing together over a three-year period a dozen leading scholars in the field, representative church leaders, and practicing filmmakers. The goal of the consultation was to discuss how the discipline of theology and film might be reframed for the next decade so that scholarship might better move forward. How should those in the field respond to pressing questions regarding scope, method, filmography, and theological underpinnings? Sponsored by the generosity of the Henry Luce Foundation, the consultation met twice (2004 and 2005) to assess current scholarship and address how the field might be strengthened, corrected, or changed.

An initial result of this deliberation was a major revision of my basic textbook for the field, *Reel Spirituality: Theology and Film in Dialogue* (2006). I am in debt to the careful criticism and positive suggestions of this group, as they both critiqued the first edition and provided helpful perspective regarding the change and development required to move the discipline to its next level of maturity.

A second result was the resolve to explore in greater depth particular means by which the discipline of theology and film might gain maturity as it moves forward in its endeavors. The third year of the consultation thus turned to a focus on particular problematic aspects of the discipline that were felt to be in need of strengthening, and essays were commissioned. This book is the result of these deliberations, a collection of essays by scholars presently working in the field. But even here, it is important to note the impact of practitioners, of those filmmakers and church leaders who helped shape the dialogue as they shared in the earlier consultations.[5] If the book reflects a particular bias, it is the filmmaker's commitment to let the film's narrative itself and our experience with it shape the conversation. Despite criticism from some quarters that such a narratological approach to film is naive and perhaps arbitrary, to talk about a film's meaning apart from the cinematic experience itself (its image, word, music) is to miss the heart of the enterprise.

Readers will note that the chapters of this book have been grouped together to make six larger sections. Each represents an aspect within theology and film studies in need of correction or strengthening in our view. In particular, the Luce consultation identified six needs: (1) to move beyond a literary paradigm; (2) to broaden the film selection, particularly to include world cinema; (3) to extend the interdisciplinary conversation beyond the disciplines of film studies and theology; (4) to take into account the role of the viewer in meaning formation; (5) to reaffirm normative criticism; and (6) to bring insights from the wider theological tradition into the theology and film conversation. Here then is a self-reflective critique by those working in the field. What follows is what we believe necessary to successfully reframe the discipline.

Section 1: Moving Beyond a "Literary" Paradigm

Some have criticized the discipline of theology and film for its heavy concentration on narrative.[6] But this is to misunderstand the nature of the problem, as filmmakers Craig Detweiler and Barry Taylor argue in their essays that follow.[7] It is not story per se but the reduction of film interpretation to literary techniques that is the problem. After all, the vast majority of commercial film is narrative in structure, rooted in storytelling. But how that story is to be understood needs redefinition and expansion in many of the present descriptions of movies by theology and film critics. For movies are both "pictured" and "heard," not just described. Thus, there needs to be an expansion of method to include the visual and the aural, if theology and film is to escape its literary captivity.

Detweiler, a screenwriter, seeks to correct the abstract nature of much film theory by turning to film practice—to how movies are made and seen. His interest, in particular, is how the use of images helps viewers better understand the power and meaning of a film story. His goal, like Taylor's, is to understand the film as "text" in more than its literary sense: "film is sight, sound, and story; images, music, and dialogue." But rather than concentrate on music, Detweiler argues in particular for "a more visual approach to theology and film" criticism. He believes that the visual elements of film (lighting, cinematography, set design) must be reconnected to one's larger interpretive practices if both film theory and "film and theology" are to achieve renewed relevance.

In a parallel essay, Taylor recognizes that "the 'text' of any given film comprises at least three intersecting issues: image, story, and sound, all working together both to create context and to give meaning to the tale being told." Making use of film music theory, Taylor (a film composer) argues that music enhances narrative, projects emotion, provides pace and shape to the story, and literally colors the movie, aiding in the meaning-making process. It is the communication link between screen and audience. Moreover, with the introduction of pop music into cinema, another opportunity for connection with the story is achieved, the viewer's own previous experience with the music now acting as an independent source of identity construction and connection.

Section 2: Broadening Our Film Selection

A second critique of the current practices of theology and film has to do with the small and repetitive number of mainstream movies that are typically used by those working in the field. (Brent Plate labels this "the Hollywoodcentrism that resides within religion and film circles."[8]) Writing about *The Shawshank Redemption, Star Wars, The Da Vinci Code,* and *The Matrix,* while appropriate, is tiresomely overdone. Immediately following the release of *The Passion of the Christ,* five books of essays by scholars working in the field came out.[9] None sold well. But the concentration on popular movies by theology and film scholars only mirrors the viewing patterns of those in the West. It is unfortunately true that in 2005, the most successful film from outside the United States made a modest $17.1 million in the United States—the 116th biggest release—and only ten foreign language films even broke the $1 million mark. Even for Netflix, only 5.5 percent of the movies shipped in 2005 were world cinema.[10] Thus, the discipline of theology and film is presently dominated by the patterns of popular culture more generally.

It is this reality that both Gaye Williams Ortiz and Sara Anson Vaux challenge.[11] In their essays, they argue that the discipline of theology and film is not using the best films for our conversation and suggest that world cinema and other thematically rich films need greater inclusion in its filmography. Although world cinema is undervalued popularly, academically, and religiously, Ortiz argues that this was not always so, nor should this pattern be maintained. World cinema has the ability to broaden our dialogue, to help Americans in particular escape our provincialism and cultural isolation. It can allow for an openness and receptivity toward the other. Using the insights of Miroslav Volf, Ortiz calls on those working in the field of religion/theology and film to overcome the racist tendencies inherent in such exclusion, and to embrace otherness.

Vaux's essay similarly argues for the inclusion of world cinema, but her reasons are distinct from those of Ortiz. Her point is aesthetic as well as ethical. What is it, she asks, that is "worth our emotional, professional, and recreational time"? Those working in the field should "recommend a broad sampling of movies that reward repeated viewings and close analysis, yet challenge the culture." "In our field," she writes, "we should promote not only a wide range of movies but also better movies, movies that possess high quality as art as well as entertainment, and movies that make us better people."

Section 3: Extending Our Conversation Partners

Theology need not and in fact should not be the sole conversation partner with film, though this has too often been the case in the initial decades of theology and film criticism. Rooted in the human story, film invites a dialogue with other areas of the arts and social sciences, as film studies has long recognized. Think, for example, of the widespread use of psychoanalytic and Marxist approaches to film by film scholars. Such an appropriation of social scientific categories, however, has too often been absent from theology and film dialogue, at least until recently. But perhaps things are changing.

Gordon Lynch, in his chapter, suggests that there is beginning to be "a deepening awareness among some theologians" of the value of interdisciplinary engagement with media and popular culture. As an illustration of the value of such scholarship, he focuses on how "theological readings of film can be usefully informed by debates concerning contemporary cultural values and beliefs in the context of the sociological study of religion." In support of his thesis, Lynch persuasively demonstrates how the subjective turn in spirituality and religion in the West provides a framework for a theological analysis of Hollywood cinema. He argues that, like the novel in the eighteenth century, film functions today as both a cultural tool for nurturing personal emotional and aesthetic experiences and a cultural text that celebrates the turn to the self.

Terry Lindvall's chapter asserts that church history holds the promise for providing a rich cross-fertilization with studies in film history. Unfortunately, this has happened too rarely: modern film histories typically neglect the religious dimensions in film, and vice versa. Nevertheless, writes Lindvall, "the historical interpretation of films invites, or rather demands, a religious lens that helps bring the narratives and the symbols into focus." Only as a film is put into both its larger religious and historical contexts can its meaning be more fully understood by the theology and film student.

Section 4: Engaging the Experience of the Viewer

Much of theology and film criticism in its initial stage has been devoted to thematic criticism. Movies have been chosen for critical reflection because they provide perspective on Scripture,[12] or because they teach Christian truth.[13] And though such content-oriented perspectives, when sensitively done, have their place both in theology and in film studies, they are also misleading because they largely overlook the experience of film watching itself. As Clive Marsh reminds us, we "need to attend to what films actually do, rather than what religion scholars and theologians would like to think that they do." As the study of theology and film continues, it must take the viewer's experience much more seriously if it is to be true both to film as a medium of communication/communion, and to theology, which is also concerned with first-order experience.

Receptor-oriented criticism is a wide-ranging field, but in this volume, three of the participants in the Luce consultation take up aspects of this crucial perspective.[14] Clive Marsh follows up on his important initial probing in the field by reporting on a study of moviegoers in the United Kingdom in 2004.[15] While these individuals said that they went to the cinema "for fun," often "meaning making" was taking place. This meaning making was not necessarily explicitly theological or even fully coherent; it worked first by affective means. But an exchange of views was taking place, with the boundary between entertainment and education proving to be fluid. Rebecca Ver Straten-McSparran, in her chapter, further unpacks the viewer's experience by turning to the insights of Michael Polanyi, particularly his recognition of a "tacit" dimension to our knowing, one rooted in intuition and imagination. Understood in this way, movie viewing requires "faith and belief and personal commitment." As such, it has the potential to shape viewers' lives—to transform our thinking and action. This is the experience, she observes, of many who see the movie *Crash*.

Lastly, Catherine Barsotti provides an important initial ethnographic study in viewer-oriented criticism by asking how US Latinas view movies in which they themselves are reputedly being portrayed (e.g., *Bread and Roses*, 2000; *Spanglish*, 2004; and *Quinceañera*, 2006). She asks, How do these films "act as windows, however tinted, to reflect on the 'reel' portrayed and the 'real' experienced by a group of [Protestant] Latina women"? Can such movies "help us see what we sometimes can't say," and in the process allow us to "speak and understand our own stories"?

Section 5: Reconsidering the Normative

Initial efforts in theology and film criticism have often either erred on the side of didacticism, reducing the movie under consideration to mere illustration, or have remained too cautious, taking readers to the door of theological conversation, but failing to walk through that door for fear of becoming dogmatic.[16] But the subject of film and its experience for the viewer is ultimately too important not to be completed from a theological perspective, as three of the essayists in our consultation affirm.

Using the model of interreligious dialogue, theologian John Lyden argues that popular film is sufficiently religion-like to merit theological engagement. Rather than ignore popular culture, theologians should engage it in open, yet evaluative, conversation, just as they might converse with those who are from other religious traditions. Recognizing the power of movies to influence and express our values and beliefs, as well as to provide our myths, morals, and rituals, theology and film critics will through such engagement with film find help in clarifying their own theological perspective.

Mitch Avila, a philosopher who regularly teaches in the area of film, finds help in empirically informed theories of film emotion for normative, critical film analysis (does it generate, promote, or otherwise foster morally praiseworthy behaviors, beliefs, and attitudes?). By prefocusing our attention on certain features, movies activate emotional responses "while at the same time interpreting what the emotions mean and validating some coping mechanisms over others." If this is true, argues Avila, then film can either draw our attention to the wrong aspects of a situation, or it can "help us cope with negative emotions and relive (and revive) endangered ones." That is, film invites, even demands, our normative attention.

Christopher Deacy makes a complementary point by looking at how film enables us "to (re-)examine, critique, and challenge the efficacy of the work of a number of prominent twentieth-century theologians." Deacy finds film capable of facilitating quite sophisticated theological inquiry. In the movie *Christmas with the Kranks*, for example, Deacy discovers a living expression of Bonhoeffer's "world come of age." The movie does not just illustrate; it also contributes to serious theological discussion of how we might need a "religionless Christianity" today. Similarly, *Big Fish*, though not an explicitly theological film, can function as a corrective to Bultmann's overly zealous demythologizing. By helping us deal firsthand with life, such movies critique and challenge various theological paradigms, helping the church facilitate and fine-tune its theological conversation.

Section 6: Making Better Use of Our Theological Traditions

The consultation of theology and film scholars, filmmakers, and church leaders identified the need in future theology and film scholarship to make better use of their own theological traditions. Recognizing that film, like any work of art, demands first to be evaluated aesthetically, theology and film critics have often underappreciated the role their own theological tradition plays, or might play, in their critical work.

On the negative side, Sister Rose Pacatte describes well the twin influences of Puritan and Jansenist theology on the creation of the ratings system that continues to influence how Christians judge movies today. Too focused on sin to be seriously receptive to the arts, their theological legacy has caused both Protestants and Catholics to focus on a film's content rather than its context, on its data rather than its meaning. The church's present focus on content analysis—on a film's representation of sexuality, violence, and language—results "in the loss of the soul (i.e., the context of the story)" and blunts "our ability to engage in parables—stories and storytelling—the very way Jesus communicated meaningfully with the people of his times."[17]

Gerard Loughlin, on the other hand, finds in the Orthodox understanding of the iconic a key to how film "can attain to the power of religious parable," how it might be understood as a spiritual medium, "the occasion of hierophany." In particular, he turns to the Russian filmmaker Andrei Tarkovsky in order to explore the possibility of a truly spiritual cinema, "a way into the light that resides in the dark; a glimpse of the invisible in the visible, in the depths of the seen." Loughlin provides a sensitive "reading of the Tarkovskian image, an exercise in cinematic theology." Through his film images, Tarkovsky seeks not a symbol of the truth, but something more immediate, "something that does not point away from itself, but into which we are led." Though they are just themselves, paradoxically his images disclose more than just themselves. There is, or can be, in film an immanent transcendence.

Finally, as a contributor as well as the book's editor, I explore the potential of using medieval Christianity's fourfold method of biblical interpretation as a hermeneutical key for understanding how a film viewer might "see different levels of reality in one image or one situation."[18] Here might be a fruitful description of the process by which a film expresses theological truth—a movie has not only a literal but also a spiritual meaning. As Dante realized, the allegorical method of the monastics described "the very logic of the imagination." It is not just the informative but also the transformative that matters. Meaning is rooted in the particular, the givenness of the story. But it is not enough to know merely what a movie "says." One must also know what it means allegorically, ethically, and spiritually.

Notes

1. Robert K. Johnston, *Reel Spirituality: Theology and Film in Dialogue*, 2nd ed. (Grand Rapids: Baker Academic, 2006), 13.

2. Joseph Kickasola, *The Films of Krzysztof Kieslowski: The Liminal Image* (New York: Continuum, 2004), xiii.

3. Krin Gabbard, "Cinema and Media Studies: Snapshot of an 'Emerging' Discipline," *Chronicle of Higher Education,* Chronicle Review, February 17, 2006, http://chronicle.com/weekly/v52/i24/24b01401.htm.

4. Jolyon Mitchell, "Theology and Film," in *The Modern Theologians: An Introduction to Christian Theology since 1918*, ed. David F. Ford with Rachel Muers (Oxford: Blackwell, 2005), 736–59.

5. In particular, the presence of several leading filmmakers should be noted. Norman Stone (director, *Shadowlands, Man Dancin'*) and Brad King (producer, *Teknolust*) joined essayists Barry Taylor (a film music director and composer, e.g., *The Third Miracle*) and Craig Detweiler (a screenwriter, e.g., *Extreme Days*) in arguing that our discussion must be rooted concretely in the cinematic experience. Hollywood publicist and screenwriter Jonathan Bock, who markets studio movies to faith-based organizations; film educator and screenwriter Barbara Nicolosi, who runs a screenwriting workshop for faith-based writers; and Sally Morganthaler, a nationally known church consultant in worship and the arts, also participated in the multiyear discussion. Together with producer Ralph Winter (the *X-Men* and *Fantastic Four* series), who served as a consultant to the dialogue, these filmmakers and church leaders helped keep the discussion concrete and focused on the movies themselves.

6. Cf. Steve Nolan, "Understanding Films: Reading in the Gaps," in *Flickering Images: Theology and Film in Dialogue*, ed. Antony J. Clarke and Paul S. Fiddes (Oxford: Regent's Park College, 2005; Macon, GA: Smyth & Helwys, 2005), 25–48; and Melanie J. Wright, *Religion and Film: An Introduction* (London: I. B. Tauris, 2007).

7. Note the reflections on music's important role in cinema, in chap. 4 by Sara Vaux.

8. S. Brent Plate, ed., *Representing Religion in World Cinema: Filmmaking, Mythmaking, Culture Making* (New York: Palgrave Macmillan, 2003), 9.

9. S. Brent Plate, ed., *Re-Viewing "The Passion": Mel Gibson's Film and Its Critics* (New York: Palgrave Macmillan, 2004); Paula Fredriksen, ed., *On the Passion of the Christ: Exploring the Issues Raised by the Controversial Movie* (Berkeley: University of California Press, 2006); Timothy K. Beal and Tod Linafelt, eds., *Mel Gibson's Bible: Religion, Popular Culture, and The Passion of the Christ* (Chicago: University of Chicago Press, 2006); Kathleen E. Corley and Robert L. Webb, eds., *Jesus and Mel Gibson's "The Passion of the Christ": The Film, the Gospels and the Claims of History* (New York: Continuum, 2004); Shawn Landrers and Michael Berenbaum, eds., *After "The Passion" Is Gone: American Religious Consequences* (Walnut Creek, CA: AltaMira, 2004).

10. David Ansen and Ramin Setoodeh, "Lost in Translation," *Newsweek*, February 27, 2006, 52–54.

11. Note chap. 7 by Clive Marsh.

12. E.g., Robert Jewett, *Saint Paul Returns to the Movies: Triumph over Shame* (Grand Rapids: Eerdmans, 1999).

13. E.g., Doug Fields and Eddie James, *Videos That Teach 2* (Grand Rapids: Zondervan, 2002), or David Cunningham, *Reading Is Believing: The Christian Faith through Literature and Film* (Grand Rapids: Brazos, 2002).

14. Note chap. 5 by Gordon Lynch.

15. Cf. Clive Marsh, *Cinema and Sentiment: Film's Challenge to Theology* (Waynesboro, GA: Paternoster, 2004).

16. Brian Godawa's *Hollywood Worldviews: Watching Films with Wisdom and Discernment* (Downers Grove, IL: InterVarsity, 2002) might be an example of the first, while Roy Anker's otherwise superb book *Catching Light: Looking for God in the Movies* (Grand Rapids: Eerdmans, 2004) ultimately eschews the normative, remaining largely at the level of the descriptive.

17. For a discussion of the ratings system, readers should also note chap. 11 by Mitch Avila.

18. Cf. Flannery O'Connor, "The Nature and Aim of Fiction," in *Mystery and Manners*, ed. Sally and Robert Fitzgerald (New York: Farrar, Straus, and Giroux, 1969), 72–73: "The medieval commentators on Scripture found three kinds of meaning in the literal level of the sacred text. One they called the allegorical, in which one fact pointed to another. One they called the tropological, or moral, which had to do with what should be done. And one they called the anagogical, which had to do with the divine life and our participation in it. Although this was a method applied to biblical exegesis, it was also an attitude toward all of creation, and a way of reading nature which included most possibilities, and I think it is this enlarged view of the human scene that the fiction writer has to cultivate if he [or she] is ever going to write stories that have any chance of becoming a permanent part of our literature."

Introduction: Reframing the Discussion

Section I

Moving beyond a "Literary" Paradigm

1

Seeing and Believing

Film Theory as a Window into a Visual Faith

CRAIG DETWEILER

I asked several of my collaborators in this book to run through a mental Rolodex of scenes that stand out and stand up—on their own, as purely visual pleasures. This book began as a community project. Filmmakers and theologians, gathered around a love for God and a love for film, came together for two sessions of dialogue. We talked about our passions, shared our research, and tested our theories. When it came time to consider the visual power of film, I conducted an informal survey. "What cinematic images continue to haunt you, guide you, inspire you? What are the most beautiful moments you've seen in screen history?" Our most haunting images ranged from the angels circling the lovers' heads in F. W. Murnau's *Sunrise* (1927) to the "green section" of Zhang Yimou's epic Chinese action film, *Hero* (2004).[1] When I look through a list of the most popular films of all time (compiled by the fan-driven Internet Movie Database [IMDb]),[2] particular visual images also leap to mind:

Grasping a snow globe in *Citizen Kane*.

The rain pounds, puddles form, swords fly in *The Seven Samurai*.

Riding a nuclear warhead in *Dr. Strangelove*.

Benjamin and Elaine in the back of the bus in *The Graduate*.

Coconuts as horse hooves in *Monty Python and the Holy Grail*.

The boulder rolling toward Indiana Jones in *Raiders of the Lost Ark*.

The Band-Aid on the back of Marcellus's neck in *Pulp Fiction*.

The lure of a gold ring in *The Return of the King*.

The eyes on the Pale Man's hands in *Pan's Labyrinth*.

Some of the more memorable images are built upon hours of anticipation. They pay off story points planted by adept filmmakers. The memory of an entire film may be reduced to a single frame or an evocative frozen image. We relish the eerie spectacle of the *Titanic* sinking. We admire Butch Cassidy and the Sundance Kid heading toward certain death, guns blazing. We may even want to ride with Thelma and Louise in their convertible, as they soar off the plateau. Some of the more memorable images haunt us. I'd like to forget the Russian roulette in *The Deer Hunter*, the eating of a live squid in *Oldboy*, and the victim literally kicked to the curb in *American History X*. Yet we play the most inspiring scenes over and over in our heads. I never want to forget Christian's romantic serenade of Satine atop an elephant in *Moulin Rouge* or Bjork's transcendent affirmation, "I've Seen It All," amid her dire circumstances in *Dancer in the Dark*.

Why are certain scenes imprinted so concretely on our psyche? We remember every gesture and nuance. Recollection of the scene can cause us to laugh, cry, or wince at a moment's notice, even years after first experiencing it. Many have connected the psychic power of film to the principles of Freud or his disciple, Jacques Lacan. In some critical circles, film studies and psychoanalysis are nearly synonymous. The key questions remain, What gives images such power? And is that power to be feared? We have all witnessed the adverse effects when demagogues figure out how to harness it. Perhaps that is why admonitions against "graven images" remain atop the Ten Commandments. The abuse of images has led to repeated controversies within religious communities. Images are distrusted because of their ability to distract, deceive, or overwhelm. Yet why has God given us eyes to see and not just ears to hear? Can we not redeem our eyesight, especially in an image-driven era?

Moving beyond a "Literary" Paradigm

This chapter has one goal: to unpack the power of moving images. I will draw from two disciplines, both of which have relied primarily upon words. I aspire to rescue film theory from a literary paradigm. Then I want to explore film theory's potential to enhance the nascent discipline of theology and film. I recognize that such a tenuous arrangement could go bad. As in a love triangle in a gritty detective story, someone is bound to feel jilted. By the conclusion, somebody, maybe even *everybody*, could end up shot. Yet I take the risk of merging film theory with theology to free both disciplines from their bookish and elitist tendencies, which threaten to marginalize them. I admire Pauline Kael's groundbreaking ability to find a little art in apparent cinematic trash and to point out the trash often lurking amidst acclaimed art.[3] She echoes Jesus's upside-down approach to storytelling. He found goodness amidst the masses and generated anger amongst the elites. So why can't film theory reflect the populist roots of the medium it analyzes? A more visual approach to theology and film could help the emerging church forge a more integrated Christian practice, rooted in sight and sound, smells and bells, word and spirit.

A few things I don't want to do. I do not want to unspool the history of film theory.[4] I do not want to review the church's first iconoclast controversy. I do not want to chronicle the Protestant church's fear of images. Others have done each well.[5] They draw upon far more expertise in each of those complicated subjects than I possess.[6] When it comes to film theory, I recognize that I will be turning back the clock, concentrating on earlier theorists who are currently out of vogue. But just because the discipline has moved on doesn't mean it has arrived. Likewise, in theology, despite my desire to move toward a visual faith, I must consider people of faith's ongoing anxiety regarding images. We will never get to a mature understanding of "reel spirituality" without wading through the murky waters of church history. Yet I do not want to get bogged down in the muck of old skirmishes. Like Andy Dufresne in *The Shawshank Redemption*, I want to emerge on the far side of the prison of the past with my arms uplifted and my eyes open.

Theology's Fear of Images

Postmodern pilgrims must navigate a world where style trumps substance and images overwhelm words. Protestants, rooted in the valuable tradition of *sola scriptura*, are being challenged by our image-driven era.

Some may consider filmmaking an advanced form of idolatry. The more practical will purchase state-of-the-art sound systems and projectors for their sanctuaries. Iconoclastic attacks and uncritical embrace both have their blind spots. So how do we grasp the power of images without bowing down to the altar of IMAX?

My word-based faith may need to adopt a more sacramental approach to seeing and believing. Signs and symbols enhance Catholic and Orthodox worship. Candles, colors, and vestments (costumes) play important parts in Lutheran and Episcopalian liturgy. Sacramental churches are teaching sermon-centered Protestants how to worship with their eyes wide open.[7] In the Orthodox Church, icons serve as "windows to heaven," collapsing the time-space continuum, simultaneously dignifying the material world and transporting the icon viewer to a transcendent realm. Some may resist the postmodern recovery of a more visual faith. It calls up ancient controversies regarding icons. While most of the debate rages over prohibitions against graven images, much of the anxiety regarding images involves sexuality, how depictions of the body affect our body.

In his book *On Seeing*, pathologist F. Gonzalez-Crussi chronicles our ongoing fascination with the human form. Gonzalez-Crussi marvels at the ability of an image to provoke sexual arousal. He finds "that a distinguishing characteristic of human beings, one that identifies them as fundamentally different from animals, is (apart from the capacity to laugh, and to know that they must die) the ability to make love with ghosts."[8] While many claim to fear the reduction of God to an image, perhaps we actually dread the power of an image to alter our physiology. How can something as inanimate as a photograph or a movie star on a flat screen create such a stir?

The idol that today's iconoclasts may need to smash is the fear of images. In *A Grief Observed*, C. S. Lewis wrestles with his tendency to turn God into an idol. He writes, "Images of the Holy easily become holy images—sacrosanct. My idea of God is not a divine idea. It has to be shattered time after time. He shatters it Himself. He is the great iconoclast. Could we not almost say that this shattering is one of the marks of His presence? The Incarnation is the supreme example; it leaves all previous ideas of the Messiah in ruins. . . . The same thing happens in our private prayers. All reality is iconoclastic."[9] God can be counted on to smash whatever we've made too sacred. Perhaps our fear of images will come tumbling down amid our efforts to forge a postmodern faith.

We also must resist the temptation to drag each other down. In some of the most contentious eras in church history, the controversy centered on the place of imagery in worship. Yet we cannot overestimate the importance of an integrated theology of images for our electronic era. Maybe a healthy view of icons can deepen one's faith and art. As enhanced definition sharpens our televisions, surely enhanced vision can expand my appreciation of film and my understanding of God. The rich visual storytelling of Catholic filmmakers like Hitchcock, Scorsese, and Coppola suggests that a profound visual aesthetic resides within our broad Christian tradition.[10] The haunting films of Russian Orthodox filmmaker Andrei Tarkovsky invite us to look *through* our material world.[11] Calvin College graduate Paul Schrader makes movies stained by sin but ripe for redemption. Protestant, Catholic, and Orthodox Christians all follow a rabbi who challenged us to have "eyes to see and ears to hear." In the beginning was the Word, but Jesus was also the image of the invisible God. I long to see clearly. I need to develop a theology of beauty that complements (and counterbalances) my understanding of sin. Simply because our eyes may cause us to sin does not mean we must cut them out of our experience of worship (or filmgoing).

Film Theory's Blind Spots

Protestants have polished word-based religious expressions, but words have also ruled academia. The printing press fueled the rise of universities as so-called universal education exploded over the past five hundred years. Theology took root in the reading and writing of books. Film theory arose with the same educational assumptions and practices. Arguments are made and responded to *in writing*. Film scholar Noel Carroll recalls his entry into the Cinema Studies Department at New York University in 1970: "The NYU program was one of the first of its kind in the United States—an academic department of film history and theory, without a practical filmmaking wing."[12] While the PhD program was still being accredited, "one felt the pressure to demonstrate that film studies was a full-fledged academic discipline. . . . Consequently, if one were in the business of inventing a new discipline, one straight-forward strategy was to imitate a going concern like literary studies."[13] Perhaps film theory, focused upon moving images, can enhance a word-bound theology. But only when both fields have been released from a literary paradigm will they be free to truly communicate with an image-saturated society.

Any attempt to theologize via film theory is hedged with trapdoors. In *Film as Religion*, John C. Lyden challenges theologians to take film studies seriously. Yet he also acknowledges the antireligious sentiments that fuel the left-leaning field of cultural studies. Lyden warns that "the field of film studies may represent a Trojan horse out of which could pour an army of hostile soldiers who are just as happy to reduce religion to ideology as to view film in this way."[14] While I appreciate Lyden's concerns, I doubt that film theory will sneak up on many readers. Their disdain for all hegemonies is quite palpable. When I dared to defend the institution of marriage to one of my University of Southern California film school professors, I was met with much more than verbal resistance. She picked up a chair and flung it across the room, barely missing my head! Her theory was turned into a violent practice.

I acknowledge the important contributions of feminist theory, queer theory, and Marxist theory. Too often I have digested films as products, never reading the fine print on the wrapper, listing the ingredients. I have been guilty of objectifying women and propping up power structures. I have chosen the blockbuster at the megaplex more often than the subtitles at the art house. We all recognize that films with higher aspirations often suffer at the box office. Yet academia remains too removed from the realities of filmmaking. Sometimes artistic decisions have more to do with overtime pay for the crew than an interest in shooting at sundown. As a moviemaker, I know that art and commerce must merge for sustained success in the marketplace. Consequently, this chapter seeks to dip into the deepest theoretical wells, withdrawing the most accessible ideas. It may end up being too superficial for serious scholars and too intellectual for the average moviegoer. Yet, a via media seems only appropriate, given the form of mass media we are studying. It is about communication and communion, rather than isolation and irrelevance.

Film studies began as an argument between formalists and realists. This dialectic provided a dynamic push/pull across cinema history. Yet, over time, efforts to create an all-encompassing film theory have devolved into an array of competing claims, each smaller than the previous theory. George Steiner's *Real Presences* warned against scholars chasing their own tails: "It is not as Ecclesiastes would have it, that, 'of making many books there is no end.' It is the 'of making books on books and books on those books there is no end.'"[15] Steiner laments the "mushrooming of semantic-critical jargon, the disputations between structuralists, post-structuralists, meta-structuralists and deconstructionists."[16] The gap between the academy and the people seems to widen with each passing year. As our most populist

Moving beyond a "Literary" Paradigm

art form, film offers a unique opportunity to merge highbrow ideas with lowbrow entertainment. It allows for the possibility of recovering the proper understanding of theory. Steiner suggests, "A 'theorist' or 'theoretician' is one who is disciplined in observance, a term itself charged with a twofold significance of intellectual-sensory perception and religious or ritual conduct." Perhaps a return to its roots will move theory from trivia that annoys to the minutia that matters—divine vision indeed. We must restore the unity of art and reconnect the visual elements of film (lighting, cinematography, set design) to meaning and interpretation.[17]

Philosophy and theology suffer from the same efforts to divide and conquer. Plato called life a deception. Aristotle aspired to mimesis. Protestants focus on the absence of God (transcendence) while the Catholic and Orthodox traditions celebrate God's immanence. Yet my thesis (and theology) is trinitarian. Film is sight, sound, and story; images, music, and dialogue. In the theological realm, I embrace what Jürgen Moltmann describes as "immanent transcendence . . . , God in, with and beneath each everyday experience in the world."[18] Attempts to isolate or atomize film into less than the sum of its parts are doomed to frustration. Isolationism is a foolish approach to theology as well. Cinema is our most collaborative of arts. The goal of communication is communion with others.

To forge a more visual faith, I will depend upon the kindness of strangers: three scholars whose inclusive vision regarding film theory has turned them into trustworthy friends. André Bazin, Leo Braudy, and Peter Wollen each wrestled with the questions posed by the Russian formalists, but managed to create a more humane critical grid. These older film theorists (within a burgeoning discipline) wrestled with the apparatus of film before critical studies became a puzzle box trapped in a self-referential maze.

Despite the best efforts of Braudy (and David Bordwell, Kristen Thompson, and Noel Carroll at the University of Wisconsin), we still need to free film criticism from a literary (or scientific or psychological or sociological) paradigm. I want to reestablish film as a visual art. Like Braudy, I seek to bridge the gulf between the academy and the audience; to respect my elders, but to connect with the next generation of students. To further complicate matters, I add the ancient and enduring questions posed by theology: What does it all mean? Can film reveal the divine? Where is God, in both the creative process and the filmgoing experience? I have been trained in theological method at Fuller Theological Seminary in Pasadena, California. My professors, informed by their surroundings, always strove to connect their hermeneutics to the contemporary cultural context. Theology is both a timeless and timely discipline. It strives to hold a newspaper in one hand

and a Bible in the other (or in more postmodern terms, to juggle an iPod with *The Message*). As more filmgoers approach film as a religion, the need to form a more mature theology of film beckons.[19]

Toward a Religious Visuality

I am far from the first reel theologian to identify this problem. S. Brent Plate called for "a religious visuality of film."[20] He advocates an interdisciplinary approach to film analysis that respects film as film, a distinct and specific artistic expression. With a strong background in the visual arts (and an affinity for experimental and avant-garde film), Plate challenges his readers to develop the aesthetics of seeing. He suggests that seeing more clearly may also lead to living more purposefully. I admire his efforts to elevate film as art. Yet I want to push beyond the obscure and the artistic and into the blockbuster at the local cineplex. Many (especially film theorists!) may also question whether better film theory will lead to better living. While I may quibble with Plate's prescription, I heartily agree with his description of theology and film as far too bound by the word.

Plate recognized that most theologies of film have been written by academics steeped in literary paradigms. Pioneer reel theologian John R. May has blended religion, film, and literature studies throughout his distinguished career. My mentor, Robert K. Johnston, drew upon his background in theology and literature for his seminal work, *Reel Spirituality: Theology and Film in Dialogue*. Roy M. Anker's excellent *Catching Light: Looking for God in the Movies* treats film as a distinct medium, but draws heavily upon Anker's expertise in English literature. Catholic scholars like Andrew Greeley and Richard Blake might well have majored in film had that been an educational option in an earlier era. Yet they have each made major contributions to theology and film from their respective backgrounds as professors of sociology and fine art. Many of the finest thinkers in theology and film, like Adele Reinhartz, Larry Kreitzer, Margaret Miles, and Robert Jewett, bring their impressive training in religious or biblical studies to their film analysis. They have been trained in how to interpret a text, unlocking hidden or at least underappreciated meanings.

Some may consider *text* a more literary word. But film's ability to combine theater, art, music, and literature enables us to recover the Latin derivation of *text* as "weaving." Film weaves audio and visual, word and image, music and dialogue, into either a satisfying or an unbearably false whole. While narrative film bears similarities to literature as a storytelling medium, the roots of cinema are first and foremost visual. It was born out of photography, fueled by the photochemical innovations of George Eastman and Kodak. It worked as a silent medium, guiding viewers with the occasional intertitle. Silent film offered a visual Esperanto, crossing cultural and linguistic barriers. Now, with the advent of digital technology (and the demise of film stock), it was, is, and shall ever be moving *images*, not moving words.

As I reflect on my own film education, the most seminal course in the University of Southern California film program was Bruce Block's "Visual Expression." It was an invigorating mixture of art and science. Block demonstrated the power of color, lighting, movement, and space to either enhance or detract from the intended story. A controlled use of affinity and contrast can invigorate an audience and heighten the drama. Haphazard attention to what's in the frame will frustrate viewers and dilute the film's impact. Students complained about the weeks spent arranging paint chips on a color wheel. Why were we stuck comparing shades of blue when we wanted to make the next *Star Wars?* Block forced us to slow down, to master the art of still photography before we graduated to moving pictures. We learned how the eye works, how our perception changes, how the brain processes on-screen activity. For example, our Western eyes, used to reading from left to right, consider this a natural or easier path. So a film director, eager to convey the difficulty of an army's charge in battle would stage the protagonists' movement from the right to the left side of the screen. The enemy attacks from left to right, with all the intangibles seemingly going their way. John Huston's *The Battle of San Pietro* (1943) follows such screen rules even though it is a gritty documentary about combat in World War II. Only war veterans may have noticed a preponderance of left-handed soldiers charging up the hill. Huston flipped the film negative to ensure that the attack occurred from left to right. Such subtle applications of screen movement and human perception have resulted in more compelling movies.

Bruce Block also taught aspiring filmmakers how to map a film's visual story.[21] The color temperature of each sequence should match the intensity (or levity) of the drama. The visual palette rises and falls along with the plot. A clear example of this visual map can be found in the making of *The Incredibles*. Director Brad Bird and his team storyboarded each scene of the planned feature. In a behind-the-scenes look at the making of the film, a foldout map breaks out the dramatic set pieces into a series of still frames.[22] The colors shift with the mood of the story, ebbing and flowing in connection with the drama. This "colorscript" visually describes the emotional content of the entire story through color and lighting. Sight, sound, and story merge in a visual symphony. The world (or at least every sequence) is captured in a few frames.

After taking Block's class, my cinematic senses were awakened. Suddenly, every scene was loaded with practical ways to support or undercut the script. Directors ignore shapes, colors, sizes, patterns, and lines at their own risk. But when the cinematography and production design align with the script, the results are often Oscar worthy. Consider how effectively the look of *American Beauty* coincided with the story. The red roses and naked stomach contrasted on the movie poster recur throughout the film. The innocence of one American beauty (a nubile cheerleader) is juxtaposed with the red American Beauty variety of rose cultivated by a suburban housewife. Lester Burnham vacillates between the dueling beauties, emerging from the bright red door of his suburban house, tempted to throw away his marriage for a fling with an underage girl. Yet both notions of beauty are undercut by Ricky Fitts's video footage of a plastic bag, blowing in the wind, "the most beautiful thing" he has ever seen. The theme of true beauty has been developed with minimal dialogue and maximum visuals. At the conclusion of the film, when Lester has resisted temptation and come to appreciate his marriage and family, he is murdered. What should be the darkest scene in the film is bathed in luminous light by legendary cinematographer Conrad Hall. As Ricky bends over, he studies the face of Lester, lying in a pool of red blood—and he smiles. Viewers who have failed to see the beauty in a plastic bag will consider Ricky's smile perverse. But for those who have learned to see, via the script, cinematography, and production design, the scene acquires an eerie power. A criminal act turns into a transcendent moment; seeing leads to believing.

These nearly invisible choices of costume, lighting, and props work on viewers in subtle and telling ways. Visual motifs heighten those dramatic moments and sear their way into our collective subconscious. The riddle of *Citizen Kane*'s snow globe pays off when we see a sleigh labeled "Rosebud." *The Maltese Falcon* coalesces around a tiny statue, "the stuff dreams are made of." Yet clumsy or obvious clues rob us of such satisfying visual pleasures. Anachronistic gaffes in production design pop us out of the film and shatter the illusion of reality. But when sight, sound, and script come together in a carefully coordinated dance, movie magic happens. Filmmakers like James Cameron (for *Titanic*) or Peter Jackson (for *The Return of the King*) haul off a raft of Oscars (and box office gold). Let us consider the theological sensibilities that lie behind the most accomplished artistic choices.

The Theological Possibilities of Film Theory

To see clearly is poetry, prophecy and religion, all in one.

John Ruskin, *Modern Painters*, 1843

In *The World in a Frame*, Leo Braudy offers insight into the way visual style informs the substance of film. He provides "a brief history of the visible," finding a recurring tension in the history of art. Should art mirror life (be realistic) or should it create its own reality, rooted in the artist's vision? The root of the conflict is theological. Are God and the stuff he created good or just a fallen reflection of a purer form that resides elsewhere? One can hear Aristotle and Plato picking sides in the immanence versus transcendence debate.[23] The invention of photography (and film) only heightened this tension. Are movies like Plato's shadows playing on the wall of a cave? Do they dull our senses and mask the real action? Or do they offer potential catharsis, moments of divine encounter?

Pioneering Russian directors saw this new medium as an opportunity to create a new reality. Inspired by the Communist Revolution, they connected moving images to political messages. Film theorist Lev Kuleshov conducted a visual experiment. He sandwiched a shot of an actor between close-ups of various objects. He found that when the face remained the same but the objects changed, so did audiences' perceptions. For example, a close-up of the actor, followed by a shot of food, led viewers to conclude "He's hungry." Juxtaposing the actor's face with images of flowers might make audiences believe, "He's happy." The Kuleshov effect suggested that audiences fill in the psychological gaps between images.[24] Consider it the new math. With the art of editing, suddenly, one image plus one image can produce a third, independent image in our mind's eye. We are so eager to create meaning that we will fill in the blank. We are so desperate that we can be manipulated, convinced that we are seeing things. Perhaps Plato's suspicions about the cave are correct.

Sergei Eisenstein built on the theories of Kuleshov, perfecting the art of editing. In the famous Odessa Steps sequence from *Battleship Potemkin* (1925), Eisenstein splices together close-ups of soldiers marching, guns firing, and a baby carriage rolling to form a visual reverie. His techniques push audiences beyond reason. Eisenstein goes for the gut. The audience experiences a mother's anguish and a mob's indignation in one overwhelming montage. Eisenstein wants to outrage viewers, to inspire a revolution. He imposes his vision upon the actors, the film, and the audience.

A French film critic, drawing upon his Catholic roots, rejected the manipulations of these Russian theorists. André Bazin searched for "holy moments" in cinema, embracing mise-en-scènes that give audiences ample space to make their own viewing choices within each scene. Film should not limit an audience's perception; it should open up new ways of seeing. Bazin celebrated the films of Orson Welles because he crammed as much information into a single frame of film as possible. In *Citizen Kane*, viewers' eyes are free to roam around each scene, in search of subtle details and clues about characters' motivations. If Kuleshov placed his faith in the director's vision, Bazin gave choice (and voice) to the audience.

Leo Braudy picks up on the theology behind these divergent aesthetic choices. The ancient tension between the sovereignty of God and the free will of his people informs the filmmaking process. Some directors prefer a predetermined cinematic universe, where artistic decisions are made months before film rolls. Others create an open atmosphere, where actors are free to improvise, to serve as cocreators of the project. Perhaps the differences in directors' styles correspond to their understanding of human nature and audience behavior. Is an audience something to be respected or directed, cajoled or corralled? Are actors just props at the director's disposal, a means to a manipulative end? Or is the filmmaker called upon to serve the story (and the audience)? These questions have echoes in the debate about humanity's role in the Garden of Eden. Does dominion over nature allow us to exploit it or is our role comparable to caretaker, tending the garden with the utmost respect? Braudy puts the tensions in cinematic terms: "Does the director, with a commitment to the visual world, discover God's meaning in objects or impose his own?"[25] For Braudy, "open films" give viewers ample time and space, "room to breathe." They are comparatively quiet, introspective, and slow. Open films have faith in nature, in the power of objects to communicate truth. "In a closed film the world of the film is the only thing that exists; everything within it has its place in the plot of the film—every object, every character, every gesture, every action."[26] Closed films are more schematic, planned out in meticulous detail, like storyboarded action sequences. Closed films often create tension by withholding information, making characters (and audiences) the victims of terror or crime. The universe acts with malevolence. In open films, the audience is a guest, given a sense of security, collaborating on a vision *with* the director.[27]

Braudy finds that closed directors tend to be autocratic, while open directors look for unexpected opportunities arising within their milieu. Alfred Hitchcock made closed films, self-contained universes in which he

Moving beyond a "Literary" Paradigm

left nothing to chance. His meticulous storyboards worked out the editing for suspense in advance. In Hitchcock's mind, the film had already been finished before he shot the first frame. Stanley Kubrick's chilling meditations on (in)humanity like *A Clockwork Orange* and *Full Metal Jacket* were also informed by years of planning and preproduction. The results are rigorous and suffocating. We admire their theme and execution, but emerge desperate for human contact and emotional connections. In contrast, French director Jean Renoir developed a languid style that stumbles upon characters and objects amid their preexisting lives. Characters wander around within the frame, oblivious to the camera poised at a neutral distance from the action. Audiences are encouraged to discover the drama for themselves, at their own pace. Renoir's films are open-ended, pregnant with possibilities. Similarly, Krzysztof Kieślowski's ten-hour *The Decalogue* (1989) unfolds slowly, leaving the plot and the point mysterious. The narratives are connected broadly, with characters overlapping across the ten episodes. Kieślowski doesn't underline his point for viewers, but invites them into the ethical dilemmas. Patient viewers are rewarded with questions (and images!) that continue to haunt and inspire.

What is the secret behind Kieślowski's transcendent art? Joseph Kickasola traces Kieślowski's artistic shift from realistic documentaries to formalistic narratives. He suggests that Kieślowski moved from the *immediacy* of human experience (questions of everyday ethics, life and death, murder and revenge) to *abstraction* (a crack in a frozen pond, ink spilled across homework). This progression culminated in *transcendence*, even if Kieślowski disdained critics' attempts to impose metaphysics upon his elusive work.[28] Kickasola suggests that Kieślowski's use of images "organically illustrates the fault lines between the rational and the nonrational, representation and expression, concrete and abstract, universal and particular, physical and metaphysical."[29] Kickasola identifies this thin place in theological terms as "the liminal image." Kieślowski uses extreme close-ups of ordinary events like steam rising when cream merges with coffee (in *The Decalogue*) to point out the minimiracles happening all around us. Perhaps an abundant approach to images, rooted in the stuff-ness of life, can yield an openness to the spirit. The finest filmmakers can both control what happens in the frame and offer room for the audience to be moved in surprising and unexpected ways.

The either/or categories of early film theory have gradually blended. Art-house filmmakers trained in formalism rocket from Sundance to Hollywood blockbusters. They combine an appreciation for Russian montage with an admiration for American film noir. Steven Soderbergh alternates between the formalism of *Solaris* and the populism of *Ocean's Eleven* with surprising agility. Today's closed filmmakers acknowledge the evil lurking in human hearts, but offer moments of lightness and grace. M. Night Shamaylan builds upon the closed tradition of Hitchcock. His scripts are complex, interlocking puzzles, carefully coordinated down to the last shot. Shamaylan's closed films like *The Sixth Sense* and *Unbreakable* hinge upon a secret revealed, a glimpse of divine knowledge that forces viewers to reexamine what they've seen. Shamaylan offers a hard-won hope. What Calvinist did not embrace *Signs'* "everything happens for a reason" conclusion? The predetermined universe of *Signs* insures that the glass of water will be there when needed to defeat an alien intruder. A wife's senseless death and a baseball player's paralysis are redeemed in one moment of blinding insight. Her obscure final words become a divine mandate when Merrill dares to "swing away" at the alien attacker. The asthma that threatens a son's breathing becomes a God-given defense against airborne alien poison. A closed universe still allows for an openness to divine providence. Yet when Shamaylan's films become too open, too fanciful (as in 2006's *Lady in the Water*), even his most faithful audience abandons him. A little structure, rooted in everyday reality, proved preferable to a fantastical world of narfs and scrunts.

David Fincher brings a dim view of human nature to his carefully controlled, closed films. Menace lurks in every frame of *Se7en* and *The Game*. The characters (and the audience) feel like pawns in someone's predetermined schema. In *Fight Club*, Fincher's protagonist seeks to break out of his predetermined existence. Jack no longer wants to be a dull boy. He trashes his home, his career, and his possessions in an effort to forge an authentic existence. A longing for God and fathers informs every frame of *Fight Club*. The bleak, nihilistic ending leaves viewers bruised and bloodied but hungry for redemption. While Fincher strives to create a godless universe, he inadvertently leaves a God-haunted vacuum.

Director Baz Luhrmann also left nothing to chance in *Moulin Rouge*. Working closely with his production designer (and wife!), Luhrmann creates a self-contained, stage-bound musical that bristles with life. The chaotic camera moves are coordinated with frenetic dancing to create the illusion of spontaneity. The bohemian virtues of courage, truth, beauty, and love took months of backbreaking rehearsals in order to burst from the screen in well-orchestrated fury. Only after the breathtaking musical numbers did the story and my pulse settle down. For many viewers, Luhrmann's carefully orchestrated assault on their senses caused them to bail on the film. They exercised their free will and turned off the DVD. I

Moving beyond a "Literary" Paradigm

extended grace to *Moulin Rouge* and was rewarded with a thrilling meditation on the power of love, including a serenade atop an elephant.

Perhaps such hyperstylized films, crafted in an age of overabundant images, can combine the best of open *and* closed filmmaking. Maybe the postmodern era will draw upon the best of Eisenstein and Bazin, the montage and the mise-en-scène. Or we could devolve into the mind-numbing, soul-draining cinema of Michael Bay. *Armageddon* and *Bad Boys II* berate audiences, offering no time to contemplate and no content to consider. Michael Bay directs like a jealous and insecure god, who demands absolute allegiance, yet offers no compelling reason to follow. Like *The Wizard of Oz*, he has been revealed as the man behind the curtain with all bark and no bite. The failure of Bay's chase film, *The Island*, suggests that audiences want something they can genuinely sink their teeth into—a montage that matters.

The next wave of film theory may combine the best of formalist and realist traditions. A more mature theology will also draw upon each tradition's strengths, while filling in their blind spots. The abundant images in Catholic and Orthodox churches inspire my deprived Protestant eyes. But maybe my Protestant understanding of the Word can sharpen my friends' Catholic or Orthodox faith. I would like to think old either/or religious squabbling could yield to a both/and spirit of mutual appreciation (and maybe even admiration!). Form and content must work together. Liturgy and proclamation must complement rather than compete. Creeds and deeds must merge in mutual support.

So what kind of films do you like? Are you an open filmgoer, embracing a leisurely pace? Or do you prefer a tightly wound film that takes you on a wild ride? Our preferences may reveal more about our theology than we care to admit. I am not a patient cinephile. On Friday nights, I choose popcorn flicks (almost) every time. When I am tired, I like movies (and directors) that take me by the hand and slap me around. I would rather have things spelled out and wrapped up clearly. Popcorn flicks start with chaos, but end with a purgative sense of order. Is it a crime to like intricate plots and tidy endings? What does such seeing say about my believing? Braudy suggests, "Open films imply that the world outside us is complex, difficult to understand, but basically benevolent; closed films imply that it is understandable, usually malevolent, and virtually impossible to escape from." He sees their divergent worldviews as "God as the chief gardener" versus "God as the head of the spy ring."[30]

I am not sure I like that. Or at least, not sure I should like that. I wonder about the relationship between my movies and my faith. Why do I like to be manipulated by autocratic directors and shudder at the thought of subtitles? Do I go to the movies hoping to be blinded or longing to see? And what about our churches? As directors frame their artistic worlds, so pastors, missionaries, and therapists frame their ministries. Do we find a world or create our own? Do I invite people into an open space full of possibilities? Or do I lure viewers into my predefined presentation? I would like to believe nature is full of ambiguity and complexity, open to potential exploration. But I have been taught that our visual world is filled with deception and deceit. Is seeing a pleasure to be understood or a prison from which we must escape?

The closer I look at film, the more I realize the limits of my (spiritual) vision. Seeing is rarely believing. I have been taught to be suspicious—to search for cracks, to solve the mystery. And yet, the further I venture in my faith, the more mysterious and enchanted God's world appears. Can my filmgoing be reconciled with my faith? Can sitting through an artsy French, Russian, or Chinese film sharpen my spiritual antennae?

The Beauty of Integration: Icons, Symbols, Indexes

I have found Peter Wollen's *Signs and Meaning in the Cinema* to be a particularly helpful companion in our nascent efforts to formalize a "reel spirituality."[31] Wollen identifies the limits in the semiotics of Ferdinand de Saussure, but he finds helpful insights in Saussure's neglected contemporary, American logician Charles Sanders Peirce. Wollen rescues Peirce's "second taxonomy of signs," which divides signs into icons, indexes, or symbols.[32] According to Peirce, an icon resembles that which it seeks to represent. It is a sign that is similar in likeness to the object depicted. An index is more akin to a measurement, like a sundial or clock. It offers a graphic representation of another aspect of reality. A symbol exists independently of those who use it. It need not resemble what it represents. For example, a stop sign doesn't show a car stopping, yet it still communicates the concept. Like letters or brands, the symbol exists in people's minds long after our direct experience of it. It even takes on universal significance (like international road signage).

Wollen takes the theorists to task for claiming absolute truth for their corner on the idea market. For Wollen, "the aesthetic richness of the cinema springs from the fact that it comprises all three dimensions of the sign: indexical, iconic and symbolic. The great weakness of almost all those who have written about the cinema is that they have taken one of these dimensions, made it the ground of their aesthetic, the 'essential' dimension of the cinematic sign and discarded the rest. This is to impoverish the cinema. Moreover, none of these dimensions can be discounted: they are co-present."[33] Wollen advocates an integrated approach to cinema. Perhaps that same level of integration can characterize our theology and Christian practice. Instead of Catholic versus Protestant or icons versus the Word, perhaps a culmination of church history will result in a more mature and united Christian community.

At the same time, film theorists have been blinded by their own assumptions regarding the supernatural. Too many scholars see icons as frozen relics of history. They may occasionally acknowledge the purpose or phenomena associated with an icon, but rarely will they "go there" themselves. They hold its ultimate purpose at bay. Protestant theology adopts a similar distance toward Orthodox icons. To call an icon "just a symbol" is comparable to reducing it to "paint on a canvas." Yet iconographers celebrate the divine purpose and function in their work with verbal metaphors. "An Orthodox iconographer, having prepared by fasting and prayer sets about 'writing' an icon; in the Russian language, the verbs *to paint* or *to draw* are used only in connection with secular painting, including the painting of religious subject matter. Therefore, iconographers do not paint icons; they write them."[34] Perhaps the perceived gap between Orthodox and Protestant Christian traditions is smaller than imagined. Protestants acknowledge that icons point to something else, but they rarely ponder that it might mediate that reality. Icons communicate a message but do not offer literal communion. Wollen (and Peirce) rightly challenge us to think of icons as being more like an index, a means of getting somewhere. Consider them more symptomology than symbology.

A younger generation, raised on smash cuts and video games, may serve as our spirit guides. The innovations of *The Matrix* and *300* are more about style than substance. Some may be frustrated by the apparent superficiality of our digital era. I know a teacher mystified by students' enthusiasm for *Garden State* (2004). They loved the shot where writer/director/star Zach Braff puts on a shirt that matches the wallpaper. Andrew Largeman has returned to his New Jersey home for his mother's funeral. His aunt has crafted a shirt with leftover material from her final act, redecorating the bathroom. Largeman stares at himself (and the shirt) in the mirror, gazing directly into the camera. The composition is flat and balanced, like an Orthodox icon. Viewers are invited to commune with the character, to enter into his sense of isolation and dislocation. When students were asked to explain why they loved the scene, most simply said, "It was cool." What was cool? The shirt? The soundtrack? Or the way three seconds of screen time embody all the confusion surrounding Largeman's reluctant homecoming?

A grieving Andrew Largeman (Zach Braff) literally blends in with the wallpaper in *Garden State* (d. Zach Braff, 2004). ©2004 Twentieth Century Fox.

A genuine communion takes place between Andrew and his mother. Unable to truly grieve over his mother's death, Andrew retreats to the most visible sign of her departure. Among her final accomplishments and resting places was that bathroom. Staring in the mirror at his shirt, blending in with the wallpaper, his existential crisis appears in sharp relief. Where does he fit in a universe that made no sense even *prior* to his mom's death? His world has been captured (maybe even frozen) in a frame. As the icons of Orthodoxy offer access to a transcendent reality, this brief shot from *Garden State* offers a window into Largeman's tortured soul. He would desperately like to escape this mortal coil. But in the meantime, he reconnects with his deceased mother through her final project, the wallpaper. The audience enters the cramped bathroom. As Andrew stares at us through the mirror, we stare at him, *through* the movie screen. One iconic image "writes" a thousand words about dysfunction and family dynamics. That *is* cool.

What images continue to resonate with me? I could talk about Peter Parker stopping a train full of commuters on Chicago's El in *Spider-Man 2*. The tidal wave that pours through New York City in *The Day after Tomorrow* also impressed me. And *Shrek* turned out to be more than a plush toy for my son; he became a living, breathing, huggable green-skinned monster. But these digital creations all failed to transport me to a higher plane. They left me at the symbolic level, void of any additional tug on my heart. For ongoing transcendence and real transformation, three images immediately leap to my mind's eye:

1. A donkey lying down with lambs in Robert Bresson's *Au hasard Balthazar* (1966)
2. An insect crawling on its back, fighting to right itself in Abbas Kiarostami's *The Wind Will Carry Us* (1999)
3. A hat burning in a verdant field in David Gordon Green's directorial debut, *George Washington* (2000)

The box office receipts of these three films bubble under a million dollars (combined!). They are slow, ponderous meditations on the human condition—anathema to most moviegoers (and me!). Erwin Panofsky laments the problems inherent in art films: "While it is true that commercial art is always in danger of ending up as a prostitute, it is equally true that non-commercial art is always in danger of ending up as an old maid."[35] These cinematic maids (orphans? refugees? sanctuaries!) are filled with moments of quiet reflection where almost nothing happens on-screen. They are virtually plotless (much like life itself!). The filmmakers purposely slow viewers down long enough to awaken our senses to the beauty looming right before us. Each made a lasting impression on my collective visual memory. In an era of overabundant images, the challenge will be to find films that sharpen our vision. Despite the best montages money can buy, Hollywood may still need to learn that sometimes less is still more.

Conclusion: An Opportune Moment

A rational theology has had difficulty relating to the emotive motion picture. Analytical film theory rooted in literary paradigms has also struggled to encompass the complexity of the filmmaking and filmgoing experience. Both have been imperial in their claims, attracting an elite audience privy to their closed-door conversations. It is not that audiences don't hunger for a thick description of their experiences of film or theology. But we do not want to wade through too much chaff in order to sink our teeth into the ideas. This chapter has been an attempt to merge the populist art of film with two of the more elusive and absolutist disciplines, theology and film theory. In Westerns, such demands of fealty often end in bloodshed. Let's hope this chapter has resulted in something other than a gunfight at the academic corral.

We have been far too dualistic in our thinking. The choices are not film as a visual art or film as twenty-first-century literature. Film theorists want cinematic signs to be either natural or cultural, uncoded or encoded.[36] But why can we not see them as both? The most politicized film theorists have been surprised to see "mere symbolism" survive. Protestants chasing relevance cannot explain how an unchanging Catholic or Orthodox church attracts new believers. But the sacramental religious tradition has kept the iconic tradition and symbolic language alive. In the beginning was the Word, but the Word became flesh and dwelt among us. We need an idealized *and* an embodied film theory. We need an incarnational theology that calls us to heaven, but resembles our world. We cannot reduce our faith to either transcendence or immanence. Jürgen Moltmann suggests that "to experience God in all things [including cinema] presupposes that there is a transcendence which is immanent in things and which can be inductively discovered. It is the infinite in the finite, the eternal in the temporal, and the enduring in the transitory."[37] We need icons, indexes, and symbols (from both liturgy and film) to show us the way. The Father, Son, and Holy Spirit call us to move beyond dualism, into an ongoing conversation that affirms sound, sight, and motion.

We have been warned about the power of images. The Nazis demonstrated how propaganda could rally troops for the most reprehensible causes. We also know that the veneration of icons can devolve into idol worship. But none of those warnings has prevented (or even held back) the march of our electronic era. Images are threatening to overwhelm us. A recovery of visual aesthetics could launch film theory and film and theology into renewed relevance. What previous generations have separated, the next generation aspires to unite. Ways of seeing may enhance our ways of being. Better film viewing may yet inspire more careful contemplation and even deeper discipleship. We are just waking up to the possibilities of the motion picture, discovering how seeing can lead to believing.

Notes

1. Among the additional films mentioned were (in historical order) *Sparrows* (1926), *The Passion of Joan of Arc* (1928), *Amarcord* (1973), *Barry Lyndon* (1975), *The Mirror* (1975), *Days of Heaven* (1978), *Tess* (1979), *The Mission* (1986), *Grand Canyon* (1991), *The Fisher King* (1991), *The Shawshank Redemption* (1994), *Ponette* (1996), *Basquiat* (1996), *The Pillow*

Moving beyond a "Literary" Paradigm

Book (1996), *The English Patient* (1996), *American Beauty* (1999), *Gladiator* (2000), and *The Story of the Weeping Camel* (2003).

2. See www.imdb.com.

3. See her seminal essay from 1969, "Trash, Art and the Movies," collected in Pauline Kael, *For Keeps: 30 Years at the Movies* (New York: Plume Books, 1996).

4. It took Leo Braudy and Marshall Cohen *only* 880 pages to compile *Film Theory and Criticism: Introduction Reader*, 5th ed. (New York: Oxford University Press, 1998). For a more compact overview, I recommend J. Dudley Andrew, *The Major Film Theories: An Introduction* (New York: Oxford University Press, 1976), although it mostly surveys the male, Eurocentric perspective that has dominated so much of academia and film theory.

5. For a quick review of the iconoclast controversy, see Gerardus van der Leeuw's *Sacred and Profane Beauty: The Holy in Art* (New York: Holt, Rinehardt & Winston, 1963).

6. I recommend William A. Dyrness, *Reformed Theology and Visual Culture: The Protestant Imagination from Calvin to Edwards* (Cambridge: Cambridge University Press, 2004).

7. Elizabeth Zelensky and Lela Gilbert, *Windows to Heaven: Introducing Icons to Protestants and Catholics* (Grand Rapids: Brazos, 2005).

8. Jonathan Kirsch, "Peep Show: A Review of *On Seeing: Things Seen, Unseen and Obscene* by F. Gonzalez-Crussi, Overlook Duckworth, 2006," in the *Los Angeles Times Book Review*, March 26, 2006, R2.

9. C. S. Lewis, *A Grief Observed* (San Francisco: Harper & Row, 1961), 76–77.

10. Richard Blake, *After Image: The Indelible Catholic Imagination of Six American Film-makers* (Chicago: Loyola, 2000).

11. Andrei Tarkovsky, *Sculpting in Time*, trans. Kitty Hunter-Blair (Austin: University of Texas Press, 1986).

12. Noel Carroll, *Interpreting the Moving Image* (Cambridge: Cambridge University Press, 1998), 1.

13. Ibid.

14. John C. Lyden, *Film as Religion: Myths, Morals and Rituals* (New York: New York University Press, 2003), 32.

15. George Steiner, *Real Presences* (Chicago: University of Chicago Press, 1991), 48.

16. Ibid.

17. David Bordwell and Kristen Thompson literally wrote the book on the subject, *Film Art: An Introduction*, 8th ed. (New York: McGraw-Hill, 2004).

18. Jürgen Moltmann, *The Spirit of Life: A Universal Affirmation* (Minneapolis: Fortress, 1992), 34.

19. George Barna chronicles the rise of "media, arts, and culture" as the primary means of how Americans express and experience their faith in his small but potent volume *Revolution!* (Wheaton: Tyndale House, 2005).

20. S. Brent Plate, "Religion/Literature/Film: Towards a Religious Visuality in Film," in *Literature and Theology* 12 (1998): 16–38, referenced in Clive Marsh, *Cinema and Sentiment: Film's Challenge to Theology* (Milton Keynes, UK: Paternoster, 2004).

21. Bruce Block packed the basic principles of his class into *The Visual Story: Seeing the Structure of Film, TV and New Media* (Boston: Focal, 2001).

22. Mark Cotta Vaz and Brian Bird, *The Art of The Incredibles* (San Francisco: Chronicle Books, 2004).

23. I acknowledge my oversimplification for the sake of advancing an argument. The Radical Orthodox movement has challenged the reduction of Plato to an antimaterialist stance. For a quick dip into this rereading, see James K. A. Smith's "Will the Real Plato Please Stand Up? Participation vs. Incarnation," in *Radical Orthodoxy and the Reformed Tradition*, ed. James K. A. Smith and James H. Olthius (Grand Rapids: Baker Academic, 2005).

24. For an extended discussion of the Kuleshov effect, see Jon Boorstin, *Making Movies Work: Thinking Like a Filmmaker* (Los Angeles: Silman-James, 1995).

25. Leo Braudy, *The World in a Frame* (New York: Anchor, 1976), 73.

26. Ibid., 46.

27. Ibid., 49.

28. Joseph Kickasola, *The Films of Krzysztof Kieslowski: The Liminal Image* (New York: Continuum, 2004), 41–42.

29. Ibid., 38.

30. Braudy, *World in a Frame*, 49.

31. Peter Wollen, *Signs and Meaning in the Cinema* (Bloomington: Indiana University Press, 1973).

32. Ibid., 122.

33. Ibid., 141.

34. Zelensky and Gilbert, *Windows to Heaven*, 24.

35. Erwin Panofsky, "Style and Medium in the Motion Pictures," in *Three Essays on Style* (Cambridge, MA: The MIT Press, 1997), as quoted in Wollen, *Signs and Meaning*, 15.

36. Wollen, *Signs and Meaning*, 124.

37. Jürgen Moltmann, *The Spirit of Life: A Universal Affirmation* (Minneapolis: Fortress, 1992), 35.

Moving beyond a "Literary" Paradigm

2

The Colors of Sound

Music and Meaning Making in Film

BARRY TAYLOR

I think that, sometimes, the most simple tune can unlock so much more than anything else in a picture.

Lisa Gerard

Film music has often received scant attention from those who engage in dialogue between film and theology, mainly, it seems, because we theologians are "textual" people and tend to consider the words on paper, be they scriptural or screenplay, to be the locus of singular importance. That may be somewhat true from a scriptural perspective, but my argument is that the "text" of any given film comprises at least three intersecting issues: image, story, and sound, all working together both to create context and to give meaning to the tale being told. To understand a film's meaning requires more than simply paying attention to the script and dialogue on-screen. The story in a film is told by bringing a script to life: by acting, but also by scenery and by music—the meaning being offered lies woven in the fabric of these different forms of discourse converging in the darkness of a cinema. The lights go down, the curtain rises, the opening strains of music are heard, light comes streaming from the screen, and a story unfolds—this is the magic of film.

To help the reader/viewer/listener appreciate the importance of music for film, this chapter is divided into two distinct sections. The first attempts to paint a general picture of the development of film music and examines some of the key ways in which music enhances narrative, shapes emotion, and "colors" the movie, aiding in the meaning-making process. I have used the term "color" as an invitation to the reader to understand music in film not as mere sonic background in a film but rather as a catalyst for making the story come alive (much like the old expression about things that "put some color into the cheeks"). Music brings film to life by expanding the emotional arc of characters, aiding in establishing locational and particular contexts of a given film, and adding an overall thematic sense to the story that is unfolding before our eyes on the screen.[1]

The second section attempts to bring us up to date by looking at some shifts in the focus of music in film that have occurred since the early 1970s. It could be argued that the second portion of this chapter examines "postmodern music in postmodern films." Initially this was the direction I was going to take, but I realized that to invoke the dreaded "post" word is to jump into a contested field of discourse, which, in this brief introduction to film music, is simply too much to take on. It is not only a lack of space that prevents me from taking this approach, however; I also think that the postmodern conversation is not absolutely necessary in order to speak about film music in the closing decades of the twentieth century and the opening decade of the twenty-first. Instead I will simply argue that film music in the twenty-first century is often yet another example of popular culture referencing itself in other mediums.

As we made our way through the twentieth century, popular culture increasingly took on new levels of importance and influence over all aspects of our cultural life. We now live in a world dominated by popular culture (as others have argued, it is now the "amniotic fluid" of our lives), and as the canon[2] of popular culture in all forms has grown, and continues to do so, it increasingly becomes a source of inspiration as well as a resource for adding to the meaning-making process in other artistic mediums. This cross-referencing has implications that must be examined, and this will form the backbone of the second section of this chapter. Film and film music does not exist in a vacuum. The increasing use of artifacts from

Moving beyond a "Literary" Paradigm

other pop cultural expressions, particularly pop music, is affecting the ways in which meaning is created in film, partially changing the function of music in film in the process.[3]

Part One: In the Beginning . . .

Introduction

To mention a movie these days is to invite a melodic reply. Mention the movie *Jaws* and almost everyone will mimic the ominous music that accompanies the scenes before the giant shark attacks. And who can forget the triumphant theme of Sylvester Stallone's *Rocky* sagas—as Rocky races up the steps of the Philadelpia Museum of Art or rises from the edge of defeat in the boxing ring to claim victory in the face of huge obstacles? Or mention *Chariots of Fire* and its opening scene of athletes running on a deserted beach, and doesn't the synthesizer-driven melody of Vangelis's score immediately spring to mind and join the image of those athletes, giving them pace and emotion? Movie music has become a part of our collective cultural consciousness, and film themes remain in our minds in much the same way that commercial jingles and pop song melodies do.

Film and music have gone hand in hand since the inception of the movie industry. It could be argued, in fact, that music came before dialogue. Early black-and-white films may have been dialogue-free, but when shown in movie houses across America, those "silent films" were usually accompanied by music, whether it came from a simple upright piano in rural movie houses or massive organs or small chamber orchestras in the ornate theaters of metropolitan areas. A manual from 1922 for cinema organists spelled out the challenges of matching music to image on the screen:

> If you are playing pictures, do so intelligently. To give you an idea of how easily a wrong number can be chosen for a scene, a man and a woman were shown on screen in each other's embrace. The organist began playing a silly love song, only to find that the couple were in fact brother and sister.[4]

A later manual gave instructions on how to use organ stops to mimic a host of effects such as snoring, a barking dog, and thunderstorms.[5] Since those early days when music for film was outside the actual filmmaking process and left in the hands of local musicians, it has moved to the inside of the industry and developed into an integral part of the filmmaking process, film composition becoming a major part of the industry.[6]

Film craft today has a trinitarian center—at the heart of a movie three key dynamics are at work: the images, the cinematographic elements of the film that create the visual setting; the narrative sounds of character dialogue and interaction; and the music. What is perhaps surprising is the relatively little attention given to the study of film music. It remains a strangely neglected area of pop music and cultural studies in general, given the huge success of film soundtracks in the pop music charts. That may be a topic to be taken up in another arena. For now, I will examine exactly what it is that music contributes to a film and how we might respond to that theologically.

What Does Music Do?

Before we discuss exactly what music contributes to a film, it might be helpful to reflect for a moment on how music works in a general sense. Although neurobiological research suggests that there is no music center in the brain,[7] Simon Frith notes that there is little doubt that the structure of music evokes feelings in listeners that are then given emotional and metaphorical interpretations. It can make us feel tension, fear, dissatisfaction. It can convey a sense of liveliness or complacency, movement or stillness.[8] As Aristotle wrote, "What we have said makes it clear that music possesses the power of producing an effect on the character of the soul (Politics, 8.1340b)."[9] Music has a structure and a language of its own. We feel sad or happy when listening to certain pieces because there is something of those emotions created in the particular structure of the music. We often describe our feelings on hearing a specific piece of music, but what we are actually describing is something caused by our response to what is happening structurally in the music.[10] This relationship between music and feelings or emotion is a central understanding of film composers, who commonly use music to communicate particular feelings to a great range of people. If we begin with at least this basic understanding of the way music works we can then move on and explore our main question of what it is that music contributes to a film.

Two of my favorite films, particularly from a musical perspective, are the Orson Welles classic from 1941, *Citizen Kane*, and Martin Scorsese's tumultuous and deeply troubling film from 1975, *Taxi Driver*, starring Robert De Niro. What I didn't know for a long time was that the same film composer created the scores for each of those films and that those

Moving beyond a "Literary" Paradigm

films were his first and last scores respectively. The composer was Bernard Herrmann, one of the most influential film composers of all time. He composed scores for forty-eight movies, including Hitchcock's *North by Northwest* and *Psycho* (along with Hitchcock, we have Herrmann to thank for always wondering what lurks behind the shower curtain!). In an article titled "Music of the Fears" for the magazine *Film Comment*,[11] author John Broeck explored the remarkable career of Bernard Herrmann. In that article Herrmann offered some of his own insights into the purpose and function of film music. I have condensed Broeck's expansive reflection of Herrmann's work into four broad categories that I will use to outline some of the major issues to be addressed in order to answer our question.

MUSIC CREATES ATMOSPHERE AND COLORS THE FILM

In my title I alluded to this element of the role of music in film, which is another way of saying what I say here: namely, that music is the means by which a sense of time and space is achieved. In musical terminology this is called "color." Scores must delineate different places and social milieus. Color happens on a number of different creative levels. First it is associative—different instruments conjure up different images—be it bagpipes to evoke the rolling hills of Scotland or the plaintive sound of the koto used to great effect to evoke feudal Japan in *The Last Samurai*.[12] In a larger sense, musical color is the means by which the film can be set into its larger context of time, space, and history, helping establish and situate the story in an accessible way. Is the movie set in the present or the past? Are we on land or on sea? In what geographic location is the action taking place? Helping provide answers to these questions is a function of music as color. This color is established in the opening scenes along with the first camera shots and perspectives, all working together to situate the story. "A composer's first job is to get inside the drama," Herrmann said; anyone who can't do that "shouldn't be writing music at all." The film composer's task is to reinforce the cinematic images while not intruding on the action.

Color reflects the collaborative role of music and story in creating a film's meaning. Musical meaning in a film is not derived exclusively from a knowledge of musical structure. The "Asian" score in *The Last Samurai*, for example, is not understood first of all because we are familiar with Japanese folk music and culture, but by the narrative images on the screen. Conversely, the way we understand what happens on the screen is determined by what we hear. Nicholas Cook, discussing television commercials, but giving insight to this point, writes, "Music transfers its own attributes to the story line and to the product, it creates coherence, making connections that are not there in words or pictures; it even engenders meanings of its own. But it does all this, so to speak, silently."[13] For Cook, music doesn't simply bring color from the outside invading the screen, as it were, but functions instead to interpret what we see. In other words, it allows meaning to happen.

The Italian composer Ennio Morricone offers a slightly different perspective when he says that effective film music has to function like an uninvited dinner guest who, at the risk of embarrassment, should not announce his presence in the room with loud and arrogant gestures but instead should knock at the door asking permission to enter, and once welcomed, move gently into the room meeting people and warmly making him- or herself a welcome addition to the table. Regardless of the kind of film score, whether action-driven or meditative, the music must enter politely, slowly, delicately building relationship with the characters and the story and also with the audience. This coloring process also extends to the character arcs in a given film. Music can often imply a psychological trait of a character much better than dialogue can. George Bluestone claims that "film . . . cannot show us thought directly. It can show us characters thinking, feeling, and speaking, but it cannot show us their thoughts and feelings."[14] On the contrary, I would argue that music can and does show us the thoughts and feelings of a character on-screen. We are cued to murderous intent by music that evokes a certain "unhingedness," and sense a character's yearning or desire more often by music than by word.

Music Invests Particular Scenes with Strong Emotion

While musical color is meant to be unobtrusive and avoid clashing with the narrative, another role that music plays is in imparting strong emotional power to particular scenes and moments in a film. If we return to the work of Herrmann for a moment and consider his famous score for Alfred Hitchcock's *Psycho*, this particular function of film music becomes apparent. Think of the character Marion, in the shower, and try to imagine her demise and not have your mind filled with the dissonant glissandos and violent violin screams that accompany Bates's knife. It has been said that Hitchcock originally wanted no music in this scene, which seems unimaginable after experiencing it with Herrmann's score.

Moving beyond a "Literary" Paradigm

Or consider another Hitchcock-Herrmann collaboration, *Vertigo*, starring James Stewart and Kim Novak, which has more music than spoken dialogue.[15] Virtually the entire film's emotional tone is set by the music. Essentially a chase movie, *Vertigo* revolves around the complex relationship between Scottie (Stewart), an ex-detective suffering from a fear of heights, and Madeleine (Novak), a mysterious woman given to throwing herself from tall buildings. Scottie has been hired by Madeleine's San Francisco business magnate husband to follow her. Both Scottie and Madeleine are complex characters struggling with self-destructive demons, and the film is further complicated by the question of murder. It is the music, however, that opens up these two characters and makes the film compelling. It acts as a haunting memory that seems to propel Scottie deeper and deeper into scenarios threatening his very core, giving voice to the fear that has immobilized him, while at the same time underscoring Madeleine's fragile emotional state. "Vertigo is all about how a dizzy fellow chases after a dizzy dame," is how film critic Bosley Crowther described the film in his *New York Times* review in 1958, and dizzy is how the music makes us feel throughout the movie.

In film the music can also provide an emotional environment that allows for the transformation of dialogue from prose into the poetic.[16] This is, of course, not always the case; all too often dialogue is what lets a film down. Stilted and generic dialogue—a hallmark of action-based movies—is sometimes not even transcended by the most powerful film music. But there are moments when the music literally allows words to soar and transforms them from mere dialogue to seminal iconic moments.

CINEMATIC RHYTHM AND MOVEMENT—IT'S ALL IN THE MUSIC

The great composer Aaron Copland, writing about the art of film music, said:

> The other day I saw a picture that had as its setting medieval Europe. There was one scene in a cathedral, and the accompanying music was a most authentic fifteenth century motet. But the next shot was of the heroine, and the score immediately shifted to a reflection of the sweetest of Strauss waltzes, thus projecting the audience four centuries forward in as many seconds.[17]

Movement in film is the domain of music. It is the music that slows a scene down or in cases such as Copland described, shifts a whole film in a particular direction. It is not simply that actions in film require active music, it is that the whole rhythm of a film is linked to the music. Sometimes a composer can shift the focus away from a character's particular actions at a given moment. Liam Neeson as Scottish folk hero Rob Roy, in the film of the same name, running through the Scottish highlands, is accompanied by the slow beat of animal-skin drums clearly out of synch with the actual. In *Citizen Kane*, Herrmann ties the audience to the forward motion of the film by a constant key and tempo change and a recurring bass chord that attends the towering and dark gothic house where Kane resides. In *Taxi Driver*, Herrmann's last movie score, the film attempts to reveal the apocalyptic darkness lurking beneath the surface in post-hippie, post-Vietnam America. A deep sense of the loss of faith inhabits the film, and there is a sense in which the entire film feels like standing on the edge of a cliff waiting to fall off into chaos, and again Herrmann's score signals this movement, catapulting us into the mad, troubled world of Travis Bickle.

The pace and shape of a film can be dictated by the musical score. Ennio Morricone's scores for Sergio Leone's "spaghetti Westerns" (*The Good, the Bad and the Ugly* being the best known) created a pace and movement for the entire film series. The music was sparse, staccato, and iconic in nature—lots of musical space suggesting the emptiness of the Western environment. It evoked cowboys' sentiments in the audience, even though the films themselves were far from traditional Western tales, underscoring the debt Leone was attempting to pay to an entire genre of movies (Westerns). The music determined that the films unfold in a certain way—not in the traditional way Western stories were usually told but in a somewhat disconnected and fragmented manner. This approach to the score had ramifications beyond the films themselves. So iconic was the music and so strong its associations with the central character played by Clint Eastwood that it has shaped in his acting career what has turned into a lifelong rhythm for the actor's emotional arc—playing characters that are usually cool and slow (the Dirty Harry series, for instance), moving at a different pace from that of the rest of the world—methodical, emotionally cold, and often cruel.

The Communicating Link between Screen and Audience

Aaron Copland and Bernard Herrmann shared similar perspectives on the ultimate function of film music, and I will quote them at length here. Copland, in "The Aims of Music for Films," said film music was designed to "strengthen and underline the emotional content of the entire picture."

Moving beyond a "Literary" Paradigm

He quoted Virgil Thompson, whose conception was that the score of a motion picture

supplies a bit of human warmth to the black-and-white, two-dimensional figures on the screen, giving them a communicable sympathy that they otherwise would not have, bridging the gap between the screen and the audience. The quickest way to a person's brain is through his eye but even in the movies the quickest way to his heart and feelings is still through the ear.[18]

Despite the patriarchal use of language and reference to a time when color film had yet to be introduced, Thompson touches on a key issue of the function of music in film. Music connects us in profound ways to the story on the screen—providing clues to the characters, creating coherence, linking us to time and space, drawing us into the world created on-screen. Herrmann, himself a champion of Copland and others during his tenure as conductor for the Columbia Workshop, had this to say on the same subject: "Music is the communicating link between the screen and the audience, reaching out and enveloping all into one single experience." What they both seem to be saying is that music is a bridge between the two worlds that collide in the cinema: the real world of the audience and the imagined world being presented on the screen.

Part Two: The Future Sound of Color

Pop as Self-Definition and Orientation

Pop music can serve as a film's memory, instantaneously linking it with its audience, tapping into a nostalgic past or fixing the film firmly in the present.

J. Romney and A. Wootton[19]

The roots of film music composition are, as noted earlier, firmly in the classical realm. One has only to listen to the orchestral scores that dominate film music to realize the continuing connection. The majority of big-budget Hollywood films still tend to rely on the orchestral film score to signal the film's importance (which is indicative of music's acknowledged power within the movie industry). It has become the standard, or norm, for major moviemaking today.

Since the 1950s, however, another musical thread has been woven into the fabric of cinema: pop music. At first, the introduction of pop music into films was largely within the confines of the actual story. Movies like *Blue Hawaii*, starring Elvis Presley, and *A Hard Day's Night*, featuring the Beatles, are examples. In such films, the music *was* the story. But as popular music has continued to gain ascendancy within contemporary culture, it has moved, if you will, to the other side of the camera and become an integral part of newer dynamics in filmmaking that are the result of cultural and technological developments over the past thirty to forty years.[20] In the 1970s films like *Midnight Cowboy* and *The Graduate* used pop music as film score, building the rest of the film's music around popular music compositions, establishing a new relationship between film and music.

For unlike a more conventional film score, pop music is often not written exclusively for a film. It preexists. This changes the relationship between music and film. Pop music thus works in a different way from traditional film scores and introduces some new points for consideration when contemplating the role of music in film. Does the fact that the music preexists influence this dynamic? What informs the choice of a specific piece of pop music in a film? And what are the theological issues raised by this use of music?

Perhaps an exploration of the films of Quentin Tarantino can shed light on these questions. All of Tarantino's films are scored by pop music of various styles and genres, which is as much a characteristic of his films as the unique characters and story lines that populate them. Tarantino is a self-confessed pop culture junkie, and his films are loaded with oblique and opaque references to various elements of popular culture that he loves—pop music, Japanese anime, Hong Kong action films, film noir, B films, and a host of American pop cultural artifacts from just about every decade since the 1950s, particularly the sixties and seventies. This love of pop culture is a key feature of Tarantino's appeal: people who watch his movies often share similar likes and loves, and identifying the references being made is a key part of engaging with his films.

One of Tarantino's principal devices is the discussion of pop music within the story lines of his films. Thus, a person's knowledge of the particular piece of music being discussed in the film adds another opportunity for connection with the story. For instance, his 1991 movie, *Reservoir Dogs,* opens with a group of men seated around a table in a diner discussing the meaning of Madonna's song *Like a Virgin*. Our introduction to the film's characters is achieved through a discussion about pop music. The various characters offer their views on the song and on Madonna in general. Their relationship is being defined for us through their pop music discourses before we even know who these characters really are, and we, as audience members with our own opinions about the song and artists in question, make character assessments based on the contributions the actors make to the conversation. The lively conversation about Madonna's canon of songs also implies a deep friendship among these men—only later do we discover that they barely know each other, and that it was this music conversation that actually brought them together.

Tarantino often uses music in this manner as a way of establishing character identity. The effect is similar to the more traditional composition technique of assigning a particular instrument or melody or piece of mood music to a character in a film. For instance, when we hear ominous strings in a horror film, chances are that a bad person is about to show up and do something horrible to someone—the music serves as an aural cue to both the impending action and the character of the actor initiating events in the film. For Tarantino, pop music is used for a similar purpose. However, the use of pop music differs from the traditional score because we may have a "subjective history" with a pop song. Often a song is woven into the emotional fabric of the lives of moviegoers long before they hear it being used specifically in a movie. This provides a new set of dynamics within our cinematic experience: not all the audience will hear it the same way.

When I was a teenager my friends and I used to go regularly to a place called the California Ballroom in Dunstable, fifty miles or so from where I lived. Its official name may have been the California Ballroom but we all called it "Soul City." It was a huge barn of a place where two thousand or more people could see the latest soul and funk bands from America. I saw many of my favorite bands there when I was growing up. In 1974 I went to see the Philadelphia-based soul group the Delfonics, whose albums were never far from my stereo. Their 1971 Grammy winner, *Didn't I Blow Your Mind (This Time)*, written by lead vocalist William Hart, was one of my all-time favorite songs. It is one of those soul songs about heartache, love, and desire that would sound really cheesy were it not for the great voices singing the lyric. The Delfonics did not disappoint when performing the song live. I can close my eyes and recall the moment when the synthesized trumpet call, which marks the opening chords of the song, flowed from the stage and the audience, myself included, erupted into blissful euphoria. "I gave my heart and soul to you girl / didn't I do it baby / didn't I do it baby. . . . Didn't I blow your mind this time, didn't I?" We were all carried away, the cultural divide between downtown Philly and semi-rural England erased by a shared love for sweet soul music.

When I moved to America I had to leave my vast record collection behind—it is still in the bedroom at my parents' home, gathering dust. But I am lucky enough to live in the world of iTunes where any song I desire is just ninety-nine cents and a download away. Needless to say, the Delfonics made their way back into my music collection. However, it was a movie that reminded me of how much I loved the song. It showed up in Quentin Tarantino's 1997 movie *Jackie Brown*. Jackie, the central character played by Pam Grier, an actress who gained cult status through her performances in seventies-era "blaxploitation" movies, expresses her love of the Delfonics to Max (Robert Forster). Later he buys a Delfonics album and listens to it in his car. Max vicariously attempts to get closer to Jackie through the music. Not only do the characters in the movie define their relationships by this discourse about pop music, we also define our relationships by such discourse. We agree or disagree with their musical tastes, and are partly relating to the characters through their taste in music. As an avid fan of soul music, I completely understood Max's purpose in using the songs.

Tarantino's characters reveal how conversation around pop music works within a culture; it helps us define ourselves, and part of this self-definition is achieved through comparison with the musical tastes and choices of others. "I like this piece of music—they don't—therefore . . ." Music, then, becomes a "jumble of references and assumptions, a fusion of musical, cultural, historical and cinematic illusions," writes Simon Frith.

> We all hear the music we like as something special, as something that defines the mundane, takes us out of ourselves, puts us somewhere else. . . . Music constructs our sense of identity through the experiences it offers of the body, time and sociability.[21]

Pop music is loaded with meaning; it has a cultural specificity. A song can have meaning outside of its lyrics and tune, conjuring up connections with a time, place, or situation that it doesn't necessarily refer to (such as my own association of the Delfonics with a place in England in 1974).

The Song Is the Story—The Story Is the Song

> If I start to seriously consider the idea of doing a movie, I immediately try to find out what would be the right song to be the opening credit sequence even before I write the movie.
>
> Quentin Tarantino

Moving beyond a "Literary" Paradigm

Why do directors like Tarantino or Cameron Crowe, both of whom are key proponents of the use of pop music in film, pick a certain piece of music? What is it about that particular piece of pop that could make us examine a scene in a different way, and how does this work? Because of its cultural specificity and separate history, which exist before a film is made, there is a chance that pop music will bring a new level of meaning to the film. The use of soul and funk music in Tarantino's *Jackie Brown*, as we have seen, added depth to one's understanding of the movie. As an homage to blaxploitation films of the seventies, the movie used pop music to create associations with a genre, time, and place. Pam Grier, the heroine, also linked us to the genre (provided we were aware of the existence of such a genre, which again, added a new layer of meaning to the film—the viewers' awareness of pop cultural references and artifacts, giving them the advantage of bringing external information to the film experience, thus expanding the meaning potential). Add to this the additional information that the film was based on an Elmore Leonard novel (Leonard was famous for seventies crime stories) and we begin to see the potential for a multiplication of meaning in Tarantino's movies.

Blaxploitation films were often low-budget, but they were also often politically and socially charged, highlighting the marginalization of African Americans on the one hand but empowering those same communities on the other. So the film is not solely responsible for the connections it makes. It does not exist in a vacuum but rather cross-references pop culture in order to deepen its own meaning-making potentials. It becomes a part of a larger network of mood creators by using outside sources to fuel its own inner meaning. In weaving this interactive web, Tarantino often uses obscure pop songs to make his case. He seldom uses mainstream pop hits in the traditional sense—perhaps to minimize the "outside" influences— but this precludes those who have limited knowledge of the artifacts from fully relating to everything that is going on. This may explain why there is often a love or hate response to Tarantino's work. Tarantino takes a song and makes it his. He says, "If a song in a movie is used really well, as far as I'm concerned that movie owns that song, it can never be used again."[22] The question must then be asked, how does this affect the film?

Music Applied to the Narrative

"Girl, You'll Be a Woman Soon"
> *Pulp Fiction*, 1994

In Tarantino's breakout film, *Pulp Fiction*, the two central characters, played by John Travolta and Uma Thurman, define their relationship for the audience by dancing to a song. Thurman plays Mia Wallace, the wife of a crime boss that Travolta's character, Vincent Vega, works for. Vega is assigned to keep Mia company while his boss is away. She wants to go out to eat and they wind up at a diner.[23] At the diner, a dance competition unfolds and Thurman decides she wants to dance. Once again external pop cultural references begin to fly. Vega is played by Travolta, who came to fame for his role as Tony Manera, the Brooklyn guy who strikes gold on the dance floor in the movie *Saturday Night Fever*. Are we watching Vega dancing in *Pulp Fiction*? Or Tony Manera? Or John Travolta? Or perhaps it's all of them rolled into one.

Before this event both Mia and Vega are uncomfortable and forced in their relationship with each other, but intimate environments coupled with the intimacy of dancing as a couple draw them together in new ways. The lyrics of the song "Girl, You'll Be a Woman Soon" also "tell" the story of their relationship. Later, after their prize-winning dance and a drug overdose, which they keep as a secret between themselves, their relationship enters a new equilibrium. The songs tell us things about the characters they do not fully know about themselves—how and where they listen to music, and what kind of music they listen to. Film writer Jonathan Romney says that "Tarantino knows that the exact placement of a song within a movie can shape and change the nature of the on-screen story." But what Romney attributes to Tarantino is something that many smart filmmakers understand. Tarantino's particular gift is that he generates multiple layers of meaning by using pop songs to achieve this goal.

The Source of Sound and the Construct of Cool

Although Tarantino's use of pop music is complex and calculated, he always gives his viewers specific reasons within the film for the songs to be there. With him it is never enough to simply use a device like a radio, as he did in *Reservoir Dogs*, or a live band, as he did in *Pulp Fiction*. He doesn't want the songs to appear to be manipulative or send the wrong message. He uses a lot of sixties and seventies music, which immediately raises the specter of nostalgia, but his films are rooted firmly in the present. His concern seems to be in creating the concept of cool rather than simply evoking nostalgia. I said that I would not address the "post" word in this chapter, but I fear that I must say that nostalgia is simply not part of the

Moving beyond a "Literary" Paradigm

postmodern world that Tarantino inhabits or creates. This is reflected in his eclectic, and therefore "cool," musical choices.

In contemporary films, as in contemporary culture, being cool is an important issue, and again one that contributes to the overall success of a film. As Dick Pountain and David Robins write in *Cool Rules*, "What happened (in the sixties) is that hip (or cool) became central to the way capitalism understood itself and explained itself to the public."[24] While being cool may seem slight and vapid, it is a key dynamic of early twenty-first-century cultural life. Self-understanding is increasingly linked to the concept of cool, and if something is cool, then viewers will take the time necessary to explore the story presented to them, something that older filmmakers probably did not have to contend with. The use of pop music in films is one way filmmakers can raise their "cool factor" and find a broader audience for their films. This adds another dynamic to the ways in which pop music in film can contribute to the meaning-making process. It becomes a part of the decision-making process that people apply to a particular film. The music can do great harm or give added strength to a particular screen story. The rise of soundtrack CDs to the top of the Billboard music charts seems to bear witness to that.

Conclusion

Music and Meaning Making in Film

I think that, sometimes, the most simple tune can unlock so much more than anything else in a picture.

Lisa Gerard

What I have attempted to do in this chapter is briefly sketch a series of points that highlight a set of codes[25] by which we can understand the contribution that music makes to film. I will summarize them here in a more systematic way so that readers may return to the movies armed with a few tools to enhance their movie-watching experience. The first of these is the *emotional code* that music brings to a film—the ways in which music is understood to convey emotions and feelings. The emotional aspect of film music is linked, in particular, to a classical structuring in film composition. Most classical music is devoid of words, instead using its structures to convey story line and emotion.[26] Emotional codes work on two fronts: there is music created to tell the audience how to feel, and there is music created to inform us how the characters in the film are feeling at any given moment.

Pop music also has a set of emotional codes, but as we observed in the second portion of this chapter, pop songs draw from a broader palette of ideas. Their use of words separates them from most classical scores, but the language of popular music is primarily an emotional discourse anyway. As we listen, we tend to *feel* the meaning of songs, the words actually becoming emotional enhancers rather than being simply discursive.

A second set of codes, *dramatic codes*, uses music in a variety of ways to support and strengthen the narrative effect. This set of codes comes into play with regard to rhythm and motion, propelling the drama or holding it back. Unlike music used to give emotional codes, music deployed in this manner is not telling us what to feel or think, nor is it telling us where we are. It is instead focused on helping us place ourselves in the unfolding story.

The final set of codes we have referenced are *cultural codes*—the use of music to tell us where we are—to reveal as economically as possible the basic social and cultural facts of the images we are seeing so that we can get on with the story. These codes encompass place, time, geography, and cultural conventions, all of which tell us what the images and narratives do not have the time or space to tell.

Challenges to Theology

To engage with film, to do theology in this context, will require much from us. We will have to be prepared to lay aside our objective and sometimes prepackaged ideas and do our theology at the intersection of film and gospel, at the screen, if you will, "sitting in the darkness in order to find the light."[27] To acknowledge the role that music plays in the creation of meaning in film is to recognize that at least two of the central dynamics of the filmmaking process, music and images, are not discursive forms of communication. Their meanings are understood symbolically and, thus, engaging with the narrative element of the film will not be enough. Of course the narrative element invites dialogue and engagement in ways that the symbolic nature of image and music do not. But if the meaning-making element of a film comprises three ingredients—narrative, image, and sound—then our theological engagement needs to be with all three elements in order to fully enter into the story being presented.

Cinema today with its embrace of advanced technologies and special effects creates virtually fully realized "other worlds." Those worlds are

Moving beyond a "Literary" Paradigm

made by combining imagery with narrative and music, and our theological response needs to encompass all three elements. Roy Anker gives a perfect example of this in his book *Catching Light*, as he explores the construction of meaning in Krzysztof Kieślowski's *Three Colors: Blue*.[28] Blue, Anker notes, is the central motif of the film and is represented in the images, the narrative, and the music. Kieślowski wants to convey the nature and fullness of divine love, a redemptive love prodding the life of the emotionally devastated central character, Julie (Juliet Binoche), who has been battered by the crippling loss of both her composer husband and her only child in a car accident. Kieślowski accomplishes this through a pervasive use of the color blue. The color soaks virtually every frame of the film, but blue also symbolically colors the narrative and the music. The film ends on a high note because the central character learns to live and love again. Here's how Anker describes the film:

> Of greater narrative importance are those resounding musical visions, again soaked in blue, that come out of nowhere to envelop, transfix, and assail Julie with the momentousness and utter rapture of living itself. . . . These events along with the music prod Julie to realize that she cannot run from life; what the music claims about life is real and inescapable. . . . As the closing montage suggests, love of life and God go everywhere, as omnipresent as the blue that pervades the film, especially to the joy and sorrow that ever mysteriously tangle up and wrestle in the midst of living.[29]

The theology that emerges from this kind of engagement is not so much a theology of answers as a theology of engagement: a poetic evocation of the gospel rather than a prosaic recitation of truth already known and digested—a theology where blue just might be the color of love.

Notes

1. The first section will focus heavily on the works of composer Bernard Herrmann, whose musical scores offer rich examples of the importance of music to film. This is an arbitrary choice, based more on my own cinematic likes and dislikes than anything else. Fortunately, Herrmann's body of work is broad and covers a large portion of cinema history, and so works well as an exemplar.

2. See Craig Detweiler and Barry Taylor, "Introduction," *A Matrix of Meanings: Finding God in Popular Culture* (Grand Rapids: Baker Academic, 2001), for an example of what I mean when I say the "canon" of popular culture.

3. In keeping with the first section of the chapter, the second will also feature examples drawn from my own subjective engagement with film and film music. I should also warn the reader that I have a limited career as a composer of music for films, and therefore am probably unduly

fixated on music in film. Music has always been, both in and out of movies, a first love, so I write out of passion as much as anything else.

4. Quoted in Gillian B. Anderson, "The Presentation of Silent Films, or Music as Anesthesia," *Journal of Musicology* 5, no. 2 (1987): 279.

5. Ibid., 269.

6. This shift from "outside to inside" speaks to many of the influences at work in film music. Simon Frith in his book *Performing Rites: On the Value of Popular Music* (Cambridge, MA: Harvard University Press, 1996), 110, notes that cinema draws on a variety of popular and artistic traditions—vaudeville, melodrama, circus, and pantomime on one hand, and opera and ballet on the other. Frith goes on to suggest that in the popular traditions such as vaudeville and circus the music functions largely as an accompaniment to the action and is used to describe it aurally, whereas in the art forms such as opera and ballet the music produces the action. I would argue that the developments in film have shifted it away from its more vaudevillian roots, and music has followed a similar developmental arc that has changed some of the ways film music should be understood.

7. Howard Bloom, "Music Stirs More Masses Than You Think," *What Is Enlightenment?* 27 (October–December 2004): 45.

8. Frith, *Performing Rites*, 104.

9. Aristotle, *The Politics*, trans. Ernest Barker, rev. R. F. Stalley (New York: Oxford, 1998), 310.

10. In rock music chord progressions rooted in minor chord variations are common structures for the creation of music that aims to evoke the anger, frustration, and melancholy that inform the genre.

11. John Broeck, "Music of the Fears," *Film Comment* (September–October 1976): http://uib.no/herrmann/articles/music_of_the_fears/.

12. The music for *The Last Samurai* was composed by Hans Zimmer, a German composer based in Los Angeles, and was created using the pentatonic scale of Western music. It is not authentic Japanese music but rather an evocation created in ways by which Western audiences could interpret the references. For most of us, the complexity of Japanese music, which uses different forms and structures, would have been too difficult to comprehend and would therefore have had a less dramatic effect on us.

13. Nicholas Cook, *Music, Imagination and Culture* (Oxford: Clarendon, 1990), 35.

14. George Bluestone, *Novels into Film* (Baltimore: Johns Hopkins University Press, 2003), 47–48.

15. Broeck, "Music of the Fears."

16. Frith does this category more justice than I will. I recommend that the reader refer to his section on the relationship between film and opera in *Performing Rights*, 110–12.

17. Quoted in Aaron Copland, "The Aims of Music for Films," *New York Times*, March 10, 1940, www.nytimes.com/books/99/03/14/specials/copland-aims.html.

18. Virgil Thompson, quoted in Copland, "Aims of Music for Films."

19. J. Romney and A. Wootton, *Celluloid Jukebox: Pop Music and the Movies since the 50s* (London: BFI Publishing, 1995), 7.

20. The development of new technologies in both audio and visual communications, digital technology, computer animation, new editing and composing techniques, etc.

21. Frith, *Performing Rites*, 78.

22. Romney and Wootton, *Celluloid Jukebox*, 131.

23. The diner itself is a clue to Tarantino's approach to history. It is a retro-looking space inhabited by waiters who are celebrity look-alikes, and the decor and feel of the place is a compression of pop culture through the decades—no delineation, no sanctity, just everything thrown together in one huge pile.

Moving beyond a "Literary" Paradigm

24. Dick Pountain and David Robins, *Cool Rules: Anatomy of an Attitude* (London: Reaktion Books, 2000), 11.

25. I am indebted to a number of writers for these categories, which are central to popular music theory and study. In particular, Simon Frith, Nicholas Cook, and Richard Middleton, in their major works, have all offered variations on these codes.

26. This is why many contemporary films successfully integrate electronic music as a viable alternative to more orchestrally based scores. Electronic music has its roots in the later developments of classical music, which occurred at the dawn of the twentieth century. Electronic music is often described as ambient music—atmospheric music committed to evoking environment and landscape—and has been called the "classical music of the future." Mark Prendergast, *The Ambient Century: From Mahler to Trance* (New York: Bloomsbury USA, 2000), introduction.

27. Gerard Loughlin, *Alien Sex: The Body and Desire in Cinema and Theology* (London: Blackwell, 2004), 50.

28. Roy M. Anker, *Catching Light: Looking for God in the Movies* (Grand Rapids: Eerdmans, 2004), 364–401.

29. Ibid., 410.

Section 2

Broadening Our Film Selection

3

World Cinema

Opportunities for Dialogue with Religion and Theology

GAYE WILLIAMS ORTIZ

Introduction

Many people were surprised at the phenomenal worldwide cinematic success of Mel Gibson's *Passion of the Christ* (2004). Yet religion and film have long been allies in the world of entertainment. The most popular films in the early days of cinema were based on stories from the Bible: an evangelist in the 1880s predicted that moving pictures would one day be the best teachers and preachers in the history of the world. Even the Vatican, in its pronouncements on social communications, such as the 1971 document *Communio et progressio,* recognized that films can provide a useful point of contact between faith and culture.

Since the mid-twentieth century the Catholic Church, through the International Catholic Organization for Cinema, has nurtured a close bond with the film industry around the world, giving Catholic (and more recently, ecumenical Christian) awards at major film festivals such as Cannes and Venice. Interfilm, a Protestant organization connected with the World

Association for Christian Communication (WACC), has collaborated ecumenically with Catholics at film festivals since the days of the Second Vatican Council. Recently, the Catholic spirit of collaboration has been extended to groundbreaking interfaith juries in Australia and Iran. In the 2003 Brisbane Film Festival the interfaith jury comprising Jewish, Muslim, and Catholic jurors awarded a prize for the first time. The government-sponsored film industry in Iran made contact with the Vatican in 2001, resulting in the first interfaith award from a jury of Catholics and Muslims at the Fajr Festival in Tehran in 2003. The basis for interfaith collaboration in film festival awards was established over thirty years ago in Sri Lanka, where SIGNIS holds the annual national Salutation Awards for film and television production; since Buddhism is the principal religion in that country, most winners are of that faith.

This chapter will evaluate the possibility of a contemporary dialogue between world cinema and religion and theology, taking into account the history of religion in film and recent trends in world cinema. It addresses world cinema in the context of American culture, and suggests that the challenge of embracing different cultures and the Other through world cinema is one that American educators, writers, and church leaders can issue to society. It may be a small step toward tolerance, but nonetheless an important one, in that the viewing of films from around the world could offset the post-9/11 perception of cultural isolation felt by many Americans.

Defining World Cinema

> Every film is a foreign film, foreign to some audience somewhere.
>
> Atom Egoyan and Ian Balfour, introduction to *Subtitles*

In the introduction to their edited volume *Subtitles: On the Foreignness of Film* Atom Egoyan and Ian Balfour attempt to tease out the meanings associated with the word "foreign," and in doing so they confront many of the implicit biases and prejudices that Americans in particular might have in considering films made outside of the United States. On a broader cultural (and even theological) level these meanings also resonate, I feel certain, with all of us as we contemplate that which is different from us and which we have to make an effort to understand.

"Foreign" can mean "nonnatural," as in an invasive item that is "situated in an abnormal or improper place."[1] It can also refer to exotica, as Egoyan and Balfour suggest, "in an old-fashioned *National Geographic* sort of way."[2] Philip Kerr, writing about foreign film watching in *New Statesman*, describes one of the thrills of becoming an "armchair polyglot" as the indulgence in "vicarious tourism and amateur anthropology."[3] Being able to safely and distantly view different parts of the world from one's cinema seat offers a certain attraction in these days of homeland security paranoia.

Another less desirable meaning of "foreign" is "un-American," in the same way that some Americans practice patriotism through the purchase of American-made automobiles and shun "foreign" cars. *Subtitles* contributor Amresh Sinha[4] claims that foreign films hold a dubious status in American society, and that the spectators of foreign films might be identified as people who are more tolerant of multiculturalism in the United States. Thus, they are viewed with suspicion by those Americans who feel that foreign-made items, films included, are harmful or at the very least hostile to the American way of life. The current political hot potato of illegal immigration has exposed distasteful cultural biases held by Americans against "foreigners" who take advantage of opportunities and freedoms this country offers.

Foreign films, with their ability to open up the world to audiences, offer a duality of openness and threat. On the one hand, as Ruby Rich observes, subtitles "allow us to hear other people's voices intact and give us full access to their subjectivity. Subtitles acknowledge that our language . . . is only one of many languages in the world."[5] On the other hand, these films are "full of foreigners," Kerr sagely observes, and thus may repel xenophobes and monolinguists.

Americans are known for their "scandalous lack of foreign language ability";[6] hence, the necessity for subtitles for American audiences introduces another complication. As Kerr describes it, the process of reading a subtitle "adds a . . . literate quality to the whole film experience."[7] Kerr couches this characteristic in positive terms, but according to the president of a firm that monitors cinema box office performance, it is a drawback to greater American consumption of foreign film:

> American audiences generally don't want to go to the movies to read. They'd rather the experience flow over them, be spoon-fed rather than interactive. Reading dialogue takes them out of the movie, they say, shattering the illusion.[8]

Before we lose sight of the meaning of "foreign" in filmic terms, it is worth considering the part that the Academy of Motion Pictures Arts and

Sciences (AMPAS) played in institutionalizing a particularly cinematic concept of the foreign, through its rules that determine the eligibility of foreign-language film entries. AMPAS was formed in 1927, but it was not until 1948 that it officially acknowledged "foreign-language" films. John Mowitt says it was then that a Special Awards rule was rewritten to allow for "the foreign language film award for which pictures need not be in English or have English subtitles and need not to have been shown in the United States."[9] However, this apparently straightforward definition came under scrutiny in 1972, when the first Jamaican feature film, *The Harder They Come* (d. Perry Henzell), was ruled ineligible for that category. The Academy determined that the "Calypso [*sic*]" language spoken in the film was in fact an English dialect, and therefore the film had not been made in a language other than English.[10]

The term "foreign-language film" may establish a particular Anglocentric definition for movies, but for the purposes of this chapter the term "world cinema" has been selected for use because it has a more inclusive and less pejorative meaning than we have been discussing. Indeed, the annual survey of filmmaking and film festivals in *Variety International Film Guide 2005* indicates a continuing dispersion of cinematic activity literally across the globe: its World Survey section features ninety-seven countries in which films were made in 2003–4, twenty-one more than in the previous edition.[11]

The Engagement of Religion and Theology with World Cinema

S. Brent Plate, in *Representing Religion in World Cinema*, complains that scholars of theology and religion who write and teach about religion/theology and film fall into the trap of using mainly (if not exclusively) Hollywood/English-language films. He stresses the need for attention to world cinema by featuring essays that offer an "alternative voice to the Hollywoodcentrism that resides within religion and film circles."[12] Although this has certainly been a tendency noticed with some alarm by theologians who deplore the inherent dangers of commercialism within Hollywood film culture and who warn their colleagues against cozying up to it in their haste to dialogue with popular culture,[13] it has not, perhaps, always been as prevalent. In the early days of religion/theology and film scholarship, for every analysis of American cinema[14] there was at least as much written about filmmakers such as Buñuel, Fellini, Tarkovsky, Truffaut, and especially Bergman.[15] In fact, in 1976 Andrew Greeley declared a preference for European filmmakers, who at least asked "the God question" that American filmmakers would never touch, observing that at least two of these Europeans whose films were consistently religious were in fact unbelievers.[16] Greeley complained, "European directors are not afraid to speak directly about the meaning of human life and the mystery of human death—which is what religion is supposed to be all about."[17] However, the academic preoccupation with art-house cinema only contributed to the ivory-tower elitist image of theologians, culturally far removed from the everyday lives of moviegoers who preferred *Jaws* to *The Seventh Seal*.

In addition to academic writings and research, there has been a long-established theological engagement with the arts in general. Jeremy Begbie calls the arts "powerful theological interpreters," which for the past three centuries have been squeezed out of academic theology by a preference for intellectual abstraction, a theology practiced by those in colleges and universities.[18] The Roman Catholic Church has for centuries been a patron of the arts, but in the past century it has developed a relationship with the film industry in particular.[19] As the church began to appreciate the potential of film as a catechetical tool, some clergy began to incorporate films into their educational programs, none more eagerly, it seems, than Abbé Joseph Alexis Joye, who over the course of a decade used film in his small Swiss parish and developed an extensive cinematic collection that was eventually bequeathed to the Jesuits.[20] The church was also involved in producing and exhibiting film in the first decades of the film industry; there were fifty-two Catholic cinema halls in Belgium by 1912, and in Europe the popularity of parish hall screenings gave rise to the publication of film review magazines like *Eco deglio Oratori* in Italy, *Le Fascinateur* in France, and *Filmrundschau* in Germany.[21] The absence of any government regulation or restriction on early filmmaking not only allowed the Catholic Church to experiment with it as an evangelizing tool but also led to the lowering of moral standards within the film industry, especially in Hollywood; in response, the Catholic call for an organized effort to educate the public about cinema led to the establishment in Belgium of the International Catholic Organization for Cinema.

The International Catholic Organization for Cinema and Audiovisual (OCIC) was founded in 1928 following several decades of Catholic involvement in film production and exhibition in western Europe, and Catholic interest in the world of cinema has continued to be supported theologically through decades of church teaching. In 1936 the first papal encyclical to deal with the subject of film was written,[22] followed by another in 1957 that broadened papal concern beyond film to the broadcasting media.[23] These and other Vatican documents written about film offer an overarching perspective on film as a positive and empowering medium.[24] The work of OCIC was praised in many of the papal pronouncements on media in the following decades of the twentieth century, although once the organization established a presence after World War II at the major European film festivals, there were also disagreements between the Vatican and OCIC over jury prizes awarded to controversial films. However, the autonomy that OCIC fought for and won in this aspect of its work has allowed for a steady expansion of the presence of Christian ecumenical juries at film festivals and even, since OCIC's merger in 2001 with Unda (the international Catholic broadcasting organization) to form a new world Catholic association for communication named SIGNIS, interfaith juries.[25] In 2004 approximately 150 people participated in SIGNIS juries across the world, giving awards to seventy films or programs from thirty-eight countries.[26]

These juries are presented with a set of criteria for choosing films for their awards. Recently, SIGNIS and Interfilm (the Protestant "sister" organization to SIGNIS) redrafted their criteria to place special emphasis on jury consideration of less accessible films: "The jury should favor quality films whose commercial future seems uncertain as well as those about disadvantaged peoples or regions. The awards can also help independent films to find a wider audience and possibilities for successful distribution."[27]

The SIGNIS and Interfilm commitment to such a worldwide program of festival activity is meant to increase the opportunities for award-winning productions to obtain wider international distribution and exhibition. Filmmakers who receive these awards are often not known outside their regions and appreciate the recognition given by SIGNIS to their works. In 2001, for example, the Iranian (Muslim) filmmaker Mohsen Makhmalbaf received the Cannes Ecumenical Jury prize for *Kandahar*. He immediately placed that jury's logo on all his publicity materials and on the opening credit frames of his film. Kenneth Turan quotes the head of the Toronto Film Festival in saying that festivals are "an alternative distribution network" and confirming the connection between the "current critical rage for Iranian films" and "the intense exposure these works have gotten at Cannes, New York and elsewhere."[28] Festival awards undoubtedly increase the attention paid to foreign films in the contemporary world market, where distribution is the key to films being viewed outside their region of origin.

The Catholic Church's long-standing support of OCIC/SIGNIS in its film festival work is one explicit sign of the theological emphasis on engagement with the world, and especially with popular culture, that has blossomed since the Second Vatican Council.[29] However, the theological interest in film that many Catholic theologians (and filmmakers!) exhibit has not received a reciprocal response from the "secular" world of academics and the film industry, who tend to view any kind of religious engagement as suspicious—not evidence of a serious interest but rather an evangelizing tactic to be avoided.[30] The religious world's fierce engagement with *The Passion of the Christ* (2004) and *The Chronicles of Narnia* (2005), as well as its equally strong aversion to *The Da Vinci Code* (2006), has alerted Hollywood of the need to consider religion in its marketing strategy for films dealing with faith.[31]

Cultural/Religious Imperialism?

Egoyan and Balfour tell us that there has never been a better time to foster an integration of film production from different parts of the world. Indeed, the substantial increase in circulation of world film can be seen in the access that audiences have via postal film rental services such as Netflix, which has a large international film catalogue, and in the ability to order films from across the world through the Internet. The film production centers of Europe and America could seem less hegemonic in that sense, but in terms of box office a different story—the same old story—emerges: the worldwide box office figures for 2004 are topped by *Shrek 2*, *Harry Potter and the Prisoner of Azkaban*, *Spider-Man 2*, *The Passion of the Christ*, and *The Return of the King*.[32] Adrian Martin sees another telltale sign of American domination of film: he claims proof of American imperialism comes in the "vast amount of literature devoted to that film genre known as the musical," which, for all intents and purposes, is really the Hollywood musical.[33] He observes that there is no analytical text yet written offering an international history of the musical. Anytime other musicals—from, for instance, Bollywood—are mentioned in writings, Martin claims they are "inevitably marginalized in relation to the American model."[34]

One genre that seems to be on the rise across the globe is the documentary; Thomas White notes that "of the top ten highest-grossing documentaries of all time . . . eight were released between 2002 and 2004."[35] The creativity displayed by documentary filmmakers over the past five years may have been spurred by politics (*Fahrenheit 9/11*, d. Michael Moore,

2004), war (*Control Room*, d. Jehane Nouhjaim, and *The Fog of War*, d. Errol Morris, both 2004) or social issues (*Super Size Me*, d. Morgan Spurlock, 2004), but White suggests that world audiences are clamoring to see how filmmakers delve deeper into news issues than the news media either want or are able to go. The innovative nature of documentary is evident not only in content but also in technology: the iMovie software that made it possible for Jonathan Caouette to make *Tarnation* (2004) for $218.32; the DVD format that has revived classic documentary titles; and the Internet as a meeting place for filmmakers, a global distribution network, and a vehicle for the personalized viewing experience.[36]

"World film culture still seems primarily a one-way street leading to the West," writes Martin, as he stresses the need to establish a multilingual system of exchange of academic film materials.[37] Although he acknowledges some advances in making world cinema more accessible in Western markets, he sees a cultural blockage manifested both in a macro- and microlevel manner: in an example of the former, Martin notes that Asian films find it almost impossible to get breakthrough releases in Western markets, but if it does happen, then they are subjected to what he describes as "crypto-racist resistance from viewers and gate keeping reviewers alike."[38] The microlevel filter is added when, due to our education, socialization, personal history, and experiences, we privilege certain filmmaking cultures or theories over others. Sara Anson Vaux warns us that "we fail to recognize commonality at our peril," and that although non-Western filmmakers "operate in cultures with differing conceptions of social space than our own, their films suggest alternate spaces where personal and societal transformation may take place."[39]

Theology and Identity: Miroslav Volf and Embracing Difference

Martin's identification of the racist roots of a resistance to cultural difference also applies to the underside of our own religious/theological identities and preferences; just as film culture needs reminding that not everything of worth emanates from Hollywood, so the adherents of major faiths need reminding that any world religion is a mosaic of differing peoples of different cultures and ethnic backgrounds. This is especially true in the United States, the proverbial "melting pot," where Koreans tend to worship in their own linguistically familiar settings and African-American Protestants—at least in the South—worship in churches that are still as segregated from the white community as are the local cemeteries. Margaret Miles has observed that Hollywood films "help Americans entertain concretely the question of how we should live," albeit with formulaic films that offer a limited range of answers. What Americans need, she says, are "films that help Americans picture religious, racial and cultural diversity as irreducible and delightful. So many films picture diversity only to 'transcend' difference by collapsing it into sameness."[40] Can cinema help us wake up to the unconscious/subconscious bias against the unfamiliar language or the different visage of our neighbor? Can it even help foster a breakthrough of an awareness of the common search for transcendence shared between religious communities? It is through these identity issues—which reflect the kinds of societies in which we live—that theologian Miroslav Volf advises theologians to be responsible agents for peace and respectful relationships.

With the dawning of a new millennium haunted by the still-smoldering ashes of genocidal struggles in Yugoslavia, Rwanda, and Botswana—and with the specter of Darfur in our midst—Miroslav Volf declares that "various kinds of 'cultural cleansings' demand of us to place identity and otherness at the center of theological reflection on social realities."[41] He identifies economic and technological developments "of planetary proportions" as instigators of the forces within our cultures seeking to assert "tribal" identity, occurring especially when "extreme imbalances of power and wealth" combine with cultural heterogeneity.[42] Instead of dwelling upon social arrangements that proffer solutions for how society accommodates old and new (or individual and communal) identities, Volf says we must explore "what kind of selves we need to be in order to live in harmony with others."[43] There must first be individual reflection on the self's identity in order to then accept that the identity of another person is valid and deserving of respect. He suggests that our personal perspective of the Other—"from here"—must be tempered with a willingness to step outside ourselves and look at the Other "from there." This self-identification with the Other forms the basis of human relations, and Volf says that, in order to promote "just, truthful and peaceful societies," theologians have a special responsibility to foster this ability to have regard for the Other.

When theologians are not acting as helpmates of economists, political scientists, social philosophers, and so on—and it is part of their responsibility to act in this way—they should concentrate less on social arrangements and more on fostering the kinds of social agents capable of envisioning and creating just, truthful, and peaceful societies, and on shaping a cultural climate in which such agents will thrive.[44]

In the face of large-scale conflict and threats to peace in the world, we are urged to start with the self—the smallest possible scale in cultural terms. Volf posits a visualization of the self's movement toward embrace—opening the arms, waiting, closing the arms, and opening them again—as the way in which the self and the Other can create and complete interaction. The opening of the arms is a symbolic gesture that creates space in oneself for the Other to come in; it signals a desire for the Other and is an invitation, to which the Other reciprocates after the self patiently waits. The one-sidedness of the action is canceled out by the Other reaching out in turn to embrace: as Volf describes it, "If embrace takes place, it will always be because the other has desired the self just as the self has desired the other."[45] The embrace must come to an end, and the opening of arms again confirms that each has retained its original identity—and yet, the arms are open for potentially another embrace. It is a gamble or risk the self takes in opening its arms to another, who may be ally or enemy, yet Volf asserts that, whether the outcome of the embrace is to become a savior or victim, one thing is certain: "a genuine embrace cannot leave both or either completely unchanged."[46]

Cinema, as a cultural form/product that transcends national boundaries in its popularity, can be a unique and appropriate locus in the twenty-first-century world for multicultural and interreligious dialogue, and applying Volf's image of the embrace to the encounter we might have with the Other through film is an intriguing exercise. Through Volf's suggestion that we step outside ourselves, it is necessary to look at how we regard others and the truths or "verities" that we tell ourselves about them. Are these truths formed from experience, or rather, as Volf says, "so many ugly prejudices, bitter fruits of our imaginary fears or our sinister desires to dominate or exclude"?[47]

African filmmakers, Kenneth Turan says, are well aware of the assumptions and stereotypes that the West might form, and countering them in postcolonial African film production is an ability they take as a serious responsibility. He quotes Gaston Kaboré, a filmmaker from Burkina Faso, whose film *Wend Kuuni* (1982) was the first black African film to win a César from the French Académie des Arts et Techniques du Cinéma for best Francophone film: "Traditionally images have been used to dominate Africa, doing damage to the minds of colonized people, telling them they are less important. . . . But ever since we started making films, we have used cinema as a tool of liberation, liberating the individual in his mind. We need to describe our own reality by ourselves."[48]

Antonio Sison identifies this postcolonial reclamation of cinematic narrative as "Third Cinema," in which the representation of third-world peoples is authentic and true to the telling of their own history in the aftermath of colonialism. It is "anti-mythic, anti-racist, anti-bourgeois, and popular."[49] The Roman Catholic religion introduced by the Spanish colonizers was presented and upheld in Filipino culture as the normative religion, although in reality it was foreign; its appropriation by Filipinos and subsequent evolution into folk Catholicism, which in turn has become symbolic of a liberated Filipino identity, is something that is important for filmmakers to communicate in films like *Perfumed Nightmare* (d. Kidlak Tahimik, 1976). This film won ecumenical jury prizes at the Berlin International Film Festival and also found US distribution with the Francis Ford Coppola company Zoetrope.[50] Sison discusses how the Catholic penitential rite of self-mortification practiced during Lent is shown in the film to have symbolic overtones of cultural inferiority, until it is subverted by the self-empowerment of Filipinos, who find divine presence in their own liberation from the utopian visions of "the American dream" turned nightmare.

In examining our internal perspective of the Other, we see how we might have exaggerated, in a positive way, stories about ourselves and our history at the expense of the Other. Certainly the narrativity of film—its ability to tell us a story and make us believe it—has been used many times, by the likes of Goebbels and other propagandists, to pander to our sense of superiority over other peoples. On the one hand, the perception that "foreign" film is somehow primitive, less developed, of lesser quality, may be a fallacy resulting from such presumed Western or American superiority. On the other hand, that perception might be just what filmmakers in another part of the world want to foster so as to distance their work from the status quo. As Catherine Benamou explains, a national cinema trying to establish its own postcolonial identity might abandon conventional cinematic narrativity because it is seen as complicity with Hollywood moviemaking: a "cinema of disenchantment."[51] Benamou recognizes this aversion to Hollywood convention in films from Latin America, which employ gritty, in-your-face realism as well as an avoidance of narrative continuity. Although there is still some concern to make films that are transnationally commercially viable—it is a film industry, after all—the deliberate, iconoclastic break with Hollywood convention says to the rest of the world: we are not representing our experience in the way that Hollywood would; we have our own identity, and you must take our storytelling on our own terms.

However, total comprehension of everything going on in a film in which the characters speak a foreign language is difficult if not impossible for an

English-speaking viewer. The effect of subtitles on those watching a foreign film, as Philip Kerr discusses, might be to smooth out all the "nuances of speech and subtleties of expression in the original language." Because no subtitling, however competent, can catch every scrap of communication, the "sense of participating in the lives of the characters seen on screen is often diminished."[52] In this kind of detachment the self can pass judgment on the Other more easily and often harshly; Volf says that "in popular culture passing a judgment is often deemed an act of exclusion."[53] Rather than recognizing and respecting difference, the self is too quick to yield to a desire to exclude.

There are numerous reasons why we as humans are prone to exclusion and rejection of others: Volf quotes Julia Kristeva's observance that we "persecute others because we are uncomfortable with strangeness within ourselves."[54] But Volf also suggests that anything that "blurs our accepted boundaries, disturbs our identities, and disarranges our symbolic cultural maps" is a threat to our domination of the world as we see it.[55] The lack of intelligent differentiation between things that are dangerous and will hurt us and those that are good for us—in other words, having no boundaries at all—is just as undesirable as creating and keeping an uncompromising distance from anything that is different.

Maintaining a balance between individual identity and boundary maintenance is not easy, especially considering the greater cultural hybridity experienced in contemporary America. But as in Volf's model of embrace, the desire to go outside oneself must be present in order for interplay between self and Other to begin. Volf points to the apostle Paul's proclamation of faith in the crucified Christ, decentering and recentering the self so that the self is radically open to the Other. Because we have to live in the world, among other humans, recognizing that our self's identity can not only be enriched but perhaps transformed by interaction with the Other is key to encouraging world peace, which can only start, in a small way, between two human beings. One's motivation for that move toward the Other, whether it be the faith that Paul proclaimed or a humanist sense of solidarity with humankind, must be based on a desire for harmony in the world.

Conclusion

Those of us who are privileged to be a part of the conversation between religion and theology and film could exercise an option for world cinema, taking that concept from liberation theologians, who urge Christians to exercise an option for the poor; in other words, by introducing our audiences—academic, pastoral, theological, virtual—to the treasures that they might find in world cinema we could be helping to broaden their perspectives on the world. In enticing our students, our congregations, our readers to open their arms to the experience of other cultures in film we may help them become better world citizens, or, at the least, more appreciative of art from another perspective. Margaret Miles says that "film resembles religion, which is fundamentally about how one relates to a larger universe: a natural world, people within one's community, and who is framed as 'other' in order to say who 'we' are."[56] True, watching a film is not the same as meeting another person from another culture face-to-face, but it is a start. Volf says, "There can be no truth between people without the will to embrace the other."[57] A film can take us out of our "from here" perspective and immerse us in the "from there" viewpoint.

Because cinema has become a universal mode of entertainment, films from other countries could be considered prime vehicles for cultural and religious exploration, not only in content and form but also in audience reception. A film is a lens for viewers through which they can glimpse different ways of life and religious values, yet recognize a common humanity. What might that mean in terms of our ability to change the stories we tell ourselves about the Other? Consider what Ruby Rich says about the effects of hearing different voices in subtitled films:

> Somehow, I'd like to think, it's harder to kill people when you hear their voices. It's harder to bomb a country when you've seen their cities in films that you've loved. It's hard to pretend whole cultures needn't exist when you've entered the space of their own yearning and fear and hope. Subtitles, I like to think, are a token of peace.[58]

Notes

1. William Morris, ed., *The American Heritage Dictionary* (Atlanta: Houghton Mifflin, 1969), 514, s.v. "foreign."

2. Atom Egoyan and Ian Balfour, eds., *Subtitles: On the Foreignness of Film* (Cambridge, MA: MIT Press, 2004), 29.

3. Philip Kerr, "How to Become an Armchair Polyglot," *New Statesman*, September 23, 2002, www.newstatesman.com/200209230037.

4. Amresh Sinha, "The Use and Abuse of Subtitles," in Egoyan and Balfour, *Subtitles*, 172.

5. B. Ruby Rich, "To Read or Not to Read: Subtitles, Trailers and Monolingualism," in Egoyan and Balfour, *Subtitles*, 168.

6. The 1979 Presidential Commission for Foreign Languages and International Studies released its report using this description of the state of multilingual capability of the American population (Rich, "To Read or Not to Read," 162).

7. Kerr, "How to Become an Armchair Polyglot."

8. Paul Dergarabedian, of Exhibitor Relations Corporation, quoted in the *Los Angeles Times*, April 27, 2003, in Rich, "To Read or Not to Read," 161–62.

9. John Mowitt, "The Hollywood Sound Tract," in Egoyan and Balfour, *Subtitles,* 383.

10. Ibid., 390.

11. And included for the first time are Cyprus, Ecuador, Kenya, and Rwanda. Daniel Rosenthal, ed., *Variety International Film Guide 2005* (Los Angeles: Silman-James, 2005), 9.

12. S. Brent Plate, ed., *Representing Religion in World Cinema: Filmmaking, Mythmaking, Culture Making* (New York: Palgrave Macmillan, 2003), 9.

13. See David Jasper, "On Systemizing the Unsystematic," in *Explorations in Theology and Film*, ed. Clive Marsh and Gaye Ortiz (Oxford: Blackwell, 1997).

14. See Richard Blake, *Screening America* (Mahwah, NJ: Paulist Press, 1991); John May, ed. *Image and Likeness* (Mahwah, NJ: Paulist Press, 1992).

15. To name a few books, most dealing with religion/spirituality, which offer insights into Bergman's work: Arthur Gibson, *The Silence of God* (New York: Harper & Row, 1969); Robin Wood, *Ingmar Bergman* (New York: Praeger, 1969); Vernon Young, *Cinema Borealis: Ingmar Bergman and the Swedish Ethos* (New York: David Lewis, 1971); Frank Gado, *The Passion of Ingmar Bergman* (Durham, NC: Duke University Press, 1986); Charles B. Ketcham, *The Influence of Existentialism on Ingmar Bergman* (Lewiston, NY: Edwin Mellen, 1986); Robert Lauder, *God, Death, Art and Love* (Mahwah, NJ: Paulist Press, 1989).

16. Luis Buñuel and Ingmar Bergman. See John R. May, "The Demonic in Cinema," in *Religion in Film*, ed. J. R. May and M. Bird (Knoxville: University of Tennessee Press, 1982), 79.

17. Quoted in May, "Demonic in Cinema," 80.

18. Jeremy Begbie, *Beholding the Glory* (Grand Rapids: Baker Academic, 2000), xii.

19. Gaye Williams Ortiz, "The Relationship between the Catholic Church and the Film Industry" (PhD diss., University of Leeds, 2004): details the establishment and operation of Catholic organizations dealing with the medium of film in a professional and empowering manner.

20. Ibid., 12.

21. Ibid., 13.

22. Pius XI, *Vigilanti cura* (1936), in F. Eilers, ed., *Church and Social Communication* (Manila: Logos Publications, 1993), 7–20.

23. Pius XII, *Miranda prorsus* (1957), in Eilers, *Church and Social Communication*, 21–54.

24. *Vigilanti cura* says that film "inspires spectators to right living and education" (4); the recreation for body and soul that film provides is "a necessity" (16); and film "stimulates the imagination" and serves "the purpose of disseminating the right principles of the Christian conscience" (19).

25. Ecumenical juries, such as those at the festivals of Cannes, Locarno, and Berlin, are made up of members from Catholic, Protestant, and Orthodox traditions; the interfaith juries of Brisbane (Australia) and Tehran (Iran) include Jewish, Christian, and Muslim members.

26. *SIGNIS Annual Report 2004* (Brussels: Editions SIGNIS, 2005), 17.

27. "SIGNIS in Juries," in *Workshop Cinema*, a publication of the SIGNIS World Congress, Lyon, France (Brussels: SIGNIS, November 2005), 2.

28. Kenneth Turan, *Sundance to Sarajevo* (Los Angeles: University of California Press, 2002), 8.

29. See the documents "Pastoral Constitution on the Church in the Modern World" (*Gaudium et spes*) (1965) and "Decree on the Means of Social Communication" (*Inter mirifica*) (1963).

30. Ronald Holloway chides those academics who shun theologians who attempt interdisciplinary advances: "Sociology, rather than natural philosophy, is the partner of the modern theologian; likewise, the arena in which the sociologist carries on his [sic] research is the everyday playground of the movies. Thus the film historian undertaking a study of human affairs commits himself, by the act, to becoming a theologian, too," ("Be Thou My Vision," *Risk* 12, nos. 3–4 [1976]: 7).

31. See Peter J. Boyer, "Hollywood Heresy: Marketing *The Da Vinci Code* to Christians," *The New Yorker*, May 22, 2006, http://newyorker.com/printables/fact/060522fa_fact.

32. Daniel Rosenthal, ed., *Variety International Film Guide 2004* (Los Angeles: Silman-James, 2004), 10.

33. Adrian Martin, "Musical Mutations: Before, Beyond and Against Hollywood," in *Movie Mutations*, ed. Jonathan Rosenbaum and Adrian Martin (London: BFI Publishing, 2003), 95.

34. Martin, "Musical Mutations."

35. Thomas White, "How the Documentary Took Flight," in Rosenthal, *Variety International Film Guide 2004*, 43.

36. White, "How the Documentary Took Flight," 46.

37. Nicole Brenez Quintin, Mark Paranson, Adrian Martin, and Jonathan Rosenbaum, "Movie Mutations II: Second Round," in Rosenbaum and Martin, *Movie Mutations*, 180.

38. Ibid.

39. Sara Anson Vaux, "In the Mood for Cinema: Inside Religion/Theology and Film" (paper presented at the 2005 Annual Meeting of the American Academy of Religion, Philadelphia, November 20, 2005).

40. Margaret Miles, quoted in Marvin Hightower, "Religion in the Movies," *Harvard Gazette*, June 6, 1996, www.news.harvard.edu/gazette/1996/06.06/ReligionintheMo.html.

41. Miroslav Volf, *Exclusion and Embrace* (Nashville: Abingdon Press, 1996), 17.

42. Ibid., 20.

43. Ibid., 21.

44. Ibid.

45. Ibid., 143.

46. Ibid., 147.

47. Ibid., 251.

48. Turan, *Sundance to Sarajevo*, 71.

49. Antonio Sison, "*Perfumed Nightmare*: Religion and the Philippine Postcolonial Struggle in Third Cinema," in *Representing Religion in World Cinema*, 183.

50. Sison, "*Perfumed Nightmare*," 182.

51. Catherine Benamou and Lucia Sakes, "Circumatlantic Media Migrations," in Rosenbaum and Martin, *Movie Mutations*, 162.

52. Kerr, "How to Become an Armchair Polyglot."

53. Volf, *Exclusion and Embrace*, 67.

54. Ibid., 78.

55. Ibid.

56. Quoted in Hightower, "Religion in the Movies."

57. Volf, *Exclusion and Embrace*, 258.

58. Rich, "To Read or Not to Read," 168.

4

Letters on Better Movies

SARA ANSON VAUX

To my movie-loving friends, who can't get enough movie watching:

People who write on religion or theology and film have at least one thing in common: they are crazy about movies. You and I are no exceptions. A quick glance at the books and articles in the field (and a rapid scan of syllabi online) reveals an amazingly eclectic sampling of what we cinephiles consider worth our emotional, professional, and recreational time. For me, it's a whole raft of French, Iranian, Asian, British, and African films, classic and new. Oh yes, and Clint Eastwood, Westerns, and films noir. For others, it's *The Godfather*, *What Dreams May Come*, *The Matrix*, chick flicks, apocalypse served hot or cold (*Twelve Monkeys*; *Apocalypse Now*), Woody Allen, Steven Spielberg, *The Shawshank Redemption*, *Star Wars*, and the blockbusters of the day. I don't mean to imply that I don't like the movies or directors on the second list (although I do not in fact like *Dreams*). It does hint that, in this letter, I plan to present the virtues of some films I consider complex, durable, and teachable; say why I prefer to use these rather than others; and offer some ways to locate fertile material in addition to whatever we each use in our own classrooms. But first, my dream movie.

Sometimes, when I have received my fourth e-mail of the day from a colleague asking what movies I'd recommend they use to help teach (fill in the blank here), I am reminded of student teaching days: "If you run out of steam, pull out a movie." I for one am looking forward to the new Anne Boleyn/Henry VIII movie *The Other Boleyn Girl* (2007), starring Scarlett Johansson (*Match Point*, Woody Allen's newest attempt to channel Dostoevsky, which intrigued me); Natalie Portman (*Star Wars: Episode III—Revenge of the Sith*, which bored me); and Eric Bana (*Hulk*; *Munich*, two daring ventures by Hollywood directors Ang Lee and Spielberg, who are good enough to break box office rules about keeping things simple and commercial). I will be able to recommend *Boleyn* to friends for Tudor history, political theory, gender studies, economics, art history, pop culture, and sex ethics. Better still, I can design a whole course around the movie. One week on the iconography of the star, one week on adaptations (à la *Adaptation*), one week on political movies, one week on biopics and historical costume dramas, one week on the culture industry's lock on distribution channels for this movie, and so on.

In my eagerness to mine this already-golden topic, I quite forgot the weeks on Reformation theology and biblical studies and the study (possibly a joint course with Kellogg School of Management and Garrett-Evangelical Theological Seminary) of product tie-ins with the Westminster Confession, designing clergy vestments that express your theological orientation (evangelical? More Light? womanist?), and how to become a leader of a Really Big Church.

Lest I be accused of mocking our beloved field, however, let me hasten to say that, given the film's proposed director, Justin Chadwick, who codirected the superb TV adaptation of Charles Dickens's novel *Bleak House* in 2005 with Susanna White, my modest proposal for a full course on a potential Hollywood blockbuster might actually happen. Might we finally have a period movie that examines the present global crises of war and religious hatred through the lens of family tragedy in a far distant age? Could the iconic glamour of Johansson and Portman help outwit the culture industry's enormous power to saturate global distribution markets with inferior movie "product" and create widespread spectator desire to see a movie that's subversively also a work of art? (See my discussion of *Babette's Feast*, below.) Sucked into 2,500 screens by studio marketing machines, will American audiences once again experience the satisfaction of seeing a movie that rejects rather than valorizes violence and war, critiques rampant consumerism, and offers complex narratives, characters, and formal style, as they did with *Citizen Kane, Casablanca,* and *Unforgiven*? Will audiences be drawn to experience the poverty and frustration of men, women, and children who find themselves shut out of the corridors of power during the early sixteenth century? Will they connect that age with the power struggles and inequities of our own? The televised version of *Bleak House* accomplished these cross-fertilizations in its visual design, subdued and complex character portrayals, and complete refusal to sentimentalize or sanitize extreme poverty. Big budgets and major stars sometimes mute talented directors: witness the difference between the Jane Campion of *Sweetie* and *The Piano* versus the Campion of *Portrait of a Lady*. But we can hope and plan.

The sound design of the new *Boleyn* will be key. If I were called upon to advise Mr. Chadwick, I'd suggest he listen to the sound tracks designed by Alex Wurman for *13 Conversations about One Thing* and *March of the Penguins*, which expand and enrich those movies' interpretations. Clint Eastwood's original music for *Million Dollar Baby* enhances that film's intellectual and emotional appeal. A few days with the sound tracks constructed by Wong Kar-wai for his movies *Chungking Express* and *In the Mood for Love* will demonstrate the virtues of sound that catches the mood of love and longing without stomping all over spectators' responses—a mix of pop, Chinese traditional music, classical Western, and street sounds.

Or listen to the film scores for the movies of Pedro Almodóvar, who relishes the timbre of the human voice in speech and song and weaves the ancient village wails of widows and forsaken lovers into the urban beats of Madrid with its pulsing echoes of the Moors, who once anchored Spain's intellectual and artistic life. His latest film, *Volver,* evokes the seepage of music and dance into the visual field of movies in which we might (and with *Volver*, will) find enough religious or theological resonance to fill a year's worth of courses.

I won't be called to consult on the score for *The Other Boleyn Girl*, though Wurman should be. He has a matchless ear for the rhythms of contemporary urban life, the musical seductions of the classical masters Schubert and Mozart, and the ethereal summons of the life beyond that have already made him a composer of promise in the tradition of Ennio Morricone (*The Good, the Bad and the Ugly*, no. 5 in the IMDb top 250 films with an 8.9 in part because of the score[1]) and Bernard Herrmann (*Vertigo*). And music does as much as story line, visuals, or words to create a film that might belong in our storehouse of teaching possibilities. Consider the use of Mozart's Mass in C Minor in *A Man Escaped* or

Monteverde's "Magnificat" in *Mouchette*, both by French master Robert Bresson. Listen to the music for Andrei Tarkovsky's *Andrei Rublev* and the amazing score for *The Beat That My Heart Skipped*.

Or think about *Babette's Feast*, now a standard in the religion/theology and film repertoire, which seems to be outlasting *Breaking the Waves*, its provocative double. Both were derived from fellow Scandinavian Carl Theodor Dreyer's *Ordet* and *Day of Wrath*. For the first part of this letter, I've fantasized about a Tudor-era movie (the proposed *Boleyn*) that might appeal to multiple audiences, achieving highly desired crossover status freed from genteel critiques of being either "elitist" (because non-Hollywood) or "mind-candy" (because immensely popular). But we already have a fine model for such a crossover movie in user-friendly *Babette*, which demonstrates that a foreign art film set in another century can appeal to audiences unaccustomed to movies with subtitles. Its sound design floats between *diegetic*—the female protagonists in the movie sing both church music and opera, and the church congregations sing—and *nondiegetic*—outside the story world floats an unknown narrator who presents the movie's interlocking tales in a voice-over akin to the soothing tones of Morgan Freeman in *March of the Penguins* and *Million Dollar Baby*.

If we were to list all possible approaches to the field of religion/theology and film, we only would need to examine the ways that *Babette's Feast* has been analyzed since its appearance in 1987. It has been explored in the context of liturgical drama, feminist theology, biblical exposition, liberation theology, vocation and redemption, the multiple manifestations of love, the history of the Danish church, and political cinema. It is the ultimate food movie, combining meal and message, its lush representations of the sensual pleasures of food preparation and consumption recalling the common meals of the early church. "Meal" suggests the meals of heaven: the drama of the Mass, the Seder, the meals of Ramadan, the hospitality of the Sikhs, and Abraham's gracious welcoming of the three strangers in Genesis 18. Even for spectators who are not used to thinking in biblical or early church history terms, it far outclasses *Tampopo*, *Eat Drink Man Woman*, *Like Water for Chocolate*, and Lasse Hallström's *Chocolat* for the supreme visual culinary feast.

For a moment, I want to leave *Babette's Feast* and probe its rich sources, Dreyer's *Day of Wrath* and *Ordet*. Both resonate with *Babette*'s central dilemma, the opposition between religions of fury and judgment and religions of love and forgiveness. Unlike *Babette*, however, neither enjoyed wide release—*Wrath* because it was made in 1943 and suppressed due to Denmark's Nazi occupation and Dreyer's outspoken early opposition to anti-Semitism. (Dreyer fled Denmark after the movie's completion.) *Ordet* did receive wide release and critical praise in Europe when it appeared in 1955 and quickly became a greatly admired movie for budding directors. But it has not been shown widely in the United States, unlike Dreyer's earlier *The Passion of Joan of Arc*, which luckily was found in the closet of a mental hospital in Oslo in 1981 (superb marketing hook) and then attracted a talented choral director to write a score to accompany its silent showings.[2] *Joan* (by far the best of the many treatments of this famous life) has played a number of times in Chicago alone to audiences of over one thousand people each.

The narrative of *Ordet* concerns two warring Protestant sects, one full of life and joy, one dour and judgmental, who are brought together by movie's end through marriage. Inger, the pregnant daughter-in-law from one family, seeks to broker peace between the two sides while managing her fiercely agnostic husband's anger, her father-in-law's fury at his neighbor's puritanical intolerance, and her brother-in-law's belief that he, a former seminary student, is the Christ. The film (now restored by Criterion) is full of sequences that introduce debates on science versus religion, visualize delusional fancy, challenge traditional cinematic representations of time and space, and create the hermetic worlds of religious communities.

Ordet's real genius lies in its technical brilliance, which brings those persons and issues to life. In its formal tour de force, Inger, who dies in childbirth, rises from the dead on-screen. While in theory, cinema itself celebrates the dead or absent brought back to life, *Ordet* shows the young mother's corpse awakening as if from slumber. Recently I showed the resurrection sequence from *Ordet* to a church congregation as an example of a movie that accomplishes what other movies only approximate: it dares to represent the occurrence of a miracle without sentimentality (*Ghost*), avoidance (*The Passion of the Christ*), or displacement (*The Shawshank Redemption*). With DVD projection, Criterion's sharp restoration brings the drama out into the audience as if the miracle were happening among us.

Dreyer long has been considered one of the finest directors of spiritual or religious movies, along with Robert Bresson, Andrei Tarkovsky, and Sergei Paradonov. Whether we as teachers of religion/theology and film prefer films about angels (*Wings of Desire*) or pastors and nuns (*Thérèse*; *Winter Light*; *Bells of St. Mary's*), adore the holy fools of Robin Williams (*The Fisher King* and almost everything else Williams has done), or simply must connect with theological depth (*The Seventh Seal*; *The Sacrifice*; *The Sweet Hereafter*), Dreyer has been there first with vampires and the great beyond (*Vampyr; Day of Wrath*), preachers (*Day of Wrath*), saints (*Joan*), feminist theology (*Gertrude*, his last film), and the explosive combination of religious beliefs and politics (*Day of Wrath*).[3] More on other movie choices later.

Yours, Sara

To my movie-loving friends, searching for new and better movie choices:

In my last letter, I wrote about a potential 2007 film, *Boleyn*, which in theory might be made both audience-friendly and thematically complex. It would be attractive to students because of its stars and subject. It would be accessible to us as teachers whether we go with spiritual, theological, religious, or pop culture–audience reception approaches, since conceivably it might be both immensely popular (though *Pirates of the Caribbean: Dead Man's Chest* seems to have the box office locked up for a while) and satisfyingly controversial due to its sexy topics, sex and kingship, and temporal power versus church power.

I don't want to create excessive advance anticipation for this movie, however. I want rather to suggest that as we seek movies to analyze from our specialized corners in the field, we might leave our personal niches and consider alternate movie spaces and places from which to regard human experience. In particular, I would like to challenge the idea that some movies are elitist and some popular, as though the viewing public were divided between educated city dwellers and the rest of the world—those who prefer movies with subtitles and narrative complexity and those who, well, scorn such things as elitist!

In a field that purports to interest itself in people, issues, and ideas that matter, such a divide limits us severely. Study the culture industry, but don't be fooled by it. A top box-office movie lands there in part because of screen saturation and multimillion-dollar ad campaigns designed to create desire. *The Da Vinci Code* is a good example of market forces at work. *Mission: Impossible III* opened on 2,500 screens, for instance, crowding out possible showings of hundreds of other films that might have offered alternate genres or narratives to audiences.

Let's continue to study the studio machine (which, by the way, thrives on pitting so-called elitists like you and me against "real" people, except at Oscar time), but let's also resist that industry by looking into new movie possibilities. A pop culture/audience accessibility approach to religion and film can yield fascinating results, such as Clive Marsh's analysis in *Cinema and Sentiment* of the multiple reasons that *Titanic* appealed to young audiences.[4] But if we slavishly imitate film studies' theoretical preference for audience reception analysis (left over from the eighties and nineties), we are missing out on treasures newly available to us on VHS and DVD.

As teachers and pastors, we are in a position not only to study what is happening in our culture right now (what is popular at the box office) but also to recommend a broad sampling of movies that reward repeated viewings and close analysis, yet challenge the culture. For some decades, Americans (and also Europeans) have seen independent movie theaters disappear. These were the theaters where once moviegoers could have been exposed to cinema from all over the world as well as to films made by small companies. In Britain, France, and Belgium, where I have spent the past two months, movie theaters (and churches, no longer widely frequented) have been converted into condos, restaurants, bars, and offices, or torn down to build multiplexes, as has happened in the United States. The lucky few could, and do, attend film festivals or at least follow festival reports from Cannes, Edinburgh, Strasbourg, Venice, or Berlin to get ideas for movies they might want to see someday (or order for private showings).

Now multiple distribution channels have replaced the old theaters, and services such as Netflix and Facets Multimedia make it possible for viewers to visit the immense storehouses of newly restored movie classics put out by operations such as Criterion and New Yorker films. They provide mail access to such films from Iran, South Africa, or Asia, for instance, or those of Michael Powell, Joseph Losey, and Claire Denis that address the human condition from fresh perspectives with innovative cinematic language we don't see in the average blockbuster.[5]

Moreover, we possess a growing list of restored classics from around the world in every genre. *The Matrix*, *The Shawshank Redemption*, and *Crouching Tiger, Hidden Dragon* stand on the giant shoulders of German expressionist Joe May's *Asphalt*, Hong Kong Cinema director King Hu's *A Touch of Zen*, Victor Sjöström's *Phantom Chariot*, Erich von Stroheim's *Greed*, F. W. Murnau's *Sunrise*, screwball comedies such as *The Philadelphia Story*, Orson Welles's *The Magnificent Ambersons*, Jean Renoir's *La Grand Illusion*, and the films of Yasujiro Ozu, to name a few. Although I have heard some colleagues say that their students do not respond to black-and-white movies, which limits their use of the early Dreyer and Bresson or even *Citizen Kane*, this has not been my experience. Both the University of Chicago and Northwestern University have long-standing student-run movie houses that cross-program silent movies, foreign films from all eras and national industries, American movies of the thirties or the seventies, and current blockbusters. As the student boards say, "If you build (offer) it, they will come!" Student audiences have turned out in droves for movies with spiritual themes such as *Au hasard Balthazar*, *Seventh Seal*, *Andrei Rublev*, and *Vampyr* as well as for the Spielberg, Coppola, or Western series.

Perhaps we need to experiment with new ways to present such movies. This spring I was asked to deliver a spontaneous pre-movie lecture to introduce F. W. Murnau's *Faust* (1926), which was screening that evening at the student movie theater. I began by introducing the somber tones of Job's framing debate between God and Satan, discussed the ways the Manichaean oppositions between good and evil played off that ancient scenario throughout the various Faust legends and in Milton, and probed Murnau's attempt to combine what then (1924) were new cinematic techniques— for example, transparent figures—with a serious attempt to address the problem of evil. We talked about the real-life battle between good and evil: Murnau himself, world-renowned filmmaker, lured to Hollywood in the late twenties, was excoriated in the trade press for budget overruns on his masterpiece *Sunrise*. He was quickly destroyed by the studio system and died at forty-two. All this was glamorous stuff. Most surprisingly, the students loved the movie itself!

As we try to expand our ideas about (sacred) cinema space, I want to return to the false opposition between elitist and popular movies and talk a bit about the word "better." In our field we should promote not only a wide range of movies but also better movies, movies that possess high quality as art as well as entertainment, and movies that make us better people. But what do we mean by better, exactly?

As ever, Sara

The search for a better way to a fuller life: *Tokyo Story*:

"Everyone needs to see this movie. It makes one a better person," young Chicago film director Michael Smith recently commented about *Tokyo Story*, a movie that is constructed with astounding visual surprises and leads spectators toward personal transformation. In what ways might this movie guide us as we choose which movies to study with our religion/theology and film audiences? Mike assumes that watching movies is an inherently moral act. Some movies are valued over others (not simply preferred, but seen to possess desirable qualities) because they positively affect the ways viewers see the world and treat other people. Further, his use of the word "better" assumes the existence of a moral spectrum along which we might rate both movies and human actions from best to worst, with reference to a perceived and commonly accepted good that all or at least most cinema watchers might endorse.

Philosopher Stanley Cavell builds his analysis of selected movies around the question of goodness. In *Pursuits of Happiness: Hollywood Comedies of Remarriage*,[6] he points out that thinkers from Plato to John Rawls, including Emerson and Nietzsche, have struggled to define the good: what humans should prize and what they should denounce. It's an age-old search that far outdates Plato. For Christians, such moral code(s) might be summarized in the Beatitudes and in the statement Jesus made to the rich young ruler: "Why do you ask me about the good? There is only One who is good" (Matt. 19:17 New American Bible).[7] Even so, Jesus says, men and women can approach goodness. He advises the young man to "sell what you have and give to the poor" (Matt. 19:21). Elsewhere, seekers are counseled not to judge others by measures they do not want applied to themselves. Do not abandon others but sustain them. Expect the unexpected, for God's idea of goodness turns ours on its head, as the Beatitudes and Paul's "wise fool" imply. Do justice, love mercy, and walk humbly with your God (Mic. 6:8 King James Version).

Filmmakers might justifiably deny that movies exist to make viewers better people (although few would deny that they want to make better movies). Movies, they might insist, are made for pleasure or money or art. A few like Woody Allen, Krzysztof Kieślowski, and Martin Scorsese, however, openly engage morality and ethics: for example, Allen's *Crimes and Misdemeanors* and *Match Point*, Kieślowski's *The Decalogue,* and Scorsese's *Mean Streets* and *Goodfellas.* Some, like Claire Denis, Mike Leigh, Ken Loach, Ousmane Sembène, and Agnès Varda insist that personal goodness cannot exist apart from social and political responsibility.[8] We must be wary of accepting directors' stated intentions as surefire interpretive markers, since it is a long way from intent to delivery of a finished work of art. But we need not assume that cinematic political or personal seriousness excludes beauty or delight. Pleasure can accompany criticism and moral reflection: witness *Citizen Kane* and *The Decalogue.*

Seeking to find movies that might transform viewers, we cannot bypass the textual characteristics of the film itself: the sound, sights, shapes, rhythm, and aura that make a movie something other than a novel, theater piece, newspaper, advertisement, or blog.[9] We can imagine movies on praiseworthy topics—generosity, for instance, or self-sacrifice—that result in sloppy movies such as *Pay It Forward* or *Stigmata.* Wishing to show the horrors of war and the folly of intolerance, the otherwise admirable *Saving Private Ryan* and *Schindler's List* slip into sentimentality in their final sequences, blunting the promise of their tightly shot, explosive openings. What better subject to film than the life of Jesus? But the perfection of the subject does not guarantee the quality of its artistic representation: witness *The Passion of the Christ.*

More likely, we will agree what qualities characterize a good person (a sense of justice and fairness, for instance) sooner than we will reach consensus on what constitutes a good movie.[10] What makes a movie good, or at least better than, say, *The Texas Chainsaw Massacre*, apart from differences in subject matter? Here are a few more ideas for today; more in another letter. What attitudes about the world and people outside the viewer's realm of experience does this movie promote? Has it been sanitized and removed of material that might imply criticism of the viewer's own country? Does it reinforce and privilege a wealthy, monochromatic society? Does its superhero rescue the vulnerable and struggle with moral choice, or valorize brute power and imperialist ambitions? In Martha Nussbaum's words, does this movie help our students to "imagine citizenship in both national and world terms, and to negotiate multiple allegiances with knowledge and confidence?"[11] Does it stimulate generosity and reconciliation?

In my next letter, I'll talk a bit about *Tokyo Story* and a few other movies that explore this mysterious quality of movie "goodness."

Fondly, Sara

To my movie-loving friends: some movie treasures:

In a late sequence of *Tokyo Story*, a young woman bids good-bye to her newly widowed father-in-law after the funeral guests (including his children) have fled. In this 1953 feature by Japanese master Yasujiro Ozu, the camera remained steadily discreet, framing scene after scene of an urban family's awkward adjustment to their elderly parents' visit from the countryside. Music was minimal, theatrical histrionics that characterize fellow director Akira Kurosawa's favorite actor Toshirô Mifune (*Rashômon*; *The Seven Samurai*) were totally absent save for a grandson's quickly suppressed temper tantrum early in the movie. Fifty years later, the film's closely observed vignettes feel powerfully compelling, its black-and-white images crisply defined in Criterion's fresh restoration.

Tokyo Story explores a universal problem: the ejection of an elderly mother and father from their children's lives. Yet Ozu allows this uncomfortable reality to surface slowly, with subtle touches: the grandson's anger at surrendering his personal space for his grandparents' guest bed; the children's increasing irritation at losing their work and social time to entertain their parents; the absent younger son (every family has a child who deals with aging parents by never visiting them); the bizarre vacation at a spa the children arrange for their parents to get them out of their hair. As I watched this movie in a theater recently, I revisited the months my parents lived with me and the six years I cared for them when they were ill. Ozu observes, however; he does not judge, and in his fine-grained observations lie the moral lessons for the viewer.

What salient features of *Tokyo Story* distinguish it as art and as human interest? The movie educates the eye and educates the heart. It stimulates personal and societal transformation and offers a widened perspective on the world outside our own borders. *Tokyo Story* could not change the viewer (i.e., make the viewer a better human being) without its layered visual, sonic, and narrative texture. Unlike the sweeping, lyrical camera movements of Kenji Mizoguchi, whose *Ugetsu* also belongs in any discussion of spiritually rich movies, Ozu keeps the camera fixed on clean, yet claustrophobic interiors, dialogues, and social interactions: the rituals of greeting, shoes and saki, and surface deference. Inside, as it deliberately presents an old couple's journey through abandonment toward death, we witness judgment and acceptance, cruelty and grace, rejection and hospitality. Hollywood moments of heightened emotion are absent; the mother dies offscreen; the hysteria of her neglectful daughter is brief and forced.[12]

Ozu creates a world of carefully controlled yet deglamorized surfaces, creating a "strange human density which seems inappropriate to the clinically observed environment."[13] Such disparity between the interchanges Ozu records eats away at the "solid veneer of everyday reality,"[14] creating a feeling of unease that stimulates the viewer to watch more carefully, to seek points of identification in an evenly distributed emotional landscape. I'd liken this growing uneasiness to the existential dread that builds up in *Vertigo*, *The Searchers*, *Unforgiven*, or *All About My Mother*. Some measure of that dread (What is life all about?) combines with spiritual longing (What lies off the edges of the film's frame? What should I value? What are the sources of my longing for a better way of living?). All of these films present dense human worlds such as Ozu's, where profound questions of meaning spill over the edges of each frame and into the viewer's own life, where they stimulate compassion for another's suffering.

Along with dread and longing, though, comes a startling narrative payoff in *Tokyo Story*: the sequence with which this letter began. Throughout this seemingly everyday drama of parents and children threads the story of Shakespeare's *King Lear*, itself taken from an older tale. In *Lear*, the parent ages and his children reject him, but one child remains. In *Tokyo Story*, the faithful child, patient like Cordelia, attentive and loving to the old folks, is not a daughter but rather the widow of the couple's dead son. Unexpectedly, she bursts into tears in front of her father-in-law. She defies the viewer's inclination to sanctify (and thus dismiss) her as a virginal, self-sacrificing female. As the camera frames her face, its focus sharpening, the rhythm of the editing alters and we feel the bitterness of her lonely, sexless life and social isolation. Death stalks her as surely as it does the old parents, and as it does us.

Tokyo Story opens up other possibilities for transformative and accessible cinema. In Wong Kar-wai's *Happy Together*, in Alejandro González Iñárritu's *Amores Perros*, and in Robert Bresson's *Pickpocket*, we also experience a catharsis far removed from the gut-wrenching release of exploding buildings, bodies, and worlds so beloved by the thirteen-year-old boys for whom Hollywood studios design their movies. Wong has said of his Hong Kong road movie set in Argentina, "In a place which is completely strange, one can start all over again." [15] For Lai Yiu-fai (played by Tony Leung), that place is a phone booth in Buenos Aires, where he places a call home to his dad, whom he had disgraced long ago by stealing money. For El Chivo, the hit man in Iñárrito's fever dream of a movie, it's in the luxurious living room of his estranged daughter, for whom he records on her answering machine a two-and-a-half-minute confession of guilt and abandonment, and a plea for forgiveness.

In *Pickpocket*, it is inside a prison cell that Michel, the thieving protagonist, finds new life. Fyodor Dostoevsky (whose *Crime and Punishment* inspired this visually edgy, theologically challenging movie) would admire the fragmented, elliptical forms of all these movies and their unexpected bursts of light at the end. He would admire a recent Palme d'Or winner at Cannes, *L'Enfant*, based on *Pickpocket*. Biased toward gambling both with life and with the rationally unknowable but viscerally adored Divine, however, Dostoevsky might well ask, "With movies like these so easily accessible on VHS and DVD, why do spectators, film scholars, and theologians afflict themselves with so much bad Hollywood 'product'?"

Mercifully, it is at the boundaries that thought blossoms. Just as the protagonists in *Tokyo Story*, *Babette's Feast*, and *The Wind Will Carry Us* found "sacred space" in unexpected places, so also is the space of movie spectatorship changing. As I mentioned in my last letter, we now have Internet Movie Database (www.imdb.com) and mail services such as Netflix and Facets Multimedia that expose questers to a wide range of possibilities. Both services can deliver *The Circle*, a beautiful and thought-provoking movie by Iranian filmmaker Jafar Panahi that fixes its gaze on the lives of four women in contemporary Tehran. Netflix also stocks *The House Is Black*, a long-suppressed documentary about a leper house, by Iran's most famous female poet, Forugh Farrokhzad, who died in a car crash at age thirty-two. Her poetry is still widely read for its sensuous beauty, compassion for the vulnerable of the world, and radical ideas about human freedom.

The title *The Wind Will Carry Us* is taken from one of Farrokhzad's poems, "The Wind Will Take Us Away." The poet seeks to counter the "darkness blowing" with the warmth of love. The film powerfully engages issues of birth, life and death, differing conceptions of "civilization" (the village in the film may be remote, but most houses have TV), ruins as markers of past war and natural disaster or carriers of historical tradition, and ways of being—or not being—in a community. Behzad, a director, and his TV crew burst into an ancient Kurdish village to wait for a one hundred-year-old woman to die to allow them to record the exotic death rituals that follow. She begins to rally. Behzad fights with his faraway producer, battles poor cell-phone reception, and berates the young boy who was sent by the village to be his guide. His high-paced technologically driven customs clash with the village's time-honored ways (he is very much the Westerner). The film's sonic and visual rhythm depends as much on silence and long shots as it does on textured sound track and vision; at least eleven of its characters are largely unseen, including Behzad's lazy crew and the dying woman. The ancient woman's wise physician opens up the mysteries of life to the young engineer and to us, the viewers.

Where else might we fix our gaze? The "Asian Alternative" is hot in film criticism now. Within the phrase "Asian cinema" hides a wealth of cinephilic cultures—Vietnam, South Korea, Taiwan, Hong Kong—that range in storytelling style from Hitchcock to Carl Theodor Dreyer or Jean Renoir to Clint Eastwood or Alfonso Cuarón. *In the Mood for Love* is infused with a Buddhist and Christian longing for love and life, as is the sublime *Spring, Summer, Fall, Winter . . . and Spring. Hero* (Zhang Yimou) imitates what Hou Hsaio-hsien and Edward Yang capture in their films: the intertwining of intellectual curiosity and moral commitment, both directed toward the goal with which we began this chapter: to transform the world.

Late Confucianism spoke of this transformation as the "unity of knowledge and action," guiding your life by principles that equip you to address problems in the wider world. The martial arts, further, are infused with spiritual power and enlightenment. Despite the differing styles of presentation in the various Asian films that I list below (e.g., Wong's combination of traditional and pop Eastern and Western music, fragmented images, and intense color palettes contrast with Hou's distant and watchful camera), all enmesh individuals in a complicated web of familial and communal connections that affect their ability to move out into the world. Relationships cross boundaries of religion, ethnic identity, power configurations, and gender.

Well-made movies that can transform us underline the nobility and capacity of each person, the inescapable interdependence of all human beings, and the ways that consumerism attacks the foundation of living well alone and together. Some address the dark aftershocks of imperialism and colonialism (*Beau Travail*; *Chocolat* [1988]; *Ali: Fear Eats the Soul*) or totalitarianism (*Werckmeister Harmonies*; *M. Klein*; *Army of Shadows*). All are infused with the presence, or a powerful and insistent absence, of a spiritual vitality that refuses to detach itself from the physicality of the created world.

Werckmeister Harmonies' protagonist, Janus, for instance, is a holy fool somewhat akin to the young priest in Bresson's *Diary of a Country Priest*: a man who intuits the good and the beautiful like a little child. Janus's heart is stirred by the sight of a giant whale on display in the public square of his town. For him, Leviathan, brought from the depths of the sea and killed for the profit of hawkers, reveals the marvels of creation. Although this movie explores politics, philosophy, music, and commerce in various unsettling combinations, its visual beauty surpasses and defeats any attempts either to crystallize it in theory or to dismiss it as unmarketable.

Something in us is stirred by the beautiful and impelled by the good. Such is the message of one of my favorite movies from 2005, *The Beat That My Heart Skipped*, directed by Jacques Audiard. What did this little film do to justify its Silver Bear at Berlin (the equivalent of an Oscar) for Best Score,[16] art-house circulation in America, or eight Césars? Much. Its protagonist, Tom Seyr (Romain Duris), lives between the antiphonies of venality and beauty and chooses life, as Josey Wales pleads in an Eastwood classic, *The Outlaw Josey Wales* (1976).

In the opening sequence, two men talk at a bar, their faces only dimly perceptible against a black, orange, and gold background. One, a *malfrat* (bad boy), does his father's dirty real estate business, releasing rats and chasing out tenants in rundown buildings in Paris. Some reviews suggested that the hero would make a run for virtue before he finally collapsed into vice. They were wrong. The opening should have tipped me off.

The two young men just sit, one of them talking about his father's last days: that once-powerful man began to ask him for advice on everything from how to live his life to how to take care of his health. When the father became ill, the boy became father to the man, cleaning up after him and feeding him like a baby, hating it and feeling imprisoned and yet never wanting it to end. The conversational current shifts. "Do you believe in God?" "No." "This stuff was enough to make me believe." He cries, quietly. "A year later my first child was born." Death and (re)birth, the pattern of this movie.

Strange start for a two-hour action movie, more akin to Kieślowski's *The Decalogue* than to Scorsese's *Mean Streets*, which also features twenty-something hoodlums. Or is it so far from Scorsese? In *Mean Streets*, Charlie Cappa (Harvey Keitel) says: "Theology happens on the streets." "You don't make up for your sins in church. You do it in the streets. You do it at home. The rest is bullshit and you know it." Audiard steeps *Beat* in action and consequence, revealing the birth of conscience through horror and beauty.

This odd opening to *Beat* lasts a full five minutes, breaking several rules for movie sequences: capture the audience's attention with quick, flashy shots and sexy music; produce the plot hook; and build in questions that the movie must answer such as "How will the hero get himself out of this mess?" Instead, the movie turns that question toward philosophy and ethics, taking the strangeness of death as the thread that runs through the young men's antics. Combining low lighting, on-site locations, thrashing beats mixed with sublime classical melodies, and a palette of darkness edged with golds and oranges, *Beat* creates parallel expectations of dread and hope—the "fear and trembling" with which the movie opens. Death sits at your doorstep. The strutting, street-smart male (the listener in the opening sequence) also turns caregiver to his father.

Tom's beloved father is murdered, payback for Tom's seduction of a rival gang leader's girlfriend. In harrowing medium close-up, Audiard suppresses Tom's tears, setting a side view of his face against several racked shots of his father's bloody body. The horrific scene is underplayed, strung out over anguishing minutes, allowing a space to open up in our perception—and his—that he caused his father's death.

The center sequences of the movie had alternated between shots of his partnership with his father, squatter-busting with his friends, and the piano lessons he was taking to prepare for an audition with his pianist-mother's former agent. He fails the audition; his father dies. The director yields in no way to cheap sentiment.

Abruptly, two years pass, and we are treated to a reversed, canted shot of him playing superbly in a concert hall. Has the director sold out after all to the box office? The red plush seats of the hall recall his father's blood; did that death baptize him and wash him clean? But the camera pulls back to reveal an empty auditorium. Was this a fantasy shot in the style of the runway scene in Kieślowski's *Red*? No, Tom has become an impressario much like the man who had nurtured his mother's career. His client is Miao, his former piano teacher. On the way to her public performance, she kisses Tom's hand, which my students read as signaling that the two were now "dating," as they quaintly put it.

After parking their car and running to join Miao at her gala concert, Tom spots the man who killed his father. He beats him, neither on the street nor in an enclosed space but rather on the stairs in an anonymous apartment building, an unbounded space—black and white, not the lush red of the music hall or the soft blue interior of Miao's apartment—that allows him to choose the moral code by which he now will act.

The fight is shot in real time, stitching the spectator into the action as Tom battles between survival and revenge. Victorious, Tom could blow the killer's head off and walk away released, as happens with Charles Burns (Guy Pearce) in the searing Australian Western *The Proposition*. With the man at his mercy, Tom sobs for long minutes but leaves him alive. The camera cuts to the concert hall bathroom, where he cleanses his bloody face and trembling hands. His body, shot in fragments, counterpoints visually and sonically with the pianist's sublime music playing offscreen. As he takes his place in the audience, the beat of the music transforms his ravaged, suffering features into a lover's gaze, enraptured by Miao's concerto and focused on his sweetheart. He has been released at last from his demons.

In a place that's completely strange, the broad terrain of international, classic, and independent American cinema, we can make our new personal or communal cinema space a lively and life-enhancing one. Curl up with a few of my favorites.[17]

Your devoted friend, Sara

Notes

1. IMDb (Internet Movie Database), www.imdb.com, is a useful, even if not flawless, source for basic facts about movies and a portal to movie reviews. Movies are rated 1–10, with 10 as the highest mark.

2. Richard Einhorn, "The Voices of Light," was inspired by the newly discovered Dreyer film and has been performed at hundreds of screenings all over America. The Einhorn piece accompanies the Criterion Collection restored *Joan*.

3. It is little known that Dreyer, embittered by a miserable life with his adoptive parents, who were religious fanatics, rejected religious belief even as he engaged with theological and religious issues in every film in a career of over forty years.

4. Clive Marsh, *Cinema and Sentiment: Film's Challenge to Theology* (Carlisle, UK: Paternoster, 2004).

5. www.netflix.com, www.facetsmultimedia.com, www.nicheflix.com.

6. Stanley Cavell, *Pursuits of Happiness: Hollywood Comedies of Remarriage* (Boston: Harvard University Press, 1981).

7. Parallel texts: Mark 10:1–12 and Luke 9:51. The Beatitudes, which draw upon the Psalms and Isaiah, appear in Matt. 5:3–10 and Luke 6:22.

8. See Denis's *Chocolat* (1988) and *Beau Travail* (1999); Leigh's *Vera Drake* (2004) and *Topsy-Turvy* (1999); Loach's *Land and Freedom* (1995) and *The Wind That Shakes the Barley* (2006); Sembène's *Moolaadé* (2004); and Varda's *Vagabond* (1985), for instance.

9. Nevertheless, directors such as Wong Kar-wai (*In the Mood for Love*) and Pedro Almodóvar (*All About My Mother*) make ample use of other forms of communication such as ads, pop songs, kitsch, slang, and journalism to enrich their visual and sonic texts.

10. Several movies in the last decade have played with the idea of embodied goodness, most daringly, Lars von Trier's transgressive Bess in *Breaking the Waves*, who is said to have died of "goodness"; Amélie, who deals with the stresses of life by attempting to be good (with comic results); and Rosetta, a walking encyclopedia of laws for "débrouiller" (making your way in life against all odds). These female portrayals of goodness draw heavily in appearance and gesture on Gelsomina in Fellini's *La Strada* and Mouchette in Bresson's *Mouchette*.

11. This is classic Nussbaum, quoted here from an address she delivered to teachers at the Laboratory School of the University of Chicago in 2005. On citizenship, goodness, and art, see *The Fragility of Goodness: Luck and Ethics in Geek Tragedy and Philosophy* (Cambridge: Cambridge University Press, 1986).

12. Cf. *Steel Magnolias* (d. Herbert Ross, USA, 1989).

13. Paul Schrader, *Transcendental Style in Film: Ozu, Bresson, Dreyer* (Berkeley: Da Capo Press, 1972), 44.

14. Ibid., 46.

15. Stephen Teo, *Wong Kar-wai* (London: BFI, 2005), 98.

16. Music by Alexandre Desplat, who also scored *Syriana, Casanova, Read My Lips,* and *Girl with a Pearl Earring.*

17. Some life-transforming movies:

Armenia: *The Color of Pomegranates* (d. Sergei Parajanov, 1968)

Belgium: *La Promesse* (d. Jean-Pierre and Luc Dardenne, 1995), *Rosetta* (d. Jean-Pierre and Luc Dardenne, 1999), *Le Fils* (d. Jean-Pierre and Luc Dardenne, 2002), *L'Enfant* (d. Jean-Pierre and Luc Dardenne, 2005)

Britain: *The Third Man* (d. Carol Reed, 1949), *Secrets and Lies* (d. Mike Leigh, 1996), *Vera Drake* (d. Mike Leigh, 2005), *The Wind That Shakes the Barley* (d. Ken Loach, 2006)

Canada: *The Sweet Hereafter* (d. Atom Egoyan, 1997)

China: *The World* (d. Zhang Ke Jia, 2004)

France: *L'Atalante* (d. Jean Vigo, 1934), *La Grand Illusion* (d. Jean Renoir, 1937), *Rules of the Game* (d. Jean Renoir, 1939), *Diary of a Country Priest* (d. Robert Bresson, 1951), *A Man Escaped* (d. Robert Bresson, 1956), *Pickpocket* (d. Robert Bresson, 1959), *Au hasard Balthazar* (d. Robert Bresson, 1966), *Mouchette* (d. Robert Bresson, 1967), *L'Argent* (d. Robert Bresson, 1983), *Army of Shadows* (d. Jean-Pierre Melville, 1969), *The Silence of the Sea* (d. Jean-Pierre Melville, 1949), *Thérèse* (d. Alain Cavalier, 1986), *Chocolat* (d. Claire Denis, 1988), *Beau*

Travail (d. Claire Denis, 1999), *The Beat That My Heart Skipped* (d. Jacques Audiard, 2005), *M. Klein* (d. Joseph Losey, 1976)

Germany: *Ali: Fear Eats the Soul* (d. Rainer Werner Fassbinder, 1974)

Hong Kong: *In the Mood for Love* (d. Wong Kar-wai, 2000), *Chungking Express* (d. Wong Kar-wai, 1994)

Hungary: *Werckmeister Harmonies* (d. Béla Tarr, 2000)

Iran: *The House is Black* (d. Forugh Farrokhzad, 1963), *The Wind Will Carry Us* (d. Abbas Kiarostami, 1999), *Close Up* (d. Abbas Kiarostami, 1990), *The Circle* (d. Jafar Panahi, 2000)

Italy: *Battle of Algiers* (d. Gillo Pontecorvo, 1966), *Paisà* (d. Roberto Rossellini, 1946), *The Son's Room* (d. Nanni Moretti, 2001)

Japan: *Tokyo Story* (d. Yasujiro Ozu, 1953), *Ugetsu* (d. Kenji Mizoguchi, 1953), *The Seven Samurai* (d. Akira Kurosawa, 1954), *Fireworks* (d. Takeshi Kitano, 1997)

Mexico: *Amores Perros* (d. Alejandro González Iñárritu, 2000), *Children of Men* (d. Alfonso Cuarón, 2006)

Poland: *The Decalogue* (d. Krzysztof Kieślowski, 1989), *The Double Life of Veronica* (d. Krzysztof Kieślowski, 1991), *Three Colors: Blue* (d. Krzysztof Kieślowski, 1993), *Three Colors: White* (d. Krzysztof Kieślowski, 1994), *Three Colors: Red* (d. Krzysztof Kieślowski, 1994)

Romania: *The Death of Mr. Lazarescu* (d. Cristi Puiu, 2005)

Scandinavia: *The Seventh Seal* (d. Ingmar Bergman, 1957), *Cries and Whispers* (d. Ingmar Bergman, 1972), *The Man Without a Past* (d. Aki Kaurismaki, 2002), *The Passion of Joan of Arc* (d. Carl Theodor Dreyer, 1928), *Day of Wrath* (d. Carl Theodor Dreyer, 1943), *Ordet* (d. Carl Theodor Dreyer, 1955), *Babette's Feast* (d. Gabriel Axel, 1987)

Senegal: *Moolaadé* (d. Ousmane Sembène, 2004)

Soviet Union/Russia: *Andrei Rublev* (d. Andrei Tarkovsky, 1969), *Stalker* (d. Andrei Tarkovsky, 1974), *Sacrifice* (d. Andrei Tarkovsky, 1986)

Spain: *All About My Mother* (d. Pedro Almodóvar, 1999), *Talk to Her* (d. Pedro Almodóvar, 2002), *Volver* (d. Pedro Almodóvar, 2006)

Taiwan: *Yi-Yi* (d. Edward Yang, 2000), *City of Sadness* (d. Hou Hsiao-hsien, 1989), *A Time to Live and a Time to Die* (d. Hou Hsiao-hsien, 1985), *Dust in the Wind* (d. Hou Hsiao-hsien, 1986)

United States: *Sunrise* (d. F. W. Murnau, 1927), *Citizen Kane* (d. Orson Welles, 1941), *The Searchers* (d. John Ford, 1956), *Vertigo* (d. Alfred Hitchcock, 1958), *The Night of the Hunter* (d. Charles Laughton, 1955), *Goodfellas* (d. Martin Scorsese, 1990), *The Outlaw Josey Wales* (d. Clint Eastwood, 1976), *Unforgiven* (d. Clint Eastwood, 1992), *Mystic River* (d. Clint Eastwood, 2003), *Million Dollar Baby* (d. Clint Eastwood, 2005), *Flags of Our Fathers* (d. Clint Eastwood, 2006), *Letters from Iwo Jima* (d. Clint Eastwood, 2006), *Dead Man* (d. Jim Jarmusch, 1995), *Days of Heaven* (d. Terrence Malick, 1978), *The Thin Red Line* (d. Terrence Malick, 1998)

Other movies cited in the text:

Adaptation (d. Spike Jonze, USA, 2002)

Apocalypse Now (d. Francis Ford Coppola, USA, 1979)

Asphalt (d. Joe May, Germany, 1929)

Bells of St. Mary's (d. Leo McCarey, USA, 1945)

Breaking the Waves (d. Lars von Trier, Denmark, 1996)

Casablanca (d. Michael Curtiz, USA, 1942)

Chocolat (d. Lasse Hallström, USA, 2000), not to be confused with the sublime *Chocolat* (d. Claire Denis, France/West Germany/Cameroon, 1988)

Crimes and Misdemeanors (d. Woody Allen, USA, 1989)

Crouching Tiger, Hidden Dragon (d. Ang Lee, UK/USA, 2000)

The Da Vinci Code (d. Ron Howard, USA, 2006)

Eat Drink Man Woman (d. Ang Lee, USA, 1994)

The Fabulous Destiny of Amélie Poulain (d. Jean-Pierre Jeunet, France, 2001)
Faust (d. F. W. Murnou, Germany, 1926)
The Fisher King (d. Terry Gilliam, USA, 1991)
Gertrude (d. Carl Theodor Dreyor, Scandinavia, 1964)
Ghost (d. Jerry Zucker, USA, 1990)
The Godfather (d. Francis Ford Coppola, USA, 1972)
The Good, the Bad and the Ugly (d. Sergio Leone, Italy, 1966)
Greed (d. Erich von Stroheim, USA/Sweden, 1924)
Happy Together (d. Wong Kar-wai, Hong Kong, 1997)
Hero (d. Yimou Zhang, Hong Kong, 2002)
Hulk (d. Ang Lee, USA, 2003)
Like Water for Chocolate (d. Alfonso Arau, Mexico, 1992)
The Magnificent Ambersons (d. Orson Welles, USA, 1942)
March of the Penguins (d. Luc Jacquet, France, 2005)
Match Point (d. Woody Allen, USA, 2005)
The Matrix (d. Larry and Andy Wachowski, USA, 1999)
Mean Streets (d. Martin Scorsese, USA, 1973)
Mission: Impossible III (d. J. J. Abrams, USA, 2006)
Munich (d. Steven Spielberg, USA, 2005)
The Passion of the Christ (d. Mel Gibson, USA, 2004)
Pay It Forward (d. Mimi Leder, USA, 2000)
Phantom Chariot (d. Victor Sjöström, Sweden, 1921)
The Philadelphia Story (d. George Cukor, USA, 1940)
The Piano (d. Jane Campion, New Zealand, 1993)
Pirates of the Caribbean, Dead Man's Chest (d. Gore Verbinski, USA, 2006)
Portrait of a Lady (d. Jane Campion, New Zealand, 1996)
The Proposition (d. John Hillcoat, Australia, 2005)
Rashômon (d. Akira Kurosawa, Japan, 1950)
Saving Private Ryan (d. Steven Spielberg, USA, 1998)
Schindler's List (d. Steven Spielberg, USA, 1993)
The Shawshank Redemption (d. Frank Darabont, USA, 1994)
Spring, Summer, Fall, Winter . . . and Spring (d. Kim Ki-duk, South Korea, 2003)
Star Wars (d. George Lucas, USA, 1977)
Star Wars: Episode III—Revenge of the Sith (d. George Lucas, USA, 2005)
Stigmata (d. Rupert Wainwright, USA, 1999)
Sweetie (d. Jane Campion, New Zealand, 1989)
Tampopo (d. Juzo Itami, Taiwan, 1985)
The Texas Chainsaw Massacre (d. Tobe Hooper, USA, 1974; d. Marcus Nispel, USA, 2003)
13 Conversations about One Thing (d. Jill Sprecher, USA, 2001)
Titanic (d. James Cameron, USA, 1997)
A Touch of Zen (d. King Hu, Taiwan, 1969)
Twelve Monkeys (d. Terry Gilliam, USA, 1995)
Vagabond (d. Agnès Varda, France, 1985)
Vampyr (d. Carl Theodor Dreyer, Scandinavia, 1931)
What Dreams May Come (d. Vincent Ward, USA, 1998)
Wings of Desire (d. Wim Wenders, Germany, 1987)
Winter Light (d. Ingmar Bergman, Sweden, 1962)

Extending Our
Conversation Partners

5

Film and the Subjective Turn

*How the Sociology of Religion Can Contribute
to Theological Readings of Film*

GORDON LYNCH

The past decade saw evidence of increasing sophistication in theological engagements with media and popular culture—of which this book is one example. Part of this trend toward increasing sophistication has been a deepening awareness among some theologians of the interdisciplinary nature of this field. Elsewhere I have discussed the distinctive role that theology can play in the critical study of popular culture, and the distinctive contribution that theology can make alongside disciplines such as sociology, media, communication, and cultural studies.[1] In this chapter I want to focus instead on how the theological study of film can benefit from drawing on the knowledge and expertise of other disciplines. In particular, I want to focus here on how theological readings of film can be usefully informed by debates concerning contemporary cultural values and beliefs in the context of the sociological study of religion. Over the past ten years, a number of theologians and religious scholars have recognized the importance of engaging with film studies as a source of theoretical concepts and methods for analyzing film. This has led to a more informed use of approaches such as auteur criticism and mise-en-scène analysis, as well as calls for the study of film not so much as text but as aesthetic experience, following principles of Lacanian analysis.[2] As with many contemporary academic endeavors in which scholars find themselves having to learn a new disciplinary language and concepts, many theologians are still arguably at a relatively early stage in orienting their work in relation to concepts and debates in film studies. There are already promising signs, however, that this turn to film studies is bearing fruit in increasingly sophisticated theological engagements with film.

Given the importance of this turn to film studies, it is perhaps unsurprising that theologians have not seen engaging with the sociology of religion as such an important priority for informing their analysis of film. I would suggest, though, that as the turn to film studies becomes increasingly accepted by theologians, it is time to start to look beyond film studies to see what other disciplines may have to offer.

The particular angle I take in this chapter is to suggest that it is helpful to think of film as an important medium for the transmission of cultural ideologies. As such, it is important to think about how values and meanings conveyed in film texts may reflect wider patterns and trends in the values and beliefs of contemporary societies. The study of cultural values and beliefs is, of course, not the sole preserve of sociologists of religion, and it is embedded in a wider range of social science disciplines such as sociology, anthropology, cultural studies, human geography, and political science. But the sociology of religion, in its attempts to understand changing patterns of religious belief, affiliation, and practice, offers a particular set of debates, concepts, and insights that may help theologians read film in the context of broader social and cultural changes. As an illustrative case example, I will be exploring here how debates about the "subjective turn" in contemporary religion and spirituality in the West can offer a helpful frame for the theological analysis of Hollywood cinema. Before moving on to this discussion, though, some opening comments are needed about the idea of film as a medium for the transmission of cultural ideologies.

Film and the (Re)production of Cultural Ideologies

To suggest that film texts transmit cultural ideologies is hardly a novel claim. A key principle in post-1960s film studies—from Laura Mulvey's seminal article on the male gaze to the Althusserian-inspired critiques of other contributors to *Screen* magazine[3]—has been that film texts convey ideologically loaded ways of seeing and thinking about the world. The preoccupation with issues of representation among many scholars of film reflects the recognition that films are not neutral depictions of the world as it is, but convey particular cultural assumptions about social and political structures, gender, class, ethnicity, and sexual orientation. Furthermore, this ideological approach to film criticism has typically adopted the fundamental Marxist principle that such cultural assumptions are likely to be unhelpful, weighted in favor of dominant social groups and interests, and need to be identified and critiqued if they are not to be unconsciously absorbed by film audiences.

This well-established ideological approach to film criticism has been supplemented more recently by the work of theologians and religious scholars who argue that film plays an important role in the transmission of religious and moral beliefs and values. Although some of this latter work has been influenced by Marxist, feminist, black, or queer approaches to ideological criticism, much of it also introduces more specifically religious language for understanding film as a medium for cultural ideology. For example, Margaret Miles argues that film is an important source of contemporary representations of visions of the good life.[4] This point is also taken up by John Lyden, who argues that film watching constitutes a form of ritual in which audiences engage with culturally significant meanings and values.[5] Another point of connection between film and the language of religious studies is made by Joel Martin and Conrad Ostwalt, who refer to film as an important source of contemporary cultural myth.[6] Similarly, Clive Marsh recently argued that cinemagoing can be understood as a worshiplike experience, in the sense that cinema audiences are being invited to engage in sympathetic and formative, affective engagements with narratives bearing significant cultural beliefs and values.[7]

While the work of Miles, and Martin and Ostwalt, invites theologians and religious scholars to engage in the critical analysis of film texts, Lyden and Marsh point to another important area for reflection—how audiences actually make use of films. A basic assumption in much ideological criticism of film is that audiences tend to be passive recipients of the cultural ideologies implicit in particular films. The "turn to ethnography" in cultural studies more generally, however, calls this assumption into question, and suggests that audiences may interpret and make use of films in ways that are quite different from the ideologies embedded in the film text itself. John Fiske's example of observing Australian aboriginal teenagers who enjoyed watching Westerns for scenes in which the "Indians" kill the "cowboys" is a good case in point here.[8] If cinemagoing is indeed a significant ritual framework for engaging with meaning-laden narratives, then we need to understand more about what audiences bring to and take from such rituals if we are to have a fuller understanding of how films genuinely function as transmitters of cultural ideologies in people's lived experience. This task forms a central part of the project of the "turn to the audience" that must surely be an important priority for future work in the theological study of film. Drawing on broader theories and methods in audience-reception studies, theologians need to turn their attention from a pure focus on film texts to the ways in which people make use of films in their own personal, meaning-making activities.

Given the growing consensus in the theological and religious study of film that films are an important medium for the transmission of cultural beliefs and values, it is perhaps surprising that there have been relatively few serious attempts to connect the analysis of individual films with findings from the study of cultural ideologies within the sociology of religion. In reality this reflects a broader gap that currently exists between the literature on theology, religion, and popular culture and literature on the sociology of contemporary religion. Some scholars are now doing important work to bridge this gap. Lynn Schofield Clark has conducted research into the ways in which American teenagers use media and popular culture in the construction of religious identities and attitudes.[9] Christopher Partridge argues that Western media and popular culture have been a crucial resource for the shift in Western culture away from institutionalized Christianity and toward alternative forms of spirituality.[10] The work done by Schofield Clark and Partridge is important for highlighting the idea that the content and structure of contemporary media and popular culture both shape, and are shaped by, wider trends in religion and spirituality. The meaning of films can therefore not only be regarded as a focus for isolated acts of theological reflection—as in the theological analysis of other cultural "texts" such as art, novels, music, or plays—but, in sociological terms, can also be read in relation to broader trends in cultural values and beliefs as well as being understood as tools in the transformation of contemporary forms of religion and spirituality. Films have an important sociological function in shaping contemporary religious beliefs and practices—though we still have a long way to go in understanding more precisely the complex relationships between media and the construction of religious identities, attitudes, and behaviors. Through analyzing the content of films in rela- tion to broader religious and cultural patterns, however, we can develop a

Extending Our Conversation Partners

richer reading—or to use Clifford Geertz's phrase—a "thick description" of them, which gives a fuller account of their cultural significance and meanings.[11] To illustrate this point in more detail, I now turn to the debate about the "subjective turn" in the sociology of religion as a context for the theological interpretation of film.

The Subjective Turn in Modern Religion and Spirituality

There is a broad consensus among sociologists of Western religion that the postwar period has been a highly significant period of religious change and transition. In trying to make sense of these changes, a focal debate has concentrated on various theories of secularization, which make connections between social processes of modernization and the declining social significance of religion. No clear consensus has emerged from this debate about the usefulness of theories of secularization for interpreting the contemporary religious landscape. But one point that this debate has clarified is that while the period since 1945 has seen significant religious changes in Western societies, the precise nature of these changes has varied from country to country. For example, there is increasing acceptance that notions of secularization may apply better to postwar societies in Western Europe than they do to postwar America.[12] Even within this acceptance of "European exceptionalism," and the search for the particular historical and cultural factors that have promoted secularized European societies, it is still argued that within Western Europe there are significantly different religious cultures.[13] Religious changes in modern Irish society—where a still-strong residual Catholic identity has been seriously undermined in the past decade by revelations about abuse by clergy—are therefore different from the more gradual decline of institutional Christianity in England. This recognition of different national contexts (as well as emerging transnational movements) is important for developing more nuanced accounts of contemporary religious landscapes than are often offered in broad accounts of Western religion.

At the same time, while there are obvious differences between various national and regional contexts—reflecting historical, linguistic, and cultural factors—there are also some broad trends in religion since 1945 that are evident to varying degrees in most Western societies. These include a growing religious pluralism, fueled by immigration from Latin America, Africa, and Asia; the tendency of younger adults to disengage from religious institutions; the restructuring of religious groups and identities along "conservative" and "progressive" lines associated with the rise of politically engaged religious conservatism; and the impact on religious institutions of changing social attitudes to gender and sexual orientation. Along with these changes has been the rise of spirituality, the personal quest for religious meaning and significance, or what has been termed by Charles Taylor, the "subjective turn" in Western religion.[14]

The notion of the subjective turn in contemporary Western religion alludes to two important processes. The first of these is the increasing importance of individual choice in relation to religious belief and practice. For many people in Western societies since 1945, there has been a considerable weakening of extrinsic motivations associated with religious identity and observance. Despite the growth in church attendance in Britain and America in the 1950s,[15] a range of social factors (including the expansion of higher education, greater social mobility, and cultural pluralism) have since weakened the idea that to be a good member of society one should have particular kinds of religious identity or affiliation.[16] The rise of secular welfare services in this period also lessened the structural need to engage with religious institutions as sources of material support. As a consequence, individuals' engagement with religious institutions since the 1960s has become more fluid.

The idea of a lifetime commitment to a particular congregation or religious institution (what Robert Wuthnow refers to as a "spirituality of dwelling") has been displaced by an ongoing search for religious contexts and resources that are personally meaningful and helpful (a "spirituality of seeking"). Extrinsic motivations for religious observance—such as social expectations or utilizing religious institutions as structures for full participation in one's local community—have become less powerful. By contrast, intrinsic motivations—such as the search for a meaningful spirituality, an emotionally supportive peer group sharing similar values, or physical or psychological healing—have become increasingly influential in shaping people's religious choices. There are, of course, exceptions. In immigrant communities, religious institutions still play an important role in maintaining particular ethnic and cultural identities, relationships, and practices—and to be a participating member of such immigrant communities often requires maintaining involvement with some kind of indigenous religious institution (whether church, mosque, or temple). Similarly, in many smaller communities in America, the church still plays an important role in local community life—and full participation in the local community demands some level of church involvement. But more generally, and especially in larger urban areas, the subjective turn in contemporary religion has meant the growing influence of intrinsic, personal motivations for one's choice of religious affiliation, identity, and practice.

This way of understanding the subjective turn in contemporary Western religion has become particularly identified with discourses on religious consumerism. Peter Berger and Thomas Luckmann were among the first sociologists to refer to the emergence of a religious or spiritual marketplace in contemporary society.[17] Berger, in particular, conceived of the individual in modern society as being compelled to choose among the growing range of beliefs and lifestyle options available. For Berger, modern life is therefore that of the lifestyle consumer, forced to make conscious choices between different ways of understanding and living that are presented through the mass media. Making choices about one's religious beliefs and identity is simply one part of this larger process. Such language of religious consumerism has since been taken up by Wade Clark Roof, who describes the emergence of an "expanded spiritual marketplace," stimulated by the search for personal spirituality among baby boomers, that has transformed the religious landscape of America.[18] Such understandings of the individual's relation to contemporary culture are also evident in the social theory of Anthony Giddens, who argues that we live in a posttraditional society in which meanings and values can no longer be assumed, and in which we are forced to choose how to live our lives.[19]

Sometimes these trends are misleadingly referred to by theologians and missiologists as postmodern—with the implication being that the rise of personal choice in religious matters is also inherently bound up with theological and moral relativism and the collapse of belief in any grand narratives. While such connections have become almost a truism in some theological and missiological discussions, they are, in fact, highly questionable. In the 1960s Peter Berger, for example, initially argued that a culture in which people are thrown back onto their own choices tends to become relativistic and secular—because one person's choice can seem as good as any other. By the 1990s, however, Berger had abandoned this view, noting the resurgence of certain forms of religion and spirituality, and arguing instead that personal choice does not make people more relativistic or less religious, but simply changes the way in which they are religious.[20] Similarly, the importance of personal choice for contemporary religious identity does not necessarily imply the abandonment of a strong belief in metanarratives. The phenomenon of young adults in America consciously opting into neoconservative forms of Christianity or Judaism (including an upsurge in Orthodox Christianity) is indicative of how personal religious choices can be closely tied in with the desire to subsume one's identity in relation to a larger tradition.[21]

The first aspect of the notion of the subjective turn in contemporary Western religion therefore points to the growing importance of personal choice in religious matters and the emergence of the "spiritual consumer." The notion of the subjective turn, however, also alludes to a second point—namely, the growing influence in Western culture of a particular cluster of beliefs and values relating to the individual and subjective life.

Although interest in the interior life in Western culture could hardly be seen as originating with the Reformation (see, e.g., the much earlier origins of autobiography in Augustine's *Confessions*), the religious ferment of the sixteenth century nevertheless played a crucial role in stimulating Western concepts of the importance of individual, subjective life. The concepts of personal conscience and piety obviously played an important role in the thinking of leading Reformation theologians. But it was arguably in the religious practices that the Reformation stimulated that a new kind of interest in the interior life of the self became more popularized in Western culture. Colin Campbell, for example, suggested that the Calvinist doctrine of election led to a significant increase in practices of introspection (including the keeping of personal diaries) as individuals sought to search out their own inner world of thoughts, feelings, and desires for signs that they might indeed be part of God's chosen.[22]

Campbell argues that over time in the seventeenth and eighteenth centuries, this emphasis on the value of introspection became increasingly secularized and lost its earlier rationale in Calvinist theology. Instead, understanding one's inner life—and, indeed, having a rich, inner world of deep feelings and experiences to understand—became more commonly seen as a good in its own right. In the eighteenth century, this found expression in the "cult of sensibility," a diffuse cultural turn toward celebrating the active cultivation of a rich inner life. For the purposes of our discussion here, it is important to note that a vital resource for this emerging cult of sensibility was the recently developed media product—the mass-produced novel—which was not only used as a tool for the cultivation of deep emotional and aesthetic experiences but also whose pages themselves often contained celebrations of such sensibility.[23] This nascent cultural movement, celebrating the inner life of the individual self, came in time to find fuller expression in the Romantic movement of the late eighteenth and early nineteenth centuries. From the Reformation onward, then, a particular cluster of values and beliefs relating to the importance of the self and subjective life began to coalesce in Western culture.[24] This included—reflecting the turn in Enlightenment philosophy and science—an emphasis on the autonomous, rational individual, and its cultural "other"—reflected in Romanticism—the importance of the complex emotional, spiritual, and aesthetic inner life of the self. Out of this cultural nexus emerged particular values relating to the self such as the importance of freedom, authenticity, and self-expression. Such concerns with the self had—dating back to the Reformation—primarily been the privilege of middle and upper social classes, rather than lower social classes preoccupied with subsistence. The spread of Evangelical piety among the working classes, however, did offer a form of religiosity strongly oriented toward the desires and workings of the heart.

It was not until the twentieth century, however, that an onset of social conditions proved favorable for the spreading influence of cultural beliefs and values relating to the importance of the self. As Daniel Bell argues, at the beginning of the twentieth century the idea of one's individual life as a work of art, to be formed out of a creative process of self-expression, was the preserve of a small, avant-garde cultural and artistic elite. By the end of the twentieth century, Bell notes, improving living conditions, the growth of consumer culture, and the increasing social importance of leisure led to such ideas as life as a process of self-expression, and the pursuit of one's authentic self was becoming much more widespread.[25] New social practices, such as the rise of advertising and the rapid growth of the personal therapy industries, further popularized the turn toward valuing one's interior world and the quality of personal life.[26]

Within the sociology of religion, there are a number of scholars across the twentieth century who claimed that these ideas about the value of individual, subjective life had a significant effect on Western culture and religion. One of the pioneering writers in this regard was Émile Durkheim, who suggested that the decline of traditional, institutional religion in the West was matched by the rising influence of the "cult of the individual," focused on celebrating the idea of the inherent dignity and worth of the free, rational self.[27] While Durkheim recognized that the celebration of the self had the potential to promote a corrosive anomie, he also suggested that with the appropriate social and ritual structures to support it, the cult of the individual could be a viable basis for a collective moral life for future Western society.

Following Durkheim, Ernst Troeltsch wrote about the turn to privatized, mystical experience among the cultured classes of his day.[28] Georg Simmel similarly wrote about the way in which the religious impulses of the cultured classes were turning away from the traditional symbols of

Christian faith and were finding expression through "a way of living life itself," the pursuit of personal life characterized by depth, richness, and wholeness.[29] Thomas Luckmann, writing in the 1960s, spoke of the rise of a new social form of religion, displacing institutional Christianity in the West, which was focused on the development of a free, creative, and authentic personal life.[30] And Peter Berger argued that the rise of choice in the religious marketplace tended to reinforce the turn inward into the self—for where else could one find the resources to make lifestyle decisions other than with reference to one's own concerns, experiences, values, and desires?[31]

Concerns for personal development, meaning, and wholeness are also evident in the studies of post-1960s American spirituality conducted by Robert Wuthnow and Wade Clark Roof.[32] In Britain, the Kendal project, recently completed by Paul Heelas and Linda Woodhead, offers empirical evidence that forms of religion that are more accommodated to the language and values of "subjective-life spirituality" are more likely to survive and even thrive than forms of religion that preserve traditional beliefs and doctrines and do nothing to address the development of an authentic, holistic personal life.[33] This cultural turn toward the self does not necessarily imply a retreat into a self-serving narcissism, as some critics would imply. In fact, in Heelas and Woodhead's study, concern with quality of personal life among their research participants was typically bound up with a concern for quality of personal relationships with others, and in many cases, active involvement in various forms of the caring profession. As Heelas and Woodhead point out, Sheila Larsson—the epitome of personalized spirituality, described by Robert Bellah and his colleagues in their seminal study *Habits of the Heart*—was no shallow narcissist, but worked in a demanding health-care role with very sick patients.[34] The turn inward is not necessarily a turn away from constructive relationships with others, but reflects a desire for a certain quality of relationship with self and others.

In one sense, the idea of the autonomous religious consumer and the rise of cultural values about the importance of subjective-life spirituality can be seen as complementary. If Western cultural values have tended to privilege the importance of the free, rational, and expressive self, then religious consumers' choices in the spiritual marketplace will tend to be influenced by such values. Religious beliefs, practices, and groups that offer more by way of cultivating and valuing one's personal life and close relations with others will be more attractive than those that do little to address such personal concerns. This is evident not only in the findings

Extending Our Conversation Partners

of studies such as the Kendal project but also, more anecdotally, in the substantial rise of religious and spiritual lifestyle media from *The Purpose Driven Life* to *The Road Less Traveled*.

At the same time, notions about the importance of Western cultural values of subjective life call into question certain accounts of the autonomous, religious consumer—particularly notions of the morally relativistic, "postmodern" spiritual consumer that I criticized earlier. If cultural values of subjective life still provide an important moral framework within which many people in the West make their religious and lifestyle choices, then it is questionable whether we are living in a society characterized by the collapse of all metanarratives. Rather than being "posttraditional" or "detraditionalized," Paul Heelas, for example, argues that contemporary Western society retains a core tradition, focused on the significance of the self and subjective life.[35] Heelas, like Durkheim, argues that this cultural tradition has the potential to nurture thriving forms of spirituality, social concern, and a culture of respect for individual rights and freedoms. Other critics suggest that the centrality of a subjective-life spirituality in contemporary culture is a damaging, ideological structure of late capitalist society.[36] Wherever one stands on this debate, the idea that we live in a cultural context devoid of influential cultural narratives is surely mistaken, and little more than an unreflective assumption that so-called postmodern culture means the extension of a Derridean deconstructionism to the mind-set of the general population.

Reading Film in the Context of the Subjective Turn

As we have seen, the notion of a subjective turn in contemporary religion implies both the growing importance of personal choice and intrinsic motivations in religious matters, and the influence of an evolving Western cultural tradition of values and beliefs relating to the importance of subjective life. But, so much for the sociological lecture: how can this wider social and cultural context usefully inform a theological reading of film?

First, when approaching the theological study of film, it may be useful to think of the role of film in contemporary culture as potentially being analogous to the role of the novel for the eighteenth-century cult of sensibility. As we noted earlier, the novel functioned both as a cultural tool for nurturing a certain kind of attitude toward, and experience of, one's inner life, and as a cultural text that at times celebrated the value of a deep emotional and aesthetic interior life. It is reasonable to argue that the medium of fictional, narrative film in the twentieth century serves a similar function in the more recent phase of the turn to the self in Western culture. The very nature of the medium encourages it to focus on the audiovisual representation of aspects of subjective life—the virtues, flaws, desires, motivations, aspirations, experiences, discoveries, and choices of individual characters. Furthermore, through being drawn into an affective engagement with this material, audiences may be drawn into a process of reflection about their own subjective lives in relation to those of the characters represented on the screen. What do I learn about the nature of love from Jerry Maguire or about the shallowness of my desires from Lester Burnham? From the subject positions represented by characters on the screen, what do I discover about my own interior life?[37]

Such a dialogue between the viewer's subjective life and the subjective lives represented on the screen may be rarely articulated in an explicit way. But this process of engaging with and reflecting on the subjective qualities and processes of film characters is conceivably a central part of the pleasure of film watching. Genre (or computer-generated-imagery) films with shallow characterization may be experienced as unsatisfying precisely because of their limited treatment of subjective-life issues. By contrast, low-budget films can be well received critically and commercially if they offer more complex and satisfying opportunities for emotional engagement with the film's characters—whether these be in the form of humans or other, anthropomorphized creations. In the first sense of the subjective turn that we have noted, film can therefore be understood as a cultural resource for the spiritual consumer, helping to stimulate personal reflection and to deepen personal commitments to particular ways of seeing the world.

The medium of fictional, narrative film is therefore typically oriented around issues of subjective life, and as such can function as a cultural tool for eliciting significant emotional and aesthetic experiences, as well as for reflecting on subjective-life issues and choices through empathic engagement and dialogue with film characters. At the same time, film texts can also offer sympathetic ideological treatments of the cultural turn to the self.

A good example of this is Gary Ross's 1998 film, *Pleasantville*, perhaps best known for its groundbreaking use of color and black-and-white elements in the same shot. In the film's narrative, two teenagers, David and Jen, find themselves mysteriously transported back into the world of a black-and-white 1950s sitcom—Pleasantville. Initially, the world of Pleasantville appears idyllic compared to the dysfunctional and bleak future David and Jen came from. Over time, though, David and Jen begin to realize that the pleasantness of their new home excludes richer and more complex aspects of human life. With varying degrees of awareness, they introduce new qualities and experiences into this restrained world—sexuality, love, artistic creativity, emotional depth, learning—and as this happens, color begins to appear in this hitherto monochrome world. The changes in Pleasantville are not universally welcome, however, and the cryptofascist chamber of commerce tries to set in place a repressive regime that will rein back the shift toward a freer and more expressive town. By provoking both his father and the leader of the chamber of commerce into a realization of the depths of their emotional lives, David succeeds in turning even them into color, and the world of Pleasantville is irrevocably changed.

The film narrative itself traces developments in David's and Jen's self-understanding. David grows from being emotionally and sexually repressed (and therefore initially more sympathetic to the ethos of Pleasantville) to being more courageous, innovative, and creative. Jen's horizons are broadened from a preoccupation with sex, and she develops a more secure sense of self-respect and desire to develop herself through education. The film's use of characterization and its visual and narrative structure thus reflect the cultural ideology of the cult of the individual. It celebrates the value of a deep, authentic interior life, even if the price of this is the loss of a certain degree of security and comfort. Through the movie's construction of good and bad characters, through the narrative arc toward the good life along which the central characters travel, and through the movie's innovative mixing of color and black-and-white elements in its mise-en-scène, the film reinforces the value of particular understandings of the subjective life.

Obvious examples can be found of films that critique the more optimistic, expressive vision of the good life offered by *Pleasantville*—such as Tyler Derden's critique of therapeutic culture ("You are not a precious flower") in *Fight Club* or Jiao Long's discovery of the dangers of self-assertion in *Crouching Tiger, Hidden Dragon*. But these tend to be exceptions to the more general values of contemporary Hollywood film, which celebrate personal freedom, compassion, intimacy, courage, expressiveness, creativity, individuality, and authenticity. In the second sense of the subjective turn that we noted—the rise of a cluster of cultural values around the importance of the self and subjective life—particular films can thus be read as texts that transmit this particular cultural ideology.

Conclusion

Recognizing the cultural significance of Western fictional narrative film as both a tool for personal reflexivity in shaping lifestyle and religious choices, and as a medium for transmitting the ideology of the cult of the individual, provides a useful starting point for the theological analysis of particular films and the activity of film watching more generally. Some theological critics will tend to treat this connection between film and the subjective turn as the basis for a hermeneutic of suspicion for their readings of particular films. At its simplest, this can find expression in the argument that films that encourage the subjective turn—valuing personal authenticity, individuality, intimacy, and self-expression—without placing them in some kind of explicitly confessional context, are encouraging a shallow, narcissistic form of spirituality. Other theological critics—more influenced by the work of the Frankfurt School—may instead argue that films that focus simply on issues of subjective life are failing to engage with the deeper causes of human suffering, that is, the wider social and structural issues that perpetuate alienation and social injustice.[38]

Narcissism, cultural alienation, and social injustice are all clearly worthy of critique. But it is possible that theological engagements with the relationship between film and the subjective turn could also use the critical analysis of film as a way of engaging with questions of what kind of subjective life or quality of personal life we should aspire to. To see the ideology of the cult of the individual as simply problematic—and as something that an authentic spirituality should distance itself from—is to my mind an unworkable basis for a viable contemporary Western theology. Furthermore, creating an arbitrary separation between religious tradition and the cult of the individual fails to appreciate the ways in which the evolution of the Christian tradition in the West has precisely been an important source of stimulation for the cultivation of the inner life and a sense of the value of the individual self. If to do contextual theology means thinking theologically through the symbols and structures of one's own particular cultural milieu, then meaningful contemporary Western theologies will need to engage critically and constructively with the cultural legacy of Western understandings of the value of the self.

Engaging theologically with film—as an important medium for the transmission of the cultural ideology of the subjective turn—has the potential to be a leading edge of a contextual Western theology that explores the dialectic between ultimate meaning and personal life.[39] Such engagements need to move beyond superficial moral judgments about the behaviors of individual characters (e.g., Is a character a good role model or not, based on whether the person lies, steals, cheats, engages in illicit sexual activity, etc.?). A theological analysis of characters at this level serves only to reproduce existing ethical codes in the mind of the viewer. Richer, Western contextual theologies will use the analysis of film to explore questions such as the moral and spiritual significance of our emotional lives; the positive meanings of individuality, creativity, and self-expression; the roots of alienation from our true selves and from others; the meaning of genuine healing and growth; and the content of true, personal wisdom. It will examine the nature of healthy and unhealthy forms of intimacy and ask what friendship can contribute to the development of a rich, inner life. Such a contextual theology of film will therefore move beyond superficial moral critiques of characters to explore how an empathic and imaginative engagement with film texts and characters contributes to our theological understanding of an authentic, whole, and creative personal life.

Understanding the relationship between film and the subjective turn should not therefore be a reason for theologians to dismiss the moral and spiritual usefulness of film, but can instead provide a framework for a critical theological engagement with subjective-life issues in film. Through critical engagement with film texts, and audiences' experiences of watching film, theologians can stimulate important discussions in faith communities and the wider public sphere about the true nature of constructive and healthy forms of subjective life. Indeed, reflecting on particular films can provide a useful structure within which religious groups or congregations can reflect in a focused way on issues of personal meaning and wholeness. This is already starting to happen in the burgeoning movement of film discussion groups that are growing up in churches in Britain and America. Such grassroots theological reflection on film arguably offers one of the most interesting and engaging media for theological education in recent years. Ultimately, though, perhaps the most direct and formative kinds of theological reflection will take place not so much in these group settings as in the direct, affective, and imaginative engagement of the individual viewer with the flickering image in the quiet, darkened space of the cinema. It is perhaps as we learn to think about cinemagoing as itself a spiritual practice that we will really discover how to nurture personal, transformative theological encounters with film.

Notes

1. Gordon Lynch, *Understanding Theology and Popular Culture* (Oxford: Blackwell, 2005).

2. E.g., Robert K. Johnston, *Reel Spirituality*, 2nd ed. (Grand Rapids: Baker Academic, 2006); Steve Nolan, "Towards a New Religious Film Criticism: Using Film to Understand Religious Identity Rather Than Locate Cinematic Analogue," in *Mediating Religion: Conversations in Media, Religion and Culture*, ed. Jolyon Mitchell and Sophia Marriage (London: T&T Clark, 2003), 169–78; Melanie Wright, *Religion and Film* (London: Tauris, 2006).

3. Laura Mulvey, "Visual Pleasure and Narrative Cinema," *Screen* 16, no. 3 (1975): 6–18. See also Graeme Turner, *British Cultural Studies: An Introduction*, 3rd ed. (London: Routledge, 2003), 85–89.

4. Margaret Miles, *Seeing and Believing: Religion and Values in the Movies* (Boston: Beacon, 1996).

5. John Lyden, *Film as Religion: Myths, Morals and Rituals* (New York: New York University Press, 2003).

6. Joel Martin and Conrad Ostwalt, eds., *Screening the Sacred: Religion, Myth, and Ideology in Popular Film* (Boulder, CO: Westview, 1995).

7. Clive Marsh, *Cinema and Sentiment: Film's Challenge to Theology* (Carlisle, UK: Paternoster, 2004).

8. John Fiske, *Understanding Popular Culture* (London: Routledge, 1989), 25.

9. Lynn Schofield Clark, *From Angels to Aliens: Teenagers, the Media, and the Supernatural* (New York: Oxford University Press, 2005).

10. Christopher Partridge, *The Re-Enchantment of the West*, vol. 1 (London: Continuum, 2004).

11. Clifford Geertz, *The Interpretation of Cultures* (New York: Basic Books, 1973), 3–30.

12. See Steve Bruce, *God Is Dead: Secularization in the West* (London: Routledge, 2002); Grace Davie, *Europe: The Exceptional Case* (London: Darton, Longman & Todd, 2002).

13. David Martin, *A General Theory of Secularization* (Oxford: Blackwell, 1978).

14. E.g., Charles Taylor, *Varieties of Religion Today: William James Revisited* (Cambridge, MA: Harvard University Press, 2003).

15. See Dean Hoge, Benton Johnson, and Donald Luidens, *Vanishing Boundaries: Religion of Mainline Protestant Baby Boomers* (Louisville: Westminster John Knox, 1994); Callum Brown, *The Death of Christian Britain* (London: Routledge, 2000).

16. See Robert Wuthnow, *After Heaven: Spirituality in America since the 1950s* (Berkeley: University of California Press, 1998); Wade Clark Roof, *Spiritual Marketplace: Baby Boomers and the Remaking of American Religion* (Princeton, NJ: Princeton University Press, 1999).

17. Thomas Luckmann, *The Invisible Religion* (New York: Macmillan, 1967); Peter Berger, *Heretical Imperative: Contemporary Possibilities of Religious Affirmation* (New York: Doubleday, 1980).

18. Roof, *Spiritual Marketplace*.

19. Ulrich Beck, Anthony Giddens, and Scott Lash, *Reflexive Modernization: Politics, Tradition and Aesthetics in the Modern Social Order* (Cambridge: Polity, 1994).

20. See Peter Berger, ed., *The Desecularization of the World: Resurgent Religion and World Politics* (Grand Rapids: Eerdmans, 1999).

21. Colleen Carroll, *The New Faithful: Why Young People Are Embracing Christian Orthodoxy* (Chicago: Loyola Press, 2002). For a discussion of the significance of the "subsumed self" in relation to other forms of negotiated selfhood in contemporary religion and spirituality, see David Lyon, *Jesus in Disneyland* (Cambridge: Polity, 2000).

22. Colin Campbell, *The Romantic Ethic and the Spirit of Consumerism* (Oxford: Blackwell, 1987).

23. See John Mullan, "Feelings and Novels," in *Rewriting the Self: Stories from the Renaissance to the Present*, ed. Roy Porter (London: Routledge, 1997), 119–34.

24. See Charles Taylor, *Sources of the Self: The Making of Modern Identity* (Cambridge: Cambridge University Press, 1989).

25. Daniel Bell, *The Cultural Contradictions of Capitalism* (New York: Basic Books, 1976).

26. E.g., Philip Cushman, *Constructing the Self, Constructing America: A Cultural History of Psychotherapy* (Cambridge, MA: Da Capo, 1999).

27. For a helpful summary of Durkheim's rather diffuse writing on this subject, see Paul Heelas, "On Things Not Being Worse and the Ethic of Humanity," in *Detraditionalization*, ed. Paul Heelas (Oxford: Blackwell, 1996), 200–18.

28. Ernst Troeltsch, *The Social Teaching of the Christian Churches*, 2 vols. (London: George Allen & Unwin, 1911).

29. Georg Simmel, *Essays on Religion* (Yale: Yale University Press, 1997).

30. Luckmann, *Invisible Religion*.

31. Berger, *Heretical Imperative*.

32. Wuthnow, *After Heaven*; Roof, *Spiritual Marketplace*.

33. Paul Heelas and Linda Woodhead, with Benjamin Seel, Bron Szernsynski, and Karin Tusting, *The Spiritual Revolution: Why Religion Is Giving Way to Spirituality* (Oxford: Blackwell, 2005).

34. Paul Heelas and Linda Woodhead, "Homeless Minds Today?" in *Peter Berger and the Study of Religion*, ed. Linda Woodhead, with Paul Heelas and David Martin (London: Routledge, 2002), 60–61.

35. Heelas, "On Things Not Being Worse."

36. See, e.g., Jeremy Carrette and Richard King, *Selling Spirituality: The Silent Takeover of Religion* (London: Routledge, 2004).

37. The notion of media texts as a source of "subject-positions" is developed in Douglas Kellner, *Media Culture: Cultural Studies, Identity, and Politics between the Modern and the Postmodern* (New York: Routledge, 1994).

38. See, e.g., the recent critique of personalized spiritualities in Carrette and King, *Selling Spirituality*.

39. This kind of contextual theology is called for in Tom Beaudoin, *Virtual Faith: The Irreverent Spiritual Quest of Generation X* (Chichester, UK: Jossey-Bass, 1998).

6

Hollywood Chronicles

Toward an Intersection of Church History and Film History

Late on a hot autumn afternoon in Williamsburg, Virginia, I met with an upper-division class of very bright students from the College of William and Mary. The course was titled "Christian Theology and Film," and although sponsored by the religion department, it had attracted students from across the academic spectrum. During this particular class period, we were viewing two silent religious films on the life of Jesus: Sidney Olcott's *From the Cross to the Manger* (1912) and Cecil B. DeMille's *The King of Kings* (1927). Olcott's film traversed the sites of Palestine and Egypt, being in some ways an extended "actuality" film, a film documenting static scenes of holy writ. As such, it appeared to be a visual authentication of the quest for the historical Jesus, showing actual locations and facsimile characters from the Gospel accounts. With his impressive images of the pyramids and Sphinx and the walls of Jerusalem, Olcott had captured for his era the authenticity Albert Schweitzer sought in seeking the historical shell of the biblical story. The silent moving picture gave audiences the sense of "being there." One could believe in the story of Jesus because one saw his holy land and his reproduced life.

Where Olcott strove for historical credibility of space and time, showman DeMille went for the grand spectacle in his 1927 version of *The King of Kings*. DeMille's lascivious prologue, concocting a sort of romantic triangle among the courtesan Mary Magdalene, Judas, and Jesus—which author Dan Brown would have loved—sparked incredulity and humor among all the students. However, different responses to the episode in which Mary first encounters Jesus revealed a discrepancy between those who were biblically literate and those who were not.

Mary, wearing a skimpy, revealing bra, rides her zebra chariot into Jerusalem looking for this carpenter who has stolen away the attention of her Judas. She storms into the home where Jesus has just healed a blind girl on the Sabbath, and shouts, "Where is this Nazarene?" The shot cuts to Jesus speaking with his disciples. He turns toward Mary and declares, "Seek and ye shall find; ask and it shall be granted unto you; knock and it shall be opened." The comic textual incongruity is hilarious, but only to those who know the biblical reference and its context in Scripture. For those who do not, it seems a very apt reply. The juxtaposition of the biblical passage in an absurdly foreign context to support a narrative logic jolted students well acquainted with the gospel story. Others, less biblically literate, looked nonplussed.

Film History and Church History

Not only basic biblical literacy but also fresh perspectives are needed as Christian faith and tradition intersect with the history of film. The writing of such a religious film history depends in part, of course, on an informed hermeneutic. How I interpret the stories or contexts of filmmaking pivots on the basic knowledge that I hold, and unfortunately, readers of film history are rarely provided with theologically informed narratives or critiques. Likewise, we might confess that church historians are oblivious (and many happily so) to the relevance of popular culture to their tasks of mapping out theological trends and events.

Film historian Richard Maltby's investigation into the "propriety of the Christ story" as owned by Cecil B. DeMille in his aforementioned epic *The King of Kings* illustrates a positive step in demonstrating the richness possible in cross-fertilized studies of film and church history. Rather than assuming a monolithic religious response to the classic silent film, he notes the diverse and conflicted religious perspectives among Christian groups. His observation coincidentally illumines the emerging modernist/fundamentalist chasm growing in the 1920s. When one of the film's advisers, the Congregational Reverend George Reid Andrews, wandered onto the set of the resurrection scene, he mused that it must be quite consoling for those who accepted such an event literally, to which Roman Catholic Father Daniel Lord responded: "I take it literally."[1] The biographical anecdote revealed the variety of religious experiences and opinions engaged in recording the cultural phenomenon of the movies in the 1920s.

Likewise, a writing of church history in the twentieth century requires competency in the study of popular culture, and particularly, film. Do cinematic events have any impact on theological ideas or religious experiences? Reports from audiences in the 1930s indicate that when they prayed, they envisioned the visage of H. B. Warner, DeMille's actor, as the face of Jesus. The pictures of a Hollywood movie shaped the piety of congregational devotion. So, too, Mel Gibson's *The Passion of the Christ*, with its contemporary aesthetic of graphic violence, refigures the religious imaginations of another generation. One catches a glimpse of the scope and depth of cultural discourse surrounding such a religious/film historical event (or pseudoevent) in Robin Riley's *Film, Faith, and Cultural Conflict*, a case study of Martin Scorsese's *The Last Temptation of Christ*. Riley analyzes the various groups castigating, scapegoating, and defending the film, and thereby opens up multiple levels of meanings about Christology, the sacred, and the rhetorical rituals of blame and victimizing. Films contribute to shaping or tweaking theological nuances. Too easily one can point to director Ron Howard's *The Da Vinci Code* as a visual argument for the heretical doctrine that Jesus was merely human and the outlandish fabrication of a church history that posits Constantine's power plays in squashing alternative (gnostic) gospels and establishing patriarchal oppression of women. The values assumed in film narratives are those that are, unfortunately, the ones assumed and assimilated by gullible viewers. The great worth of *The Da Vinci Code*, however, is that it shocks true historians into a conversation with such an influential medium as film.

The writing of film histories continues to undergo a paradigm shift, namely the merging of social and cultural histories. Social history informs film history with its attention to and concern with studies of women, immigrants, ethnic groups, and others who left no written records or documents. In the realm of social histories, another fascinating and very curious phenomenon is the rise of local histories, which through maps,

Extending Our Conversation Partners

charts, and graphs seek to illuminate cultural processes and changes on smaller levels. Broader cultural histories emphasize the role of hermeneutics in interpreting texts and contexts. What this means for a theological cultural history is highlighting the role of religious faith and institutions as human agencies of social change. Cultural histories also showcase the functions of film and media within the realms of traditional religious activity, such as in mythmaking, agenda setting, moral formation, and identifying sources of authority.

In 1912, in an early study on the science of moving pictures, author Frederick A. Talbot averred that any episode from the creation to the resurrection could be produced to familiarize young and old with Bible stories. Talbot related one anecdote that demonstrated the power of moving pictures to certify biblical truth. A Sunday school teacher was describing the passage through the Red Sea to a group of children. As the teacher told the story of Moses, a young girl's piping voice exclaimed:

"Yes, teacher, I know that is right!"

"Why?" asked the somewhat startled teacher.

"Because I saw it!" The child explained that the previous evening she had been to a picture theater and had seen the Israelites crossing the Red Sea.[2]

A full cultural history is attuned to the impact that the production and consumption of media have upon the shaping of a religious consciousness, noting, for example, the privileged place that the sense of sight attained over hearing in the early twentieth century. Cultural historian David Morgan clearly laid out such an intersection of visual learning and religious communication in the nineteenth century in his superb *Protestants and Pictures*, a model study of the precursors of the intersection of film and religion.

Reflecting on these episodes, I wonder why modern film histories have generally neglected religious dimensions in film and why there has not been more interface between the two disciplines. The writing of history, the realm of historiography, has not heretofore invited theologically minded scholars to its table. When theologians do appear, they enter like Paul at the Areopagus, pointing out the truths behind the unknown gods of Hollywood, tracing the christological figures on Hollywood's shrouds, and identifying apt heirophanies and transcendental styles.

However, several recent trends have brought theology into conversation with the film industry and film scholarship. Most electric and controversial was Mel Gibson's *The Passion of the Christ*, a film that attained financial blockbuster status to the chagrin of Hollywood insiders. The money spoke, and the film industry recognized, as DeMille had in the 1920s, that religious audiences could buy tickets as well as anyone else. Likewise, the cunning strategy of film advertising invited concerned church groups to enter into dialogue with the controversial falsehoods of *The Da Vinci Code*. *Entertainment Weekly* quoted actor Tom Hanks as saying that the movie "may end up helping churches do their job. If they put up a sign saying: 'This Wednesday we're discussing the gospel,' 12 people show up. But if a sign says: 'This Wednesday we're discussing the Da Vinci Code,' 800 people show up." A Vatican call for a boycott notwithstanding, the marketing campaign proved remarkably successful, attracting record numbers of ticket buyers.

Second, historiography is being reshaped by scholars like John Lyden, who envisions film as a potential rival and competitor, and even an idolatrous substitute, for religion. The notion of film as religion hints of a parentage with graven imagery, the theater, and idolatry, cultural phenomena that have historically induced a schizophrenic ambivalence in church leaders. But such entertainment media, from the medieval miracle and morality plays to the apocalyptic imagery of German artist and mathematician Albrecht Dürer, have also contributed to the mission and ministries of the church.

The historical interpretation of films invites, or rather demands, a religious lens that helps bring the narratives and the symbols into focus. Adam Potkay's *The Bible as the Root of Western Literature* reveals how indebted the great works of Dante, Milton, and others are to the biblical tradition. He expertly connects Shakespeare's *The Merchant of Venice*, for example, to the apostle Paul's tension between law and grace. Edmund Spenser's *Faerie Queen* and John Bunyan's *Pilgrim's Progress* are similarly tied to the Reformed theologies of Luther and Calvin. The obvious question that arises is, to what theological ideas, debates, or themes are films connected? Likewise, to fully appreciate, and even understand, films pregnant with references and doctrines grounded in the Hebrew and Christian Scriptures, one must seek out a conversation between two nonintersecting histories: film history and church history.

Toward a *Kinoheilsgeschichte*

My present concern is to outline key questions and issues in giving birth to writing a religious film history. This project is more than pinpointing ostensibly religious works, such as those on Jesus films and classic biblical subjects, or such hagiographies that embellish the lives of saints or priests as in *Brother Son, Sister Moon* or *Going My Way*. It aims at writing film history that takes a fuller view of the role of religion in general and Christianity in particular as salient variables in shaping film scripts and images. As such, I propose the following criteria.

The writing of a religious film history (what I playfully call a *kino-heilsgeschichte*) requires a multiple hermeneutic of film. (See, e.g., Robert Johnston's essay on the medieval quadriga in chap. 15.) How we interpret the texts of film dictates what we will write about. How we see shapes how we interpret. And how we understand the context of the film, both in its historical setting and in its creative and economic production, shapes how we see. At the outset, however, we viewers must confess our all-too-fallible biases and try to see the film as fairly as possible. I must be aware of my prejudices even as I approach the films, lest I succumb to a Procrustean mode of interpretation. (In the classic Greek myth, the hero Perseus comes upon an inn owned by the crafty Procrusteus. He offers one bed of a predetermined size to any weary traveler seeking rest for the night. However, if the person sleeping on the bed is too short, he is stretched to fit the length of the bed; if she is too tall, her legs or head are cut off. Thus, a Procrustean hermeneutic makes all evidence fit one size, one limited perspective projected onto the text.) We must not force an interpretation on any film text, but we might measure it according to its own historical context.

The different readings of the text of Peter Weir's *The Truman Show*, for example, can reveal how the film fits in the oeuvre of Weir's transcendental work and how it can divulge contemporary concerns and changing views of spirituality at the end of the millennium. Weir's works (*Picnic at Hanging Rock, The Year of Living Dangerously, Witness*) hint at worlds of mystery and difference. For some critics like Brian Godawa, the film signifies the need for a simple true person to escape from God's sovereign control and find personal autonomy in liberating the self.[3] Such a Pelagian theme fits well with David Bordwell's classical Hollywood narrative cinema, in which individual protagonists, usually male, assert their will and function as causal agents to win a battle, get a girl, or achieve a goal. However, Weir seems to be doing something different. His hero struggles against Christof, a villainous "prince of the air" waves, to discover a world beyond his material existence, a supernatural world. When the one authentic person he has met in his plastic Platonic cave prays that God will help him, Truman finds the strength to seek what lies beyond his artificial environment. In the waning moments of modernity, Weir allows the spiritual to break in, amid cheers from a host of ordinary witnesses watching and rooting for the pilgrim's progress into a super "real" world. Other scholars like Robert K. Johnston see the artistic vision of Weir and help to circulate questions around the elements in Weir's world and in the contemporary religious landscape that contribute to this fresh parable of a man being saved from his shadowy existence. Put in such a context, the film opens up an understanding of the postmodern spiritual condition.[4]

Underlying a fuller understanding of film texts is this task of viewing them in their religious and cultural context. Unfortunately, we often discover that a paucity of knowledge about the Christian tradition subverts even a simple recognition of biblical significance. That film and other media have supplanted literature, and specifically the Bible, in providing a template for interpreting the contemporary world is beyond much debate. In fact, even a film reviewer for the journal *Film Comment* worried that we may have lost our intellectual grounding and historical perspective. Critic Richard Crinkley attended a showing of Bruce Beresford's painfully cheesy adaptation of *King David*. As he watched David dance before the ark of the covenant, wearing only an ephod, his boredom was broken up by the unexpected laughter of several boys sitting behind him. He asked why they had guffawed so loudly at that scene. "Oh," explained one of the boys, "we know where they got that idea of the Ark thing. That came from Spielberg."

Cinema literacy has superseded biblical literacy. The simple pleasures of superficial film viewing do not require an understanding of historical facts or religious traditions; however, knowledge of the past augments ordinary pleasures. The significance of silent film director Lois Weber's protest films against the injustices of labor and abortion is deepened when one understands them in relation to her calling to be a missionary. Frank Capra's encounter with the mysterious little man from God rebuking him for not countering the fascist propaganda of Hitler places his populist message films in a brighter light and more urgent purpose. The historical religious contexts of films themselves invite a deeper pleasure. Hugh Hudson's contemporary classic *Chariots of Fire* is a satisfying film; yet understanding the context of the Sabbatarian movement and the simmering prejudices of anti-Semitism during the 1924 Olympics enhances the gratifying value of the film. Understanding the deeper relevance and experiencing the fuller pleasures of such a film does require information not only on its historical significance but also on its religious history.

As another example, Roman Polanski's *Rosemary's Baby* stands not simply as a mere creepy horror story masquerading a satanic incarnation nor as a political allegory suggesting a social conspiracy of evil surrounding such an innocent occasion as the birth of a baby; rather, the film can be viewed in the contexts of the European loss of faith as portrayed in the religious films of Ingmar Bergman and Luis Buñuel and of the writings of John Robinson and the Death of God movement. Polanski intentionally incorporates the infamous *Time* magazine cover on God's death to connect his fictional narrative to current events. "If there is no God," wrote Dostoevsky, "then everything is permissible," even the cinematic advent of the devil in the flesh. Historical religious context offers a hermeneutical key to discover the significance of such a film beyond its entertainment thrills and gratifications. It is a film about theodicy that shadows the waning faith of the late 1960s.

Historiography begins appropriately with both an acknowledgment of facts and a clarification of ideological assumptions. Legends too easily grow up within the merry task of writing history, even religious history. Biases influence which documents and arguments are given preference. Thus, writers of a religious history must examine both their materials and their own conceptual frameworks upon which they ground their work. Early film histories focused on the great-man tradition, while later film histories read history through the perspectives of key films, directors, or stars. Alternately, psychoanalytic, Marxist, and feminist readings shape how we interpret film texts. Such perspectives, while useful, have dictated which sources are privileged and which are neglected. Methods and assumptions determine what critics look at and how the mass of data of films and accompanying material are interpreted.

The religious film historian can wisely learn from the perspectives of these other ideological approaches. Film history need not always be written by the winners. Rather, an argument on what to see and how to look at it becomes a worthy task, an argument that can esteem those works usually deemed less honorable. I would argue, for instance, that director Chris Columbus's zany, slapstick comedy *Home Alone*, with a close-up insert of old man Marley's stigmata and his subsequent conversation with little Kevin in a church during Christmas, carries more theological gravity than either Ron Howard's *The Da Vinci Code* or TBN's *Omega Code* movies. One does not expect the holy in the midst of a light comedy, and it arrives more significantly than in specious religious spectacles. But one argues such issues to discover the worth of various films and to valorize them, especially in trying to formulate a reliable, credible, and cogent account of the past.[5]

One must wrestle as well with whether one constructs or exegetes the meaning of the texts. In his essay on historiography in *Cinéma et cie*, historian Tom Elsaesser raises such concerns about the construction of history.[6] Not only should religious film historians examine their own subjectivities, but they should also reconsider the cultural and personal factors of their sources. Bias against independent religious films, for example, distorts any kind of careful and fair analysis of materials thought to be sentimental, trivial, or exploitative. Such blatantly dispensational films as the Mark IV production of *A Thief in the Night* might be worthy of cavalier dismissal, but the text should be considered in light of its purpose and effects as much as its aesthetic and technical constraints.[7] Here is a nontheatrical film that has allegedly been used as a means for thousands of conversions through manipulative techniques of suspense and fear; yet while it is rarely part of a canon of critical analysis, it fits aptly in Michael Lieb's category of the media of eschatology in *Children of Ezekiel*.[8]

The twin dangers of historicism (historical revisionism) and subjectivism need to be questioned, as much as discerning the underlying ideologies of any work. The virtue of partisan critical works as diverse as authors Margaret Miles and Ted Baehr is that their theological premises are clearly writ large and deliberately unconcealed. Yet perhaps most importantly, theological film scholars must bring, along with their rigorous critical engagement, what Charles Musser so aptly called "a sympathetic, humble openness to the material and a readiness to accept a body of work on its own terms."[9] Such a posture approximates what former Fuller Seminary provost and theologian Russ Spittler once identified as an attitude of "critical loyalty" to one's material and tradition.

Historiographical approaches should negotiate numerous histories. The study of the writing of religious film histories needs also to attend to the diversity of histories. History is an eclectic discipline, borrowing from many others. Film historian Sumiko Higashi writes of a colleague who ironically remained the only nonwhite person attending a film history conference on race and the diverse writings of film history. The question raised was, Who gets to write about what and why? If no religious traditions are represented, who defines the topic, the salience, and the significance of texts? The need for a fresh interdisciplinary writing involves not only demographic differences, but also a category we might call theographics, wherein we seek to understand how different theological traditions (i.e., Roman Catholic, Reformed, etc.) might approach the interpretation of films. Working in cooperation, both film historians and church historians can find fascinating points of intertextual convergence.

Extending Our Conversation Partners

In their groundbreaking work *Film History: Theory and Practice*, Douglas Gomery and Richard Allen summoned colleagues in film studies to expand their study of film as an art form to include technological, economic, and social perspectives. Likewise, in a special 2004 issue of *Cinema Journal* that focused on film history, author Lee Grieveson asked whether film histories will "traverse other histories"; in other words, whether in a larger view of cultural meanings, film would find itself informed by diverse scholarly disciplines as much as by its own aesthetic traditions.[10] Implicit in both challenges was recognition of the need to attend to religious voices. Some cultural historians have already refocused attention on the interface of religion and film. For example, Francis G. Couvares examined the plural perspectives of religious groups (Roman Catholics, liberal Protestants, fundamentalists, etc.) in articulating diverse views regarding certain films. In fact, even among conservative groups, divergent opinions clashed. Revivalist and evangelist Billy Sunday, for example, promoted movies that honored what he saw as good civic values, while others like C. H. Jack Linn damned them as the "devil's incubator."

Key to this interchange of intellectual disciplines is the contribution of theological studies as a ground for interpreting the place of film in the lives of people. Film historiography requires a sense of church history. Roman Catholic scholars have capably chronicled the role of the church in setting forth the Production Code in the early 1930s and in shaping the religious worldviews of filmmakers like John Ford and Martin Scorsese. One of the premier texts to merge the histories of Roman Catholic religion and film is Theresa Sanders's *Celluloid Saints*, a brilliantly insightful convergence of hagiography and film studies. Other historical frameworks, like feminist theory, helpfully note the religious place of women in film, such as Barbara Stanwyck in Frank Capra's *The Miracle Woman*, as an Aimee Semple McPherson evangelist hostile to the mainline church of her father and open to revivalism. Yet one generally finds a paucity of research on films and their relation to the mainline Protestant tradition. While scholars like William Romanowski and James Gilbert are altering such a dearth, there is more to be uncovered and addressed.

Additionally, Steven Ross points out that in finding new ways of writing cinema history, one should celebrate the contradictions and ambivalences that do exist in merged histories, as they often exist in one's own mind.[11] In other words, the history of religious people and film is not neat and tidy. This new practice of historiography should be viewed as essentially dialogic and collaborative, as one's colleagues in other disciplines question and diagnose the false, the sham, the pretentious, the pompous, the obscure, and even the verbose in our own writings.[12]

This fertile historiographical approach will also incorporate nontraditional film archival material. Appropriately, film historians have turned to engage sources beyond film archives—city directories, public records, local newspapers, and even editorials. Troves of historical data also exist in religious realms as well as in such less-established venues in film. Rarely probed alternative sources in religion such as religious journals, printed sermons, or spiritual meditations now contribute to a broader view of cultural history. Societies, classes, or groups marginalized from the mainstream Hollywood cinema presumably left few published written records and thus had no written history. Fortunately, in addition to religious documents, an oral history trend investigating "orphan films" and local film projects has begun to alter such shortcomings, seeking to rescue the nonliterate and marginal from the condescension of traditional history. However, while barriers between academic and popular studies of history are being overcome with fresh approaches to oral history, some important questions remain. How reliable are oral sources? What significance and relevance should be given to testimonies and personal reflections regarding film? How should historians deal with oral traditions concerning religious reactions to film? How should historians treat social and religious memories, and how should historians deal with reported uses and functions of film by religious bodies?

Religious Film Histories

That a religious film history exists is no longer in question; the issue has become, How does one appropriate this diffused and widespread approach to film without yielding to exercises in trivia and irrelevance? One such possible heuristic approach, headed up by Arthur Knight, is the Homer Project, which seeks to document an international history of moviegoing, exhibition, and reception. Sponsored by the International Cinema Audience Research Group, the project aims at excavating the ways in which audiences in local communities have appropriated film for sundry uses. Writings from religious periodicals as well as correspondence between religious leaders and Hollywood personnel, such as that between evangelist Billy Sunday and entertainers like Cecil B. DeMille and William S. Hart, housed in the Billy Graham Center at Wheaton College, have illumined the intersection of the two realms. Other materials such as meditations on movies in journalist G. K. Chesterton's "Fear of the Movies," Christian mystic Thomas Merton's *The Seven Story Mountain*, and C. S. Lewis's *Experiment in Criticism* adumbrate theological reflections on film that are being discussed in a plethora of books and articles.

What also needs to be examined closely is the correspondence between church and film industry. Unexamined records of the Protestant Film Commission, for example, corresponding to the documented history of Roman Catholic dioceses, particularly of Los Angeles, need to be located and opened. Local historical archives, especially newspapers and maps, frequently reveal a religiously aware and centralized population, especially in the early years of moviegoing. Churches, in geographical relation to theaters, give us a sense of spatial relations and cultural proximity. Certain studies like those of historian Dean Rapp and cultural scholar Bill Romanowski serve as vanguard studies. In this new historical turn, religious discourses and practices do traverse the history of film and the history of other media as Janet Staiger observes. As a compelling example, one might investigate the synergetic connection between the Calvinist film Westerns of Broncho Billy and William S. Hart and their backdrop of nineteenth-century evangelical novels.

The writing of film history must also include studies of the people who watched the films. Traditional audience studies in uses and gratifications (U&G) looked at why people use media and analyzed the personal and psychological components that determine the reasons people choose to watch certain media (i.e., information, personal identity, social interaction, entertainment, etc.). U&G theory suggests the functions that media play in fulfilling people's needs and what influence the media have in attracting target audiences by way of satisfying certain needs. From a broader social context, reception studies foreground what people see in the media and the meanings that people construct as they interpret media texts. The focus of reception analysis is on specific content (e.g., an end-times film) and on specific social contexts (e.g., a group of Southern Baptists). It probes the meaning of the film through in-depth interviews (rather than U&G questionnaires).

Recent trends emphasize how audiences resist Hollywood's constructed texts and find their own, often oppositional, interpretations to the film. Such a theoretical perspective in New Audience Research assumes that audiences are active producers of meaning, not mere consumers who tailor the significance of the media to fit their social and religious worldview. The work of Everett Rogers and William Brown investigates the concept of entertainment/education, assessing how global cultures use media to teach pro-social and religious values. Presently, scholars like Clive Marsh are asking such questions as "What do people do with film?" from a theological perspective. The creative appropriation of film by audiences will affect the writing of film history, particularly in the indirect ways in which messages are mediated by institutional church organizations or public spokespeople. In 1934, for example, both Cardinal Dougherty of Philadelphia and William O'Connell of Boston shaped what was acceptable viewing for their own congregations. More recently, church leaders like those at Calvary Chapel in Costa Mesa, California, work with distributors to arrange movie screenings in churches, following a practice set up in the 1910s by Methodists, Presbyterians, Episcopalians, and others.[13] In identifying the nexus of media histories with all their constellations and webs of relations, audiences must be taken into account, with the recognition that this audience is defined not only by gender, race, and class, but also by Christian faith and tradition.

Film history is a crucial part of twentieth-century church history. So far we have emphasized the place of religion in the writing of film history. However, what is lacking even more is the inclusion of film and media history into the annals of church history. Silent American film invaded churches and was incorporated into religious education, missions, preaching, and evangelism. The 1919 Methodist Centenary in Columbus, Ohio, for example, instituted a program of film exhibition worldwide. Pioneers like D. W. Griffith viewed silent films as a universal language that could usher in the kingdom of God.

In less visionary ways, the Hollywood community has affected the public image of American religious life. While biographers and historians dealing with the life of Aimee Semple McPherson opine on the alleged kidnapping scandal, they generally ignore the published testimony of actor Milton Berle on his reported affair with the flamboyant evangelist in a hotel room. The religious scandals provided the raw narrative material of which Hollywood movies were made, from the aforementioned *The Miracle Woman* to John Schlesinger's *The Day of the Locust*, both tipping the hat to Reverend McPherson, shaping a stereotype of female evangelists. More significantly, the films of Ingmar Bergman may have shaped theological imaginations in the 1960s more than the writings of theologian Paul Tillich. The influence of films on sermon construction in the early twenty-first century is also marked by the development of such Web sites as Movie Ministry, started by entrepreneurial scholar Dr. Marc Newman, who weaves theological reflections in with specific film clips for use in emergent churches. Church history may do well to consider the subtle influences of media upon its own image and theology.

Extending Our Conversation Partners

Conclusion

If as Frederick Turner observed, "Each age writes the history of the past with reference to the conditions uppermost in its own time," our age has become attuned once again to a religious view of history. A question remains: In the nature of a totally secularized history of film, is there any thread of divine activity, a series of signs and clues as to the meaning of God's work in and through historical situations? As God instructed Moses to use the suspect image of a brazen serpent to provide healing and restoration for a grumbling and dying people, could there be a sense of God supplying hints and directions for an ailing people through other more kinetic graven images? As God sent dreams to Pharaoh and Nebuchadnezzar, might he not have communicated to his people through the dreams of other pagans?

University of Texas professor Marvin Olasky has called for a new paradigm that acknowledges the theological origin of the craft of American journalism, rooted in the Protestant Reformation. Part of his argument calls for the religious motives of historical figures to be fairly portrayed. He also argues for the unveiling and analysis of underlying worldview assumptions of the histories themselves. And he calls for recognition of the dominant religious movement, Protestant Christianity, that formed the context for the development of such journalism. Within a generation of the origins of journalism, the religious elements were written out of the records, marginalized and ignored by a new superstructure and material base of "progressive, liberal materialism" dictating data and methods for study. Such misconceptions about religion in journalism history (reflected as well in the study of religion and education, as brilliantly narrated by George Marsden in his *The Soul of the University*) have their parallel misconceptions in film history.[14]

Two of the classic film history texts in our field illustrate two tendencies of historiography. On the one hand, Robert Sklar's perennially successful *Movie-Made America* provides a brilliant and entertaining cultural narrative, observing the ebb and flow of historical events and moments as they influence the film industry's output. In particular, Sklar chronicles the stories of Walt Disney and Frank Capra as social forces that shaped the 1930s and beyond, inventing the dominant myths of American society and diffusing them through their respective animated and populist film productions. Religion enters the narrative as a Victorian aunt, repressively dictating the Breen Production Code and protesting any immoral or blasphemous graven images daring enough to assault America's sensibilities.

On the other hand, Larry May's profound social history, *Screening Out the Past*, probes the birth of mass culture and the motion picture industry with an astute awareness of the theological underpinnings of American society in the first decades of the twentieth century.

Sklar's work is knowledgeable and compelling, but ultimately secular and lacking the full perspective of religion's role in film history other than as a censor (which, alas, history may show was its fundamental role). May integrates within his film history the realities of Protestant progressive reform movements, spiritual biography, and other religious trends. As such, he contributes not only to an understanding of film history but also to an understanding of American life in the teens and twenties.

A "historical turn" in film historiography is perhaps beginning to occur. Film journals, frequently the swallows of a new spring paradigm, have devoted issues to the place of religious discourse and events in the study of film. Two entire issues of *Film History* have been devoted to the subject of early and classic film history and religion. Historian Garth Jowett introduced the Reverend J. J. Phelan's 1919 book, *Motion Pictures as a Phase of Commercialized Amusement in Toledo, Ohio*, which offered insights from a progressive religious mind dealing with creating an ideal church, social amusements, and problems in caricatures of the Protestant ministry in public motion pictures.[15] Editor Daniel J. Leab followed with an official "Film and Religion Issue" of *Film History*, defining key uses of film as a tool for proselytizing and of film as a means for exploiting religions.[16]

Again, in an introductory essay within the issue of the *Velvet Light Trap* devoted to the relationship of religion and film, Heather Hendershot addressed the academic film community on how the relationship between religion and the media continues to be a marginal topic due to the "typical liberal university professor mindset," which "often does not acknowledge the worldview of the religious right as textured, 'livable' and for those who live within it, 'natural' and 'reasonable.'" Media scholarship, she thinks, has not kept pace with global industries, texts, and audiences for whom religion is a central issue, and film scholarship must grapple with these issues.[17] In a separate essay that followed in the same journal issue, Hendershot invited further research into the media culture of the religious right in her "Onward Christian Soldiers?" pushing for salient angles beyond both textual analysis and industrial analysis of "zealot figures" and the Family Channel. In particular, she centers her inquiries on the overlooked significance of pleasure and belief and how they play in religious audiences' relationship to mediated texts. Hendershot recognizes that what is missing is an understanding not only of the diversity and heterogeneity of Christian groups but also of the nonadvocacy entertainment media of conservative Christians that constitute the nonpolitical bulk of the Christian cultural products industry. As such, she opens up research into crossover products like the VeggieTales children's videos and the relevance of audience spirituality, faith, and a sense of community as genuine sources of motivation and energy for media participation.[18]

Hopefully, this review of historiography can remind us of what is missing when we write (or read) the existing texts on film and church history. Just as I could benefit greatly by having a certified, Freudian psychoanalyst sitting beside me during a showing of Hitchcock's *Vertigo*, so also the presence of church historians like Duke Divinity School's historian Grant Wacker and theologians like Robert Johnston would enhance my viewing of popular films like *Kingdom of Heaven* and *The Chronicles of Narnia: The Lion, the Witch and the Wardrobe*. What I wouldn't give to watch Kieślowski's films with Professor Joseph Kickasola by my side, or view any of the Roman Catholic hagiographic films with scholar Theresa Sanders whispering footnotes in my ear. Such encounters simply revive my hope that we may see traces of *kinoheilsgeschichte* in future records in the study of film history. Perhaps then my students could see hints and rumors of angels in their texts as well as in their lives.

Notes

1. Richard Maltby, "The King of Kings and the Czar of All the Rushes: The Propriety of the Christ Story," *Screen* 31, no. 2 (Summer 1980): 188.

2. Frederick A. Talbot, *Moving Pictures* (Philadelphia: Lippincott, 1912), 317.

3. Brian Godawa interprets the media manipulator Christof as a God figure; I see him as an Accuser, a literal and figurative "Prince of the Air," who deceives the innocent and "damns" God. Brian Godawa, *Hollywood Worldviews* (Downers Grove, IL: InterVarsity, 2002), 45.

4. Robert K. Johnston, *Reel Spirituality: Theology and Film in Dialogue*, 2nd ed. (Grand Rapids: Baker Academic, 2006), 267–90.

5. I am much influenced here by Jacques Barzun and Henry F. Graff's classic text, *The Modern Researcher* (New York: Harcourt, Brace, 1957) and Robert C. Allen and Douglas Gomery's *Film History: Theory and Practice* (Boston: McGraw-Hill, 1985).

6. Thomas Elsaesser, "Writing and Rewriting Film History: Terms of a Debate," *Cinema et cie* 1 (Fall 2001): 24–33, 110, 128.

7. Two of the better writings on evangelical films in context are James Gilbert, *Redeeming Culture: American Religion in an Age of Science* (Chicago: University of Chicago Press, 1997), 121–46; and Heather Hendershot, *Shaking the World for Jesus: Media and Conservative Evangelical Culture* (Chicago: University of Chicago Press, 2004), 145–209.

8. Michael Lieb, *Children of Ezekiel: Aliens, UFOs, the Crisis of Race, and the Advent of End Time* (Durham, NC: Duke University Press, 1998).

9. Charles Musser, "Historiographic Method and the Study of Early Cinema," *Cinema Journal* 44, no. 1 (2004): 102; see also Richard Abel, "'Don't Know Much About History' or the (In)vested Interests of Doing Cinema History," *Film History* 6, no. 1 (1994): 110–15.

10. Lee Grieveson, "Woof, Warp, History," *Cinema Journal* 44, no. 1 (Fall 2004): 119–26.

11. Steven Ross, "Jargon and the Crisis of Readability: Methodology, Language, and the Future of Film History," *Cinema Journal* 44, no. 1 (Fall 2004): 130.

12. Robert Sklar, "Does Film History Need a Crisis?" *Cinema Journal* 44, no. 1 (Fall 2004): 134.

13. Elise Soukup, "Hollywood: Praise the Movie," *Newsweek* (November 21, 2005).

14. Marvin Olasky, "Historiographical Essay: Journalism Historians and Religion," *American Journalism* (Spring 1989): 41–52.

15. Garth Jowett, "Introduction: *Motion Pictures as a Phase of Commercialized Amusement in Toledo, Ohio*," *Film History* 13 (2001): 231–328.

16. Daniel J. Leab, "Film and Religion Issue," *Film History: An International Journal* 14, no. 2 (2002): 119–20.

17. Heather Hendershot, "Religion and the Media" *Velvet Light Trap* 46 (Fall 2000): 1–3.

18. Heather Hendershot, "Onward Christian Soldiers?" *Velvet Light Trap* 46 (Fall 2000): 4–11.

Extending Our Conversation Partners

Section 4

Engaging the Experience
of the Viewer

7

On Dealing with What Films Actually Do to People

The Practice and Theory of Film Watching in Theology/Religion and Film Discussion

CLIVE MARSH

In some quarters of film studies attention has shifted in recent years away from directors' interests and intentions, and away from what happens on-screen to what happens off it—in the experience of the viewer. Not surprisingly, this shift to the consumer may be seen as good news for those keen to claim and investigate the religious and theological significance of film watching in contemporary Western society. For it may be easier to focus largely on what viewers bring to their film watching than on what films contain or what directors intend. In this way, the personal lens through which viewers watch films, or the cognitive world/schema within which they process what happens to them, becomes important. Suddenly, though, the films themselves may cease to matter. The charge readily leveled against much theological interest in film—that films are simply exploited for theological ends—can be voiced again.

The only way of countering this persistent doubt about the legitimacy of undertaking theological conversation with film as something more than a leisure pursuit for theologically interested film buffs (or film-enthusiastic theologians) is to demonstrate with empirical evidence how films actually work. Elements of viewer response that may too easily be overlooked in film studies may thus prove to be of great interest in religious studies and theology. And those engaged in cultural studies—a discipline that too easily carries a secular or antireligious agenda—may then find that they could speak profitably to religion scholars and theologians after all.

The need to attend to what films actually do, rather than what religion scholars and theologians would like to think that they do, has been well expressed by Christopher Deacy. His book *Faith in Film* makes use of viewer reviews found on such Web sites as the Internet Movie Database (www .imdb.com).[1] In a more recent article, he questioned further the extent to which scholars are tempted to read films on behalf of the audience, using the theme of redemption as his case study.[2] His point is well made.[3] Using movie databases may, however, still not get us far beyond what those who are already religious are doing with films. The Internet reviewers cited may, of course, be film watchers who are already religious. Until the academic study of religion, philosophy, and worldviews manages to gain access to what happens on the part of ordinary viewers who, as paying consumers, go to be entertained, then little headway will be made.

This chapter makes a small contribution to inquiry into the complex affective and cognitive processes that occur at the point of the consumption of film. Using analysis of a small amount of the data collected by a freelance journalist, Charlotte Haines Lyon, on a research project conducted in the United Kingdom in the summer of 2004, this chapter offers insight into how films are actually consumed. Admittedly, the research is limited in that only certain kinds of people agree to be subjects in such studies, and that only certain kinds of people fill in forms. It is thus limited in a different way from that of Deacy. But it is a start. It was not known beforehand what philosophical outlooks participants held, or whether they were even interested in theology, philosophy, or ethics at all.[4] The self-selection of the subjects of the research was thus not ideologically prescriptive. A snapshot of who was watching films in the United Kingdom in the summer of 2004, and what for, was gained by the research. And it was a more detailed picture than is obtained by market-driven consumer research.[5]

In this chapter I merely draw four conclusions from the insights and reflections supplied by the participants themselves in their end-of-project forms before going on to draw out some pointers for further inquiry.[6]

Conclusions

1. *Whatever people say they go to the cinema for, they often get more than they expect.* What do people go to the cinema for? Mostly, for fun. A particular word that keeps appearing in regular cinemagoers' accounts of their practice is that they want to "escape." Escapism can refer to both the practice of cinemagoing itself and the kind of film that is watched. Here are some examples from the 2004 UK research on the point of cinemagoing:

It's a point in time when you can escape away from reality. (Respondent 3)

Films are pure escapism and enjoyment and totally separate from reality. (Respondent 8)

I use movies to escape from life's sometimes dullness. (Respondent 9)

For me film is an escapism activity, for me to forget about things for a couple of hours and enjoy the movie. (Respondent 25)

"Reality" or "things" presumably refer to working life, everyday routine, or life's troubles. Respondent 9 talks of using film for this purpose, thus suggesting a sense of control on the part of the cinemagoer.

While for Respondent 8 films are, by definition, "escapism," for others there are different levels of escapism, corresponding to different types of film. Respondent 10, for example, remarks:

The majority of films I see are not realistic . . . or historical. They do not affect my life in any way.

Here, the implication is that realistic or historical films *might* exert an influence. But by choosing not to see such films, escapism remains a primary purpose of the practice of cinemagoing. Interestingly, Respondent 30 comments:

I was inclined to divide all films into two categories: 1) Escapist films which I enjoyed but analysed or reflected on very little; 2) "interesting films" which

I watched on the basis of recommendations (usually on DVD though) and reflected greatly on—both during and after the film. Since being married (in the last year), the films I have watched at the cinema have been almost entirely in the former category and so this project has made me even more aware of the recent change in the extent to which I reflect on films.

Cinemagoing can thus be seen as an escapist activity, and it is further enhanced if prior decisions are being made by the viewer about *which* films are watched and which films avoided. A particular kind of (avoidance) experience is often being anticipated. Nevertheless the value of such "escapism" is interpreted in different ways. In response to the question "Do you consider that films affect your life?" for example, Respondent 3 prefaces the cited comments about escapism with the observation "Yes, to a certain degree." This is in contrast to Respondent 5's judgment that "Films are fantasy so don't affect my life." Respondent 9 expands the point about escaping life's dullness: "But I also like them for having emotions thrown around in a short time." The escapist intent, in other words, is accompanied by an explicit desire to experience a range of emotions. In this person's view, cinemagoing has the purpose of giving the viewer a good emotional shake-up. For Respondent 21, even though

> the majority are just a (hopefully) fun way of passing an hour or two, . . . if they are good, then I suppose they have positively affected you by lifting your spirits.

The lifting of the spirits may easily be equated with enjoying the feel-good factor. But this may be too simple a reading of the evidence. Good films may not, of course, always be feel-good films. Even so, the refreshing, recreational function of cinemagoing, whether or not deemed escapist, should not be downplayed in religion/theology and film discussions.

Thus far, I have been addressing what viewers appear to be in control of, and what they *think* is happening and *choose* to consume films for. The fun/entertainment/escapism factor is undoubtedly the dominant, even if certainly not the sole, reason given by cinemagoers as to why they go. But it is also clear that it is not necessary to overstate other evidence (e.g., that some people go for purposes of education or intellectual stimulation, or that some people avoid blockbusters in search of indie or thoughtful films) to show that even in the context of an escapist intent, much else is going on in multiplexes.

The evidence for this conclusion is contained in the tensions apparent in respondents' reflections, between the escapist intent and the clear recognition on the part of many that film watching affects viewers in their life beyond the cinema, and forces them to think about life's big questions. Respondent 35 offers a striking example of such tensions. Despite stating clearly both that "Films always naturally divide into those you need to discuss with someone afterwards (e.g., *The Passion of the Christ*) and those you watch purely for enjoyment and escapism (e.g. *Shrek*)" and [in response to the question "Do you consider that films affect your life?"] "No. They are an enjoyable way of passing the time—sometimes stimulating but actually just a pleasant pastime," the respondent goes on to note, in response to the question "Do you think that films ever help you think about life's big questions?"

> Yes (this may contradict [my earlier answers] . . .)—films like *The Passion of the Christ* do—in the right discussion forum—lead to interesting theological discussions. Others, like *Capturing the Friedmans*, do focus the mind on a particular subject. The main problem is that part of the answers discussed to "life's big questions" disappear in the haze of the post-cinema pint!

Others recognize that more may go on for them as regular cinemagoers even when they do not necessarily distinguish between escapist and thoughtful (or "good") films.

> A good film can change your emotions in the short-term and can change the way you think about things in the long. (Respondent 38)

> If you enjoy the film you will take away all that you need to. . . . I think sometimes you can put yourself into the film. The character can be "so what you're going through," it fits like a glove. (Respondent 41)

More subtly still, at least one respondent (36) states clearly that films are not an influence on life, but then declares immediately:

> But my emotions can be temporarily swayed or my attention drawn to an aspect of my behaviour of which I was not previously aware.

Yet this is surely striking evidence of film's influence!

My first conclusion, then, confirms what many working in religion/ theology and film assume: that much is going on for viewers, at many levels, when they go to the cinema. Much is active for viewers: they go for particular reasons and feel to a large extent in control of what is happening to them. Escapism is a dominant motif in their declared purpose in cinemagoing. But the de facto function of what occurs is much more complex. This leads to a second working conclusion:

2. *Entertainment is taking the place of religion as a cultural site where the task of meaning making is undertaken.* It is now a commonplace sociological observation that meaning making is happening in many places in Western society. Some people do their meaning making via religious practice. But religion is one channel among many. Whatever the theological, philosophical, psychological, or cultural significance of such a change, it is occurring, and the shift needs logging, accounting for, and analyzing. For some years Stewart Hoover and other researchers at the University of Colorado have been noting how patterns of media consumption affect the way religious meaning making happens.[7] Film is part of the package of media that Hoover identifies. "Religion" as a concept comes under challenge as a result. Those who regard themselves as religious do their meaning making in relation to a range of resources and practices that is wider than they realize. This being so, what constitutes a "religious" or "theological" worldview may be less easy to track and define than is commonly thought.

Conversely, analysis of how people consume media and how they participate in a wide range of social practices shows more similarities to how people construct religious identities than is often recognized. Indifference or hostility to religion may be mixed up with very religion-like practices and a very human desire to find or construct meaning. A number of examples of sites where meaning making happens can thus be cited. Sport, for players and watchers, shapes the life cycle, creates contexts for the experience and exploration of elation and disappointment, and celebrates the stretching of human experience to extremes and to new heights. Contemporary music—sometimes too easily referred to as providing "the soundtrack of our lives"—offers the words through which a great many people construct their personal narratives or articulate things that happen to them (recall the movie *Moulin Rouge*). Television is a conversation partner, the relative who's always around, chatting in the corner of the room. Through its soaps, it lays out in melodramatic form the dilemmas of daily living and a range of options for dealing with them, in the form of the various responses of (and to) stock characters. Stand-up comedy (live, on TV, or on DVD) supplies the public preachers of today: those who offer striking observation on the everyday and trenchant comment on our social and political life. Through satire, comedians can be today's

Engaging the Experience of the Viewer

prophets. Organized religion is often less interesting, certainly less entertaining, and therefore often less expected to be of much help to daily life (except in times of crisis) than such pastimes.

Cinemagoing and film watching are social practices that occur within this rich mix of diverse and complex contexts of meaning making. The 2004 UK research merely confirms this.

> I rarely choose to see films that I don't think are capable of changing my life. What is the point of seeing a film that you don't think will challenge you? (Respondent 13)

> They make you think about issues sometimes you'd never even consider. They can also be educational, and the type of things in films which stir up emotions in you teaches you things about yourself. (Respondent 17)

> I think that some films affect my life because they force me to think about bigger issues that may not affect me directly. (Respondent 24)

And the same respondent also adds:

> They can make me reflect on my relationships, my direction in life and my place in the world.

And as a final example:

> I enjoy going to see films that challenge, or that give me an experience that is distinctive from other films I've seen, such as the blockbusters. . . . How much I reflect on a film also depends on the film . . . and how much reflection I think it really needs. . . . I think films do affect my life. Watching them is one of my main enjoyments in my life, and it wouldn't be if they didn't affect my life at all. (Respondent 33)

This cluster of quotations from contemporary cinemagoers thus indicates that meaning making happens in the cinema in a variety of ways: through encounter with issues, through challenging of the mind, as a resource for personal psychological and social development, as an aid to establishing a direction in life. Furthermore, as the final quotation shows, there is a link between the enjoyment of the experience and the recognition of its value as a stimulus for reflection.

Taking these first two working conclusions together, then, we are faced with evidence that the cinema is a place where much occurs for viewers, even while the primary purpose for going remains entertainment or escapism. Not surprisingly, religion and theology cannot but be interested in what is going on in any context where encounter with issues, challenging of the mind, personal psychological and social development, and establishing a direction in life are taking place. But if film often avoids religion, and theological reflection usually becomes explicit only as a result of what viewers already bring, then the question of how *theology* can play much of a *public* role inevitably arises. In other words, viewers may be engaged in the (often subconscious) task of meaning making, and yet be enabled to identify this only when asked (e.g., via a research project!). Meanwhile, religions may be variously considered as sources of truth and ways of life (for their sympathizers) or dangerous sets of practices (by religions' opponents and by the puzzled). Yet the complex, if subtle and incidental, practice of meaning making is occurring nevertheless in the context of people's participation in a range of pastimes.

3. *Cinemagoing reveals different types of meaning making at work in Western societies.* So what can be deduced about contemporary meaning making, and how does the film-related form of this meaning making inform the work of theology and religious studies? First, meaning making may not necessarily or primarily be cognitive. Cinemagoing habits may shape a person's week. They may thus help structure life. Meaning making needs "habits." Whether or not a person consciously chooses to be cognitively stimulated or challenged emotionally, an entertaining trip to the cinema does these things too. And a habit of film watching feeds this need. Furthermore, because films often work first by affective means, it is usually not cognitive processing of a film's content and impact that occurs first for a viewer.

Second, meaning making may not be explicitly philosophical or theological, or fully coherent, even when it is a more cognitive undertaking. Meaning making occurs in an increasingly pluralistic framework.[8] Supporters of independent, art house, "European," or "world" cinema (i.e., the kinds of films multiplexes often do not show and so films that must await release on DVD to be viewed) may object to this point. Arguably, the dominance of Hollywood (and the United States generally) in the making of films seen in cinemas throughout the West means that actually the worldview of cinemagoers may end up being rather uniform. But even though greater diversity of available films would be welcome, this objection does, I think, underplay both the diversity of US-based films themselves and the critical capacities of viewers.

Third, we need to accept that the range and diversity of sites of contemporary meaning making may be very, very far from theism of any kind even when a sensitivity to spirituality may become explicit for viewers. Sensitivities to religious difference often lead to such a stark understating of the role of religion in life (the negative aspect of political correctness) that Western cinemagoers could be forgiven for thinking that humans really are secular creatures. The evidence of the postmodern turn, however, shows that quite the opposite is the case. Spiritualities of all kinds blossom, and the importance of religion globally is impossible to dispute. But it is very common now to hear the claim that "I'm a spiritual person, but I've no time for religion." Thus, though religion, in formal terms, may be sparsely represented in film, and sometimes treated in hostile terms by viewers, the necessity to reconnect spirituality/religion/theology with film watching *because* it is a site of meaning making could not be more urgent.

Fourth, though the identifiable sites of contemporary meaning making may not be coherent or theistic, this does not mean that they are not value-laden (even, at times, value-driven). Films frequently do "have a point to make." In this way, a cinema becomes a context in which viewers are invited to reflect on an opinion presented in relation to an issue.[9] Even then, however, the "exchange of views" between film and viewer will not be solely a cognitive matter. Nor need it be explicitly theological (that depends both on director/film and viewer). The identification, exploration, and commendation of any value system, religious or not, is always a mix of cognitive, aesthetic, ethical, and affective components.[10] My point is simply this: the cinema is one place where such ideological exchanges are clearly occurring. I am not, of course, claiming a singular role for the cinema in the contemporary practice of meaning making. I am merely highlighting the fact that cinema is on the list of sites where meaning making happens.

4. *Resistance to social control and to didacticism are so strong in Western societies that viewers are sometimes reluctant to own up to what cinemagoing actually does to and for them.* The 2004 UK research indicates one further striking feature of cinemagoing and meaning making, which not only the religion/theology and film debates need to heed but religions too (perhaps Christianity especially): there is evident aversion on the part of cinemagoers (and thus cinema managers) to being preached at or compelled to reflect or be taught when they are trying to enjoy themselves. In the UK research this aversion was expressed in a number of forms.

When Charlotte Haines Lyon first sought the assistance of one or more cinema chains through which to undertake the research, one independent chain replied aggressively, declaring a basic opposition to any form of activity that might annoy customers or prove commercially detrimental. This may have been an excuse. Perhaps a strong religion/secular division was at work in the mind of a regional manager. But the presenting reason was clear: commerce and meaning making do not mix.

At the second stage—having received permission from the Ster chain to stand in foyers and approach people—Charlotte still faced the task of getting people to agree to undertake what was quite a demanding three-part research task (initial form, a form for each film watched, plus a concluding questionnaire, for all of which participants were to receive a small payment). Some who were approached wanted nothing to do with it (the fun/escapism/enjoyment factor presumably being even greater than for those who became respondents). A number wanted to know whom the research was for. Intriguingly, there was very little opposition to, or suspicion of, the project per se, even when it was revealed that the Methodist Church in Great Britain was ultimately the funding body. By contrast, gratitude was expressed at the directness with which information about the research was given, and *reassured that they would not be expected to toe any particular line*, participants proved relatively easy to attract.[11] At this second stage, then, it is important to note that respondents needed to know that they would have the freedom to say—within the constraints of the research forms (already available for inspection at this stage)—*whatever they wanted to say*. In this respect they could see that it would not distort their intended experience, but could only enhance it.

The third stage of aversion to didacticism is, however, evident in the responses themselves. Though some cinemagoers clearly do go expecting to be educated, this is not a primary purpose for most. Respondent 17 is therefore unusual: "They make you think about issues sometimes you'd never even consider. They can also be educational." The reassurance many respondents needed at the stage of agreeing to undertake the research project is reflected in their insistence on the escapist element in their cinemagoing. Despite the fact that they then go on to reveal more about what happens to them, either *via* their escapism or *in addition* to it, the respondents are clearly pleased to express what it is they think is happening to them and what their intentions are. But it is as if the process of being released from any assumption that their experiences of participation in the research or their responses are somehow going to be controlled or prejudged opens the door to clarifications (revelations, even?) about what is going on in the cinemagoing experience.

All this said, analysis of the evidence of what people actually say when reflecting on the process as a whole, and when processing what happened to them when watching (and being encouraged to reflect on) individual films, leads to the conclusion that meaning making *is happening* whether or not this is a main intention behind film watching. Why people sometimes want to deny this or play it down in favor of the dominant declared reason for cinemagoing (escapism) is a question that opens a fresh avenue to explore.

Admittedly, little conscious learning may happen until cinemagoers are encouraged to reflect. Some respondents clearly enjoyed being prompted; others got bored—though they stuck with the project because they agreed to do it and were being paid! But on the basis of the available evidence it is neither far-fetched nor wishful thinking on the part of such research to claim that philosophy, theology, and ethics are happening as furtive, incidental activities amid enjoying a supposedly escapist activity. This observation produces a working thesis: as a form of popular culture, society is perhaps implicitly expecting films to carry more than they are meant to (and can?) carry. This tentative conclusion broadens out into wider socioreligious and sociopolitical questions such as these: Is this level of expectation inevitable when religious communities are numerically weak? Though it is recognized that religion is a vitally important global matter, if "religion = fundamentalism = terrorism" is a dominant assumption, then where are critical discussions about ideologies and values happening? If popular culture (and popular films) offer, in practice, very little thoughtful fare (and you have to hunt beyond multiplexes for such good-quality films), then how can we expect meaning making to occur? In which and from which settings (communal, ideological, political) do people get their values and commitments, and on whom do they test out their existing and emerging commitments?

In the case of the respondents, some of these questions can be addressed in a limited way through cross-referencing their responses to films with the information they supplied about their lifestyles. But, in truth, more information still would be needed (e.g., concerning their ethical, political, and religious commitments) to gain a fuller picture. Are they conservative or liberal? Are they Jewish, Buddhist, Muslim, or Christian? Are they Episcopalian, Methodist, Baptist, Roman Catholic, or Orthodox? The evidence does, however, suggest that the freedom to think and believe (and thus to choose thoughts and beliefs) is very strong on the part of the respondents. Furthermore, the freedom to choose *when* to be educated and influenced is equally strong. The assertion of such freedoms may, of course, overestimate the extent of the freedom that does exist and underplay what happens subliminally, or incidentally (with the de facto cooperation of the film viewers). But the sense of freedom that the viewer needs, both for entertainment to remain entertainment, and for any learning or personal development or intellectual stimulus to be an enjoyable and welcome experience, deserves utmost respect.

One Significant Consequence and Four Key Themes

Combining these four simple conclusions carries a major consequence for religious groups. In thinking, for example, of what the observations mean for Christian churches, it is clear that the fluidity of the boundary between entertainment and education may apply equally to the boundary between entertainment and worship. Perhaps worship has always been more entertaining than has been sufficiently acknowledged. Recognizing this now, however, at a time when Christianity has less cultural power or impact than it once had in the West, may lead churches to assume (mistakenly) that they should try to *be* more entertaining. The lesson of the cinema may, however, be quite the contrary. In the same way as the cinema should not try to educate, but accept, while entertaining, that it may also educate, so also the churches should accept their primary purpose (the worship of God) and not try to do something different in order to attract people (e.g., entertain).

The consequence of the shift of focus away from Christianity as a (or even the main) site of primary meaning making in the West, however, poses a major question as to what churches are to do in relation to film. Theology/religion and film debates over the past four decades have addressed this question in many different ways. Attention has been paid to art films that evoke spiritual experiences in the cinema. These are, however, not the films that most people watch. Traces of Christianity have been identified in all sorts of films. But such an approach appeals to the already religious, and the traces may not be spotted by many cinemagoers (and when they are, then the enjoyment may be spoiled). More generally, attention to the human condition or to ethical concerns has suggested that films provoke exploration of the kind in which theologians cannot but be interested. True, but are people interested in what theologians have to say, given that you do not have to be a theologian to be interested in the human condition?

Engaging the Experience of the Viewer

All of these approaches are legitimate in their own way. One of the main difficulties when churches get hold of films, or attempt to evoke discussions about films, is that the fourth conclusion reached earlier in this chapter (cultural resistance to didacticism) is rarely heeded. Church discussions about films can too easily imply exactly where these discussions must head, that is, what the right conclusion might be (and thus the right reading of a film). As is now widely recognized, however, good films, like good literature (and like the Bible), are capable of multiple, but not limitless, readings. That's what makes them good (and, at their best, classics). If churches are to participate publicly in this new context of meaning making, in which the world of entertainment—not just the arts—plays a prominent role, then it will need to work out how it can facilitate such open-ended, exploratory inquiry. Such inquiry already happens in many educational settings, formal and informal. The problem here is that when religion and theology are not specifically on the agenda in such groups, they rarely get attention.[12] The question of how religion and theology can again feature in an informed way in public discussion of all that films do to people and the questions and issues they raise for people is one that churches, then, need to address directly and urgently. For churches to do this, three things will be needed: a better grasp of orthodoxy's range, greater humility than is often displayed in the handling of Christianity's riches, and an acceptance that doctrine does change. There is not space here to argue that case fully. It need simply be said that who God is, where God is at work, and how God is to be understood in the world as well as the church always seem to catch Christians by surprise.[13]

In addition to this major consequence for churches of the 2004 UK film research, four themes emerge that merit further exploration. The first offers a much more positive interpretation than is often given of the motif of escapism evident in cinemagoers' declared purpose in film watching. I have begun to speak of a necessary *discipline of displacement* at work in human life. By this I mean that the psychospiritual significance of a desire to step out of one's routine is worth highlighting as part of the theology/religion and film discussion. When the multiple functions of film watching are acknowledged, it could be argued that in choosing "fun," people are actually *choosing more* because of the actual impact of film watching upon them. Some people, as the evidence shows, explicitly acknowledge and declare the wider purposes of film watching. Others reveal the impact more incidentally through their reflections on individual films. My contention is that this creation of space within the routine of life, by being shown to be more than the entertainment that is sought, is fueled *by the very fact* that more occurs for cinemagoers than they bargain for. They continue to seek the form of escapism that film watching supplies precisely because it offers much more than mere fun. In other words, there is evident value in the detachment brought about by the social practice of cinemagoing. As a discipline of displacement, it functions on a regular basis in the same way that vacations sometimes do for holiday makers and, it should be stressed, as worship does for Christian believers.[14]

A second theme extends the first. Unlike TV in the home, which can easily be turned off, left to hum in the corner of a room, or moved away from, cinema provides a context in which it is less easy to lose concentration. The attention needed to do justice to a well-made film develops powers of concentration. The *attentiveness* that can come with regular film watching can itself be seen as the cultivation of a practice that enhances spiritual development of the viewer.[15] At a time when the subhumanity of information overload and multitasking threatens to lead to the disintegration of persons, any activity that reverses the process is surely to be welcomed. This is not a reactionary resistance to technological development. It is more a recognition that it cannot always be a good thing for a person to be attempting simultaneously to watch TV and speak to someone on a mobile phone, while texting someone else via a computer screen. An activity that welcomes technology (and uses it to good effect) yet resists some of the forms of multiple bombardment of the senses in favor of the development of a more concentrated, meditative activity can be a good thing. The same insight is perhaps reflected whenever film critics praise—with apparent relief—films that eschew complex computer-generated imagery and offer more traditional filmic techniques (facial close-ups, good acting) evident in human dramas.

Third, a debate is needed about what counts as *good entertainment* and whether there is anything that religion/theology cannot do business with. I am reluctant to enter this debate, I must admit. Theology in particular has been (and often still is) much too picky about what counts as art (often concluding—wrongly—that it is only that which counts as art, not popular culture, that theologians should be in dialogue with, despite the fact that religions have long depended on popular culture in order to work).[16] But even though theology can always do more with a wider range of forms of media and the arts than it has often recognized, it would be silly to suggest that anything and everything (and any and every film) is worthy of extended theological debate. Perhaps, at the very least, in acknowledging that religions have, and have had, their own role as forms of entertainment (whatever else they achieve), and that entertainment does more than

Engaging the Experience of the Viewer

entertain, we can also remind ourselves that there is light entertainment too. It is as if the entertainment industry itself has always been clear that there are different forms of escapism. In the theology/religion and film debate, then, it is wise not to prejudge what might be useful. If you start from a viewer perspective, you simply have to allow for many surprises as to what films do to people and make people think about.

Fourth, the issue arises as to the *communal/social settings* in which personal/spiritual development (outside of churches and academic settings) is actually provoked. One of the respondents (35) was explicit that discussion may need to be provoked and shaped. The respondent suggested that reflection would happen "in the right discussion forum." In other words, some of what the research has uncovered, that is, what has gone on in respondents' heads and what has only been uncovered because of the research, might have remained in respondents' heads, or perhaps at most as the subject of the postfilm, pre-pint conversation. Churches understandably want to capitalize on the fact that those emergent and potential conversations could be provoked more often (and lead to some very interesting places), and want to be the forums in which they are conducted. I have already offered words of caution about how churches do this.

Nevertheless, the need for contexts in which people can talk beyond the cinema about their responses to films appears to be culturally vital. Forums for such discussion could prove a crucial feature of public life. Film groups, in whatever setting they emerge, could have a social and ethical function similar to the book groups that have emerged of late.

In addition, there is simply too much anecdotal evidence from cinemagoers about "the conversations you hear on the way out of the cinema" to suggest that it is only because of formal discussion forums that films exert a huge impact on people. Formal discussions may admittedly extend what has begun. But formal discussions of varying kinds (in educational settings, as film groups/clubs) do not appeal to all.[17] Whatever filmmakers intend or think ("I want to entertain people, that's all"), it is, then, worth considering the nature of the settings in which film discussion actually occurs for ordinary cinemagoers. Filmmakers (and especially distributors) might look to make an impact on cinemagoers largely for commercial reasons ("I want to get my film talked about" [and then more people will want to see it, and more money will be earned]). But the known loss of control about what is discussed and in what contexts is a powerful reminder both that viewers contribute hugely to the making of meaning, and that the discussion can become part of a viewer's method of constructing a personal narrative. There is much more work to be done on exploring how that happens, and happens most profitably, in a way that does not turn an enjoyable, entertaining medium into something unduly worthy and controlling.[18]

Final Comment

I agree with Deacy, then, that we need to take viewer responses seriously. But the manner and context of the processing of viewer responses is a very complex matter. Deacy would not dispute this. His own work is addressed largely to the academy, urging theologians and religion scholars to take film seriously and, in doing so, to bear in mind who is actually watching film and what is happening to such people. I agree totally. My own comments here are addressed primarily to churches and to how cultural life shapes up beyond the academy. How are churches to be involved in that? And how is the *fact* of what films are doing to people actually to be addressed culturally? These are big questions. But they need to be asked with some urgency, for the sake of ethical, political, and religious life. The escapist entertainment that the cinema provides is that serious.

Notes

1. Christopher Deacy, *Faith in Film* (Basingstoke, UK, and Burlington, VT: Ashgate, 2005).

2. Christopher Deacy, "Redemption Revisited: Doing Theology at Shawshank," *Journal of Contemporary Religion* 21 (2006): 149–62.

3. Nevertheless, Deacy is less clear and consistent in his methodological approach in *Faith in Film* than he might be.

4. Indeed, the cinema chain that assisted in the research provided advice as to the best nights on which to target the maximum number of twenty- to thirty-year-olds, the age range whose views were in particular being sought by the research.

5. Charlotte and I are currently in the process of sifting the data more fully and hope to publish a fuller account of the findings in due course.

6. The project, which was conducted with the cooperation of the Ster cinema chain, secured data on the filmgoing habits, and the detailed responses of films watched, of forty-seven cinemagoers during a three-month period in the early summer of 2004. All participants completed three questionnaires: a lifestyle questionnaire at the start providing data about themselves; a second, recording their reactions to between four and eight films watched at the cinema during a defined three-month period; and a third, reflecting on the whole process.

7. See now, most recently, Stewart M. Hoover, *Religion in the Media Age* (London and New York: Routledge, 2006).

8. We may call this "fragmented," too, though interestingly this implies that there was a unity before. This is, I think, only a half-truth, which in the case of much Christian reading of the past takes a rather rosy view of what Christendom entailed.

9. In other words, a thematic approach to religion/theology and film would be possible, indeed logical, here. My point is simply that this is not always how films work, and is certainly not always how *theological reflection* on film works. Life would be all the poorer (and unduly

compartmentalized) if religion and theology only ever dealt with what was identifiably religious. Religion and theology are about life.

10. This is one of the main points of my *Cinema and Sentiment: Film's Challenge to Theology* (Milton Keynes: Paternoster, 2004).

11. £5 was paid for every completed form (i.e., between £30 and £50 for their involvement in the project). Even so, it remained a considerable commitment. Participants would receive no payment without completing the whole project.

12. And in the United States, of course, in many educational contexts religion and theology would be actively excluded.

13. I have explored the christological shape and content of (worldly) divine presence extensively in my two recent works, *Christ in Focus: Radical Christocentrism in Christian Theology* (London: SCM, 2005) and *Christ in Practice: A Christology of Everyday Life* (London: Darton, Longman & Todd, 2006).

14. My father-in-law was on occasion chaplain to a holiday camp and reported intriguing cases of people who, whatever their intention on going on holiday (rest, fun, pleasure) either ended up needing support when acting in ways they regretted or, more pertinent here, found opportunity for reflecting on the direction of their lives. The *Shirley Valentine* experience is, in other words, more far-reaching than often supposed (and not only experienced by middle-aged women). Furthermore, displacement and revelation often belong together, as is recognized by T. Gorringe in *Discerning Spirit: Theology of Revelation* (London: SCM, 1990).

15. I have considered "attentiveness" as one of a number of themes in chap. 5 of *Cinema and Sentiment*.

16. I have explored this question briefly in " 'High Theology'/'Popular Theology'?: The Arts, Popular Culture and the Contemporary Theological Task," *Expository Times* 117 (2005–6): 447–51. See also G. Lynch, *Understanding Theology and Popular Culture* (Oxford: Blackwell, 2005), and K. Cobb, *The Blackwell Guide to Theology and Popular Culture* (Oxford: Blackwell, 2005). The latter contains a helpful annotated bibliography of related works (pp. 324–34).

17. And any kinds of formal groups often end up as middle class in culture.

18. *Participations* is an online film studies journal that looks at viewer response in theory and practice (www.participations.org).

8

Polanyi's Personal Knowledge and Watching Movies

REBECCA VER STRATEN-McSPARRAN

In L. A. nobody touches you. You're always behind this metal and glass. I think we miss that sense of touch so much that we crash into each other just so we can feel something.

Crash, 2005

Introduction

In the darkness of the theater we imperceptibly lean forward into the film as the music rises and the opening credits begin to roll. We are suddenly focused, our senses integrated and heightened as we listen and pour ourselves into the world of the story. What does this unique experience "do" for us? Does it alter us only during the time we are in the theater? Does it have potential for transforming our thinking and actions? If so, how does it do this?

Michael Polanyi, a scientist and philosopher, had much to say about how we come to know the world through our experience and how it alters and transforms us. As a scientist, he rejected the traditional scientific model for describing how we come to know, decrying it as an empty and sterile description of the world, one devoid of real meaning. For humans, he says, our goal is meaning, and our ability to pursue meaning comes from a passion to discover. Powerful discovery, the "Eureka," propels us from one discovery to another. The underlying requirement for such discoveries is faith, a passionate commitment to pursue a hunch or potential truth. I would like to suggest that this theory of "personal knowledge" works well as a paradigm for engagement with film, using the film *Crash* as a case study.

Beyond *Crash*, and specific films, Polanyi's epistemology has a greater end. He ultimately draws together art (I posit cinema as art) as the penultimate realm of knowing and religion as its pinnacle. Although Polanyi was not known to be a religious person, he held theology to be the height of what it is to have meaning and to know.

Michael Polanyi's Epistemology

It was Polanyi's genius to anticipate, and participate in, the demise of modern epistemologies, and to create a constructivist epistemology before its time. Michael Polanyi's purpose was to elucidate a structure for knowing that overcame the critique of objectivism and scientific doubt. Although he was a scientist, a reknowned professor of physical chemistry who for years corresponded with Einstein, he became frustrated with what he saw as the destruction of belief through the trenchant objectivism of the philosophers of science. He believed it incorrectly reduced all knowledge to scientific knowledge and arrogantly presumed that universal doubt was the "universal solvent of all error," which would leave only pure truth behind. In contrast, he says:

> We owe our mental existence predominantly to works of art, morality, religious worship, scientific theory and other articulate systems which we accept as our dwelling place and as the soil of our mental development. Objectivism has totally falsified our conception of truth, by exalting what we can know and prove while covering up with ambiguous utterances all that we know and *cannot* prove, even though the latter knowledge underlies, and must ultimately set its seal to, all that we *can* prove. In trying to restrict

our minds to the few things that are demonstrable, and therefore explicitly dubitable, it has overlooked the a-critical choices which determine the whole being of our minds and has rendered us incapable of acknowledging these vital choices.[1]

Polanyi's interest shifted from questions about chemistry and gases to broader and more philosophical questions of knowing. In a unique move, the University of Manchester allowed Polanyi to move from holding the chair of physical sciences to the chair of philosophy, where he spent the remainder of his career.

As a scientist, Polanyi struggled with the prevailing model of scientific knowledge. His concern with science is that it acts as if it follows a strict set of rules by which experiments and ideas are discovered and verified, but that is not in fact the case. Of key significance to Polanyi's philosophy is the *process* of knowing, which entails much more than mental observances. Long before any set of experiments begins, the scientist's mind roams over what she is doing and suddenly "sees" a connection between two ideas that she has never before seen. It is a heuristic moment, a moment of joyful discovery. She has a hunch about what it could mean, and it drives her on to experiment to see if it really works. For Polanyi, this moment of discovery is the genesis of scientific experiment and verification rather than a critique of objectivism and scientific doubt. He was fascinated with what knowledge looks like if discovery is its most important form.

Einstein, Polanyi's friend, recognized the unique place of discovery in the scientific process. "The supreme task of the physicist," he wrote, "is the search for those highly universal laws from which a picture of the world can be obtained by pure deduction. There is no logical path leading to these laws. They are only to be reached by intuition, based upon something like an intellectual love. . . . Here be mystery."[2] Although Einstein did not pursue his belief that intuition was central to discovery, Polanyi made intuition his starting point, and his ideas are developed through the required struggle of personal discovery, with personal commitment and faith being central to his structure.

Polanyi believed that discovery occurs when two distinct and separate "ideas" or experiences suddenly "connect" in a new way so that a person "sees" something he has never before seen. Following the initial moment of "seeing," the person has a hunch of its deeper meaning, driving him to commit to a course of action (the "struggle") with faith that it will yield yet a deeper knowledge. "Seeing" requires identifying clues and developing skills that integrate the parts to a whole. Only in this way is the joint

Engaging the Experience of the Viewer

meaning discovered. Polanyi calls this "tacit knowledge." There can be no discovery through tacit knowledge without an accompanying desire or caring, as well as a passionate belief that there really is something out there to know: the focus. This desire or caring is joined with subsidiary clues brought to bear on the focus, being imaginatively integrated into a whole new joint meaning through intuition.

All knowing has a heuristic center, according to Polanyi, in which each struggle and ensuing personal commitment and faith brings the person to a new level of awareness. Polanyi posits a many-leveled world in which each level is drawn up into another level of awareness, incorporating the previous level's parts into a greater whole. One way of understanding Polanyi's levels of awareness is to consider how our understanding of the whole changes when viewed from one, two, and three dimensions.

Polanyi and Film

Polanyi's theory of "personal knowledge" works well as a paradigm for engagement with film. Films draw us into a world in which we do not know what is going on. If it is a good film, we will be caught in its web of discovery, bit by bit, until the final moments of the film reveal the ultimate "Aha!" Suddenly all the parts are integrated into a whole new meaning. The film *Crash* offers a good model for discovering a profound way to engage with film and to understand the particulars of Polanyi's process of personal knowing.

The DVD jacket of *Crash* has this description of the film:

> *Crash* tracks the volatile *intersection* of a multi-ethnic cast of characters *struggling to overcome their fears* as they *career in and out* of each other's lives. *In the gray area*, between black and white, victim and aggressor, *they will all collide*. [italics added]

This summary of the film is fascinating because it includes the key elements of Polanyi's theory of how we come to know.

For Polanyi, discovery occurs when a connection is made between two ideas, a connection that has never before been seen or understood by the "knower." In *Crash* it is in the "volatile intersection" of characters that life-transforming discoveries are made when their lives "collide," or connect in unexpected ways. The "gray area" of these connections produces new discoveries, internal and external, which change the characters' lives.

One of the stories in *Crash* begins with a white officer stopping a successful black director and his wife in their Lincoln Navigator. Something of a sexual nature has been going on while the husband was driving. The upset wife mouths off to the questioning officer, who then physically searches them, touching the wife intimately in the guise of "checking" her. Feeling violated, the wife is angry with the husband not only for giving in to the officer but for apologizing so that he will let them go. We see in the husband's eyes his recognition (Polanyi's intuition) of the disparity between her point of view and his action (connection). He chooses to apologize to get out of the situation. The next day, the director, at work, is forced to make a black actor use street language, although the context did not require it. The sudden awareness (connection) of his actions and struggle to submit is again evident in the director's eyes, but again he submits. Later that day, when a gang member attempts to steal his car, not recognizing that the director/driver is also black, the director refuses to be forced out of his own car. Police notice the erratic driving and trap the car. The director grabs the thief's gun, hides it under his jacket, and jumps out of the car to confront the officers, knowing that the hidden gun will incriminate him. He refuses any longer to kowtow to anyone because of his race. The fierce look of discovery and commitment to his action is written on his face and ensuing actions (connection $\Rightarrow$ discovery = personal knowledge). Each of the "collisions" that occur between the characters becomes the genesis for new connections and discoveries.

While the characters in the film are making connections and consequent life-altering discoveries, I as viewer am making those same discoveries with them. Never before having been searched by a cop, I feel the helplessness that the director feels when the only apparent action possible is to sacrifice his dignity and submit to the cop. He is the victim. When I experience with him the demands of his boss to change the actor's accent, I slowly become aware that the director is passively accepting his situation. He is in some sense responsible for the situation. He has chosen to submit in order to get what he wants: a paycheck and a name in the industry. There is a choice. When the director is later angry with the young gang member who attempts to steal his car, and the cops stop them, he becomes the aggressor, willing to kill the cops for the injustices committed and to cover for the gang member. He carries a gun that he might use or will incriminate him. As I experience this process I feel and understand the complex emotions of a person very different from myself—his anger, his embarrassment, and even his protection of a member of the community of which he is only tangentially a part. I suddenly have a new lens through

Engaging the Experience of the Viewer

which to see and understand the complex black experience. Compounding this story is that of the director's wife, who is violated by the cop's search and later forced to trust the same cop to save her life as her car is engulfed in flames. I am drawn into the world of the characters, living vicariously through their experience. As they struggle, find catharsis, and ultimately are transformed, so too I struggle, breathe with relief, and also am transformed in my understanding and intention.

For Polanyi, there is more to this discovery, however, than just connections. The discovery comes through a myriad of clues that must come together to have a joint meaning. He calls these building blocks of discovery "tacit knowing."

Polanyi had many ways of describing "tacit knowing." One is similar to identification. If your child is singing in a choir, you eagerly seek his face through the rows of children. When you see his face, you know it instantly. You can't tell how you know his face, all the particular features and parts, but you could pick it out among hundreds of faces. You know the parts and depend on them to locate his face in a crowd, but you can't articulate them. They are known tacitly by you.

Another way to describe this concept of tacit knowing is through skill. As long as a child focuses on all of the particulars of learning to ride a bicycle—balance, pedaling, keeping the handle bars straight—she wobbles. She can concentrate only on trying to keep the bicycle going and usually falls at least a few times. She has what Polanyi calls subsidiary awareness. As she learns the rhythm and balance of riding, she skillfully adapts to all sorts of bodily clues without having to attend to them. Her subsidiary awarenesses then merge into a focal awareness of freely riding a bicycle down the road. As she attends to the road, all of the subsidiary awarenesses come into play, but she is barely aware of their existence, if at all. Most important in this concept is that this kind of knowledge may not appear to be as strong a knowledge as a "scientific fact," but it is indeed knowledge: the child knows how to ride the bicycle, the person knows how to hammer a nail, the parent knows the child's face. This knowledge may be limited, but it is valid knowledge, even though the particulars are not specifiable and no scientific procedure would make them valid. We focus on the whole by attending from the parts to the whole. By integrating the parts to the whole, we discover their joint meaning.

In a similar way, watching a foreign film with subtitles is initially awkward. We move back and forth from words to image. But as we become immersed in the story, we do not even notice that the words are there and that we are reading them.

Each story in *Crash* has connections and discoveries of its own. Each story becomes a subsidiary clue, bringing, bit by bit, the whole story into focus. Just as a parent searches for her child's face in a choir, so the characters of each story line of *Crash* try to identify the clues that make sense of their particular story, as does the viewer. For example, a young Latino locksmith is replacing locks in the district attorney's home and overhears his wife saying she will have the entire job redone in the morning. She assumes that his tattoos and shaved head mean he is a gang member. Later, the same locksmith tries unsuccessfully to explain to a Persian shop owner that it is the door, not the lock, that is broken. The shop owner does not understand or fix the door. The locksmith becomes increasingly frustrated by clues of racial bias and barriers. In a beautiful and tender scene with the locksmith's five-year-old daughter, it becomes evident to the viewer that the locksmith is no gang member but a caring and faithful father. Nonetheless, when the Persian shop is broken into and destroyed, he locates the locksmith and shoots at him, accidentally "hitting" the man's daughter instead. At this moment, the depth of the racial barriers existing between the characters is excruciatingly revealed to the locksmith. By integrating the parts into the whole through subsidiary clues, he has painfully discovered their joint meaning. So, too, for the viewer, as the interweaving of stories and victim/aggressor theme continue building with each connection and progression of the film.

The skill used to put together these clues is exemplified in the story line of the district attorney's wife in *Crash*. At first, she is walking down the street in Westwood with her husband, a bit upset that he is on the phone constantly with his assistant, a black woman. She exhibits a barely perceptible fear when seeing two young black men walking down the street. In minutes, they steal her car at gunpoint. When she arrives home to see a locksmith who looks like a gang member fitting new locks, her anger explodes. The next day, the details of her life—her garden (tended by Latino gardeners), dishes wrongly placed by her Latino housekeeper—make her feel like her world is falling apart. At the height of her frustration she suddenly sees what is happening inside herself and tells her best friend, "I am angry all of the time and I don't know why." Finally, when she falls and needs to go to the hospital, her friend is too busy getting a massage to take her. The housekeeper, instead, takes her. Skillfully, the wife who has everything weaves together the clues of her anger and sadness to recognize how friendless, how arrogant, and how loveless she is. Humbled by this knowledge she hugs and holds her Latina housekeeper, telling her that the housekeeper is indeed her best friend. In the arms of the housekeeper the wife experiences forgiveness and catharsis. In this story, I as viewer experience a deepening of compassion and new understanding for poor and rich alike—a justice of sorts. I push and pull from the parts of stories to gather clues that bring me into a larger room of comprehension of worlds that are not my own.

Polanyi says there can be no discovery through tacit knowledge without an accompanying desire or caring, as well as a passionate belief that there really is something out there to know. Discoveries are made not by using a formal procedure, but by the intuition scientists or artists use when they discover a new pattern or connect two ideas into a new whole. Subsidiary clues are imaginatively integrated into a whole new joint meaning, or the focus. It is similar to a Magic Eye picture with hidden dolphins: the subsidiary clues eventually disappear and all we see are the dolphins.[3] It is the same whether we are learning to ride a bicycle, discovering uranium, or uncovering the reasons for our anger. This is at the core of all knowledge. Without it we would have no kind of knowledge at all.

A World Undivided

Polanyi insists that this process of discovering through connecting hunches and through tacit knowledge is the same in both science and the humanities. Beginning with the physical world, he constructs his epistemological theory in a way that eliminates a dichotomized world:

> If . . . personal participation and imagination are essentially involved in science as well as in the humanities, meanings created in the sciences stand in no more favored relation to reality than do meanings created in the arts, in moral judgments, and in religion. . . . To have, or to refer to, reality—in some sense—may then be a possibility for both sorts of meanings, since the dichotomy between facts and values no longer seems to be a real distinction upon which to hang any conclusion.[4]

Polanyi's view is very un-Cartesian: he sees no separation of unseen intelligence peering out upon a visible world.[5] We live at varied levels of reality and move from level to level depending on what the situation calls for. The key point is that all persons can be drawn into a higher level where meaning is more important than material. Although all levels have validity, they are partial, not whole, until shaped by the highest level. These levels are shaped by two opposite tendencies that Polanyi calls dwelling in and breaking out. As these two tendencies are held together in the person, their reality and relation to truth grows.

We find meaning by paying attention to that one thing, indwelling it, by fully entering into its "world" just as Lucy enters Narnia, just as we enter into awareness of living and moving in a God-bathed world, or as we indwell the story framed by the curtains surrounding the cinema screen. Once we act with faith, pressing through the struggle, we begin to "know" it in a much fuller measure and see things we could never have seen by retaining objective distance.

Polanyi suggests that we alternate dwelling in the world of our story and breaking out of it. Being able to hold these tendencies together forms meaning, and causes us to grow in relation to reality and truth. In *Crash*, we are fully absorbed in one of the stories when it dramatically collides with another story, pulling us into the new story they create together, all the while making new connections from the old separate stories to inform the new story. At times the movie pulls us out of one story to stand back and look at the whole through a night scene of all of Los Angeles or of snow falling. In that moment of pulling back, or "breaking out," reflection on the connections involuntarily floods our minds. With each experience of indwelling a world, whether a story from *Crash* or seeing the dolphins within the designs of the Magic Eye, we absorb that story and adapt our larger story to fit the new information.

Necessary to understanding Polanyi's work is Jean Piaget's theory of cognitive development through his study of children. I would suggest that this is indeed the core of Polanyi's theory, giving all the ways of human knowing organic unity and congruity with our physicality. Polanyi speaks of a "many-level world." A brief description of Piaget's theory[6] will clarify how knowing begins and make sense of the movement and beautiful unity of Polanyi's many-level world.

From birth onward our minds, bodies, and communal relationships develop by the information we receive from the external environment and our internal and outward response and/or action in response to that environment. It is the interplay, the "push-me, pull-you" of the human being with its environment and relationships that never ends until one dies. This process is described in three phases: assimilation, accommodation (Polanyi calls this "adaptation"), and equilibration. The process begins when the child (or adult) receives information. It is taken in and "placed" in a file where it seems to fit (four legs, "nice doggy"—then it says, "Moo"). Once it is found that it fits or must be moved, it is accommodated into the entire structure of the child's perception, and rests (equilibration) until the next

Engaging the Experience of the Viewer

challenge. Part of this process is to perceive things that do not fit, fitting them into one's schema through connecting ideas and then comparing them to the constants or the perceived tradition of the community.

The two- to four-year-old child has a unique sense of causation called "magical thinking." Because the sun shines in when Daddy opens the blinds, opening the blinds causes the sun to shine. Through anthropomorphic thinking, things are endowed with personhood. When the sun disappears at night, it is "sleeping" behind the mountains or under the water. One of the most beautiful moments in *Crash* occurs when the locksmith returns home after a confrontation with a Persian shop owner. He walks into his young daughter's dark and quiet bedroom and sees she is not in her bed. Knowingly, he kneels beside the bed and looks underneath it. She is hiding, and he understands her fear. The father tells her the story of an invisible cloak he was given as a small child by a fairy to protect him from bullets, like the ones that went through her bedroom window in their last home. Although this new neighborhood is safe, would she like to have the cloak? The father tenderly takes the invisible cloak from his shoulders and ties it around her neck, lifting her hair so that it is not caught under the cloak. A few days later, when the Persian shop owner locates the locksmith's home and confronts the father with a gun, the little girl runs out and jumps into her daddy's arms. It happens so quickly, the shop owner shoots anyway. The slow dawn of horror and grief on the parents' and shop owner's faces is one of those rare moments in film when the viewer is inseparably woven into the web of the story. Only a moment later does the father realize she is not hurt: the gun, unknown to the shop owner, had a blank in it. The child simply, calmly hugs her daddy's neck, saying, "It's okay Daddy, I'll protect you. . . . It's a really good cloak."

Between four and seven a child begins to understand that everything is not purely as it appears or is perceived. When a straw is in water, the preoperational child will believe that the straw is broken since it appears to be in two pieces. At the stage of concrete thinking, the child will understand that it is one straw even though it looks like two. The child can conserve thought. A cookie broken into many pieces and spread out is still understood as the same size as a small whole cookie beside it.

At the same time that visible perceptions are changing, inward awareness of self within the community is growing. The boundaries between self and others are more clearly marked. Exploring issues of justice and fairness through group interaction is the project of groups of children at this age. This is why games, sports, and competition figure highly in elementary schoolchildren's lives. The processes of assimilation, accommodation, and equilibration continue across all arenas of the child's life: perception, developing morality, behaviors, relationships, creativity, spiritually, and so on.

Jean Piaget's research in developmental psychology and genetic epistemology was directed toward one question: How does knowledge grow? He concluded that the growth of knowledge is a progressive construction of logically embedded structures, each incorporating the lower logical levels into higher and more powerful structures of knowledge. This means that the logic of children is completely different from that of adults. Even more importantly, Piaget began with physiological structures, but embedded within them were the seeds of all areas of human development: the physiological, psychological, social, moral, artistic, and spiritual.

One can never return to an earlier perception of the world. Human development is not reversible. Each new level of understanding incorporates into itself all earlier perceptions and brings those perceptions to a new vision of the whole. This is to indicate that there is an underlying congruent reality toward which all development moves. If Piaget indicates this, Polanyi states it and takes it further.

Each of Piaget's stages of knowing begins with the same structure of discovery (heuristic vision) that Polanyi has identified for the adult knower, requiring participation, a faith and belief, and personal commitment to propel us into deeper knowing. It is personal knowledge. Like Piaget's child, as we explore, assimilating information, then adapting or accommodating it to the larger schema of what we know, we are increasingly enabled to have a more complete understanding of an underlying congruent reality. It is similar to understanding the existence of different dimensions. A globe in a three-dimensional world would be seen as merely a circle in a two-dimensional world. For Polanyi, each higher level of organization integrates the particulars of a lower level into a meaningful whole that has a principle of integration that cannot be perceived or discovered on the lower level. The gradual emergence of meaning is revelatory.

A poignant picture of a lower level being integrated into a higher level of meaning begins in *Crash* when a young cop watches his partner inappropriately touch the director's wife. Disgusted and idealistic, he tries to find a new partner with whom to ride. It is not as easy as he imagines. Even the black chief stands behind the cop's actions because the chief could lose his position if it came to light. Undaunted, the younger cop offers a humiliating story in order to ride by himself. The guilty cop shakes his hand and pulls him aside, saying, "Wait until you've been on the job

Engaging the Experience of the Viewer

a few more years. . . . You think you know who you are. You have no idea." Later, the young cop acts heroically to save the director's life during his moment of honesty and rage at the police who have stopped him. The young cop offers him pure grace and simply says, "Go home." Only a few hours later, when off duty, the young cop picks up a black youth on a lonely road at night. The cop is edgy with the youth and doesn't believe his story, or that he really does like the country music playing on the radio. When the youth, seeing the St. Christopher medal on the dash, laughs and begins to pull something out of his pocket, the cop shoots him, killing him. He finds in the youth's hand a St. Christopher medal that he had pulled from his pocket. In panic he drags the youth to a ravine and burns his own car. The young cop had no comprehension of what the older cop meant when he said, "You think you know who you are. You have no idea." The particulars of the lower level (older cop's first action and his statement; younger cop's own cold-blooded murder of the youth and subsequent cover-up) are integrated into a higher level, a meaningful whole, as he finally understands. It is shameful. It is revelatory. It is the demon that has been lurking unwittingly inside. He sees himself in an utterly new way, and he will never be able to return to innocence.

Crash and similar films with intersecting stories that create a larger story give particularly good insight into Polanyi's many-level world, where the gradual emergence of meaning is revelatory. To experience a film with one narrative focused on racial issues can be conscience-raising and shocking, but to see and live into the experience of racial tension, discrimination, and misunderstanding in its myriad forms of subtlety and aggression holds the capacity to alter one's vision. It helps us understand ourselves and our culture, the impact of our small actions and the collective meaning of our behaviors, at a deeper level than we have heretofore been capable of perceiving. We "dwell in" and "break out" at such a fast pace within the larger story of *Crash*, that we are hammered with the truth of it. It does need to be said, however, that there always exists a choice for the viewer: to be changed or not to be changed. If we do not choose to change through what we have discovered, no enduring knowledge occurs.

We have explored Michael Polanyi's philosophy of personal knowing, using *Crash* as a model for explaining how we engage with film, how our knowledge grows cognitively and affectively by interacting with film. As suggested above, films with intersecting stories such as *Crash*, and similarly *Magnolia*, offer the best examples of Polanyi's thought, having many stories within one story so that the "dwelling in" and "breaking out" process is transformative in our thinking. In a different way, this process is experienced with uniquely structured films such as *Memento, Fight Club*, and *Eternal Sunshine of the Spotless Mind*, for we are constantly struggling to integrate the clues offered into a larger whole. The depth of struggle that occurs within the viewer to piece together the whole is the primary indicator of the potential for transformation. Even basic narrative films, such as *Usual Suspects, Million Dollar Baby*, and *Munich*, require our participation, our integration of clues that continually become subsidiaries with each new discovery, until we've discovered the final answer to the problem posed by the film.

This push-me, pull-you interaction with film always begins with who we are to begin with, and then how we add to our knowing, how we are changed. It is constructive; it is also (or can be) transformative. Such a constructivist philosophy as that of Polanyi seems particularly suited to a postmodern culture that has trashed rationalism and idealism. Perhaps here was part of the appeal that helped garner for *Crash* its Academy Award for Best Motion Picture.

Cinema and Theology as Knowing

We will now shift from exploring engagement with a particular film to inquiring where cinema as art fits into Polanyi's system of knowing, and how cinema is connected with theology, or religion, given that he believes there is a hierarchy of knowing. This is significant because there is no other nonsectarian, constructive epistemology that posits art and then theology as the highest modes of knowing. That he even connects the two is astonishing.

Remember that Michael Polanyi was first a scientist, a chemist who chaired the chemistry department at the University of Manchester and who carried on a correspondence with Einstein for many years. He became so enthralled with pursuing this framework of knowing, however, that he moved from a chair of chemistry to a chair of philosophy and held that position for the remainder of his career. Important also is the fact that although an Eastern European Jew, he was not known to be highly religious. At one point he became a Catholic, but later he would confess to no specific belief system as his own.

All discovery, for Polanyi, begins with intuition and imagination, integrating clues perceived long before any rational and logical processes occur. Imagination is central not only to discovery but also to Polanyi's understanding of how we find meaning. Meaning is more than the sum

Engaging the Experience of the Viewer

of scientific parts, so his many-level world of knowledge moves beyond fact to find meaning. For example, the scientific explanation of Hurricane Katrina would pale in comparison to the horror and meaning of the actual experience. It is through tacit knowing, the imaginative power by which the particulars of sense are integrated into their meaning, that we can know intangible realities. Without these we cannot truly live or know our world. Only then do we participate as feeling, responsible persons.[7] Metaphor, theater, film, poetry, and painting are the arts that push the imagination beyond ourselves to discover the intangible realities that bring us meaning. The push-me, pull-you interaction that takes us to higher levels of meaning continues to expand through the arts.

Although he does not write a lot about cinema alone, Polanyi specifically places it within the arena of art.[8] As with paintings, the more abstract and complex the film (that is, the more work it makes the viewer do), the more it qualifies as a work of art. Much can be gleaned from his understanding of art. First, the arts do not depend for their meaning upon symbolic operations; instead, they rely on their sensuous content. The emotional life that art draws out is primordially ingrained in the emotions of wordless creatures, such as monkeys and babies, echoing some experience of early, shapeless emotions. "Art, like mysticism," writes Polanyi, "breaks through the screen of objectivity and draws on our pre-conceptual capacities of contemplative vision."[9] Nonetheless, it carries the same structure as scientific knowing and other kinds of knowing in that thought processes take opposing or unrelated ideas and join them for a new meaning. It is worth quoting Tilda Swinton, the White Witch of Narnia, in her San Francisco Film Festival keynote address:

> My friend, the great Italian cultural critic, Enrico Ghezzi, . . . remembered the invitation to reverie that a visionary cinema can provide, the invitation to become unconscious. I think the last film in which I experienced this kind of ecstatic removal was at a screening in Cannes of the Thai film "Tropical Malady." [I felt] for one split second, that I had fallen asleep, that only my unconscious could have come up with such a texture of sensation.
>
> Can I be alone in my longing for inarticulacy, for a cinema that refuses to join all of the dots? For an arrhythmia in gesture, for a dissonance in shape? For the context of cinematic frame, a frame that in the end only cinema can provide for the full view, the long shot, the space between, the gasps, the pause, the lull, the grace of living.[10]

The artist "indwells" a universe of her own creation. She creates it with the universal intent to share it with others, believing that it will transform their thought as well. Each viewer identifies with the art, or film, on his or her own terms. Paul Thomas Anderson in directing the film *Magnolia*, or Fellini in *8½*, had particular notions of what they were communicating to their audiences. Viewers understood these films at various levels of understanding. The more work the art makes the viewer do, the more valid it is as art and as a knowing experience.

Subsidiary clues and patterns underlie the focal creation of all art. Some art has only a few clues (paintings) to point us toward the focal creation (discovery) and some, such as film or theater have many: actors, directors, producers, crew, production equipment, and location, not to mention music score, screenplay, visuals, sound, editing, and so on. Unique to a work of art is that the clues drawn together to provide the focal point of awareness are necessarily cut off for the receiver or viewer. The personal nature of the creation disappears. Polanyi says,

> This, in fact, is the principle that turns every discovery, invention, or work of art into a sort of reality with life, so to speak, of its own—into a body of living thought severed from continued dependence upon the personality of its maker and thus capable of being understood by other personalities.[11]

All art has an artificial frame—theater stage with curtains, cinema screen, picture frame, poetic rhythm or structure of words, and in this way the artist is able to detach it from himself and offer it to the world. And thus the receiver may enjoy the art as a personal, received entity that has the power to touch or change us. Also, by this artificial frame we are able to experience, for example, murder in a film and not react to it in the same way we would a murder in real life. We can respond to the clues offered to our imagination, putting them together in a joint meaning that differs from experiences of our normal lives.

The basic structures of discovery are the same in artistic ventures as in scientific pursuits. Faith is the prerequisite. Again, a quotation from Tilda Swinton's address is apt:

> The thing is for me . . . filmmaking . . . has always been an act of faith. Not only in the sense in which one needs a certain amount of conviction to get the films made in the first place, but in the more amorphous sense in which one takes one's faith to the cinema as to the confessional: the last resort of the determined inarticulate, the unmediated, the intravenous experience of something existential, transmuted through the dark, through the flickering of the constant image through the projector onto the screen. The sharing of private fantasy, the very issue of the unconscious made in light.[12]

Engaging the Experience of the Viewer

In art, however, the joining of ideas in a metaphor will continue to ignite an imaginative fire in those who receive it, and as such will continue some of the life that served to create it, sometimes for centuries.

For Polanyi, the truth of poetry and art is more significant than the truth of science because it offers more meaning than our material structures. Moreover, while poetry and art force the imagination to great heights in joining two incompatible ideas, the most significant truth must be said to come from theology. The realm of discovery for Christians, says Polanyi, is worship. As an act of worship, theology is an indwelling, not an affirmation. He concurs with Augustine that believing is prior to understanding. "It resembles . . . the heuristic upsurge which strives to break through the accepted framework of thought, guided by the intimations of discoveries beyond our horizon. . . . It is like an obsession with a problem known to be insoluble, which yet follows, against reason, unswervingly, the heuristic command: 'Look at the unknown!'"[13]

For Polanyi, the desire to look at the unknown is "an urge to make contact with a reality which is felt to be there already, waiting to be apprehended."[14] I am reminded of the Carl Sagan film *Contact*. Jodie Foster's character seeks to communicate with "something" out there. She is sure it exists, even though she does not see it as related to Christianity. The moment finally arrives for her to explore this through an apparatus designed to potentially put her in contact with other worlds. She is stunned and overwhelmed by the hyperreality of the contact she makes. It appears to last eons. When the experience ends and she returns, she tries to explain all that has happened and eagerly shows the tapes that document her experience. The only proof she ends up with, however, is an eighteen-hour tape showing only static. The world she indwelled for only a few hours was more real, and transforming, than her normal world, but those around her did not believe, and so could not understand. Like true science and like Foster's character, Polanyi believes that Christianity should be more like a society of explorers than a community frequently dominated by rule and dogma.

The highest meaning and the highest mystical vision, for Polanyi, are made possible only by letting our categories of normal seeing go, so that we see all things as features of God.[15] Once seen in this way, we can never return to our earlier categories of understanding.

Michael Polanyi's epistemology is fascinating in its entire vision. It demands construction, struggle, faith, and personal commitment, recognizing a many-leveled, hierarchical world as intrinsic to its meaning. This many-leveled world, or hierarchy, is not made of ideal forms, but is taken, instead, from our own developmental schema, our own biology. Indeed, even current string theory in science states that there must be eleven to twelve dimensions in existence for our cosmos to function. Polanyi masterfully weaves together a cosmic tapestry of meaning divided for thousands of years by the systemic distinctions between Aristotelian and Platonic thought. That this cosmic tapestry displays art and Christian theology in its most meaningful and highest realms is astonishing. For Polanyi, as in art and cinema, only in a more whole and complete way, "God becomes the integration of all the incompatible clues that move us deeply and help us pull the scattered droplets of our lives together into a single sea of sublime meaning."[16]

Notes

1. Michael Polanyi, *Personal Knowledge* (Chicago: University of Chicago Press, 1974), 286.

2. Albert Einstein, *The World as I See It* (New York: Covici, Friede, 1934), 125; as cited in Drucilla Scott, *Everyman Revived: The Common Sense of Michael Polanyi* (Grand Rapids: Eerdmans, 1995), 32.

3. Esther Lightcap Meek, *Longing to Know: The Philosophy of Knowledge for Ordinary People* (Grand Rapids: Brazos, 2003), 48.

4. Michael Polanyi and Harry Prosch, *Meaning* (Chicago: University of Chicago Press, 1975), 65.

5. Scott, *Everyman Revived*, 150–51.

6. Barry J. Wadsworth, *Piaget's Theory of Cognitive Development* (New York: David McKay, 1971).

7. Scott, *Everyman Revived*, 176.

8. Polanyi and Prosch, *Meaning*, 114.

9. Polanyi, *Personal Knowledge*, 199.

10. Tilda Swinton, The 2006 San Francisco International Film Festival "State of Cinema" Address, May 4, 2006, www.sf360.org.

11. Polanyi and Prosch, *Meaning*, 85.

12. Swinton, "State of Cinema" Address.

13. Polanyi, *Personal Knowledge*, 199.

14. Michael Polanyi, *Science, Faith and Society* (Oxford: Oxford University Press, 1946; Chicago: University of Chicago Press / Phoenix, 1946), 35; as cited in Scott, *Everyman Revived*, 189. Polanyi, *Personal Knowledge*, 199; as cited in Scott, *Everyman Revived*, 189.

15. Polanyi, *Personal Knowledge*, 199.

16. Polanyi and Prosch, *Meaning*, 156.

9

Películas—
¿A Gaze from Reel to Real?

Going to the Movies with Latinas in Los Angeles

CATHERINE M. BARSOTTI

Introduction

Sitting in the library of a San Francisco Bay Area suburb,[1] I find myself, a second generation Italian-American woman, reflecting on the conversations that I have been a part of over the last several months with some very dynamic women in Los Angeles County.[2] Our conversations had originally been birthed out of the particular desire by the Los Angeles chapter of the Fraternidad Teológica Latinoamericana,[3] a group of Protestant theological educators, pastors, and students, to share with our sisters and brothers of the Americas, who happen to live south of the current US border, some of the Latino/Hispanic[4] reality(ies) in the United States. An ambitious project, ¿no? For how do we begin to describe *la realidad* of a community of people who are in fact a community of communities?

The overall task of discussing Latina/o reality in the United States involves numerous key dynamics. First, to speak of someone's reality implies discussions of identity, and in the Latina/o context this conversation is long, continuing to draw questions from numerous fronts. Latina/o historians, philosophers, and sociologists, as well as theologians (Catholic and Protestant) have debated the nature of this identity. Do we speak of the hybridity, the *mestizaje*, the *mulatez*, or perhaps the *criolo*-ization of US Latinas/os? Or do we speak of a legacy that contains colonizer and colonized within the same identity? Is there a *la raza cósmica* as Vasconcelos and others have suggested?[5] And how do we talk about the reality of marginalization of the "remnant" space[6] of Latinas/os living on the ever-growing "margin" of Euro-American US communities? Protestant Latinas/os face a double margin, as they live on the also ever-growing margin of Catholic Latina/o communities. Finally, since this essay will focus on Protestant Latina women, we must also include the marginalization that women often face vis-à-vis the Latino male in work and church spheres. When that marginalization hits its paralyzing low, *la realidad* can be felt in the rising rates of domestic violence.

Demographics

There are numerous ways of approaching this task. First, we can begin with some of the societal reality about US Latinas/os reflected in the torrents of demographic data. These include the following highlights. As of July 1, 2005, the US Census Bureau estimated the Latina/o population at 42.7 million (about 14 percent of the nation's total population), making Latinas/os the fastest-growing segment of the population and accounting for 49 percent of national population growth from July 1, 2004, to July 1, 2005. This growth is coming predominantly (62 percent) from natural growth (births minus deaths), with 38 percent taking place through immigration. Contrary to popular misconceptions, roughly 60 percent of US Latinas/os are native-born. Among the 40 percent who are foreign-born, 10 percent are naturalized citizens, and of the remaining new immigrants almost half entered the country legally. Latinas/os are not only the fastest-growing segment of the US population, they are the largest minority group, the youngest, and often, the poorest.[7]

According to the National Council of La Raza, a research and advocacy group, the socioeconomic disadvantages facing Latinas/os include the lowest high school graduation rate in the nation (58 percent of Latinas/os 25 years old and older graduated from high school compared to 85 percent of whites and 79 percent of blacks), a 12 percent graduation rate of Latinas/os from college, and the highest rate of working poor (given that 68 percent of the Latina/o population 16 years old and over are in the labor force, compared to whites at 66.2 percent and blacks at 63.5 percent, yet 22.8 percent live in poverty, a rate three times higher than white families). Furthermore, more than one-quarter of Latina/o children live in poverty, while Latina/o families headed by a single mother have the highest rate of poverty among all census groups. And the number of single Latina women has increased from 37.5 percent in 1990 to 41 percent in 2004. The 2000 census also disproves further stereotypes by revealing that the majority (71.8 percent) of Latinas/os who speak Spanish at home are also proficient or fluent in English.[8]

This demographic snapshot of US Latina/o experience displays some of the racial, gender, socioeconomic, and ethnic inequalities that form *la realidad* in the United States, but in the shape of numbers, not faces. In the adjoining library study room a gentleman from Mexico (who later told me of his undocumented arrival four years ago with his wife, leaving their children with family in Mexico so that they could try to make a better life for the entire family) is being tutored in English by a white suburban housewife (who later told me of her volunteer work several times a week to tutor English). In the midst of spelling and grammar lessons, the two of them are having lively conversations about family, religion, and culture— including what they would be doing for the US Thanksgiving holiday, and what movies they had recently seen. Hearing them talk about movies, I was playfully inspired to check the Worldometers Web site, which gives world statistics in real time. Under the education section of the site, the following statistics flashed before my eyes: up to this moment in November 2006, there had been 844,011 books published and 467,019,600 newspapers circulated, while 11,337,884,000 people had visited movie theaters.[9]

Film

Such is our world these days; world migrations and globalization have brought people into contact, whether it is sitting side by side talking to each other, or sitting side by side watching movies about each other.[10] Both experiences are filled with communication and miscommunication. Through both we construct meanings and impressions of "the other." Even if we are never personally involved in this global migratory movement, most of us have been impacted by the global reach of not only the US film industry but of other countries (e.g., Argentina, France, Germany, India,

Iran, Japan, Korea, Spain) and their filmmakers (e.g., Mexican directors Guillermo del Toro, Alfonso Cuarón, and Alejandro González Iñárritu left their mark on filmmaking and filmgoers in 2006).

Thus, given the assignment to reflect on the current reality of Latina women in the United States (again, a task much more complex than an essay by one person could possibly capture), I suggested to my colleagues that we could interact with a popular culture product (film) as a way to get into the theme and its multiplicity of facets and questions. We would interact with movies made in the United States or other countries and accessible in the United States and beyond, but which *portrayed the lives of Latina women in the United States*. The films would act as windows, however tinted, as a group of Latina women involved in Protestant churches, ministries, or schools reflected on the "reel" portrayed and the "real" experienced.

The Voices of Latina Women

A further narrowing of such a broad topic was accomplished, as all of the women who participated in the reflection were single women living in Los Angeles County. Out of the nine women who participated in some way, only one was a single mother. The rest were single, never married, and without children. Certainly this would frame the viewing and the conversation in distinct ways; but likewise, the filmmakers had framed the conversation in their own ways. It was time for a conversation between the social constructs. As noted above, single Protestant Latina women live multiple marginalizations daily. Perhaps the films would evoke[11] reflection on these personal realities. Perhaps the films would allow them to see and hear the commonalities that begin to give shape to a larger current reality for many Latina women in the United States. Even if the "reel" portrayals were unrealistic or skewed portrayals from those outside the community of Latina women, could they somehow be useful in calling out new voices, or rather real voices that could now speak *la realidad*? For films "help us see what we sometimes can't say."[12]

Why Film?

The Power of Story—Seen around the Globe

In the Gospel of Matthew, when queried by his disciples as to why he spoke to the people in parables, Jesús said "Por eso les hablo por

Engaging the Experience of the Viewer

parábolas: porque viendo no ven, y oyendo no oyen, ni entienden. . . . Pero bienaventurados vuestros ojos, porque ven; y vuestros oídos, porque oyen."[13] Movies have been called modern-day parables.[14] Even if one is not willing to give our current movies such a descriptor, most would recognize the immense power movies have to evoke the viewer's response.[15] Films are certainly cultural products, but just how much do they also impact culture? Are they similar to Jesus's parables, which reflected culture but also sought to shape the culture of his day?

Films are ubiquitous throughout the Americas, and the younger generations speak the language of film. This year the Los Angeles Latino International Film Festival celebrated its tenth year by showing over one hundred films of "quality cinema by us or about us in Spanish, English, Portuguese, German and Polish."[16] In the United States, Latinas/os went to the theater to see an average of 9.8 films in 2005, compared with 7.8 for African Americans and 7 for whites, according to the Motion Picture Association of America.[17] Certainly Spanish-speaking viewers around the world are not immune to film. Spaniards are especially proud of their filmmakers, and film watching is a leading form of entertainment, with close to $750 million spent at the box office in 2006. With the exception of spikes in revenue during the months of May and July, box office receipts remained steady in 2006 for the following Latin American countries—Mexico: $8 million to $9 million per week, Argentina: $1 million to $2 million per week, and Chile: $500,000 to $1 million per week. Conservatively these three countries spent $500 million at the box office in 2006.[18]

Certainly the reader is familiar with the testimonies of such people as Martin Scorcese, Paul Schrader, Sam Peckinpah, Jodie Foster, Kevin Smith, George Miller,[19] the Mexican directors noted above, and others who talk about the power of cinema in their own lives. But today, from multiple corners of our world, and not just from filmmakers, we see people engaging film as they reflect on life. Chilean writer Alberto Fuguet's 2003 novel, *Las Películas de Mi Vida*, presents (through his protagonist) his memories of growing up in California and Chile in a series of movie descriptions.[20] He uses films such as *Fiddler on the Roof*, *Willy Wonka and the Chocolate Factory*, *Earthquake*, *Logan's Run*, and *Close Encounters of the Third Kind*, but not as mere synopses of events. Rather, Fuguet shares with the reader his emotional response to how the films connected to his actual life experiences. Somehow the films helped him explain his world and his feelings about moving to and from the United States.

The Narrative Imagination of Latina/o Theology

It is not my intention to suggest a false dualism between high culture (e.g., philosophy and theology) and pop culture (e.g., film). The discourse of philosophers and theologians should be put into conversation with everyday life (*lo cotidiano*[21]). Methodologically, Christians through the ages have consistently considered the Bible, the church's history and tradition, and reason as key sources for reflecting on created life and the Creator. With the Protestant Reformation, additional sources were recognized. These included experience and culture.

Latina/o theologians have nuanced their theological method and these traditional sources by emphasizing not only the narrative nature of Scripture but also the stories of their lives and faith. Thus, they have focused on the everyday experience of the whole people of God, and the ways of knowing that come through culture and its stories. And stories invite our imagination. Justo González has talked about theological method using his tradition's Wesleyan Quadrilateral of Bible, tradition, experience, and reason. But he is uncomfortable with the use of "reason," believing it to be too limited a word for the ways in which we know. Thus he suggests that imagination is an important aspect of doing theology.[22] The use of the imagination allows the theologian to get at the affect, which has often been discounted in traditional theological methodology. Pentecostal theologian Samuel Solivan calls for not only right thinking (orthodoxy) and right action (orthopraxis) but also right feeling (orthopathy).[23] Likewise, Gloria Anzaldúa, Ada-María Isasi-Díaz, Yolanda Tarango, and Jeannette Rodríguez argue that women's experience, affect, imagination, and resultant cultural production are key elements in Latina/o reality and theology.[24] One of the women who participated in the film conversation and who read the first draft of this essay echoed these writers when she commented that "intuition, imagination, affect—it is our language."[25]

For all these reasons—the narrative nature of Scripture and Latina/o faith and theology; a theological methodology that values culture and experience; the often marginalized nature of women's cultures, epistemology, and experience; and the possibility of popular culture to help us break open traditional conversations in ways that include the affect, imagination, and experience of women—we set out to create a space for conversation about the reality of Latina women in the United States by interacting with film. Visual stories about Latina women and their experiences in the States would be the imaginative catalyst for reflection on life.

Engaging the Experience of the Viewer

Methodology

As noted above, our first task together was to form a small group of Latina women who might be interested in such a personal and corporate project.[26] We began with six women who expressed interest in such an undertaking. Eventually the women involved in the project would be ten (including myself). Though these women come from various Protestant denominations[27] and different countries of origin (Mexico, Venezuela, Colombia, Peru, El Salvador, Guatemala, Puerto Rico), they do share numerous similar characteristics. They are all single, between the ages of thirty and fifty; one is a single mother. They all attend local churches; some are leaders of ministries and several hold clergy positions. Likewise, these women all have a moderate to high level of education and work in professions such as graphic design, real estate/mortgage banking, higher education, office management, and social work. Most of the women came to the United States as teenagers or young adults, but one came as a nine-year-old.

The initiating group began to work on developing a list of movie titles that dealt with Latina/o themes or were aimed at a Latina/o audience (see list at end of chapter). From this larger list the group narrowed the films to those that actually dealt more directly with Latina women in the United States, especially in Los Angeles.[28] Initially a weekend retreat was planned for those who could join together for two days to view and discuss selected films. The six films selected and viewed were: *Luminarias* (d. José Luis Valenzuela/screenwriter Evelina Fernández, 2000), *Bread and Roses* (d. Ken Loach/screenwriter Paul Laverty, 2000), *Real Women Have Curves* (d. Patricia Cardoso/screenwriter Josefina Lopez and George La Voo, 2002), *Spanglish* (d. James Brooks, 2004), *Maria Full of Grace* (d. Joshua Marston, 2004), and *Quinceañera* (d. Richard Glatzer and Wash Westmoreland, 2006). These six films represent a variety of filmmaking as they come from Latina/o, European, and Euro-American[29] filmmakers; female and male filmmakers; and studio settings plus independent collaborations. These six films combined generated over $80 million in box office receipts (and had combined budgets of over $80 million).[30] While these dollar amounts suggest that none of these films were "blockbusters," it does suggest the number of people involved in the making and viewing of these cultural products.

The initial group watched each of the films together. After viewing each film, the women took fifteen to twenty minutes to write a reflection on the film, using a form containing four clusters of paired questions and lots of blank space for journaling of their reactions, reflections, and commentaries. Afterward the group embarked on a forty- to sixty-minute discussion of the film, using some of the written questions but also going wherever the group's discussion naturally led. I, as facilitator, took notes on the group conversation, noting repeated points of agreement or disagreement, and new personal insights that the individuals within the group had through the experience. After the discussion the women gave me their written responses as further documentation of their reflections and commentaries.

At the conclusion of the weekend, this group chose three of the six films viewed for their particular relevancy to and compelling nature for single Latina women living in Los Angeles (it was unanimous that none of the films captured the Latina/o reality in the United States for reasons discussed below). These three films were *Luminarias, Bread and Roses*, and *Spanglish*. While these films are very different from each other, together they formed a kind of triptych that the women thought represented various aspects of subgroups within the Latina/o community in Los Angeles. Each dealt with aspects of culture, class, religious belief and practices, and acculturation that are present in the large, diverse group that Latina women represent. Some of these films were then viewed by women who could not attend the retreat. A couple of viewings were done in small groups, for which the same protocol was used as for the weekend retreat (i.e., written responses followed by group discussion). Two of the women individually viewed the films and sent me their written responses, and in a couple of cases we had lively phone conversations. Again, I reviewed these responses with an eye toward their similarities and differences with former conversations and what new personal insights emerged.[31]

The Films—Brief Synopses

So as to give the reader an idea of the films viewed, a brief synopsis follows for each of the six films. I will begin with the two films from 2000. In *Luminarias* a group of friends—four single, fortyish, second- and third-generation Mexican American women (who self-identify as Chicanas) with careers (lawyer, psychologist, painter, boutique owner)—gather regularly at Luminarias, a restaurant in Monterey Park, to commiserate and encourage each other as they face loneliness, relationship difficulties, identity challenges, and emotional survival in Los Angeles.

Bread and Roses focuses on Maya, a young, single Mexican woman who crosses the border with "coyotes" and is undocumented. She makes

Engaging the Experience of the Viewer

her way to Los Angeles to find her sister Rosa, who helps her get a job as a janitor in a nonunion company. As union organizers work with the janitors (who include persons from Mexico, El Salvador, Guatemala, and Nicaragua, as well as Eastern Europeans, Asians, and African Americans) for justice in wages, working conditions, and benefits, the sisters are pulled apart as each seeks to survive the "harsh realities" of life for them in Los Angeles.

From 2002, we viewed the film *Real Women Have Curves*. The film tells us the story of Ana,[32] a second-generation Mexican American, who is juggling her dreams of college with the expectations of her more traditional parents. Torn between "mainstream ambitions and her cultural heritage," she reluctantly agrees to help out in her sister's downtown sewing factory for the summer.[33] There she admires the hardworking Mexican and Mexican American women and their teamwork, but even as their solidarity grows, she realizes that leaving home for college is an important step in her own identity development as a Latina living in the United States.

We viewed two films from 2004, *Spanglish* and *Maria Full of Grace*. Again, these films represent two very different experiences of Latina women in the United States. The first, *Spanglish*, is the story of Flor, who comes to the United States (no mention is made of documents) hoping to find a better life for herself and her young daughter.[34] She is hired by an affluent but dysfunctional family to be their housekeeper. As she deals with the clash of cultures and values, while learning English, we see the strength of this Mexican woman and her culture vis-à-vis this troubled family. However, when Flor is forced to live with the family over the summer, she insists that her daughter be allowed to join her. The family happily consents, since they love Flor and her centering presence. However, once the daughter, Christina, begins to interact with the family, Flor knows it will be a challenge to maintain family and cultural values in the midst of a swirling US society.

Maria Full of Grace is the story of pregnant seventeen-year-old Maria, who lives in a small village in Colombia and works in a flower factory to support her family. When she is fired, she accepts an offer to work as a drug mule. Flying to the United States with sixty-two pellets of cocaine in her stomach and with several newfound friends, she arrives to find the plan gone awry. She is left to her own devices and the help of other Colombian immigrants to survive the drug cartel and the streets of New York. While her closest friend returns to Colombia, Maria chooses to stay and make her way in the United States.

Finally, we viewed a 2006 film by going to a local theater together and discussing the film over dinner. This film, *Quinceañera,* focuses on Magdalena's life in Echo Park, a community of Los Angeles. As she approaches her fifteenth birthday and begins preparations for her Quinceañera, she finds out she is pregnant. Kicked out of her house by her father (he works as a security guard and pastors a local storefront church), she creates a new family with her great uncle and cousin. While it may seem a rocky road to adulthood in this changing neighborhood, we see Magdalena teaching others about what it means to be a twenty-first-century Latina in Los Angeles, as she models self-respect and reconciliation to her family, church, and community.

As the reader can see from these descriptions, the films are all very different, and yet have similar themes about how Latinas make their way in the United States. Some of the films are more concerned with the process of survival amid great adversity, while others focus on the process of acculturation and identity formation. In all the films, women are portrayed as having to make difficult choices between two worlds—their former and their present worlds, or their world and their parents' world. These choices are made in different ways. Regardless of a predominant focus on Mexicans and Mexican Americans, each of the films identified some aspect of the experiences of the Latina women who viewed them, or aspects of the reality they see in their churches, places of work, and communities.

Constructed Meanings, Critique and Conversations about *La Realidad*

I have referred to these films as tinted windows, for each of the filmmakers offers the viewer their constructed reality about, or view of, Latina women. While some of these movies were not made by Latina/o filmmakers, they all resonated in some way with the Latina women viewing them. However, the women were quick to name what elements in the films resonated with their own experience or the experience of their Latina friends and family, and what elements did not. The films were so accessible through the visual images, music, narrative, and thematic power that the women's affect was engaged. They were eager to dialogue with the "reel" to get at the "real." The women were quite able to exercise a "hermeneutic of suspicion" that would shine light on the "hidden stories."[35] Unlike many a lecture or thesis about Latina women's reality, the films invited these women to tell their stories.

Critiques

CONFLATING IDENTITIES AND REALITIES

Perhaps the first clear observation that most of the women made was that each of the films portrayed a particular culture and not Latina culture generically, nor even a plurality of Latina/o cultures (cf. Latina/o scholarly debates over *mestizaje* or *la raza cósmica*, noted above).[36] Thus, the women from Central or South America or the Caribbean had trouble relating to the struggle and rage of Chicana or Mexican American second-generation women, while the first- and one-point-five-generation Mexican women in the group could more easily identify with those feelings. As a group, though, we realized how mainstream US society and its films equate Latina with Chicana or Mexican American women. Thus, talking about Latina women often gets conflated with talking about Mexican American culture and religious expression.[37]

It was obvious to the women that the film industry reflects "mainstream" US society by not seeing and understanding the particularities of Latinas/os in the United States. Though people of Mexican descent make up 63 percent of the Latinas/os in the United States, the group felt that films should not neglect the cultures of the many other groups within the Latina/o community in the United States.[38] Yet many of the women appreciated the other varieties (regarding education, class, and marital status) of Latinas portrayed in the films and suggested that the films presented realities of which many Anglos are not aware.[39] However, after viewing several of the films, they noted that prejudices arise among Latinas from different countries of origin, and between them and Anglo women. One woman remarked that such movie viewing helped her "examine her own stereotypes about others" and confront her own discriminatory practices, to which several others nodded in agreement.[40]

SEXUALIZED PORTRAYALS OF LATINA WOMEN

The films were also critiqued for misrepresenting these Latinas and/or their realities (or those of their communities/churches). One such criticism, which is often leveled not just by Latinas but also by numerous feminists, is the way women are sexualized by the media. While most of these films did not do this overtly, *Luminarias* in particular received mixed reactions from the women viewers. (The screenplay for this film was written by Evelina Fernández, a Chicana raised in Los Angeles.) When the Latina woman was not overly sexualized, beauty was emphasized. *Spanglish* was a particularly nonrealistic portrayal of Los Angeles Latina housekeepers.

Numerous scholars, sociologists, and journalists have documented how many housekeepers experience a much more difficult work life than the protagonist of the film.[41] The viewing women were quick to point out that the protagonist (played by Paz Vega, a Spanish actress) did not look, sound, or act like the Mexican housekeeper she was supposed to be. As they put it, she looked and acted more like a "runway model."[42] She was tall, slender, beautiful, and perfectly dressed. She never looked tired or dirty and was never observed cleaning anything.[43] However, they did appreciate that the housekeeper was the heroine of the film, as she truly "modeled" health and strength vis-à-vis a fractured Anglo family.[44]

Failure to Include Religious Belief, Practice, or Leaders

Another criticism focused on the "white saviors" in some of the films, as if the Latina/o community didn't have its own leaders and heroines. *Bread and Roses*, for example, depicted a white male union organizer leading the fight for workers' rights (however, these viewers noted that, to the filmmaker's credit, Latina women were also key leaders in the fight for justice). But the film went even further in the wrong direction, some of the women said, because it did not include any religious leaders from the Latina/o community involved in this struggle for justice. Most of the women found this depiction completely unbelievable. They referenced the historic work of César Chávez, or the current work of their own local pastors in mobilizing their congregations to impact the legislative process for just immigration reform.

Additionally, the films made by Europeans or European Americans included little or no religious beliefs, practices, or commitments in the stories. "For years Latino church leaders, Catholic and Protestant, have lamented the abysmal lack of attention given to Latino religion by historians and social scientists. A certain secular mind-set allergic to the topic of religion has tended to ignore or bracket this reality."[45] The same critique can certainly be leveled at some older modernist filmmakers, and Ken Loach (*Bread and Roses*) and James Brooks (*Spanglish*) are prime examples of such lacunae. Younger Anglo filmmakers, such as Joshua Marston (*Maria Full of Grace*) or Richard Glatzer and Wash Westmoreland (*Quinceañera*), included some religious practices in their films. Perhaps because they actually have lived within Latina/o communities or in Latin America, they understand the importance of everyday spirituality in such communities.

The Latina/o filmmakers included religion as a visible element in the lives of their characters. The religious world shown was obviously that of Roman Catholicism. However, the most recent film, *Quinceañera* (2006),

Engaging the Experience of the Viewer

portrayed both Catholic and Protestant religious practices and views of life. Regarding the Protestant depiction, one woman commented, "I could identify with Magdalena as a daughter of a pastor—living a role in the church, but experiencing other things in the larger society."[46] But even the Latino filmmakers' films did not engender long or deep conversation about faith by the Latina women viewers. Perhaps since the religious expression was mostly Catholic and our group was mostly Protestant, a vicarious connection was absent. Perhaps the "reel" portrayals were not convincing or complex enough for serious engagement. In addition, these initial viewings and discussions were mostly about "unpacking" a film's power and meaning and then dialoguing with it through the telling of the group members' own stories.

Resonances

But beyond this critique of the films viewed, the women noted many characteristics across cultures that were common to a Latina reality and with which they could relate. The most obvious factors included (1) a reverence for the extended family, (2) a continued desire and struggle to preserve cultural roots and practices, (3) the importance and role of religion, (4) the value placed on the community and the solidarity felt within and across Latina/o communities, (5) hard work, and (6) a passion for life displayed in the presence of color, music, food, and stories in the lives of Latinas/os. Noticing the stories told by characters in the films helped the viewers connect with how Latinas/os live in a narrative world, and see that these stories can often make survival in a hostile place possible (e.g., in both *Quinceañera* and *Spanglish* characters relate stories about overcoming adversity, identity formation, and survival in a new culture). Soon the women were sharing their own families' stories—stories marking cultural identity and survival.

LIFE AS STRUGGLE

But deeper issues were also noted as representing realities within the particularities of their own lives. The viewers insisted that struggle is a common reality for Latina women. Whether it be the struggle of poverty, civil war, economic or political oppression in their countries of origin; the struggle to get to the United States; the struggle to carve out a place for oneself here; the struggle to find work; the struggle for human rights and dignity; the struggle to navigate multiple worlds; the struggle to maintain traditions and not to lose your roots; the struggle to differentiate yourself and create new traditions; or the struggle to feel at home, to feel comfortable, these women saw themselves and other Latinas/os like them as having emerged from struggle. And this emergence has made them strong. They tenaciously strive to protect and create a better life for their loved ones and themselves.[47] Most agreed that overcoming struggles, including identity struggles, has been or is currently part of their lives in the United States.

Frustration and Celebration

Some of the women identified with the frustration or even rage felt and expressed in some of the movies, as characters interacted with the majority Anglo culture in the United States.[48] One woman suggested that the life of a Latina woman is a "drama" filled with emotions as they navigate life.[49] Another commented about the "weariness of always feeling like you have to prove yourself."[50] But they also noted that the ability to survive, laugh, and even celebrate within the darkest of situations is a strength within Latina/o peoples. Self-respect is a characteristic they saw as key to survival in the United States.

"Viviendo en dos mundos"

Overall, many of the women talked of the films' very real portrayal, regardless of context, class, or culture, of "viviendo en dos mundos."[51] The constant navigating of two worlds can create women who are survivors and strong leaders regardless of the apparent marginalization the society might perpetuate.[52] To belong and not belong is a daily experience. Yet almost all of them commented that to return to their countries of origin would also result in a "ni acá, ni allá" feeling.[53] They have chosen to continue living in multiple worlds in order to carve out something new for themselves, their families, and their communities.

Invisible to Anglos

Linked to the above discussion was the sense of being invisible to Anglos, as expressed in the film *Bread and Roses*. Two janitors cleaning the floor of an office building are literally stepped over by the Anglo workers, as if they are invisible. One janitor says to the other, "Somos invisibles—this uniform makes us invisible."[54] Many of the women could identify with this feeling, even in the midst of the demographics noted above regarding the growth and visibility of Latinas/os in US society.

Harsh Realities

Other negative components of their reality were also noted as being accurately portrayed in some of the films, such as infidelity within marriage relationships, physical and verbal abuse, abandonment, financial problems, fear, and emotional manipulation. Some positive key elements, such as family, were also examined in a new way, a hybrid way, as Mexican American women in the films were faced with some of the negative aspects relating to family. Some characters, like the Latina women viewers, knew what it was like to "go against your family, especially the influence of the mother" or the "torture of 'betraying' your family." To depart from the norms established by the family meant to a certain extent "treason."[55]

The Variety of Responses

Stepping back, the reactions of these Latina women viewers might be categorized in several ways with regard to whether the films portrayed *la realidad*. First, the women often had very personal identifications with some of the film stories or particular characters. They relived some of their own experiences through the characters of the films, and refelt the respective emotions. So in one sense, the films portrayed reality very well.

Second, when the films didn't connect to a viewer's own story, they often connected to the experiences of other women they knew within their community (an example of the solidarity mentioned above). They could say, "I know what that is like because I have a friend at work, or in my church, or in my neighborhood that has had that experience. It might not be my reality but I know Latinas for whom it is."[56]

Third, there were times when the films, in the women's view, completely missed or misrepresented a certain aspect of their reality. In addition to the numerous examples given above, a further example is worth mentioning due to the current US immigration context, and because of the anger and pain this portrayal generated among the women. While Ken Loach's *Bread and Roses* was made in 2000, its portrayal of Maya's deportation to Mexico—because of her robbery of a convenience store in order to help a friend unjustly fired by the janitorial company—was like throwing salt on an open wound in 2006. The women could not believe that this character would have committed such a crime. Furthermore they saw this portrayal as the stereotypical way Latinos in the United States are criminalized by the larger society. As one woman wrote, "The North American film industry ends up highlighting the stereotype of the delinquency of Latino culture."[57]

Finally, through the use of a variety of films, the Latina viewers were able to address different aspects of their own marginalized reality: their reality as Latina women who live and work on the margins of Euro-

American US society; their reality as Protestant Latina women who believe and practice their faith at the margins of a Latina/o community that is predominantly Roman Catholic; and as single, Protestant Latina women who often serve or sit in the pew on the edge of their churches, due to their gender and marital status. These women walk in worlds that are the borderlands between many demographics and sensibilities.[58] They are women who have developed the ability to hold apparent contradictions within themselves and to live within such complexity in society. So, all of the movies viewed, even the ones that had elements that were critiqued, were appreciated by the women.

Suggested Conversations for the Future

It seems that the way in which these single Protestant Latina viewers interacted with the films connected directly to the demographic reality noted above, but even more so with *la realidad* of Latina/o theology in the United States. Some of the films and many of the women raised the same issues with slightly different accents. They repeatedly raised the important issue of identity for the Latina/o community in the United States. But this is a larger question for all of the Americas and the world. What does identity mean in a global world of local communities, perspectives, and theologies?

Will metaphors and words such as *mestizaje* and "hybrid" suffice, or will there be new words and metaphors coming from Latinas' contexts that will lead the way?[59] Maybe these Latinas who live in multiple borderlands and navigate many margins have something to teach us regarding what life is about in the twenty-first century. As one of the women said after reading this essay, "Living in the margin is common to all Latinas/os, but perhaps it is even more exaggerated for us single Protestant Latina women. But we want to speak to the center from the margin."[60]

Might their voices and lives have something to teach us about walking with God in a pluralistic religious world? And will these women be allowed to shape the Latina/o Protestant religious world, which often makes them invisible? These viewers saw aspects of themselves in each of the films, since most of the protagonists were single Latinas. What does it mean for these women, and for the church, that they see themselves as strong leaders at the cinema but often don't know where to look to see women like themselves at church? Who will have eyes to see and ears to hear these single Latina women?

Engaging the Experience of the Viewer

We were overwhelmed with how much we learned about each other by watching these films and discussing them. Some of us had been friends for many years, yet through this experience we heard new stories. Visual stories helped us speak and understand our own stories. Even when told "wrongly," or when it does not accurately depict the viewers' reality, a "reel" story can help us articulate our real story. These women recognized the filmmakers' movies as particular windows on reality. So the women were not shy about adding their own touches to the windows, when needed, or even dismantling the windows altogether. But just as often these filmic stories did bear the weight of *la realidad*.

These movies had a prophetic role, too, for in the discipline of critiquing stereotypes we had to face ourselves. Good film can model a respect for others and their cultures. Through the history of humankind, this kind of respect has been woefully lacking. Perhaps the aesthetic of film can nurture an ethic of respect. Ethics and aesthetics must go together. Our Latina/o sisters and brothers have centuries of understanding, creativity, and practice, as well as misunderstanding and pain, to help the global church in its integration, proclamation, and service in the world. In a world of highly politicized debates and rhetoric of pride, intolerance, domination, and hate, it will be our artist/prophets who will lead us.

Pope John Paul II, a poet and playwright himself, who had several of his plays turned into movies, talked of "the *via pulchritudinis* [path of beauty] as the best way for the Christian faith and the culture of our time to meet."[61] He also asserted in his *Address to the Festival for the Third Millenium*, December 1999, "The cinema enjoys a wealth of languages, a multiplicity of styles, and a truly great variety of narrative forms. . . . It can contribute to bringing people closer together, to reconciling enemies, to favoring an ever more respectful dialogue between diverse cultures."[62] And that is one reason I go to the movies with my Latina women colleagues.

We may have taken only one step on the path of beauty, but the experience has given us confidence for the journey.[63]

List of Movies with Latina/o Themes

Alambrista (1977)

El Norte (1983)

The Milagro Beanfield War (1988)

Como Agua para Chocolate (1992)

Mi Vida Loca (1993)

The Perez Family (1995)

A Walk in the Clouds (1995)

My Family, Mi Familia (1995)

Cilantro y Perejil (1995)
Lonestar (1996)
Luminarias (2000)
Americanos: Latino Life in the United States (2000)
Bread and Roses (2000)
Amores Perros (2001)
Tortilla Soup (2001)
In the Time of the Butterflies (2001)
Y Tu Mama También (2001)
El Crimen del Padre Amaro (2002)

Frida (2002) [México]
Real Women Have Curves (2002)
Chasing Papi (2003)
Un Día sin un Mexicano—A Day without a Mexican (2004)
Spanglish (2004)
Maria Full of Grace (2004)
The Motorcycle Diaries (2004)
The Three Burials of Melquiades Estrada (2005)
Quinceañera (2006)

Notes

1. Per US census data, this city of roughly 68,000 moved from 91 percent "White/non-Hispanic" in 1990 to 80.4 percent in 2000. During the same period people of "Hispanic origin" grew from 7 percent to 7.9 percent; www.ci.pleasanton.ca.us/business/development/demographic=profile .html.

2. Per US census data, Los Angeles County moved from 41 percent "White/non-Hispanic" in 1990 to 32 percent in 2000. During the same time people of "Hispanic origin" grew from 38 percent to 45 percent; http://planning.lacounty.gov/doc/stat/LA_Population Ethnicity.pdf.

3. Occasionally throughout this essay Spanish words and punctuation will be used. Since the reader will be able to discern the meaning from the context, no translations will be given.

4. The discourse in the United States around the use of a term/label for the groups of people who share the Spanish language and other historical, political, social, and cultural legacies is prolific and debated by philosophers, sociologists, historians, journalists, artists, and theologians. Cf. David T. Abalos, *Latinos in the United States: The Sacred and the Political* (Notre Dame, IN: University of Notre Dame Press, 1986); Rodolfo Acuña, *Occupied America: A History of Chicanos*, 3rd ed. (New York: Harper & Row, 1998); Elizabeth Conde-Frazier, *Hispanic Bible Institutes: A Community of Theological Construction* (Scranton, PA: University of Scranton Press, 2004); Geoffrey E. Fox, *Hispanic Nation: Culture, Politics, and the Constructing of Identity* (New York: Carol, 1996); Roberto S. Goizueta, *We Are a People! Initiatives in Hispanic American Theology* (Minneapolis: Fortress, 1992); Juan González, *Harvest of Empire: A History of Latinos in America* (New York: Penguin, 2000); Justo L. González, *Mañana: Christian Theology from a Hispanic Perspective* (Nashville: Abingdon, 1990); Jorge J. E. Gracia, *Hispanic/Latino Identity: A Philosophical Perspective* (Malden, MA: Blackwell, 2000); Denis Lynn Daly Heyck, *Barrios and Borderlands: Cultures of Latinos and Latinas in the United States* (New York: Routledge, 1994); Ada María Isasi-Díaz and Yolanda Tarango, eds., *Hispanic Women: Prophetic Voice in the Church* (San Francisco: Harper & Row, 1988); Luis D. León, *La Llorona's Children: Religion, Life, and Death in the U.S.-Mexican Border-*

Engaging the Experience of the Viewer

lands (Berkeley: University of California Press, 2004); Edward James Olmos, Lea Ybarra, and Manuel Monterrey, eds., *Americanos: Latino Life in the United States = La Vida Latina en los Estados Unidos* (Boston: Little, Brown, 1999); Rubén Rosario Rodríguez and Jeannette Rodríguez, "Teología: Latino/a Contributions to Systematic Theology," paper given at the Annual Meeting of the *American Academy of Religion*, November 2006); Fernando F. Segovia, "Hispanic Americans in Theology and the Church," *Listening* 27 (Winter 1992); and Ilan Stavans, *The Hispanic Condition: Reflections on Culture and Identity in America* (New York: HarperCollins, 1995). Otto Maduro of Drew University suggested at the 2006 Annual Meeting of the American Academy of Religion that, though all words are social constructs with fluid contextual meanings, this does not imply a "sin pensar" use, but rather all words should contain warning labels, like cigarette warning labels. So here is my warning label: For the purposes of this paper, I will now use the term "US Latinas/os" because of my focus on bilingual Spanish-speaking women from numerous countries of origin in the Americas and Caribbean who now live in the United States, and because this term coincides with uses found in other print and visual media.

5. See also the National Council of La Raza Web site's "Twenty of the Most Frequently Asked Questions About Hispanics in the U.S.," www.nclr.org/content/faqs/detail/396.

6. Isasi-Díaz and Tarango, *Hispanic Women*, 117. The reasoning behind these authors' use of the word *remnant* is worth noting: "We refuse to use *minority* or *marginalized* since these labels communicate the way the dominant group sees us. The biblical concept of remnant seems to describe us better: a hermeneutically privileged group with a significant contribution to make. The function of the remnant in the Bible was to challenge the structures. This is in keeping with the way we understand our task as Hispanic Women: we do not want to participate in present oppressive systems, but rather we want to change those systems."

7. US Census Bureau, *Facts for Features*, "Hispanic Heritage Month: Sept. 15–Oct. 15, 2006," www.census.gov/Press-Release/www/releases/archives/facts_for_features_special_editions/007173.html; Rodríguez and Rodríguez, "Teologia."

8. The National Council of La Raza Web site's "Twenty of the Most Frequently Asked Questions," and US Census Bureau, *Facts for Features*, "Hispanic Heritage Month."

9. While the accuracy of the Worldometers Web site is beyond my expertise, numbers noted are illustrative of the ever-changing face of global literacy and communication in which film has become a significant player. Data collected November 22, 2006, 2:55 pm. See www.worldometers.info.

10. According to one pollster, viewers in the United States watched on average thirty-eight movies in theaters, homes, or planes in 2003 (57 percent of all Americans watched *Finding Nemo*; 45 percent saw *Pirates of the Caribbean: The Curse of the Black Pearl*; and 42 percent saw *Bruce Almighty*). Among adults, 95 percent saw at least one movie that same year, while only 47 percent read one book the previous year. Robert K. Johnston, *Reel Spirituality: Theology and Film in Dialogue*, 2nd ed. (Grand Rapids: Baker Academic, 2006), 25.

11. *Evoke* comes from the Latin word *evocare*, from e-, "out," and vocare, "to call," and thus means "to call out" or "to call forth." Synonyms include "rouse," "illicit," and "summon," Webster's New Twentieth Century Dictionary of the English Language, unabridged 2nd ed.; Online Etymology Dictionary, http://etymonline.com, s.v. "evoke." My choice of this word is important as Latinas have their own strong voices. There is neither need nor liberation in speaking for them, in "giving them voice." See, for example, Isasi-Díaz and Tarango, *Hispanic Women*, and bell hooks in Norman K. Denzin and Yvonna S. Lincoln, eds., *Handbook of Qualitative Research* (Thousand Oaks, CA: Sage Publications, 1994), 70–82.

12. Marlene Dermer (director and cofounder), Los Angeles Latino International Film Festival, 2006 Program Book, 2.

13. Mateo 13:13, 16, Reina-Valera Version.

14. See also Herbert Jump, *The Religious Possibilities of the Motion Picture* (New Britain, CT: South Congregational Church Private Distribution, 1911), reprinted in Terry Lindvall, *The Silents of God: Selected Issues and Documents in Silent American Film and Religion, 1908–1925* (Lanham, MD: Scarecrow, 2001), 55–56; Matt Rindge, "Modern Parables: Jesus' Wisdom in Contemporary Film," *Christianity and Theatre*, Fall/Winter 2004:23–31.

15. The ongoing and complex discussion regarding film's context, text, and viewer response has a long history as illustrated by the debate between the Frankfurt School and British Cultural Studies.

16. Dermer, Los Angeles Latino International Film Festival, 2006 Program Book, 2.

17. Lorenza Muñoz, "Filling Theater Seats but Not Movie Jobs," *Los Angeles Times*, October 15, 2006.

18. *Variety* Web site; their International Department and Film Box Office display box office receipts for the following Spanish-speaking countries: Argentina, Chile, Mexico, and Spain; www.variety.com/index.asp.

19. For examples see Johnston, *Reel Spirituality*.

20. Fuguet was born in Chile but lived in Encino, CA until he was twelve years old, when he suddenly moved back to Chile. *Time, Newsweek,* and the *New York Times* have all taken notice of this Chilean/United States writer. Rayo-HarperCollins published his book *Las Películas de mi Vida* because they wanted to "publish books that reflect the Hispanic experience in the U.S." His books feature frequent references to the respective popular cultures of the two countries. See Marcela Valdes, "Split Screen," *Críticas*, October 1, 2003, www.libraryjournal.com/article/CA330165.html.

21. "Lo cotidiano" has been discussed by numerous Latina/o theologians as a source of theological reflection. However, most of this conversation has been directed at popular religious practices, art, music, celebrations, literature, or "testimonios." Very little work has been done regarding film or other media that have Latina/o themes, or are aimed at the Latina/o market, and which form part of the everyday lives of today's Latinas/os.

22. Justo González, "Theology and Its Sources: Scripture, Tradition, Experience, and Imagination," in *The Ties That Bind: African American and Hispanic American/Latino/a Theology in Dialogue*, ed. Anthony B. Pinn and Benjamin Valentin (New York: Continuum, 2001); and González, *Mañana*.

23. Samuel Solivan, *The Spirit, Pathos and Liberation: Toward a Hispanic Theology* (Sheffield, England: Sheffield Academic Press, 1998).

24. Dr. Rodríguez made her comments at the 2006 Annual Meeting of the American Academy of Religion. See also Gloria Anzaldúa, *Borderlands = La Frontera*, 2nd ed. (San Francisco: Aunt Lute Books, 1999); Ada María Isasi-Díaz, *En La Lucha = In the Struggle: A Hispanic Women's Liberation Theology* (Minneapolis: Fortress, 1993); Isasi-Díaz and Tarango, *Hispanic Women*.

25. Respondent at the regular meeting of the Los Angeles chapter of the Fraternidad Teológica Latinoamericana, November 29, 2006.

26. All of the women who participated were given an informed-consent form to sign. All films were viewed in Spanish or with Spanish subtitles. All written documents, including the questions regarding the films, were produced in Spanish. All focus groups were conducted in Spanish.

27. One of the women is an involved Catholic parishioner, but is attending a Protestant seminary, and is thus conversant with Protestant theology and ethos. The other women are part of historic mainline (Presbyterian, Methodist) or evangelical Protestant churches.

28. As Father Allan Figueroa Deck suggests, much work in Latina/o history, sociology, religious studies, and theology focuses on Texas, Miami, New York, or Chicago and much less on California or Los Angeles, although "at least a third of all US Latinos are found there"; "Their Distinctive Presence," review of *Latinos and the New Immigrant Church*, by David A. Badillo,

Engaging the Experience of the Viewer

America: The National Catholic Weekly 195, no. 18 (December 4, 2006). Actually, 2004 Census Bureau estimates suggest that the figure is closer to 35 percent.

29. Some of the Euro-American filmmakers have lived in Latin American or in Latina/o contexts, while others have not.

30. The budget totals and total US box office receipts for these films were based on the budgets and box office numbers listed for the individual films on the Internet Movie Database (www.imdb.com) and www.boxofficemojo.com.

31. The major themes discussed below come directly from the women. Any theme or issue that I may have noted during my experience of the films was not included in this reflection unless also commented on by others in the group. Occasionally I have given some background data so as to give some larger context in which to place the women's comments. However, I mostly refrained from such insertions of cultural, sociological, or film studies data, as well as theological interpretation, so as to stay with the commentary of the women. This ethnographic conversation with film focused on the women's current reality. In the future we hope to reconvene our group so as to explore more deeply the issues/themes raised and to further our theological reflection and praxis. In a way, this group can be likened to Paulo Freire's consciousness-raising community groups or to Comunidades de Base, in which the Bible and daily life intersect in theological reflection and praxis. In this case, we hope to "do theology" with the resources of film (culture), experience, Christian community, Bible, tradition, reason, and imagination.

32. The actress, America Ferrera, is currently portraying Betty in the US remake of *Ugly Betty (Betty la Fea)*.

33. Internet Movie Database plot summary, www.imdb.com/title/++0296166/plot summary.

34. *Spanglish* alone generated $55 million of the box office proceeds of the six films viewed ($80 million total), with 22 percent of the proceeds coming from the international market. Summary box office figures, www.boxofficemojo.com/movies/?id=spanglish.html.

35. See, for examples, Daniel R. Rodríguez and David Cortés Fuentes, eds. *Hidden Stories: Unveiling the History of the Latino Church* (Decatur, GA: Asociación para la Educación Teológica Hispana, 1994); Elizabeth Conde-Frazier, "Testimonios: Narrative, Agency, and the Latina Woman," unpublished paper presented to the Fraternidad Teológica Latinoamericana in 2002; Jeanette Rodríguez, *Stories We Live: Hispanic Women's Spirituality = Cuentos que Vivimos* (New York: Paulist Press, 1996).

36. Numerous panel discussions and papers presented at the 2006 Annual Meeting of the American Academy of Religion debated this topic: e.g., "Beyond Mestizaje: Revisiting Race, Syncretism and Hybridity," "Post-colonial Notions of Mestizaje and Race," "Hybrid Cultures or Multiculturalism: Navigating the Contested Spaces of Mestizaje Discourse(s)."

37. Similarly, Latinas/os, such as Michelle Gonzalez, Jeanette Rodríguez, and Nestor Medina, within the theological academy, have talked about the "Mexicanization" of US Latino theology.

38. Of the six films we viewed, only one had a non-Mexican or non-Mexican American protagonist, and one movie had minor characters from Spanish-speaking countries other than Mexico. In this small sample this equates to roughly 17 percent of the protagonists. When surveying the larger list of films in the list of movies at the end of the chapter, one sees that the percentages are about the same.

39. Given their own social location, they especially appreciated seeing educated professional Latina women being portrayed, even if the portrayal included elements outside of their reality.

40. Focus group, 8/25/06 translated from Spanish.

41. Pierrette Hondagneu-Sotelo, *Doméstica: Immigrant Workers Cleaning and Caring in the Shadows of Affluence* (Berkeley: University of California Press, 2001); Frank Cancian and

Julieta Noemi Lopez, eds., *Orange County Housecleaners* (Albuquerque: University of New Mexico Press, 2006); Barbara Ehrenreich and Arlie Russell Hochschild, eds., *Global Woman: Nannies, Maids, and Sex Workers in the New Economy*, 1st Owl Books ed. (New York: Henry Holt, 2004).

42. Focus group, 8/25/06 translated from Spanish.

43. Compare this portrayal with that of Amelia, the housekeeper in Mexican director Alejandro González Iñárritu's recently released film *Babel* (November 2006), who looks and sounds Mexican, dresses to work, and work hard she does. She too is a heroine, but in a much more tragic way. Unfortunately the film came out after the focus groups met and this essay was in draft form.

44. Both Hondagneu-Sotelo's and Cancian and Lopez's work (see note 41) found that many Latina housekeepers are shocked by the state of the families (distant relationships between parents, rude and undisciplined behavior by children) for whom they work. In this sense *Spanglish* depicts reality.

45. Deck, "Their Distinctive Presence," 2006.

46. Focus Group, 8/25/06 translated from Spanish.

47. The documentary and photo-journal *Americanos* highlights this desire. Olmos, Ybarra, and Monterrey, *Americanos*.

48. "We are love, we are rage, we are a mix. Life hurts but you have to make love stronger." From the film *Luminarias,* 2000. Andrea says this to her son, Joey, as he is getting ready to go to his prom. Andrea is played by the actress and screenwriter of the movie, Evelina Fernández.

49. Focus group, 10/26/06 translated from Spanish.

50. Focus group, 8/25/06 translated from Spanish.

51. Focus groups, 8/25/06 and 10/26/06 translated from Spanish.

52. Some of the women use the word "mujerona" to describe such women and themselves.

53. Focus group, 8/25/06, meaning "neither here nor there."

54. Dialogue from *Bread and Roses,* 2000.

55. Focus groups, 8/25/06 and 10/26/06 translated from Spanish. Cf. Anzaldúa, *Borderlands = La Frontera,* 1999.

56. Focus group, 8/25/06 translated from Spanish.

57. Written comments received 11/28/06 from one participant.

58. Numerous Latino theologians, sociologists, historians, or activists speak of the margins occupied by Latinas/os or Protestant Latinas/os, and some speak of the margins that Catholic Latina women occupy, but none that I know of have focused on Protestant Latina women who are single. Cf. Isasi-Díaz and Tarango, *Hispanic Women*; Daisy L. Machado, *Of Borders and Margins: Hispanic Disciples in Texas, 1888–1945*, American Academy of Religion Academy Series (New York: Oxford University Press, 2003); Arlene M. Sánchez-Walsh, *Latino Pentecostal Identity: Evangelical Faith, Self, and Society*, Religion and American Culture (New York: Columbia University Press, 2003).

59. *Feijoada*, the Brazilian national dish, is a delicious stew. From its domestic origin in the kitchens of Brazil it has made its way to the hallowed halls of academia as a new metaphor to describe Brazilian society with its mix of mixed-race peoples. Stephen Engler, "Mesticagem, Brasilidade, and Feijoada: Extending Brazilian Writings on Hybridity," paper given at the Annual Meeting of the American Academy of Religion Conference, November 2006.

60. Respondent at the regular meeting of the Los Angeles Chapter of the Fraternidad Teológica Latinoamericana, November 29, 2006.

61. Johnston, *Reel Spirituality*, 51.

62. Quoted in Peter Malone and Rose Pacatte, *Lights, Camera . . . Faith! A Movie Lover's Guide to Scripture: A Movie Lectionary—Cycle A* (Boston: Pauline Books & Media, 2001), xi.

63. Quiero dar miles de gracias a las mujeronas que me ayudaron en este proyecto. Un besito a Claudia Mendoza, Thelma Herrera, Yliana Gallegos, Flor Graterol, Rosario Ibarra, Emma Rodriguez, Margarita Flores, Ana Gan, y Jackeline Vives.

Section 5

Reconsidering
the Normative

10

Theology and Film
Interreligious Dialogue and Theology

JOHN LYDEN

Theology and Religious Studies

In my book *Film as Religion: Myths, Morals, and Rituals* (2003), I argued that popular culture and media, and especially popular films, function in many ways that are similar to the ways that religion functions.[1] I proposed a model for interpreting film in relation to religion that does not so much view them through the familiar opposition of "culture" and "religion," but rather suggests that they be seen as two forms of religious influences interacting in much the same way that different religions interact. If religion is a part of culture, then there is no way to completely separate religion from culture—and if those aspects of culture that are usually viewed as nonreligious or opposed to religion meet many of the same functions of what we call religions, then we also cannot really separate culture from religion. Both operate through symbolic systems of meaning, and one can identify the forms of myths, morals, and rituals within both. Arguably, then, the dialogue between popular culture or film and religion can be seen as an interreligious dialogue.

Advancing this thesis puts me in a curious position in regard to the emerging field of "*theology* and film," which is the subject of this volume. On the one hand, it may seem that my proposals put my approach within the area of "*religion* and film" studies rather than within that of *theology* and film. As support for this, one might note that I have criticized some theological approaches to film as too narrow, as I have held that one should look to more that is "religious" in films than simply their parallels to Christian theology. But I am not ready to accept this alleged dichotomy between "religious studies" and "theology." I do realize that there are academic departments defined as one or the other, with some very different assumptions about method, truth, human reason, and so on. If asked to summarize and defend that difference, I would probably define "religious studies" as the field made up of those who study religion *descriptively* in order to understand what it *is* and how it works, for example, what people believe, and why; and "theology" as the field made up of those who study religion in order to make *normative* claims about what people (at least of a particular religious community) *ought* to believe. As such, theology is more particularistic, and also usually interested in transcendent or at least transhistorical truth claims. And although I will admit that this distinction is an important one in certain contexts, I have ultimately found it inadequate as a description of the two fields, for there is considerable overlap between these tasks, which can never be fully separated.

In support of my suggestion that one cannot fully distinguish the approaches of theology and religious studies, I refer to an analogous discussion in Paul Tillich's work regarding theology and philosophy. Tillich claimed that all theologians need to be philosophers, and all philosophers need to be theologians. For while theologians profess to study the *meaning* of being and philosophers the *structure* of being, one cannot really separate one task from the other.[2] Theologians must use the categories of philosophy to analyze being (Aquinas needs his Aristotle, Augustine his Plato, Barth his Kant and Hegel), and so are "anonymous philosophers"— but it is also true that philosophers must advance particular claims about truth and meaning and so are "anonymous theologians." Both tasks are necessary and are ultimately complementary rather than contradictory.

Clearly, not all philosophers and theologians have been willing to admit this. Theologians are suspicious of philosophical agendas being imported into religious doctrine; most notably, Karl Barth insisted that all philosophi-

Reconsidering the Normative

cal concepts used by the theologian be made subordinate to Scripture's object, the Word of God.[3] Barth also recognized that theology is human speech just as philosophy is, and that it cannot claim to be God's Word. At the same time, Barth insisted that God, through the grace of God, uses sinful human language (whether as theology, philosophy, or whatever) as the medium to express God's Word, in spite of its inadequacy to the task.[4] What Barth had more trouble admitting was that there could be a genuine interchange of ideas between theology and philosophy, and that he may not have been only appropriating philosophy for theological purposes but in fact was also affected by it in developing the content of his theology.

Philosophers, also, do not usually take well to being called prototheologians. But to profess an "objective" approach based on "reason" and "logic" instead of "faith," as philosophers once did, has been shown to be suspect in that there is no perspective that stands outside of particularistic assumptions. And so individual philosophers as much as theologians have a point of view, albeit perhaps one not identified with a set of assumptions held by a particular religious tradition. Of course, most contemporary philosophers would not claim a perspective of "absolute reason" as did some of their forebears, but they might insist that they are able to examine philosophical questions without being beholden to a religious tradition as theologians are. Here they need to be reminded that, even without a formal commitment to a tradition, they have hosts of assumptions that are analogous to those of Christianity or another religion.[5]

One can see the relevance of Tillich's distinctions to the relationship between theology and religious studies. Just as Tillich noted that one cannot do theology without doing philosophy, nor the reverse, so one cannot really do theology without doing religious studies, and the religious studies scholar cannot completely avoid being a theologian. Theologians need to let the religious studies agenda into their own constructive tasks, including gaining a better understanding of other religions and the disciplines used to study them (including sociology, history, anthropology, etc.). One cannot construct a decent theology simply by focusing on internal norms, such as coherence with Scripture or tradition; one also needs to be able to deal with the data of the world and its cultures, taking account of their diversity and being responsible to the norms of scholarship (such as gathering all relevant facts and analyzing them logically and consistently) as one studies other religions, other cultures, and other ways of thinking about them.

The charge to theologians to also be scholars of religion implies a charge to scholars of religion to admit that they are also theologians of a sort. Scholars of religion, in spite of a professed desire to understand and describe religion as it is, inevitably have their own assumptions regarding religious truth and hence make normative claims about religion as well. Clearly, scholars of religion will admit to accepting the norms of good scholarship (that is, that one should attempt to gather all relevant data, assess it fairly, seek to understand it, and so on) just as natural scientists have such norms of honesty, thoroughness, and consistency governing the tasks of responsible data gathering and the construction of theories to explain data. But even natural scientists make assumptions about religion that affect their work, for example, whether religion is compatible with the conclusions of science or not. Religion scholars, even more so because their subject is not natural science but religion per se, will have numerous assumptions about the nature of truth in religion. Scholars of religion may believe it to be fully explainable by empirical causes, and so in principle exclude transcendent ones; they may assume all religions share a similar form or content, which is defined by their categories; and so on. Taken together, these ideas form a set of theological assumptions that are not the product of scholarship but the premises to it. They may not correspond to the theology of any community or recognized religion, but they are theological in nature nonetheless, and cannot claim any greater objectivity than the assumptions of a Christian theologian. Scholars of religious studies have often insisted that their scientific or historical approaches allow them greater objectivity and the ability to transcend the arbitrary assumptions of theologians, since the latter are based on faith rather than reason. But once again, Tillich would remind us, we cannot avoid having both a faith (an ultimate concern, a point of view, a commitment of our being) and reason (the ability to analyze and develop points of view conceptually).[6]

This recognition that theology and religious studies cannot be totally separated does not mean that we need to abandon our separate fields. We will continue to be more expert in one field than another, but we can also be more conversant with the conclusions of other fields and be able to engage in intelligent dialogue with them. Thus the theologian and the religious studies scholar need to understand what the other is doing, and recognize the validity of the other field without necessarily accepting every conclusion the other advances. After all, I do not need to accept all the conclusions even of the others in my own field, and the fact that I lack expertise in a different field should not mean that I have no right to an opinion about its conclusions, as long as my opinions are well-informed and attempt as fair an evaluation of the other as I can provide. Academians can often be very intolerant of such judgments made by those outside their fields, but it is crucial that we be able to engage in this sort of interdisciplinary dialogue unless we wish to establish separate academic bunkers that permit no passage between them. If we cut ourselves off in this way, we have no ability to engage in a shared quest for truth that requires the ability to hear and assess each other's conclusions.

Here it will also be clear that the theologian or religion scholar who does film studies is in a similar position. I am no expert in film studies and probably never will be, but I can study the scholarship of film and make my own evaluations of it from the vantage point provided by my own field as well as by my general ability to analyze and critique academic scholarship. In this way, all scholarship is enlarged as we create dialogues between academic fields and so create new ways to understand things. Academic fields can sometimes be even more resistant to dialogue than religions, concerned as they are with safeguarding departments and sometimes unexamined assumptions. But dialogue we must if we are to advance our understanding, since remaining impervious to dialogue will leave us unchallenged in our assumptions and unable to develop and deal with new experiences and new data.

Interreligious Dialogue and Theology

So far, I have advanced a case for dialogue on the basis of a certain understanding of the structure of knowledge, and the fact that all disciplines have distinctive assumptions and a particular point of view (a faith) as well as the ability to converse on the basis of shared assumptions (reason). On this basis, theology and religious studies need to see that their differences are not absolute, just as interdisciplinary dialogue should include such partners as film studies and religious studies, anthropology, history, and the natural sciences. There is also, however, a case to be made for interreligious dialogue from the perspective of theology itself. By training I am a Christian theologian, and my interest in film stems in no small part from my self-identification as such. It is precisely out of concern for the future of Christianity, as well as other religions, that I encourage interreligious dialogue as an essential task of Christian theology. Any legitimate developments in Christian thought will have to take account of the fact that Christianity exists in a religiously plural world, and in fact that it always has; it has now become almost impossible to deny this. Of course, there are those who refuse to accept this religious pluralism; in this way, fundamentalisms are born out of a perceived need to defend a particular viewpoint without regard to dialogue, insisting that their own religious truth claims can be made as absolute claims, or as the only possible truth claims, never stopping to consider whether other truth claims might be viable. But if we take the fact of pluralism seriously and wish to still do Christian theology, it will have to be done in a way that can continue to make particularistic truth claims while acknowledging the real challenges posed by religious diversity.

Interreligious dialogue, then, is not simply the making of interesting comparisons between religions in order to increase our general understanding of how religions function. No, interreligious dialogue only occurs *between religions*, and so presupposes that those involved in it have a stake in how it comes out. It is then essentially a theological task, on each side, as normative claims about truth are made by each participant. Each partner has a point of view that he or she is desirous of defending, and although one hopes the partners are ready to hear and learn from the others as well, even to change their own views through the dialogue, no religious participant will regard what happens to his or her own view as a matter of indifference. I may have to believe different things about myself, my religion, and about other religions, if I am genuinely open in dialogue. This is both frightening and exhilarating; it carries risk, but also possibility. Just as Christian theology has had to learn to be open to the scientific analysis of Scripture, as well as to the conclusions of the natural and social sciences, so Christian theology also must be open to hearing the views of other religions, unless it is to keep its head in the sand and deny the existence of everything outside of itself—once again, fundamentalism has tried this, but has had to pay a heavy price in its inability to relate to any other views.

It should be made clear from the outset, however, that this openness to other views—whether scientific, historical, or those of other religious traditions—in no way implies a blind acceptance of those views without evaluation or judgment. Those who fear dialogue seem to fear just this sort of acceptance, an empty tolerance that can make no truth claims of any sort because truth, in our postmodern world, has been declared to be relative. But this can never happen, in that we will always make judgments in any case; we cannot accept every point of view as true, because there are contradictory views among them. What is at issue is only the basis on which we make those judgments. Dialogue and openness presuppose that an informed judgment is best, one that is not so defensive that it cannot hear challenges. If we listen, we may be changed, Christian thinking about its central doctrines may even change, but we need not fear the demise of Christian truth claims—for if they are in fact true, they will survive all challenges.[7]

If we accept another religion as a dialogue partner, then, it means being open to what it has to say without prejudging it. We need to determine how it functions religiously before we can evaluate it. As Jonathan Smith has observed, we should not merely ask of another religion, "How is it like-us or not-like-us?" It might be argued that all dialogue has to start with this, but if we are confined by this question, we will never gain any real comprehension of the religion. If it is seen only as "like-us," a mirror image of ourselves, it is not other, and cannot be understood as such. On the other hand, if it is merely "not-like-us," it is so alien we cannot relate to it at all, and we again fail to understand it. The history of religious interaction is rife with this sort of simplification, which has alternately seen other religions as "anonymous" followers of one's own tradition (as Native American religion, e.g., was often viewed as a primitive form of Christianity) or as demonic cults. But it has on occasion been possible to transcend this dichotomy through genuine listening to the other that results in real understanding and an acknowledgment of both the similarities to and differences from one's own religion.[8]

Being nonjudgmental, however, does not mean withholding all judgment forever, as total relativism would require. If we refuse to make judgments about another out of a supposed need for tolerance, we may be reduced to the position of sympathetic listeners who are never able to move to analysis, out of fear of imposing our values on the other. Such an approach results in a pointless relativism that simply observes the other but cannot relate to it or even learn anything from it; essentially, this makes the other "not-like-us" all over again, although this time it does not demonize the other as evil but simply counts the other as irrelevant. This does not allow for any real dialogue with the other that can result in changes to our self-understanding or our understanding of the other. Genuine dialogue presupposes that there is truth to be gained through dialogue, that is, truth exists as distinct from the individual religions so that we can consider to what extent each coheres or refers to that transcendent truth. On the other hand, total relativism allows for no truth outside of a particular viewpoint, and if each view can only refer to itself as a standard for truth, we have no shared concept of truth on the basis of which we could compare our understandings to determine to what extent they are similar or different. If each religion is its own standard only, there is no point in comparisons between them.

Real dialogue, then, acknowledges that just as I must admit the other has a viable claim to truth, I can make my own claim for truth. It is acceptable, and indeed necessary, that the observer have a religious position. There is no Promethean standpoint outside of religion altogether. My view may be eclectic or iconoclastic in regard to historic religions, but it is a position nonetheless. Even the supposedly objective scholars of religion, as we have seen, make assumptions regarding the views they study. One must acknowledge this viewpoint and its effect on one's view, to the extent that it plays a role in how I see the other. In this sense, it is necessary to admit prejudices not as impediments to the process of understanding, but as its preconditions, as Hans-Georg Gadamer has pointed out.[9] I need to be able to see similarities between my views and the views I study that are not my own, but I also need to acknowledge the differences in perspective. Only through this sort of open recognition can the dialogue partners actually gain in understanding of each other, and be transformed in the process.

Interreligious Dialogue and Film

Film as Religion

The relevance of the preceding to the dialogue between theology/religion and film may still be in question. Granting that there is no absolute distinction between theology and religious studies, that dialogue between religions is crucial to their self-understanding, and even that there is no absolute distinction between culture and religion, still it may not be so clear that something like popular film is sufficiently "religion-like" to merit a dialogue such as other interreligious dialogues. After all, there is no self-identified community of religious adherents of film. We can observe the religion-like character of their devotion, films' religion-like affect on them, even the temporary communities and ritual observances formed by film viewing. But in general, there will not be a community to have a dialogue with, if by that we mean a group that will identify itself as a "religion" and seek dialogue with us.

In this way, the interreligious dialogue that I propose, between popular culture and theology/religion, will not be exactly like some other dialogues. There will not be a high priest of film sitting across the table from a Christian theologian as they examine the similarities and differences in their viewpoints. Even if we should find someone willing to take on such a role, he or she would not be able to speak for all filmmakers or

Reconsidering the Normative

filmgoers. There is not *one* religion of film; there are filmic religions. This means that film viewing has religious aspects to it, and there are religious elements in filmgoing, but they are often diverse and contradictory. There is not one set of values or myths purveyed by films, and even a single film permits multiple interpretations. Furthermore, the dialogue does not involve a Christian church on the one hand and a community of filmgoers on the other hand. Christians are already implicated in popular culture, so the dialogue must take place within our individual psyches as well as within our religious communities. Churches need not only to ask, "What are *Christians* supposed to think or feel about this film," but also "What do we think or feel about this film?" As a filmgoer, we are all already practicing the religion of film every time we go to the movies, and the latter question acknowledges this fact. If we are Christians, asking this question does not stop us from being Christians, but it acknowledges that there are multiple sets of religious influences on us, and indeed we all have diverse sets of religious myths, morals, and rituals operative for each of us. There is not one set of these that makes one Christian or not, anymore than there is one set of myths, morals, and rituals that defines the filmic religion. Christianity is not some monolithic entity that exists apart from other cultural and religious elements; it is a particular set of such, defined by certain historic traditions, but ever changing as it interacts with other cultural and religious elements.

The relevance of the model of interreligious dialogue is that it allows us to ask what the film is trying to do for us or to us, religiously speaking, apart from questions about the extent to which it coheres with Christianity (or any other religious tradition) or in what ways it is a fit dialogue partner for what we identify as our own religious tradition. This allows for the sort of analysis of the functions of films that I attempted in *Film as Religion*. What was not present there was an analysis of how this knowledge of the filmic religion might impact Christian theology. Because I have here defended the importance of interreligious dialogue to theology, I would like to now suggest some things that Christian theology might learn from the filmic religion. This will necessarily be sketchy and brief, but I can here suggest some of the ways that Christian theology might develop as a result of this dialogue.

The Dialogue between Christianity and Filmic Religion

In *Film as Religion* I identified seven genres of film, not as an exhaustive list but as a suggestion about how to discuss the ways different sorts of films act on us. For each of these, I noted how the films provide liminal experiences of escape from our everyday reality and a catharsis of emotions that may help us return to normalcy afterward. What I may not have done well enough was to articulate how the worldview and values advanced in a film go beyond mere cathartic entertainment. If it is only a temporary fantasy release from the world, it has little impact on how we live or think outside the movie theater. In the same way, if a religion only offers a brief escape from our troubles, "hope for the hopeless," then it really is only the "opiate of the people," as Marx believed. But if religion changes our views of how the world is and how it ought to be, then its liminal world echoes back on our own to make some difference.[10] This difference can be assessed as the "message" of the religion to its adherents, and films have messages to their followers as well. In what follows, I will look at two themes that are found in filmic religions as well as in Christianity, to see how the interreligious dialogue between them might inform the way we view these themes. They are violence and hope.

Violence in Film

Westerns and action films, in particular, tend to legitimate violence as necessary, viewing the world largely in dualistic terms as a struggle between good and evil. In these films, those who do not see the necessity of using violence to fight evil are fools to believe that evil can be defeated without it. Pacifists are impractical or cowardly, and are often the first victims of the evil forces they underestimate. On the other hand, the one who uses "righteous violence" to save the community may suffer for doing so, because society cannot contain within itself the one who is tainted by this violence. In this sense, he is a scapegoat who bears the punishment for using the very violence that the community has deemed necessary for its salvation; he is isolated and rejected precisely because of this role.[11]

To put this view into dialogue with Christianity, we can ask, How does this differ from Christian views of the one who takes our place to pay for our sins? For one thing, the savior of the Western/action film is clearly not a sinless savior, so he is legitimately punished in a certain sense, but he is also clearly one of us, representing and personifying our own sins instead of being the sinless one punished unjustly in our place. The message of the Western/action film is that violence is legitimate and necessary, whereas the message of Christianity is that violence is no longer needed since the sinless one has died to end the power of all sin and violence. At this point, it is tempting to moralize about the violence of movies in

Reconsidering the Normative

comparison with the pacifist ethics of Jesus. But here we must recall that Christians do not all tend to be pacifists, suggesting that they are already beholden to the theology of the Western/action film, and that the biblical message has been muted in their own religious practice. This has always been very clear during wartime in the United States in particular, since during these times Christians (and others) are particularly supportive of violence. The present "war on terror" is certainly no exception. This is not necessarily because people are seeing too many Westerns or action movies, but rather because the values of these films have already been internalized by Christians in spite of their apparent disconnect from the values of biblical Christianity. There are political and sociological reasons why Christians support values that legitimate violence, and why Christians are susceptible to media manipulation when it gives further support to such values. Analysis of films also shows us that these values are well expressed in popular culture and provides us with a forum for examining them.

Thus far, this analysis could be provided by ideological criticism, and it would not seem essential to recognize the religious power of film to come to such insights. However, there are certain advantages to doing so. One is that of recognizing the power of images that are linked to religious symbology, so that if one admits the content of the film is *religious*, it can be seen how the filmic religion has come to be so effective and in fact may be displacing the values of other religions. The films suggest that meaning and purpose are found through violence, that revenge is redemptive and satisfying, and that those who kill for us are righteous. This is a religious message and hence a powerful one.

Second, creating an interreligious dialogue with the film that explicitly recognizes its religious content can help Christians to see more clearly the differences between the theology of the New Testament and the theology of the Western film. If we fail to see the extent to which films influence and express our beliefs and values about issues as critical as the justification of violence, we will be ill-equipped to step back and critique those values.

Third, understanding how the film functions religiously in providing myths, morals, and rituals also allows us to see that it functions in diverse ways for different people. There is no automatic blueprint of meaning that is read from a given film for all viewers; I argued in *Film as Religion* that it is not the case that all violent films encourage or approve of violence, or that they necessarily create people more willing to sanction violence.[12] This is important to recognize even or especially if we are to be critical of popular culture, since a critical analysis will have more validity if it does not dogmatically insist that there is only one way to read a film. Such a dogmatic view opens itself to easy refutation when it is pointed out that not all people who enjoy Westerns or action films approve of violence; there are even pacifists who watch and like them, perhaps because they appreciate the heroes who see injustice and are courageous enough to fight it, even if they do so (regrettably) with violent means. We need to realize that there are many meanings that can come from a film, and be sensitive to them, in order to give a more sophisticated analysis of how films function for audiences. Christians, then, may watch violent films but receive from them messages that do not sanction violence, but that express other values that may be distinct from but not antithetical to Christian values, such as courage, hope, and honor.

Hope in Film

A second theme found in many popular films is hope. In romantic comedies, we have the message of hope that true love can be found by those who seek it, if they are willing to commit to it and take the risk of having faith in it. In *Film as Religion* I pointed out that this myth may have produced unrealistic expectations for relationships, which when frustrated leave people without an effective "myth" by which to work on a relationship. Instead, the quest for an ideal relationship may lead people to give up on real relationships and embark on a series of failures.[13] This may be claiming too much, but the myth of romantic perfection does seem to be part of the message conveyed by these very popular films. Hope is also a theme in melodramatic tearjerkers, especially classic women's films in which the main female character suffers unjustly but is able to overcome her suffering and go on, even in the face of loss. *Titanic* is a modern example of this genre: it showed that women can be strong and survive through empathy and believing in themselves rather than trusting in wealth and power.[14]

In the case of both romantic comedies and tearjerkers—both of which tend to be marketed to women and appeal mainly to them—there is an appeal to the hope that things can be better. And they usually are by the end of the film. The neat endings supplied by such films belie the messy character of real life, which does not always satisfy us in the same way. Popular films often give us an ideal world filled with unrealistic hopes that are magically fulfilled by the time we leave the theater. This lack of realism, however, is itself part of the religious character of films since they portray an ideal world that we can juxtapose with the real world, and that we can aspire to achieve. If we expect these ideals to be fully actualized

Reconsidering the Normative

in our experience, they may mislead and give false hopes that cannot be literally fulfilled—but as myths, they provide a model of how reality might be, and a portrait of something we can strive toward.

This is true of Christian ideals as well; for while Christian theologians may point out that the biblical story includes a real recognition of the need for pain and suffering (the cross) rather than the simplistic happy endings of popular films, it is also true that the Bible provides a rather neat and happy ending in the resurrection of Jesus Christ and the hope for his second coming. Suffering does not have the last word in the Bible. As with most films, people like happy endings and want to believe that there is more to life than suffering. This hope enables them to cope with their lives, by believing in an ideal that transcends what can normally be found in the world of ordinary reality.

The hope offered by popular films differs from that of Christianity, but it is a hope nonetheless, and its religious character should be recognized. Thus we can admit the similarities between their myths as well as their differences, and we may think differently about both in the process. For example, we can admit a similarity in that happy endings are not bad even when they are unrealistic, for they are necessary ideals for all religions; and we can acknowledge differences, in that popular films tend to place their hope in human beings rather than in God. At the same time, these hopes need not be totally rejected, for although they are less than ultimate from a Christian point of view, it is not bad in itself to have some self-confidence and courage, or to believe that humans can truly love each other.

Conclusions

It is my hope that Christian theologians who are interested in popular culture will see the relevance of viewing films-as-religion to their own task; such an analysis of popular culture will enable Christians to engage in a genuine dialogue with culture that transcends simplistically embracing or rejecting it. No matter what our religious perspectives may be, we need to understand what popular culture is doing in order to assess it, and we need to be able to make informed critical judgments based on careful listening to the messages of filmic religions as well as honest and fair critique. I hope to see more of this type of analysis in the years to come as we develop a multiplicity of methods for viewing and understanding popular culture, from theological as well as other points of view.

Notes

1. John Lyden, *Film as Religion: Myths, Morals, and Rituals* (New York: New York University Press, 2003).
2. Paul Tillich, *Dynamics of Faith* (New York: Harper, 1957), 89–95; Tillich, *Systematic Theology*, vol. 1 (Chicago: University of Chicago Press, 1951), 18–28.
3. See, e.g., Karl Barth, *Church Dogmatics*, vol. 1, part 2, trans. G. T. Thomson and Harold Knight (Edinburgh: T&T Clark, 1956), 729–40.
4. Karl Barth, *Church Dogmatics*, vol. 1, part 1, trans. G. T. Thomson (Edinburgh: T&T Clark, 1936), 188–90.
5. Nicholas Rescher is one philosopher who has admitted that different philosophical positions may be equally tenable because they are based on different assumptions that cannot be proven true or false. One must choose a point of view about certain philosophical questions even while admitting that other views are equally plausible and defensible if they are consistent with their own assumptions. He has developed this view, known as "orientational pluralism," in *The Strife of Systems* (Pittsburgh: Pittsburgh University Press, 1985). S. Mark Heim adapts this approach to interreligious dialogue in *Salvations: Truth and Difference in Religion* (Maryknoll, NY: Orbis Books, 1995), esp. 133–44.
6. Tillich, *Dynamics of Faith*, 74–80. I do not think that Tillich's basic point here requires the assumption of a universal concept of human reason; rather, reason here stands for intellectual thought functioning heuristically as conceptual analysis, which may take diverse forms in different cultures.
7. John Cobb has claimed that Christian loyalty to Christ itself requires interreligious dialogue, since the affirmation that Divine Wisdom is present in Jesus "cannot mean that Jesus is the only channel through which God is present in the world." If Christians affirm the relevance of Christ to all, they must be open to other faiths as places where that same Wisdom might be revealed, albeit in different ways. John B. Cobb Jr., "Toward a Christocentric Catholic Theology," in *Toward a Universal Theology of Religion*, ed. Leonard Swidler (Maryknoll, NY: Orbis Books, 1988), 89.
8. Jonathan Z. Smith, "Adde Parvum Parvo Magnus Acervus Erit," in *Map Is Not Territory: Studies in the History of Religions* (Leiden: Brill, 1978), 240–64. I discuss Smith's point in Lyden, *Film as Religion*, 109–13.
9. Hans-Georg Gadamer, *Truth and Method* (New York: Seabury, 1975), 245–74.
10. Lyden, *Film as Religion*, 102–4.
11. Ibid., 91–92, 142–43.
12. Ibid., 101, 152, 156.
13. Ibid., 179–90.
14. Ibid., 171–78.

11

From Film Emotion
to Normative Criticism

MITCH AVILA

Contemporary analytic philosophy of film is marked by two distinct developments. The first is the near absence of discussion of ideology and ideology critique—what was perhaps the single most important subject matter of twentieth-century film theory. The second is the growing importance of cognitive science for aesthetic theories of emotion. Empirically based theories of emotion are easily one of the most significant and rapidly expanding areas of contemporary aesthetics. In this chapter I propose that the notable lacuna created by the collapse of ideology critique—that is, the current dearth of normative critical analysis of film—can be usefully addressed by turning to philosophical theories of spectator emotion. Theories of spectator emotion informed by cognitive science not only are excellent resources for understanding how films reliably produce affective responses, but in addition direct our attention to significant aspects of film that contribute to—or oftentimes, frustrate—the creation of just societies and ethically mature agents. The simultaneous waning of ideology critique and the waxing of scientifically informed theories of emotion provide us with the unprecedented opportunity to create a practice of film critique that combines an empirically defensible model of spectator emotion with nuanced and thoughtful normative reflection.

From Ideology to Psychology

Once the most common scholarly treatment of film, ideology critique consisted of analyzing the complicity of film in fostering the entrenched, ubiquitous social injustices that characterize late capitalist culture. Over the past several decades, film scholars have produced a voluminous body of literature that is impressive for its quality, innovation, and scope. As Noël Carroll noted, "One has the feeling that the study of mass art in the humanities is almost virtually co-extensive with the study of ideology."[1] Explanations of how film is "an agency of ideological manipulation, a means by which ostensibly oppressive systems, notably capitalism, sustain dominion,"[2] run a wide gamut. On the one end is *ideological formalism,* the position that film, through its use of such things as perspective, projection apparatus, editing techniques, and narrative structure is inherently ideological because it positions the subject as a Cartesian ego. Louis Althusser is the main theorist of this view, and Noël Carroll characterizes this methodology as the dominant approach in film studies today. Related approaches include Laura Mulvey's psychoanalytic model, a Freudian interpretation of the pleasures of male spectatorship replete with references to castration anxiety, fetishism, and voyeurism. This way of approaching film falls under what Carl Plantinga calls "ideological stoicism," a Brechtian approach that argues for a retreat from affective involvement with film.[3]

It is not difficult to explain the collapse of ideology critique as the primary mode of philosophically informed film criticism. There are three problems. First, the political situation has changed. Ideology as a concept was deeply rooted in its Marxist origins. Its purpose was to explain the stubborn failure of the proletariat to adopt a revolutionary consciousness. As a concept employed in a broader theoretical framework, ideology was *for* bridging the gap between theory (what dialectical materialism predicted) and observation (what actually occurred). When dialectical materialism collapsed, we no longer regarded it as either a plausible theory of social reality or of social justice, and thus ideology became an orphaned concept. Ideology is like "phlogiston" and "ether"—once theoretically necessary hypotheses, but now conceptual dead ends. Likewise, once we abandon the idea of ideology, there is no use for the practice of ideology critique.

Second, most of what passed for ideology critique was not rooted in science. Like the collapse of dialectical materialism, the eclipse of Freudian theory by more empirically based approaches has meant that critical approaches informed by psychoanalysis are now far less plausible. And third, ideology critiques of film could not account for our actual experience of film. Such critical approaches—for example, the claim that film positions us as Cartesian subjects—fail to account for our actual experience of viewing film, given that most of those who seriously reflect on film can easily distinguish between those films that have important social value and those that do not. Nor could these accounts explain the critical engagement that audiences regularly have with the films they view.

Similarly, it is not difficult to see why analytic philosophers of art have turned to empirically based psychology as a resource for creating a fully adequate theory of aesthetic emotion. A long-standing puzzle in aesthetics has been the question of how to explain spectator emotional responses to fictional scenarios (the so-called paradox of fiction, or mimesis). Why do we have emotions for fictional characters, for example, feeling sad for Anna Karenina or glad for Luke Skywalker? These characters are not real, and yet we respond to them as if they were real—but only partially, since we don't flee the theater when Freddy Krueger shows up or call the police when Judah arranges for the murder of Dolores. Film theorists have turned to cognitive science as a resource for answering this long-standing puzzle. Aaron Meskin and Jonathan Weinberg argue that any fully adequate theory of fictional emotion (including emotions generated by film) must account for four puzzling but basic features of our emotional engagement with film: (a) *phenomenological and physiological robustness* (the fact that from the first-person point of view we feel robust affective responses); (b) *fiction-directed affective intentionality* (the fact that the emotion is "experienced as directed at the characters, events, and situations of the film"); (c) *behavioral circumscription* (why audiences "will display a small but significant set of relevant behaviors, but will fail to demonstrate other behaviors that would be expected of someone experiencing its nonfictive analogue," e.g., why we cry but don't run from the theater); and (d) *the intimate yet ambiguous relationship to nonfictive affect and emotion* (the frequently made observation that there is some ambiguity about whether or not the emotion is itself "real" or "fictional"—do we "really" fear the monster?).[4] Empirically based research into emotions can go a long way toward explaining these puzzles about our emotional responses to fiction by explaining the structures and mechanisms that generate affective responses under ordinary circumstances. Put simply, if we know which neurological processes trigger affective responses in nonfictional situations, we ought to be able to explain which subset of these responses artworks such as film are capable of reliably generating, and the cognitive and noncognitive affective responses that are likely to follow.

My claim here is that this model of spectator emotion is especially valuable when it comes to the normative, critical analysis of film. By "normative, critical analysis" I mean interpreting and critiquing particular films and film genres with an eye to determining whether a film (or genre of films) generates, promotes, or otherwise fosters morally praiseworthy behaviors, beliefs, and attitudes, both on the level of individual viewers and society at large. At the very least, recent work on spectator emotions provides us with a set of sophisticated tools for interpreting films, that is, understanding exactly how films are capable of reliably producing the affects that they do. If nothing else, this body of work should improve our interpretative practices. But given that the emotions play such an important role in our moral engagement with our environment, empirically based and scientifically informed theories of film emotion can and should be part and parcel of the larger project of normative critical analysis.

Theories of Affective Response

In this section, I give an overview of several major theories of emotion that are important for contemporary analytical aesthetics. Although I will only discuss those views that I regard as being significant—and thus plausibly true—I am not defending any of these theories as conceptually adequate or empirically justified. Rather, the point is to provide the reader who may not be familiar with this literature with an overview of the field. As I hope to show later, in spite of the fact that there are ongoing debates among scholars working on art and emotion, there is sufficient agreement and overlap to contribute to the larger project of creating a robust critical theory useful for the normative analysis of film.

Cognitive Theories of Emotion

The standard view of emotions is the "cognitive theory of emotions."[5] On this view, emotions have two components: the first, the cognitive component, is a belief, thought, or judgment about persons or facts; the second component is a feeling or bodily state that results from the cognitive belief. Both cognitive and physiological elements are necessary conditions for emotions, but neither is sufficient. For example, suppose I am angry at Eric. That anger is felt in the body as certain changes in blood flow, galvanic skin response, tension, alertness, and so on. Why do I feel this way? Because I believe, say, that he has carelessly and recklessly damaged my car. My emotional state of anger is dependent upon and determined by my cognitive belief that Eric was careless, that my car has been damaged, and that this has harmed my interests. Without the belief, it is just a feeling, not an emotion.

Defenders of the cognitive theory of emotions put a great deal of emphasis on the fact that emotions are *about something,* what is called *intentionality.* (A mental state is said to be "intentional" if it refers to or is about something external.[6]) Robert Solomon defends what he calls the Deweyian-Sartarin view of emotions in which intentionality is the central feature:

> Essential to this view is the idea that emotions are *intentional,* which means that they are directed toward objects (real or imaginary) in the world. They therefore involve concepts and cognition, including recognition. Of course, they also involve neurology and physiology, and there may therefore be an instinctual and hard-wired biological basis for intentional states. . . . But what this notion of "intentionality" tends to do is break down the Cartesian barrier between experience and the world, between the "inner" and the "outer." (They may be merely imagined, or remembered, or, in extreme cases, hallucinated.) . . . But in the more usual case, in which Harry loves Sally, in which Fred hates spinach, in which Woody is jealous of Alan, the intentionality of emotion is clearly directed at something real and in the world.[7]

The view that emotions are intentional is important for a number of reasons. Most importantly, it provides criteria by which emotional states can be evaluated. If, for example, there is no reason to be fearful of *that* object, then an affective response of fear is inappropriate. However, if the object is something of great value, then certain kinds of affective responses (such as awe) are appropriate. This feature of intentionality allows the cognitivist to hold that we *ought* to feel wonder in the presence of great physical beauty, that we *ought* to feel pity or sympathy for an individual in pain, that we *ought* to feel joy when those we love achieve great accomplishments, and so forth. Emotions, rather than being irrational or nonrational, are instead appropriate responses to the world around us. Robert Nozick, for example, argued that emotions are bodily responses to real, subject-independent values instantiated in the world.[8] While not many philosophers have been willing to defend the objectivity of value, emotions are quite plausibly the proper kind of response that complex biological/neurological organisms such as ourselves *should have* to the world around us.

Another advantage of the cognitive theory of emotions and the importance it places on intentionality is its ability to explain the range of human emotion. Although there are a limited number of physiological states, the wide array of cognitive beliefs accounts for nuanced discriminations between anger and irritation, reverence and admiration, and pity and compassion. Even if it is true that there are only a small number of primitive or primary emotional responses (as critics of cognitivism will argue), the wide range of finely distinguished emotions can be defended as appropriate given the complexity of our intellectual judgments about particular situations. This in turn allows us to explain the variations in emotions from culture to culture insofar as affective responses depend on culturally determined judgments.

Most importantly, the cognitive model of emotions helps to explain why we need emotions to begin with. Emotions focus our attention on select, highly significant features of our environment and align the body with our cognitive appraisal of the world. Fear is useful when danger lurks, just as compassion is helpful when others are suffering. We need emotions because some elements of our environment demand attention, and our bodies and minds must be readied to respond. Carroll argues:

> The emotions glue our attention to those features of the object of the emotion that are apposite to the emotional state we are in; it encourages us to survey the event for further features that may support or sustain the prevailing emotional state in which we find ourselves; and protentively, our emotively charged state shapes our anticipation of what is to come by priming us to be on the lookout for the emergence or appearance of further details subsumable under the categories of the reigning emotion.[9]

This in turn helps explain how narrative fictions work, that is, how they reliably create emotional states. Carroll proposes the view that narrative texts are "criterially prefocused."[10] While in everyday life, our emotional and cognitive processes identify relevant details of the world that demand an emotional response (the possibility of danger, the happiness of a loved one, and so forth), in fiction, the situation has been "prestructured" for our attention. The author or director directs our thought toward certain aspects of a situation eliciting predictable emotional responses. If I care about a character (a sacrificing mother whose child is gravely ill), then by focusing my attention on a particular fact (perhaps a shot of the "empty cradle"), film directors reliably generate emotional responses (in this case, an empathetic response of shared grief). Carroll argues that the reliability of fiction in producing particular emotional responses is not mysterious and can be easily explained by the shared culture of author and audience.

> Authors of narratives, including mass fictions, are able, fairly reliably, to induce the emotions they set out to evoke—especially basic emotions (like anger, fear, hatred, and so on)—because they share a common background (cultural, but biological as well) with their audiences, both in terms of the criteria relevant to the experience of certain emotions as well as in terms of what it typically takes to elicit concern for given characters and their goals. Inasmuch as authors generally share a common background, cultural and otherwise, with their audiences, they may use themselves as detectors to gauge how audiences are likely to respond to their texts.[11]

Criticisms of Cognitive Theory

The cognitive theory of emotions has been criticized by both psychologists and philosophers, although most critics retain certain features of the theory. In this section, I consider the work of three recent philosophers of art who offer alternative theoretical models of emotion with important implications for aesthetics. Jenefer Robinson proposes a two-stage model, according to which emotions are given culturally determined labels only after bodily affective responses occur. Craig DeLancey defends a hierarchical, modular view of the mind, in which emotional responses occur largely independent of cognitive reflection. Finally, Greg Smith defends the "mood-cue approach," according to which films rely on moods to orient spectators toward proper emotional responses that are generated by automatic, subcortex processes.

Jenefer Robinson argues that empirical research supports a two-stage model, the "appraisal/reappraisal model."[12] In the first stage, the "affective appraisal" (or "primary appraisal") stage, environmental stimuli automatically produce physiological changes in light of an individual's needs and desires. These "rapid, automatic, and unconscious" responses alert us to significant changes in our environment. Robinson argues that this stage is "non-cognitive," by which she means both the environmental triggers that produce the emotion and the fact that this appraisal stage is not marked by the higher-order cognitive processes that are the hallmarks of mature human thought. The second stage, the "reappraisal" (or "secondary appraisal") stage, is a cognitive *re*appraisal of our environment. Here, the individual's (rational and intellectual) cognitive processes evaluate the situation, sometimes modifying the initial emotional response. Robinson summarizes her view this way:

> Emotions are processes, in which a rough-and-ready affective appraisal causes physiological responses, motor changes, action tendencies, changes in facial and vocal expression, and so on. The function of non-cognitive affective appraisals is to draw attention automatically and insistently by bodily means to whatever in the environment is of vital importance to me and mine. These affective appraisals can be automatically evoked not only by simple perceptions such as a sudden loud sound, but also by complex thoughts and beliefs. The reason why we experience emotions as passive phenomena is that we are never fully in control of our emotions: once an affective appraisal occurs, the response occurs too. We can influence our emotions only indirectly through subsequent cognitive monitoring.[13]

In her model of a two-stage affective response, Robinson incorporates a great deal of the work by psychologists Zajonc, LeDoux, and Lazarus, as well as the well-known Schachter and Singer experiment in which subjects were injected with adrenaline and then placed in various social situations that resulted in divergent emotional states.[14] Without going into the specifics of this research, one key feature is Robinson's claim that emotions are labeled *after* the bodily affective appraisal occurs, a process open to a great deal of error and mistake.

> In human beings, the end of an emotion process—or one stream of a more complex emotion process—is often marked by a conscious judgment cataloguing the emotion in recollection: people label their emotions with one of the emotion terms available to them in their own language and culture. Naming one's emotion and what caused it is, however, notoriously unreliable.[15]

According to Robinson, cognitivists like Solomon and Carroll are "engaged in after-the-fact classification of emotional processes, using the resources of ordinary language and the terms of folk psychology."[16]

Of what importance is Robinson's view for film spectators? A key feature of her account of cognitive *re*appraisal is the adoption of mechanisms for coping with negative emotions. Coping mechanisms include action, avoidance, and reinterpretation. An example is helpful. Suppose I am angry with a friend because I believe I was not invited to his wedding. My immediate affective appraisal generates anger, but on reflection, I cope with this anger by either taking action (phoning for an explanation), avoidance (turning my thoughts toward other friends), or by reinterpreting the meaning of his actions (it's a small wedding and only close family are invited). Figure 11.1 is taken from chapter 7 of Robinson's book and illustrates the two-part appraisal stage along with the cognitive reappraisal stage (which is the stage at which the coping mechanism appears).

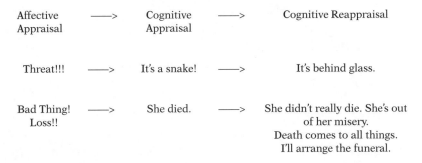

Figure 11.1, Robinson, "Appraisal and reappraisal: the coping mechanisms"[17]

How does this help us understand spectator emotion? In my view it helps explain why we voluntarily view films that generate unpleasant emotions: because coping with these unpleasant emotions is pleasurable (or at the very least, satisfies a need humans naturally have to anticipate how to cope with inevitable loss and unhappiness). Films provide us with useful strategies for coping with unpleasant emotions. Just as films generate emotions (or primary appraisals) by prefocusing our attention, they also narrate coping strategies for responding to these unpleasant emotions. Films show us "scripts" for responding to anxiety, fear, grief, and shame, and part of the pleasure of viewing films is experiencing the catharsis that results from simulating effective coping strategies. This answers one of the main puzzles in aesthetics—why we view films (or other art objects) that produce unpleasant emotions. For Robinson, the apparent paradox of tragedy (why we voluntarily watch or read tragedies) "may be resolvable by focusing on how tragedies both present painful material and at the same time provide the resources for us to cope with this material."[18]

In his book *Passionate Engines: What the Emotions Reveal about Mind and Artificial Intelligence*, Craig DeLancey, like Robinson, argues that the affective responses have an automatic precognitive component, although he attempts to preserve emotions as intentional. DeLancey defends what he calls the "Affect Program Theory," a view of emotions that depends on a hierarchical theory of the mind. "This is a modular view of mind in which certain capabilities are seen as more fundamental to autonomy, and are likely to be required by other (hence, dependent) capabilities. In particular, many of our affective capabilities . . . are more fundamental than, and can and do often operate independently of, the kinds of capabilities that are typically taken to constitute 'high cognition'; and in turn many cognitive abilities make use of, and may require, these other subcognitive abilities."[19] Incorporating the work of neuroscientist Jaak Panksepp, DeLancey argues for a view of emotions in which there are genetically predetermined "underlying circuits" that structure and organize "subroutines" and modify our sensitivities to the surrounding environment while interacting with the higher-cognitive processes of the brain and consciousness.[20] Emotions that fit this model are called "basic emotions" and for DeLancey include "fear, anger, joy, sadness, disgust, seeking/curiosity, social distress, lust, care, and play" (other theorists have similar but divergent lists of "basic emotions").[21]

DeLancey gives six reasons to reject "strong" cognitive models of emotions. The first is the confusion of cognition with affect, by which DeLancey means the failure of theorists like Solomon to adequately distinguish affects (with their autonomic bodily responses) from mere beliefs (which do not necessarily produce such bodily changes). Second, the cognitive model cannot account for the fact that direct neural stimulation can produce affective states, seemingly quite apart from any cognitive content or intentional belief. Third, there is the problem of emotional states in animals (the problem of homology). Psychologists regularly study basic emotions such as fear in rats, cats, and dogs: the "fear" these animals experience cannot be due to an intentional belief, and thus the cause must lie in some noncognitive process common to both humans and animals. Fourth, DeLancey points out that the emotions begin in infancy and can be seen as developing into adulthood—observations that do not easily fit the cognitive model. Fifth, there is evidence of neuro-anatomical differentiation, that is, that there are anatomical structures in the cortex and subcortex that correspond to specific emotions such as fear. Finally, there is the commonly recognized phenomenon of displacement, in which we go "searching for an object" for our emotional state (something to direct the emotion toward), a behavior observed both in everyday life and in experimental settings.[22]

Despite the fact that the basic emotions depend on autonomic processes that operate independently of higher cognitive faculties, DeLancey defends the view that the basic emotions are rational insofar as the emotions help maintain consistency of belief and persons possess conscious criteria that warrant the belief. DeLancey is careful not to reject the intentional model of emotions outright. Thus he is able to argue that basic emotions "must properly categorize" an event or state of affairs: "A threatening event must be recognized as the danger it is, an infuriating state of affairs must be seen to be such, and so on."[23] He further argues that the basic emotions can be shaped by learning, are revisable, can be "generalized" from particular instances to generic situations, and are subject to various constraints, such as the kind of action the emotion produces or the intensity of the affective response.[24] So despite the fact that DeLancey defends a hierarchical model of the mind with semiautonomic lower-level modules, emotions turn out to be rational in important ways (albeit in ways logicians might not appreciate).

For our purposes, what is interesting about this account is DeLancey's solution to the paradox of fiction. He argues that it is an acquired skill—one that animals and small children do not possess—to be able to understand the difference between fictional and actual content:

> The child has the ability to entertain propositional contents, and treats them all as the same value, and . . . from our perspective this treatment is quite like the kind of commitment we reserve for belief. The child must in turn learn to separate out some thoughts as warranted beliefs, others as fictions. . . . To have beliefs and acknowledge them as warranted is a learned and special skill; and just so, to entertain content for content's sake, while being aware that it is merely entertained because it is unwarranted, is a learned and special skill. . . . That is, there are not dog dramas and there can be none, because we cannot train a dog to separate mere pretending from actual activity.[25]

Greg Smith's approach to film emotion is much different from that of Carroll, Robinson, or DeLancey. In *Film Structure and the Emotion System,* Smith proposes what he calls the mood-cue approach. In his view, the primary effect films strive for is to produce a mood, which is an "orienting state that asks us to interpret our surroundings in an emotional fashion."[26] One advantage to Smith's model is that moods are easier to create than emotions for two reasons. First, because moods are lower-level emotional states, less concrete emotional cuing is necessary—the task is first of all to create an emotional orientation. Second, this allows for a great deal of redundancy of emotional cues, which in turn assures that audience members from different backgrounds and with different personal histories will still acquire the proper emotional orientation and that the cues that accomplish this need not be foregrounded.

> Redundant cues collaborate to indicate which emotional mood is called for. The viewer need not focus conscious attention on each of these elements. Some of these cues activate the associative network of the emotions, and

this creates a low level of emotion. If a film provides a viewer with several redundant emotive cues, this increases the likelihood of moving the viewer toward a predispositionary mood state.[27]

The cues that create this mood include such fundamental component elements of film as facial expressions, set design, music, camera angle, and narrative structure. Smith argues that this way of creating emotions (through orienting moods) explains the success of film as a form of mass media insofar as it produces consistent emotional responses in audiences that have very different emotion scripts and prototypes.

How do films use moods to create spectator emotions? Narratives are, of course, reliable processes by which this occurs. However, one underappreciated way of generating spectator emotions is what Smith calls "emotion markers" ("configurations of highly visible textual cues for the primary purpose of eliciting brief moments of emotion").[28] Emotions created by emotion markers vary from those created by narratives, which rely on the achievement (or frustration) of narrative goals and obstacles. These goal-oriented (or diegetic) emotions are structured by the narrative and are typically foregrounded in most films. Emotional markers, however, create brief bursts of emotion, usually unrelated to (that is, not required by) the narrative structure of the film, although they serve an important purpose: they reward the viewer's mood orientation and thus help sustain the mood.

> For the viewer engaged in an appropriate mood, [the emotional markers] give a reward that helps maintain the predisposition toward expressing emotion. Few texts can rely only on narratively significant moments to provide mood-sustaining emotion. Most have to provide markers to shore up the mood the text has created, even if the markers have little or no effect on the overt diegetic aim: the character's achievement of a goal.[29]

From Spectator Emotion to Normative Criticism

It is not difficult to use these models of spectator emotions as part of normative critical approaches to film that assess and evaluate the ethical and moral adequacy of specific films and film genres. To do so requires, first, a set of normative claims about what makes actions or states of affairs good or bad, what has value and what does not, how to adjudicate competing or conflicting moral goods, and how to prioritize our responses to various degrees of evil in the world. Such a set of normative claims might of course be generated by a purely rationalist normative theory, but for our purposes it is enough to note that most living, community-based moral traditions have sufficiently cohesive and coherent sets of ethical judgments to satisfy this requirement. Second, it is also necessary to possess a model of the human person in which affect is a central capacity insofar as both cognitive and noncognitive processes, whether primarily mental or bodily, are seen as normal and healthy ways of responding to the agent's environment. In my view, it is readily apparent that most religious traditions easily meet these two conditions given that faith communities have rich, living ethical traditions that include models of the person that emphasize a psychosomatic conception of the self. Indeed, traditional Judeo-Christian morality can readily incorporate this model of the emotions into its robust moral traditions, which are several thousand years old.

One example of this, easily seen, is the Catholic tradition of virtue ethics that builds on Aristotelian foundations. It is only a small step from the moral ideal of a virtuous person to recent theories of cognitive and noncognitive affect. Consider Aristotle's discussion of the importance of "seeing" for moral excellence ("seeing" being our primary mode of engagement with film and thus notably apposite for our purposes). "The excellent person," writes Aristotle, "is far superior because he sees what is true in each case."[30] Why does Aristotle claim that the virtuous person *sees* what is true? Aristotle uses the verb *aisthēsis*, or "perception," to refer to both the sensory capacities of the five senses and, in an extended sense, to the perception of what is morally significant and notable at some particular time and place. The well-trained perception of the excellent person sees "what is really so"—in short, they see well. And it is crucial that they do so, because seeing well is a necessary precondition to exercising virtue. One always exhibits virtue in concrete, particular situations—but this particularity and concreteness makes general rules inapplicable. Because the person of virtue is unable to depend on rules as a guide for action, one must learn to see well by developing and training one's perceptions. It is only a short distance from this model of moral virtue to Robinson's appraisal/reappraisal model and DeLancey's defense of the emotions as rational. In both cases what was previously regarded as a premoral or amoral process (mere emotional response) turns out to be morally significant when subject to discipline and training (learning to "see well").

Another example from the Judeo-Christian tradition is the biblical language of the "heart." The heart, which comprises emotions, intellect, and will, is portrayed in the Bible as the seat of moral character. Morally upright persons respond with a "pure heart"; that is, their emotional and intellectual states are harmoniously aligned such that they respond immediately and transparently to the needs of others around them and to the demands of the moral law. If emotions focus our attentions, then the emotional intelligence of morally upright people points to the most salient features of the environment—they see the world as God would have us see it. Duplicity is condemned because this implies an inner contradiction between what the person feels and what the person believes is correct. Instead of affective responses that reveal the unified commitment of the body, mind, and emotion to a single moral vision of the world, the duplicitous person experiences the self as divided and in conflict. (In my view, Paul's famous report in Romans of his inner conflict only makes sense against a background in which the unity of the self—in terms of reason, emotion, and desire—was the assumed normative ideal.)

Contemporary theories of spectator emotion are much closer to affirming this type of traditional biblical model of moral personhood than are philosophical or rationalist normative theories (such as Kantianism or utilitarianism) that are notably suspicious of any role for emotions in moral judgments. Contemporary theories do so by emphasizing the constant interplay of bodily affect and cognitive reflection, creating a model of the person as embodied agent, emotionally and attentively attuned to the environment. We need only add to this research a conception of moral excellence and social justice to produce a normative, and yet empirically based, model of human moral agency—one that not only describes how and why we have the responses to the world that we do have, but also gives practical advice about how to become mature moral agents. For example, rationalist moral theories have often portrayed the self as a free, independent moral calculator whose agency is exercised through a will capable of being moved by reason alone. Such models of moral agency have always run counter to the tendency of religious traditions to emphasize moral training and discipline (as opposed to abstract, rational calculation).

Work in the cognitive theory of emotions opens up the possibility for a more sophisticated discussion of the moral excellence exemplified in religious traditions and texts. For example, one key place emotional transparency and immediacy are evident is in the Gospel stories of Christ. Throughout the Gospels, Christ is portrayed as being acutely attuned to the proper or most morally significant aspects of his environment, while those around him are emotionally glued to the wrong aspects of the situation. While the disciples fear the storm that threatens them, Christ is serene in his awareness of God's providence. Where others respond with repulsion and disgust to disease, Christ sees suffering and responds with compassion. While Judas is obsessed with his perception of Mary's wastefulness, Christ contemplates an act of beauty (John 12:1–8). Again and again, Christ is represented as possessing an emotional sensitivity to his environment that leads to his immediate correct response, while others (most often the disciples) are hampered by emotional responses that misdirect their attention and paralyze their will. Put differently, the trope "the mind of Christ" captures in very simple form a rich and complex ethical ideal. The pilgrim aspires to have the mind of Christ, that is, to have the emotional intelligence and sensitivity of Christ, attentive to what Christ would see, and ready to respond as he would act. And, importantly, the theories of emotions I have been discussing readily explain what it would mean to have "the mind of Christ" for embodied, culturally embedded persons like ourselves (as opposed to the free-floating, transcendent spirits imagined by some philosophical theories).

I am not claiming here, however, that normative film criticism should adopt a religious orientation. Given that film is a mass art, it is more appropriate to critically analyze film from a *public* rather than *parochial* or *religious* point of view. Given the irreducible pluralism that marks contemporary society, such public film criticism can play an important role, especially if it turns out that particular films threaten even the modest, thin conception of the good that grounds public civility and tolerance. Having said that, I would emphasize that the Judeo-Christian tradition has important moral resources that theorists of emotion typically lack, mainly normative ideals by which to judge and assess autonomic affective processes. Theorists of emotion who rely heavily on psychological research often characterize various aspects of the process of generating emotions as amoral because emotions occur prior to cognitive reflection. We should reject this claim, however, in part because it is false to assume that moral correctness or failure is a function of volition or of other cognitive processes. It *just is* the human condition.

Normative Film Criticism Reconsidered

Let me conclude with some reflections on the importance of empirically informed theories of film emotion for critical film analysis. Perhaps the most important conclusion we can draw from this literature is that we can safely put aside any claims that film generates "quasi" or "fictive" emotions. Whatever else can be said about these emotions, they are generated using the same neural routines and mechanism that produce ordinary affective responses. In particular, the accounts of Robinson, DeLancey, and

Smith converge on the view that the primary, basic emotional responses are given interpretative content by higher-order cognitive processes that follow temporally. Importantly, this is the same process by which films reliably generate emotions in spectators: an undifferentiated physiological appraisal is given content by such formal devices as narrative or emotion-orienting mood. In my view, we should reject the claim that film emotions are fundamentally unlike other human emotions and proceed on the more reasonable hypothesis that film emotions are coextensive with the ordinary emotional lives of humans.

This does not imply, however, that the emotions generated by films should be evaluated in exactly the same way as nonfilm emotions. For example, while I might in general encourage my children to not be "angry" or "fearful," I wouldn't automatically condemn film-viewing experiences that generated emotions of anger or fear. I might even encourage them to view films that create anger and fear. Why is this? One reason is clear enough: because emotions are intentional, anger and fear are sometimes appropriate affective responses. For example, anger toward social injustice might, all things considered, be the appropriate affective response, one that ought to occur more regularly in ordinary real life. Another reason is that film emotions are typically *for* something, that is, they have a purpose distinct from that of everyday emotions. So, for example, a film might generate anger for the purpose of narrating a coping mechanism. It is here that normative criticism can play an important role. We can and should make moral assessments of whether the emotion generated is the proper response, whether the object toward which the emotion is directed is a suitable object for that particular affective response, whether the coping mechanism is a morally defensible one, and so forth.

This is especially true when we recognize that emotions are to a significant degree learned responses. These are associative processes that reinforce the connection between certain physiological states and corresponding cognitive evaluations and bodily responses, including scripts for action and reactions. Films activate latent potentialities in viewers for these kinds of emotional responses while at the same time interpreting what the emotions mean and validating some coping mechanisms over others. Emotions that follow cognitive reappraisal are clearly learned and thus are modifiable via reflection and experience; automatic affective appraisals can also likely be modified through training and discipline. Because there is no clear dividing line between film emotions and nonfilm emotions, neither is there any clear dividing line between the learning that occurs inside and outside the movie theater. We ought to direct our attention

Reconsidering the Normative

to cognitive reappraisal processes and consider carefully not the initial emotions of grief, fear, or anxiety but how films narrate coping strategies for handling these emotions. This requires investigating how films create emotional catharses in audiences and whether or not these accord with our best reflective confessions and moral traditions.

Normative film criticism must also be cognizant of how a film's formal structures prefocus our attention on certain features of the environment that *the filmmaker regards as significant.* This opens up two possibilities: that our attention will be drawn to the wrong aspects of a situation or that the film will help us to be responsive to elements of situations we pass over too quickly. In the first case, there are numerous examples of spectator emotions distracting us from important, relevant facts. The developing romance in *Pretty Woman* obscures how Julia Roberts's character is both commodity and consumer. The emotional catharsis of *Guess Who's Coming to Dinner* blinds audiences to the film's reestablishment of patriarchal authority by severely silencing female voices. The emotional climax at the end of *Vertigo* thrills us, but rarely is anyone outraged by Scotty's systematic erasure of Judy's identity. In the second case, however, just as many other films focus our attention on features of our world we might not otherwise observe carefully enough: the senseless destruction of war (*Gallipoli*), the enduring beauty of the world (*Days of Heaven*), and the joy of being embodied (*Singin' in the Rain*). Either way, normative evaluation of the film's "criterial prefocusing" is inescapable, whether commendable or not.

An empirically informed theory of film emotion can also inform our evaluation of film at the social or cultural level. Film is a mass art and aims to generate particular sets of emotions in a broad spectrum of society, although certain genres aim for particular demographics (teens, twenty-something women, families with small children, etc). One particularly important feature is how films are directed toward addressing the needs of their intended demographic. Granted these "needs" might be fairly banal (e.g., the need to do something with your preschooler that can be intellectu- ally stimulating on multiple levels), but I would argue that quite often our selection of films to view corresponds with some deeply felt need to cope with negative emotions, both individually and collectively. Consider the importance of *Star Wars*—with its myth of the lone individual destined to defeat the faceless, dehumanizing machine—for America's national psyche after Vietnam. Or the significance of *Roots* for a nation struggling with the legacy of slavery. Or, to use my favorite example, the importance of *Who Framed Roger Rabbit*—with its killer fluid and ghettoed cross-dressers—in preparing America to emotionally address the AIDS epidemic.

Film critics should evaluate how particular genres of film and contemporary themes are indicators of broad cultural and social changes. I think it is arguably the case that young men view violent films of destruction in part to shore up weak ego boundaries by subordinating the Other. Tragic romances, perhaps, appeal to women struggling with the emotional deadness of their own relationships. At other times, we need films to help us feel what we know to be true—the triumph of forgiveness over vengeance, the enduring pleasures of marriage and family, the spark of divinity in each person—outlaw emotions in a post-Christian society. Some emotions are fragile, and film helps keep these emotions alive. The point here is that we can learn much about our society and ourselves by considering how films help us cope with negative emotions and relive (and revive) endangered ones.

Films affect us in complicated ways, and evaluating them fairly is difficult. Violence is not always bad; love is not always good; sexuality can be degraded or celebrated. Rigid rating systems and classification schemes miss what is most important, including how films use catharsis to teach us how to deal with negative emotions. There are plenty of nihilist films without nudity or profanity, just as there are plenty of films about love that treat romantic love as a kind of fate that magically happens when we discover our soul mate. Communities of faith need to evaluate films not solely in terms of keeping tally of profanity, acts of violence, and nudity (although these are worth noting) but also by assessing the adequacy of a film's emotional message—its valorization of certain emotional experiences, its cognitive interpretation of the emotions' meaning, and the script it offers us for responding to negative emotions.

In the end, as important as emotions are for film and as important as emotions are for a full human life filled with robust engagement with the world, our cognitive and rational thought processes remain essential to our evaluation of film. We must be intentional about opening up spaces for careful reflective criticism of film, both to warn us of its dangers and to help us embrace its potential as a tutor of the emotions. Paradoxically, though, reason functions here not to enthrone its own regime, but to return emotions to their central role as a vital component of our moral engagement with the world.

Notes

1. Noël Carroll, *A Philosophy of Mass Art* (Oxford: Oxford University Press, 1998), 245–90.

Reconsidering the Normative

2. Noël Carroll, *Theorizing the Moving Image* (Cambridge: Cambridge University Press, 1996), 275.

3. Carl Plantinga, "Notes on Spectator Emotion and Ideological Film Criticism," in *Film Theory and Philosophy*, ed. Richard Allen and Murray Smith (Oxford: Oxford University Press, 1997), 373.

4. Aaron Meskin and Jonathan M. Weinberg, "Emotions, Fiction, and Cognitive Architecture," *British Journal of Aesthetics*, 43, no. 1 (2003): 19–20.

5. This section summarizes the position set out by Carroll in *Philosophy of Mass Art*, 245–90.

6. See Craig DeLancey, *Passionate Engines: What the Emotions Reveal about Mind and Artificial Intelligence* (Oxford: Oxford University Press, 2002), 87–89.

7. Robert Solomon, "The Politics of Emotion," *Midwest Studies in Philosophy* 22 (1998): 6–7.

8. Robert Nozick, *The Examined Life: Philosophical Meditations* (New York: Simon & Schuster, 1989).

9. Carroll, *Philosophy of Mass Art*, 264–65.

10. Ibid., 265.

11. Ibid., 267.

12. For a summary of this view, see Jenefer Robinson, "The Art of Distancing: How Formal Devices Manage Our Emotional Responses to Literature," *The Journal of Aesthetics and Art Criticism* 62, no. 2 (2004): 153–62.

13. Jenefer Robinson, *Deeper than Reason: Emotion and Its Role in Literature, Music, and Art* (Oxford: Clarendon, 2005), 97.

14. Robinson references the following sources: R. B. Zajonc, "Evidence for Nonconscious Emotions," and Joseph LeDoux, "Emotional Processing, but Not Emotions, Can Occur Unconsciously," in *The Nature of Emotion: Fundamental Questions*, ed. Paul Ekman and Richard Davidson (New York: Oxford University Press, 1994); and Richard Lazarus, *Emotion and Adaptation* (New York: Oxford University Press, 1991).

15. Robinson, *Deeper than Reason*, 97.

16. Ibid., 98.

17. Ibid., 198.

18. Ibid., 226.

19. DeLancey, *Passionate Engines*, viii.

20. Ibid., 24.

21. Ibid., 28.

22. Ibid., 37–43.

23. Ibid., 131–32.

24. Ibid., 131–33.

25. Ibid., 113.

26. Greg M. Smith, *Film Structure and the Emotion System* (Cambridge: Cambridge University Press, 2003), 42.

27. Ibid., 43.

28. Ibid., 44.

29. Ibid., 45.

30. Aristotle, *Nicomachean Ethics* 1113b30.

12

From Bultmann to Burton, Demythologizing the Big Fish

The Contribution of Modern Christian Theologians to the Theology–Film Conversation

CHRISTOPHER DEACY

While recently teaching an undergraduate module titled "Death of God? Christian Theology and the Modern World," one of the questions I asked my students, in the specific context of a seminar on Latin American liberation theology, concerned the extent to which theology should be thought of as a contextual discipline that can only be conducted and understood in ways that, as Gordon Lynch puts it, "take seriously the particular context and experiences of those engaging in theological reflection."[1] Although the discussion that followed was fruitful, I could not help feeling that, in talking in a European university about the nature and impact of a distinctively South American phenomenon over the last forty or so years, a crucial point was being missed. For, while it may be appropriate to enter into a discussion about the merits of neoorthodox theology, evangelical theology, liberal theology, postmodern theology, or "death of God" theology, liberation theology is not simply another way of "doing theology" in the modern world. As Gustavo Gutiérrez showed in 1971, with publication of his groundbreaking work *A Theology of Liberation*,[2] a new kind of theology is involved, which does not amount to just doing theology in a new way. Since the Latin American situation is qualitatively different from the European situation,[3] a completely different conceptual framework is required.[4] In South America, unlike in Europe, the important thing is not to reflect or philosophize but to *do* the right thing, rather than merely think it. In asking my students, therefore, to reflect critically on the significance of liberation theology, I was asking them to do something that, while appropriate for the curriculum, insufficiently took into account Martin Luther's dictum that one becomes a theologian "by living, by dying, and by being damned—not by understanding, reading, and speculating."[5]

With this in mind, the aim of this chapter is to suggest that, since theology is so inescapably contextual (rather than being in the business of generating what Gordon Lynch calls "universal, timeless concepts that will be equally valid or helpful in all times and places"[6]), this will necessarily impact the way in which the theology-film conversation is understood today. At first sight, any correlation between theology and film may appear overstretched. After all, it is one thing to claim that theology is in principle adaptable and amenable to new perspectives and horizons that emanate from the specific milieu in which it has arisen, as is the case with a theology of liberation. However, it is by no means clear that the way in which audiences engage with, and appropriate, films has so far succeeded in a redrawing of the boundaries within which theology is traditionally practiced. Nevertheless, this chapter will explore the possibility that, once we move beyond a more superficial understanding of how films can be used to illustrate theology,[7] films can themselves facilitate quite sophisticated theological activity.

On a pedagogical level, it is surprising just how many opportunities arise in the course of teaching a theology module that is not explicitly film-based to do theology through film. In my "Death of God?" course, for example, greater opportunities, by virtue of being less contrived, tend to arise for doing theology through film than in an explicit module on theology and film. In the latter, an often artificial dichotomy will be set up between theology on the one hand and film on the other, in a manner comparable to H. Richard Niebuhr's five models of Christ and culture,[8] with a view toward establishing where possible convergences may be located. Whereas, in a theology and film module, I might have reservations concerning students' ability to engage theologically with films since they may come to the module without a background in theology, this is not the case in a module on modern Christian theology, where the theological tools are provided before a film is employed as part of the conversation dealing with the ideas of the likes of Bultmann, Tillich, or Pannenberg. The rest of this chapter will examine how, then, in the twenty-first century, films can (and should) be used not so much to illustrate theology but to enable us to (re)examine, critique, and challenge the efficacy of the work of a number of prominent twentieth-century theologians.

The Contextuality of Film

Upon winning the Best Actor prize at the April 1995 British Academy of Film and Television Arts (BAFTA) awards ceremony for his performance in *Four Weddings and a Funeral* (d. Mike Newell, 1994), Hugh Grant made reference in his acceptance speech to one of the other films in competition that year, *Pulp Fiction* (d. Quentin Tarantino, 1994).[9] Although the speech in itself contained no explicit (or for that matter implicit) theology, it recently came to mind during the aforementioned class on liberation theology. Searching for a way to explain how liberation theology is culture-specific, to the extent that the particular circumstances that led the Roman Catholic bishops from South America who met in 1968 at Medellín in Colombia to apply the insights of Vatican II to their own predicament—one-third of the population lives in abject poverty—I found myself curiously reminded of Hugh Grant's address at the London Palladium more than a decade ago. In his speech, Grant comically explained to his fellow nominees that *Pulp Fiction* might have performed better on a night in which *Four Weddings* took home most of the trophies if Quentin Tarantino's film had been set and filmed not in the sun-drenched metropolis of California but in the leafy suburbs of Sussex. Besides being a reference to the fact that British films tend to eclipse their American counterparts at British award ceremonies, what struck me most about what Grant said is that one could not imagine *Pulp Fiction* being set anywhere other than America, just as *Four Weddings* is a quintessentially English phenomenon. The idea that either film could be transplanted from one continent to another would be no less absurd, I suggested to my students, than that liberation theology could be relocated from Medellín, Colombia, to Maidstone, England, or Brasília, Brazil, to Broadstairs, England. When one considers that the theologies of

Barth, Bonhoeffer, and Moltmann were shaped by the particular cultural and political events that surrounded them—Moltmann, indeed, served in the German army for six months during the Second World War before surrendering in 1945 to a British soldier and becoming a prisoner of war, while Bonhoeffer was executed that same year in a Nazi prison camp after attempting, through the Confessing Church, to remove Hitler from power—it becomes clear that theology cannot be other than contextually bound. Exactly how film can contribute to this process of theological reflection and engagement, however, needs to be addressed.

On a superficial level, it might be useful to examine how paranoia and conspiracy thrillers such as *The Parallax View* (d. Alan J. Pakula, 1974) and *The Conversation* (d. Francis Ford Coppola, 1974) shed light on the cultural malaise that swept through America in the early to mid 1970s, at the tail end of the death of God movement. In reinforcing, through the lens of often dislocated and psychopathically lonely antiheroes (of whom *The Conversation*'s Harry Caul [Gene Hackman] is an exemplar), what Robert Kolker calls "fears of lost control over political and economic institutions, whose discourse insisted that no matter what efforts are made, an unknowable presence . . . will have its way and exert its ineluctable power,"[10] it is not surprising if there is no room in this climate for God. The specific context of what William Hamilton and Thomas Altizer meant when they proclaimed the death of God less than a decade earlier[11] may have been intrinsically theological, in the respect that it related specifically to the incarnation, during which they believed God started to die through taking on human form, entering human history, and firsthand experiencing sin, suffering, and mortality. But it is notable that Hamilton believed that this process was reflected in nineteenth-century literature, thereby underscoring the theologico-*cultural* dynamics at work. Writing in *Playboy* in August 1966, Hamilton suggested that "perhaps the most unforgettable image of the dying God in our language is that of Ahab finally fixing his harpoon in Moby Dick's side, as the two of them sink together, both of them God, both of them evil."[12] In reading Kolker's assessment that many 1970s films illustrated a certain ambience of "impotence and despair, and signaled disaster, a breakdown of community and trust so thorough that it left the viewer with images of lonely individuals, trapped, in the dark, completely isolated,"[13] it need not be wide of the mark to investigate how films are also potentially capable of documenting a social, cultural, and theological process of which Herman Melville's 1851 novel may be seen as something of a literary precursor.

Cupitt and Bonhoeffer meet the Kranks

A case in point is the theology of Don Cupitt, which is both a development of the ideas put forward by death of God theologians—not least Richard Rubenstein's claim that "we live in the time of the 'Death of God'"[14]—and a useful portal into the present theology-film conversation. Cupitt's starting point is that, since the Enlightenment, there has been an ebbing of the sea of faith to the extent that, nowadays, Christians are embarrassed if one suggests that God intervenes directly in history. Referring, for example, to "the myth of a supernatural redeemer," he argues that it can no longer be "presented with full seriousness," and so we cannot accord much credibility to the "Christian creeds that incorporate it in its original and most uncompromising form."[15] Cupitt suggests that while people still subscribe to the myth, as evinced by their singing of Christmas carols, "the authority of the myth has been visibly deteriorating around them."[16] The kernel of Cupitt's argument is that many people who claim to believe in God are often quite secular in their worldview, as betokened by the fact that while many people today have appropriated such Christian virtues as showing concern for the sick, hungry, and oppressed, they are critical of doctrines relating to original sin, the disciplining of children and subjection of women, as well as prohibitions against nakedness, homosexuality, and contraception.[17] We have thus, he contends, invented our own autonomous ethic rather than accepting one prescribed for us by religious authorities.

That traditional forms of religion are increasingly relegated to the margins of life, with no more than a veneer remaining, is encapsulated well in Joe Roth's seasonal film comedy *Christmas with the Kranks* (2004), based on John Grisham's 2001 novel, *Skipping Christmas*. The film concerns the ultimately unsuccessful attempt on the part of an affluent American couple from the Chicago suburbs, Luther and Nora Krank, to forego the rituals of celebrating Christmas in order to set sail, instead, on a Caribbean cruise. Aside from the film's implicit message that nonconformity (delineated in this film as individualism and a failure to subscribe to the collective neighborhood task of erecting a one-hundred-pound snowman on their rooftop) amounts to subversion and even heresy, *Christmas with the Kranks* also propounds the idea, in tandem with Cupitt's theme in *The Sea of Faith*, that the traditional functions of religion have been displaced by secular agencies. Christmas may once have been a Christian festival, but this film ostensibly celebrates the ceremonial and sacramental allure of Christmas but without, as Roger Ebert points out, "a single crucifix,

... a single crèche, ... a single mention of the J-name." Accordingly, "no matter what your beliefs or lack of them, you can celebrate Christmas in this neighborhood, because it's not about beliefs, it's about a shopping season."[18] This is exemplified in the film by the portrayal of a Roman Catholic priest, Father Zabriskie (Tom Poston), who manages to be able to spend Christmas Eve at the Kranks's annual pre-Christmas party with seemingly no congregation to attend to on one of the busiest nights in the Christian calendar. Commercialism is given more status than Christology, and the kerygma has been supplanted by kitsch.

What is useful about the film is how it is living proof of what Dietrich Bonhoeffer spoke about earlier in the twentieth century concerning how the world has come of age and can do without religion. As a barometer of our modern cultural values, *Christmas with the Kranks* is a theologically important film, even if there is a dearth of theology within the film itself. In an age when theologians often identify the theological value of a film on the basis of the preponderance of Christ-figure motifs to which it bears witness,[19] in this instance an absence of explicit theology in the film provides it with the distinction of not simply bearing witness to, but actually contributing to, a serious and sophisticated theological discussion about how, for Bonhoeffer, "God is being pushed more and more out of life" and that "we are moving towards a completely religionless time."[20] Bonhoeffer's distinction between superficial religiosity and genuine Christianity—as identified by the dichotomy between cheap and costly grace—cannot so much be read into a film like *Christmas with the Kranks*. It is more the case that such a film can be employed to elucidate the difference between how genuine Christianity entails faith with involvement, whereas "cheap grace" entails not the "justification of the sinner in the world" but "the justification of sin and the world,"[21] and involves not the call to obedient, costly discipleship but mere passive and complacent assent to a doctrine or creedal formula.

Since Bonhoeffer believed that the trappings of religion were a barrier to true and authentic faith, film can facilitate what for Bonhoeffer was a priority for theology—namely, allowing the gospel to address humans in a secular age, and to do so without requiring them to become religious. To fully understand this process, it must be stressed that when Bonhoeffer referred to the need to espouse a "religionless Christianity," he did not mean a Christless or Godless Christianity. On the contrary, Bonhoeffer believed that authentic Christianity was not concerned with increasingly redundant rituals and elaborate metaphysical teachings (both of which enabled people to escape the challenge of the gospel), "but to be a man.

It is not some religious act which makes a Christian what he is, but participation in the suffering of God in the life of the world."[22] In other words, being a person for other persons, and discovering the importance of others, was the kernel of the Christian faith. As he wrote from prison to his friend Eberhard Bethge:

> To feel that one counts for something with other people is one of the joys of life. What matters is not how many friends we have, but how deeply we are attached to them. After all, personal relationships count for more than anything else. . . . What is the best book or picture or house, or any property to me, compared with my wife, my parents, or my friend?[23]

Seen through this lens, film can play a vital and pivotal role as a conversation partner with modern theology. Robert Johnston tells us in *Reel Spirituality* that after seeing *The Year of Living Dangerously*, his wife, Catherine Barsotti, became so immersed in the pain and poverty of Jakarta, as depicted in Peter Weir's 1982 film, that she could not escape the question that Billy Kwan (Linda Hunt) asks Guy Hamilton (Mel Gibson): "What then must we do?" In Barsotti's words:

> I left the theater with that phrase and the amazing eyes of the children of Jakarta burned onto the screen of my mind. . . . It became a turning point, a recovery of sight. The next week I returned to my project at work, appraising a hospital, but I saw the world differently. Within weeks I applied for a leave of absence and within months left for Mexico to work as a short-term missionary.[24]

What is remarkable here is not simply that the film, which addresses the fall of the Sukarno government in Indonesia in the mid-1960s, resonated so strongly, but that, in addition to the aforementioned missionary work, it could prompt someone to "give myself to the youth of my church and community, to the financial and political struggle to build a shelter for women and children in my city, and to study in the area of cross-cultural theology and ministry."[25]

It would, of course, be facile to suggest that films function in an identical way for all audiences. Neither Vincent Canby in the *New York Times* nor Pauline Kael in the *New Yorker* were quite so enamored, for example, with *The Year of Living Dangerously*. Canby felt that the film "has all the correct impulses but no real grasp of the humane irony that separates sincere fiction from possibly great fiction,"[26] while Kael (despite finding the film engaging) felt an "aversion to its gusts of wind about destiny"

Reconsidering the Normative

and "truth versus appearance."[27] What is important, however, is that Weir's movie exemplifies Bonhoeffer's belief, as presented in *The Cost of Discipleship*, that "as Christ bears our burdens, so ought we to bear the burdens of other human beings."[28]

Since Bonhoeffer was of the view that the church had forgotten the "costliness" of God's bearing our flesh, it may not be surprising if alternative agencies beyond the church are sometimes more suitably able to enter into a theological conversation about what it means to be human. This is not to say that Peter Weir was intentionally bearing witness to theological concerns—in my view, it is futile to go down this path—but merely that secular agencies can be no less effective in enabling audiences to reflect (and engage) theologically. Since, for Bonhoeffer, the church was too often caught up in transcendental and otherworldly matters, it tended to neglect the fact that the God of the New Testament is not an omniscient, omnipotent, omnipresent deity, but a powerless and suffering God "who conquers power and space in the world by his weakness."[29] Indeed, he believed that through the incarnation "God allows himself to be edged out of the world and on to the cross," such that "God is weak and powerless in the world, and that is exactly the way, the only way, in which he can be with us and help us."[30] With this in mind, the church should reconsider its relationship to the secular world, thereby rendering the distinction between the sacred and the secular an artificial and somewhat outmoded one. So long as the distinction is made, the church and a medium such as film will always be seen as being in some sense in opposition to one another, both ostensibly promoting a different and irreconcilable agenda. In Bonhoeffer's eyes, the forging of just such a separation denies the unity of God and the world as achieved in Jesus Christ, since in reconciling himself to the world through the incarnation, God began the process of reconciling the world to himself. There is, for Bonhoeffer, no God apart from the world, no supernatural apart from the natural, and no sacred apart from the profane. Reading Bonhoeffer today makes clear that films can play a vital role in the way in which theology is practiced and understood.

This is no less the case even when films do not neatly tie in with the kind of theology with which links are being advanced. Fred Burnett has shown, for example, how Mel Gibson's character, Martin Riggs, in *Lethal Weapon* (d. Richard Donner, 1987) "is the living embodiment of Bonhoeffer's person who has come of age"[31] and can do without religion. Burnett insightfully shows how films do not have to presuppose the Christian faith or contain, through their dialogue and images, anything that explicitly correlates with theology to be theologically rich. In Burnett's words, "What Riggs knows and portrays is that any current solutions to evil in the world will not come from God but from humans, or more precisely, from Riggs himself."[32] This ties in with how, for Bonhoeffer, "there is no longer any need for God as a working hypothesis, whether in morals, politics or science, . . . in religion or philosophy."[33] Accordingly, Riggs's secular and nonreligious stance functions well as a filmic representation of what, over forty years earlier, Bonhoeffer was attempting to encapsulate in some of his writing about the way we have been forsaken by a supernatural and all-powerful God, leaving the onus of how we live our lives squarely upon our own shoulders.

Riggs's suicidal behavior—his death wish, indeed—may not directly address how, for Bonhoeffer, it is Jesus's "being a person for other persons" that is the key christological and theological concern. However, Bonhoeffer's concentration on the flesh-and-blood Christ of the New Testament, with the attendant motifs of self-sacrifice and suffering, provide a useful counterpart to the nihilistic and self-destructive Riggs, who perhaps has not yet quite "come of age," since he is in constant search for a set of values and commitments by which to orient his increasingly suicidal and narcissistic life. It would be out of place to propose that Bonhoeffer's theology would provide such a meaning system, but *Lethal Weapon*'s depiction of the contemporary existential crisis reaps rich theological dividends when interpreted as a filmic exposition of the challenge presented by the gospel. It may not provide us with obvious theological answers,[34] but the film can help us establish the questions and flesh out the contours of the debate.

Films can also go further in suggesting in a more systematic way how theology is able to function in the modern world. Martin Scorsese's *Mean Streets* (1973) exposes the failure of the Roman Catholic Church to adequately impart redemption on the "mean streets" of New York's Little Italy, just as *The Mission* (d. Roland Joffé, 1986) is a film I use in my classes on liberation theology to show how the Catholic Church may historically have been seen in Latin America as complicit in the slave trade. In contrast, a theology of liberation radically changes the way in which the church understands the plight and dignity of those who are disempowered. Bonhoeffer's union of the sacred and the secular is a useful corrective, however, to those of us working in the theology-film field, to help us appreciate that a film does not need to concern the role of the church to be significant theologically. There may be serious problems afoot here, not least in the light of Clive Marsh's perception that "trying to maintain a serious interest in popular culture for serious theological purposes is not

Reconsidering the Normative

always met with seriousness in theology."[35] However, since theologians must necessarily live both in the church and the world, any major separation of the two "distorts both the task of Christianity's self-understanding and self-presentation, and the task of theological construction itself."[36]

This is not a new phenomenon. It is notable that Harvey Cox, arguably Bonhoeffer's greatest champion in the 1960s, quotes Amos Wilder in *The Secular City*:

> If we are to have any transcendence today, even Christian, it must be in and through the secular. . . . If we are to find Grace it is to be found in the world and not overhead. The sublime firmament of overhead reality that provided a spiritual home for the souls of men until the eighteenth century has collapsed.[37]

For Wilder, artists and poets are now more important than ever in dealing "at first hand with life, beyond the fences of social or religious propriety."[38] In the forty years or so since Wilder was writing, it is, arguably, filmmakers no less than artists and poets who can contribute to this conversation. While, as Marsh rightly counsels, this "does not justify every cultural product as an equally valid or equally revelatory work of God," it does "invite caution before popular culture is devalued, or too easily labeled as trite, or 'kitsch.'"[39] A film such as *Christmas with the Kranks* may in itself exhibit kitsch and be said to be an aesthetically impoverished film, with what one critic has called its "strained farce, laboured slapstick and sickly sentimental finale,"[40] but the film discloses too much about our preoccupations and values not to command any attention from theologians as well as from cultural commentators.[41]

This is not to say, however, that popular culture is intrinsically amenable to a conversation with theology. Paul Tillich is often cited as a theologian whose work most enables a fruitful dialogue between theology and film to arise, in the light of his contention in *Theology of Culture* that neither the religious nor the spiritual realm "should be in separation from the other" since both "are rooted in religion in the larger sense of the word, in the experience of ultimate concern."[42] But Tillich's theology also underscores the dangers inherent in presupposing that so-called secular phenomena constitute a religious significance per se. Despite being seen as someone for whom, in Lynch's words, "any form of belief that genuinely provides the basis for a person's or community's life could be understood as 'religious,'" and "if religion is the search for and expression of 'ultimate concern,' then culture is itself a manifestation of this fundamental religious orientation,"[43] Tillich was also quite limited in his understanding of the parameters of this process.

While in principle "everything that has being is an expression, however preliminary and transitory it may be, of being-itself, of ultimate reality,"[44] Tillich did not believe that every manifestation of popular culture has or bears witness to this dimension of depth. When Tillich argued that "ultimate reality becomes manifest in works of art,"[45] he had in mind not cinema but the paintings of Van Gogh, Munch, Derain, Marc, Heckel, and Nolde. Despite the significance of his claim that "I always learned more from pictures than from theological books,"[46] he believed that "the rediscovery of the expressive element in art since about 1900 is a decisive event for the relation of religion and the visual arts" and "has made religious art again possible."[47] The cinema is not accommodated at all in his schema, thus making it difficult to apply his theological insights to, for instance, a legal thriller that has been adapted from a John Grisham novel, along the lines of A Time to Kill (d. Joel Schumacher, 1996) or Runaway Jury (d. Gary Fleder, 2003). In Bonhoeffer's case, no such tensions seem to apply, especially in the light of Grisham's tendency to sketch eminently flawed, dysfunctional, and human protagonists whose character trajectories tend to involve materially obsessed, unscrupulous lawyers being transformed by suffering and destitution into selfless, humble, and more responsible individuals who cherish the joys of the families and friendships that they had hitherto spurned. It may be a stretch to forge too great a correlation between Bonhoeffer and Grisham, but at least there is scope for dialogue, whereas it is much more difficult to enter into the theology-film conversation with someone who believed that, unless one sees God as the ground or structure of all being, a certain idolatry is at work. Tillich believed that "the renewal of religious art will start in co-operation with architecture"[48] rather than with film, and he did not entertain the possibility that other media and artistic forms, which fail to satisfy our deepest spiritual needs, may also be capable of making a contribution.

Bultmann Meets Burton: The Way Forward

However, one of the most powerful ways in which the theology-film dialogue can move forward is with respect to the work of Rudolf Bultmann, arguably the greatest New Testament scholar of the twentieth century. Underlying Bultmann's thinking was the inescapably mythological and prescientific worldview within which the Gospel writers were function-

Reconsidering the Normative

ing.[49] For Bultmann, "Man's knowledge and mastery of the world have advanced to such an extent through science and technology that it is no longer possible for anyone seriously to hold the New Testament view of the world,"[50] not least because it is no longer intelligible to confess in creedal formulas that Christ "descended into hell" or "ascended into heaven" if in our post-Copernican universe one no longer shares the underlying mythical world picture of a three-story world. Accordingly, Bultmann saw it as his mission to clear away "the false stumbling blocks created by modern man by the fact that his world-view is determined by science,"[51] and he did this through his appropriation of Heideggerian existentialism[52] and his program of demythologization. The goal was to attempt to set free the true and authentic gospel message, which has for too long been submerged in the language of mythology, thereby ensuring that the kerygma could once again be heard. For Bultmann, such a process entailed not so much eliminating the myth as reinterpreting and translating it, and in so doing, making it clearer to modern men and women what the Christian faith is all about.

At first sight, the relationship of Bultmann's theology to the modern theology-film conversation may not be readily apparent. Indeed, Bultmann's disdain for the way the mass media can control us and lead us away from appropriating God's grace,[53] thereby ensuring that we remain in bondage to death, suggests that popular culture is more of a barrier than an invitation to undertaking theology. However, I propose that Bultmann's program rests on a misguided understanding of the role that the mass media—not least the medium of film—is capable of performing, and it is also somewhat flawed in its claim that myth—a staple not just of the New Testament but of many popular films—is an impediment to the way in which the Christian message can be most effectively communicated.

Regarding the first point, our increasingly celebrity- and consumer-oriented society, perhaps typified by the *Big Brother* television phenomenon, might be said to correspond to what Bultmann had in mind when he saw technology and the media as instruments that prevent us from properly encountering ourselves as human beings and ensure that we live an inauthentic existence. But Bultmann's assumption rests on a monolithic interpretation of the mass media—one that assumes that all it does is propagate illusion and cause us to immerse and lose ourselves in worldly and insecure concerns. When one bears in mind that the world of film noir, for example, is enmeshed in alienation, paranoia, and despair, where, in a film such as *Kiss Me Deadly* (d. Robert Aldrich, 1955), we are confronted with protagonists who are journeying on "a downward path to a miserable death or annihilating despair,"[54] we have a no less erudite understanding of the human condition than that which Bultmann was attempting to disclose. Since authenticity is seen to involve, in John Richardson's words, "a turning-towards those nullities"[55] from which an inauthentic existence flees, and when one "most directly and unflinchingly"[56] confronts and faces up to one's "own Being"[57] rather than detaching oneself from it, is film not capable of documenting this process? There may be something transitory and ephemeral about the role that the mass media often performs, but it does not always cause us to be transfixed and incapacitated by transitory concerns. Can film not provide us with a full and authentic awareness of the contingency of the world rather than prevent that awareness? Since, as Livingston writes, "it is only by meditating on such limit-situations in life that we can be awakened to decision, to freedom and, hence, to authentic existence,"[58] films can be no less conducive to this enterprise than the appropriation of a secular philosophy—existentialism—which is now somewhat dated and has merely succeeded, in the eyes of some scholars, in "dissolving the substance of the Christian Gospel . . . into some sort of self-understanding subjectivism."[59]

Film is especially powerful for evoking in the spectator what Jacob Golomb terms "the pathos of authenticity,"[60] and is capable of engaging spectators' attention and provoking them to evaluate their own being and define the mode of their existence through an authentic encounter with chaos, guilt, and the inevitability of death. The fact that, as John Berger puts it, "no other narrative art can get as close as the cinema does to the variety, the texture, the skin of daily life"[61] militates against Bultmann's dismissal of its properties. Needless to say, films that tend to rely on special effects and other technical transformations may be more diversionary and bring about the situation where, as J. Dudley Andrew sees it, we "attend to the movie and not to the world."[62] But even in films of a more escapist and fantasy orientation, it is possible to find much that is germane to the present discussion, linking as it does to my second critique of Bultmann—his contention that myth is a stumbling block to the way we understand the Christian message. It may have been Bultmann's premise that mythological language and thought forms are nowadays obsolete, and that it is "impossible to use electric light and the wireless and to avail ourselves of modern medical and surgical discoveries, and at the same time to believe in the New Testament world of spirits and miracles,"[63] but as Karl Jaspers rightly noted in 1962, Jesus's resurrection was as implausible and problematic in the first century as it is today.[64] For Jaspers, "mythical thinking is not a thing of the past, but characterizes

Reconsidering the Normative

man in any epoch"[65]—a statement mirrored in G. B. Caird's assertion that "myth is a pictorial way of expressing truths that cannot be expressed so readily or so forcefully in any other way."[66]

In looking at Tim Burton's recent film fantasy *Big Fish* (2003), which draws on the power of myth to propel the narrative forward, it is possible to find a powerful critique of Bultmann's program. *Big Fish* consists of a series of extravagant fairy tales recounted by an aging father, Edward Bloom (Albert Finney), who is dying of cancer. Over the years a rift has developed between Edward and his son, William (Billy Crudup), who has become exasperated by his father's seeming inability to tell the truth. On one level, it is easy to empathize with William's frustration. Stories concerning witches, werewolves, circus-performing Siamese twins, and twelve-foot giants are, in a literal sense, too fantastic and the product of an overfertile imagination. When a rational and skeptical son is told that on the day of his birth his father was wrestling in the sea with the legendary and uncatchable Big Fish, which he then caught by offering it a wedding ring, rather than—as the son later learns—that his father was away on business trying to eke out a meager existence as a traveling salesman, it is perhaps not surprising if a breakdown of communication has occurred. So long as William's point of reference is the literal preposterousness of his father's stories, this estrangement will persist.

Yet at the heart of *Big Fish* is William's transformation, as he comes to realize that "it is impossible to separate the man from the myth, the story from the reality."[67] The son learns that, rather than dogmatically insisting on truth over fiction, the two are often at their best when intertwined, with the myth a powerful and stimulating medium for articulating the unqualified love that Edward has for his family. As Sutcliffe puts it, "his father's extravagant birth story celebrates the mystery of life and the power and challenge of love, and points to the child as being of special significance,"[68] in a manner that is congruent with biblical heroes such as Moses, Samson, and Jesus, whose extraordinary birth narratives are effective (and arguably unsurpassed) narrative ways of drawing attention to their special status. The mythological thus has an intrinsic importance and does not require, as Bultmann believed, a process of demythologization in order for the truth that is being conveyed to be understood. Indeed, as Karl Jaspers wrote in *Kerygma and Myth*, "the mythical figures are symbols which, by their very nature, are untranslatable into other language,"[69] and are only accessible in this way and cannot be translated rationally. In a similar fashion, Edward Bloom sees the rational tendency to judge a story's truth with reference to its basis in actuality as a sterile approach that imparts "all of the facts and none of the flavor." Edward Bloom would, no doubt, have concurred with Jaspers, in his critique of Bultmann, that "how wretched, how lacking in expressiveness our life would be, if the language of myth were no longer valid!"[70] It is notable that Jaspers even goes so far as to denounce the demythologization program as "almost blasphemous."[71]

If Bultmann were around today, it would be interesting to see how he would respond to Tim Burton's presentation of myth, which, if demythologized, would leave us with just an empty shell. *Big Fish*—though not an explicitly theological film—is a useful corrective to Bultmann's overzealous deconstruction agenda, illustrating as it does that all demythologization does is take away a story's essence and vitality. At the end of the film, William fully immerses himself in the vocabulary and power of the mythological, in order to give his dying father a death narrative that is in keeping with the exuberant birth story he had earlier espoused. In so doing, he has ensured that Edward's spirit lives on. On a literal level, of course, Edward is dying in a hospital bed, connected to various medical apparatuses. But what gives the film such an emotional charge at this point is William's gracious giving of a "good story to help his father die." It involves Edward being released into a river, surrounded by all of his family and friends, and becoming "the big fish he always was."[72]

There may be a certain exaggeration of reality going on here, but this depends on what we mean by "reality." As Sutcliffe observes, "Physical reality may have proved susceptible to the story-teller's hyperbole, but what we might refer to as emotional reality has been accurately expressed—more accurately than if it were constrained by literal reality."[73] The redeeming power of storytelling is the film's raison d'être and ties in with how, as Heinz Zahrnt suggests, "without myth faith would be speechless."[74] Bultmann may have seen mythological language as obsolete and bound up with a worldview to which we no longer subscribe, but Mircea Eliade has shown us how, in certain cultures, myths are "indispensable" for the ways in which "they enable communities to find meaning and value in life."[75] Writing in 1955, John Macquarrie suggested that "twentieth-century man has been ready to swallow myths that are much more improbable than any that are to be found in the Bible."[76] Although this claim precedes *Big Fish* by nearly fifty years, the willingness of audiences to swallow whole a film narrative that, to paraphrase Bultmann, bears witness to an anachronistic worldview that scientific thinking has left behind, demonstrates just how far film can be used not merely to illustrate but also to critique and challenge various theological paradigms. Whether we are reading Bultmann or watching Burton, an engagement with *Big Fish* is an invaluable theological lesson in how we should be seeking not to destroy but to restore the language of myth.

Conclusion

What may have first appeared to be a juxtaposition of two irreconcilable and ontologically disparate pursuits—the work of a number of influential modern Christian theologians and the "secular" medium of film—has resulted instead in a redrawing of the boundaries within which both theology and film can be understood. Much work has been published over the years about how film is one of many contemporary agencies that has challenged traditional religious institutions and even taken on their functions. For instance, in 1985 Margaret Miles wrote that Christian churches "have relinquished the task of providing life-orienting images,"[77] and she followed this up, just over a decade later, with the assertion that the representation of values in American culture may be seen to occur most persistently not in the church or synagogue but in the movie theater, where people now gather "to ponder the moral quandaries of American life."[78] This was reiterated in 2004 by Christine Hoff Kraemer: "In some cases, the communal viewing of a film in a darkened theater and the lively discussion it inspires have become a more vital site of spiritual exploration and reflection than the mainline church service."[79] Clive Marsh has also recently written that the multiplex may be the modern cathedral and that those who work in film "may be functioning more authoritatively or at least more influentially than bishops."[80] This is all very persuasive, not least in the light of statistics, from which we learn that by the end of the twentieth century "only 7.5% of the population in England attended church on a regular basis"[81] and that in Australia, "the past two decades have seen the virtual disappearance of people under the age of forty from mainline churches."[82] In both cases, scholars have suggested that since institutionalized faith is on the decline we may be entering (or have already entered) some kind of post-Christian era, where noninstitutionalized forms of spirituality or religiosity have taken the place of the churches. The popularity of yoga, devotion to fitness regimes, and the preponderance of "mind, body, spirit" sections in mainstream bookstores all testify to the fact that alternative agencies may be taking on religious functions in the modern world.

In this article, however, I have sought to show that, rather than replacing religion, film has proven itself adept at facilitating and fine-tuning a theological conversation that is already taking place, albeit within scholarly circles. Outside the academy, it is undoubtedly true that people who pay to see movies at the cinema or on DVD will not be particularly stimulated by any conversation concerning the way in which *Christmas with the Kranks* or *Big Fish* can be used to shed light upon—even to critique—the way in which Cupitt, Bonhoeffer, or Bultmann undertook their theologies. Yet while ordinary filmgoers may not be privy to the conversations going on within theology, the need for theologians to be attuned to the sort of dialogue that films can foster should be taken more seriously. Whatever the religious or religion-like properties of the cinema, whereby, as I have argued elsewhere, groups of people file into a theater at a specified time, choose a seat, and prepare with others for what could be said to amount to a religious experience,[83] it does not follow that the only meaningful way in which the theology/religion-film debate can be conducted today involves assessing, in psychological or sociological terms, how cinema has become a functional equivalent of religious activity. That films may be addressing questions that churches are no longer meaningfully asking is of course an important issue, but it tends to overlook the very real and vital sense in which theology is an intensely contextual discipline that has always—and not just in recent years since the advent of the theology/religion and film field—depended upon an analysis of the close and inescapable interplay between theology and culture.

As I suggested at the beginning, just as a theology of liberation cannot be adequately understood outside the specific cultural, historical, political, and economic milieu within which it arose, so no theology can ever exist within a vacuum. Irrespective of whether Bultmann or Bonhoeffer drew on films in the course of constructing their theologies, we cannot, in a film-permeated Western culture at the beginning of the twenty-first century, understand their work today outside of the matrix of our own political, social, and cultural influences. Not only is it impossible, in my view, to do theology without constantly finding an intersection with popular culture (as when I recently found myself able to explain the distinctiveness of South American liberation theology most effectively in the light of a Hugh Grant speech). But we cannot even watch a Tim Burton film without encountering a critique of Bultmann's program of demythologization, which is no less insightful than what Karl Jaspers and John Macquarrie were espousing half a century ago.

Notes

1. Gordon Lynch, *Understanding Theology and Popular Culture* (Oxford: Blackwell, 2005), 96.

2. First published in English as Gustavo Gutiérrez, *A Theology of Liberation: History, Politics, and Salvation* (Maryknoll, NY: Orbis Books, 1973).

3. It is notable that all the other theologians we have looked at in class are European, mostly German-based, thinkers, such as Barth, Bultmann, and Pannenberg.

4. The basic questions that concern theologians in Europe and Latin America are so radically divergent because the type of questions asked by the former—"Does God exist?" "What does it mean to live a 'worldly holiness'?" "Is God Wholly Other, with no point of consciousness existing between God and humans?" "What is the nature of revelation as distinct from reason?" and "What does it mean to define God as the ground of all being and as ultimate concern?"—are peripheral to the latter, who are working in a continent where there already exists a framework of faith and where belief in God is normative.

5. Quoted in James C. Livingston, *Modern Christian Thought: From the Enlightenment to Vatican II* (London: Collier Macmillan, 1971), 347.

6. Lynch, *Understanding Theology*, 96.

7. As characterized by the abundance of literature on Christ-figure motifs in film.

8. For more on this, see H. Richard Niebuhr, *Christ and Culture* (London: Faber & Faber, 1952).

9. The ceremony took place on Sunday, April 23, 1995, at the London Palladium.

10. Robert Philip Kolker, *A Cinema of Loneliness* (Oxford: Oxford University Press, 1988), 64.

11. See William Hamilton and Thomas Altizer, *Radical Theology and the Death of God* (New York: Bobbs-Merrill, 1966).

12. Quoted in L. Miller and Stanley J. Grenz, *Fortress Introduction to Contemporary Theologies* (Minneapolis: Fortress, 1998), 83.

13. Kolker, *Cinema of Loneliness*, 64.

14. Richard Rubenstein, *After Auschwitz: Radical Theology and Contemporary Judaism* (Indianapolis: Bobbs-Merrill, 1966), 151.

15. Don Cupitt, *The Sea of Faith* (London: BBC, 1984), 10.

16. Ibid.

17. Ibid., 30.

18. Roger Ebert, "Christmas with the Kranks," *Chicago Sun-Times*, November 24, 2004, http://rogerebert.suntimes.com/apps/pbcs.dll/article?AID=/20041123/REVIEWS/41116002/1023.

19. See, e.g., Anton Karl Kozlovic, "The Structural Characteristics of the Cinematic Christ-figure," *Journal of Religion and Popular Culture* 8 (Fall 2004), www.usask.ca/relst/jrpc/art8-cinematicchrist.html.

20. Quoted in Miller and Grenz, *Fortress Introduction to Contemporary Theologies*, 70.

21. Dietrich Bonhoeffer, *The Cost of Discipleship* (London: SCM, 1959), 41.

22. Dietrich Bonhoeffer, *Letters and Papers from Prison* (London: Fontana, 1963), 123.

23. Ibid., 128–29.

24. Quoted in Robert K. Johnston, *Reel Spirituality: Theology and Film in Dialogue*, 2nd ed. (Grand Rapids: Baker Academic, 2006), 287–88.

25. Quoted in ibid., 288.

26. Vincent Canby, "The Year of Living Dangerously," *New York Times*, January 23, 1983, http://movies2.nytimes.com/mem/movies/review.html?res=9951A0C0173BF932A35750 C8BF67.

27. Quoted in John Walker, ed., *Halliwell's Film Guide*, 3rd ed. (London: HarperCollins, 1995), 1277.

28. Wayne Whitson Floyd, "Dietrich Bonhoeffer," in *The Modern Theologians*, ed. David Ford with Rachel Muers, 3rd ed. (Oxford: Blackwell, 2005), 51.

29. Bonhoeffer, *Letters and Papers from Prison*, 122.

30. Ibid.

31. Fred Burnett, "The Characterization of Martin Riggs in *Lethal Weapon 1*: An Archetypal Hero," in *Screening Scripture: Intertextual Connections Between Scripture and Film*, ed. George Aichele and Richard Walsh (Harrisburg, PA: Trinity, 2002), 266.

32. Ibid.

33. Bonhoeffer, *Letters and Papers from Prison*, 121.

34. In this respect, it is helpful to encounter a theological reading of a film that challenges a theological paradigm rather than—as is the case with the Christ-figure literature—attempts to simply illustrate an elementary narrative thread.

35. Clive Marsh, *Cinema and Sentiment: Film's Challenge to Theology* (Carlisle: Paternoster, 2004), 144.

36. Clive Marsh and Gaye Ortiz, "Theology beyond the Modern and the Postmodern: A Future Agenda for Theology and Film," in *Explorations in Theology and Film: Movies and Meaning*, ed. Clive Marsh and Gaye Ortiz (Oxford: Blackwell, 1997), 254.

37. Quoted in Harvey Cox, *The Secular City* (New York: Macmillan, 1966), 228.

38. Ibid.

39. Marsh, *Cinema and Sentiment*, 144.

40. Neil Smith, "Christmas with the Kranks," *BBC Movies*, December 1, 2004, www.bbc.co.uk/films/2004/12/01/christmas_with_the_kranks_2004_reviews.html.

41. As Harvey Cox puts it, "Secularization rolls on, and if we are to understand and communicate with our present age we must learn to love it in its unremitting secularity" (*Secular City*, 3). Seeing secularization as a process distinct from secularism, Cox feels that it "represents an authentic consequence of biblical faith" (ibid., 15), the seeds of which go as far back as the creation narrative in Genesis, where God gives Adam and Eve the task of cultivating and making use of the created order. For Cox, once we move beyond "inherited metaphysical and religious meanings," this can have a liberating effect as humans are thereby turned "loose to compose new ones" (ibid., 94), with all the attendant possibilities for maturity and responsibility that this can entail. That film may be part of this process is implicit in Cox's theology, not least in light of his concern that the theologian must avoid the danger of being concerned with merely "high" culture. For Cox, developing ideas that Bonhoeffer himself would very likely have advanced had he survived the Second World War, a balance must be struck by theologians between an uncritical reception of popular culture and remaining in their ivory towers. Cox explicitly advocates moving "beyond a culture dominated by print," with what he calls "its inherently elitist characteristics," to the point where electronic media has the potential to "facilitate a more democratic and more participatory society than we now have" (Cox, "The Seduction of the Spirit: The Use and Misuse of People's Religion," in *Theological Aesthetics: A Reader*, ed. Gesa Elsbeth Thiessen [London: SCM, 2004], 254).

42. Paul Tillich, *Theology of Culture* (New York: Oxford University Press, 1964), 9.

43. Lynch, *Understanding Theology*, 29.

44. Paul Tillich, "Art and Ultimate Reality," in Thiessen, *Theological Aesthetics*, 210.

45. Ibid., 211.

46. Ibid., 216.

47. Tillich, *Theology of Culture*, 74.

48. Ibid., 75.

49. This is epitomized by the belief in a three-decker cosmos containing heaven above, the underworld below, and the earth somewhere in the middle, to which both God from on high and demons from beneath have access.

Reconsidering the Normative

50. Rudolf Bultmann, "New Testament and Mythology," in *Kerygma and Myth*, vol. 1, ed. Hans-Werner Bartsch (London: SPCK, 1953), 4.

51. Rudolf Bultmann, "The Case for Demythologising," in *Kerygma and Myth*, vol. 2, ed. Hans-Werner Bartsch (London: SPCK, 1962), 183.

52. Bultmann found the most appropriate medium for liberating the New Testament message to be the philosophy of existentialism, as formulated by Martin Heidegger. According to Bultmann, Heidegger's philosophy had "all by itself" discovered and encapsulated what the New Testament was telling us, through its anachronistic worldview, about the human condition. While acknowledging that there is no absolutely perfect system, Bultmann said Heidegger's philosophy "offers the most adequate perspective and conceptions for understanding human existence" (*Jesus Christ and Mythology* [London: SCM, 1966], 55) by virtue of its delineation of human beings as existing "in a permanent tension between the past and the future" ("New Testament and Mythology," 24), which we can either accept responsibility for and live out authentically or lose ourselves to the variety of outside pressures that try to deny our individuality and freedom.

53. Bultmann's argument is that when the New Testament mentions the existence of demonic powers ruling our world and of our being "fallen" creatures, this says something vital about human existence that we can understand in the modern day. Due to our passion for material things and the influence upon us of the mass media, we are alienated in a comparable way because external objects and influences—albeit technology instead of supernatural demons—exert an undue sway over our lives. The goal for Bultmann is to learn to be dependent for security not on the world but on God, and in so doing make the transition from an inauthentic to an authentic existence.

54. Michael Walker, "*Film Noir*: Introduction," in *The Movie Book of Film Noir*, ed. Ian Cameron (London: Studio Vista, 1994), 16.

55. John Richardson, *Existential Epistemology: A Heideggerean Critique of the Cartesian Project* (Oxford: Clarendon, 1991), 194.

56. Ibid.

57. Ibid., 195.

58. Livingston, *Modern Christian Thought*, 350.

59. Miller and Grenz, *Fortress Introduction to Contemporary Theologies*, 51.

60. Jacob Golomb, *In Search of Authenticity: From Kierkegaard to Camus* (London: Routledge, 1995), 19.

61. John Berger, "Every Time We Say Goodbye," *Sight and Sound* 1, no. 2 (June 1991): 16.

62. J. Dudley Andrew, *The Major Film Theories: An Introduction* (Oxford: Oxford University Press, 1976), 110.

63. Bultmann, "New Testament and Mythology," 5.

64. Karl Jaspers, "Myth and Religion," in Bartsch, *Kerygma and Myth*, vol. 2, 134.

65. Ibid., 144.

66. Quoted in Maurice Wiles, "Myth in Theology," in *The Myth of God Incarnate*, ed. John Hick (London: SCM, 1977), 154.

67. David Sutcliffe, "Virtual Literalism: *Big Fish*," in *Flickering Images: Theology and Film in Dialogue*, ed. Anthony J. Clarke and Paul S. Fiddes (Oxford: Regent's Park College, 2005, and Macon, GA: Smith & Helwys, 2005), 85.

68. Ibid., 92.

69. Jaspers, "Myth and Religion," 144.

70. Ibid.

71. Ibid.

72. Sutcliffe, "Virtual Literalism," 92.

73. Ibid., 87.

74. Heinz Zahrnt, *The Question of God*, trans. R. A. Wilson (London: Collins, 1969), 246.

75. Quoted in David Fergusson, *Bultmann* (London: Geoffrey Chapman, 1992), 129.

76. John Macquarrie, *An Existentialist Theology: A Comparison of Heidegger and Bultmann* (London: SCM, 1955), 245.

77. Margaret Miles, *Image as Insight: Visual Understanding in Western Christianity and Secular Culture* (Boston: Beacon, 1985), 152.

78. Ibid., 25.

79. Christine Hoff Kraemer, "From Theological to Cinematic Criticism: Extricating the Study of Religion and Film from Theology," *Religious Studies Review* 30, no. 4 (October 2004): 243.

80. Marsh, *Cinema and Sentiment*, 3.

81. Lynch, *Understanding Theology*, 166.

82. Peter Horsfield, "Electronic Media and the Past-Future of Christianity," in *Mediating Religion: Conversations in Media, Religion and Culture*, ed. Jolyon Mitchell and Sophia Marriage (London: Continuum, 2003), 271.

83. See Christopher Deacy, *Screen Christologies: Redemption and the Medium of Film* (Cardiff: University of Wales Press, 2001), 4.

Reconsidering the Normative

Making Better Use of Our Theological Traditions

13

Shaping Morals, Shifting Views

Have the Rating Systems Influenced
How (Christian) America Sees Movies?

ROSE PACATTE, FSP

I am to give a talk on the dizzying subject—"What Is a Wholesome Novel?" I intend to tell them that the reason they find nothing but obscenity in modern fiction is because that is all they know how to recognize.

Flannery O'Connor[1]

In my December 2005 column "Eye on Entertainment" for *St. Anthony Messenger* magazine, I wrote:

MILLIONS (A-2, PG) deserves to become a family Christmas classic. Reviewed here in April and newly released on DVD, it centers on an English boy who finds a bag of cash at Christmas. The lad is visited by saints, who inspire him to help poor people.

One reader soon wrote to the editor:

Please allow me to strongly disagree with the recommendation of the movie *Millions* as a "family Christmas classic." The review does not warn families of the Internet pornography scene. The two boys enjoying the picture of a woman's breast violates the dignity of women. It encourages boys to pursue this form of entertainment. This scene alone disqualifies it as a family friendly movie. The offensive scene is an insult to the morality of any God-loving home, no matter the religious affiliation. I beg your publication to retract this recommendation and clearly warn families away from its viewing. I truly expected more of a Catholic publication. It is clear from this review alone that I cannot trust your movie reviews.

Mrs. W.
Maryland

When the letter was published in *St. Anthony Messenger* in February, 2006, an e-mail message about it soon arrived:

In reference to the letter "Not Quite a Classic" to the editor in February (2006) issue, I must commend Sister Rose's response regarding the movie *Millions*. Sister Rose is absolutely correct in her explanation of the meaning of the segment of this very enjoyable movie. . . . I was, however, waiting for Sister Rose to point out a scene in the movie that I felt was irresponsible of the producers to include but that once again illustrates the climate of our times. I refer to, of course, the scene where the father is sleeping with the young woman with whom he has just recently met and could not have possibly forged any type of commitment. This is extremely misleading to young people watching this. I think *St. Anthony Messenger* was remiss in not warning parents of this small but important scene. We have to be careful of the subtle messages movies give us.

Thanks
Ms. M. H.

Although no mention is made of film ratings in these exchanges about the perceived sexual content—and diverse readings—of Danny Boyle's British-made 2005 film *Millions*, these comments led me to ask one question, which led to others: Why do some people judge and react to a film by images of the human body without considering the context of the story in which they are presented, as demonstrated by Mrs. W's letter? What accounts for the divergent readings of the two women and myself about the film *Millions*? What view of morality, and therefore, of God, may have prompted these readings? Why is the implied meaning about the human body as represented in the same film contested? Is it because of a valid concern for what children watch, or is an appeal to an inarticulated standard, or some kind of fear, involved? Why did these two viewers fixate on the body and sex when the overall meaning of the film was of greater value than a negative reading of the image of the woman in the bra on the Internet (which, if the woman had left the DVD on and seen the entire sequence, would have revealed a positive message; in a subsequent letter to me she stated that her sons had turned off the TV knowing what her reaction would be if she had walked in at that moment), or that the father was engaged in illicit sex? Why do Christians often see content over context, the tree instead of the forest?

To help guide people in their film selections, *St. Anthony Messenger* lists both the Motion Picture Association of America (MPAA) ratings and those of the United States Conference of Catholic Bishops' Office for Film and Broadcast (USCCB/OFB) ratings or classifications for each film. The magazine routinely publishes the Catholic classifications chart with the column to assist readers' understanding of those ratings. But have ratings or film classifications been a mixed blessing in regard to how moviegoers choose films and then make meaning from the film they have chosen? What has been the effect of the change from the Hays Production Code to a classification system by the MPAA in 1968 on how filmgoers choose and make meaning from films?

This chapter is an attempt to explore the question of how the ratings and classifications of the MPAA, which replaced the Hays Production Code in 1968, and the USCCB, which replaced the Legion of Decency ratings system in the mid-1960s, may have contributed to the current focus of Christians in the United States on the sexual, violent, and obscene language content (now including alcohol, smoking, drugs, and body parts and functions) as the key factors in judging the value of a film rather than its meaning, which is rendered by interpreting and judging a film by the story's context and by the social context in which a film exists. A key aspect of this question requires a look at the purpose of the MPAA and USCCB/OFB classifications and how they morphed into what they are today.

To do this I will look at how the US classification or ratings systems came about through the religious, theologizing community. This requires an exploration, albeit limited, of the moral ambiguity and ambivalence toward leisure and theater as found in the writings of our Puritan forefathers (whose direct descendants are today's Presbyterians and evangelicals), the influence of Jansenism on Catholicism in the United States in the formation of contemporary attitudes of Catholics, and the similar ambivalent expression of moral teaching toward cinema found more recently in the teaching of the Catholic Church. To frame my appraisal of this theology-

and-film issue, I will use quotations from C. S. Lewis, a Protestant novelist and writer, and Flannery O'Connor, a Catholic novelist.

My premise for this exploration is that I suspect that the influence of Puritan and Jansenist theology in early American life led to the creation of ratings systems that influence how Christians view movies today. I propose that this is because we are taught, not taught, and sometimes untaught how to communicate and make meaning from stories, whether on the printed page or through sight and sound, through the focus ratings provide.

Puritanism and Leisure

There is a saying that "the only consistent thing about [entertainment] is that it is inconsistent." I have heard from people who strive to be conscientious about their media consumption according to moral standards rooted in their faith life. They complain that just as they were beginning to like a television show, for example, it changed and added sex or some other unacceptable element. These same people, however, live freely and often very comfortably, in a capitalist political economy that permits and profits from television shows and movies that often do not reflect what they believe are objective moral values. They do not seem to perceive, and therefore do not question, a connection between the aspects of leisure experienced in mainstream media on the one hand and American public life on the other. I believe that these connections are, however, self-evident and interdependent.

The Age of Reason in seventeenth-century Europe and the Enlightenment in the eighteenth century are credited with removing faith or objective truth as the basis for morality and right living and replacing it with reason based on an arbitrary choice of premise. The roots of American moral inconsistency about leisure can be traced in large part to this overarching era and to the ambivalence of our Puritan ancestors toward pursuits such as theater.

In *Puritans at Play: Leisure and Recreation in Colonial New England*, author Bruce C. Daniels notes:

> For a society remarkably consistent in its commitment to a primary purpose, early New England pursued its grand goal with a high degree of ambivalence over strategies, values, and secondary purposes. A series of conflicting impulses lay under much of this ambivalence: Puritans believed

in conformity to doctrine but also in liberty of conscience; they worked for material prosperity but wanted to avoid worldly temptations; they prized social communalism but asserted economic individualism. . . . As a result, Puritan society was profoundly ambivalent—partly because of divisions between individuals but even more because of unresolved conflicts with them. On many matters, Puritans wanted to have things both ways, to eat their cake and have it, too.[2]

This certainly extended to ideas about leisure and recreation (including reading, music, and theater), which the Puritans eventually endorsed but always tempered with cautions. Daniels quotes Benjamin Coleman, an early eighteenth-century Puritan writer, as saying, "'I am far from inveighing against sober mirth; on the contrary, I justify, applaud, and recommend it. Let it be pure and grace, serious and devout. All which it may be and yet be free and cheerful; . . . mirth may and generally does degenerate into sin; 'tis ordinarily the froth and noxious blast of a corrupt heart.' In its overall thrust, Coleman's work rehashed what must have been a familiar message to New Englanders: Have fun, but not too much."[3]

Puritan—that is, Calvinist—thought, theology, and morality, which prevailed in New England from 1620 through the Revolutionary War until 1780, was gradually eroded due to the emergence of major cities over the original settlements, villages, and towns, and when "regional identity became submerged in a national polity."[4] The original New England preachers, who interpreted the Scriptures literally, followed Calvin's idea that "the mind was so limited by its finitude and so darkened by sin that its efforts to attain knowledge of God apart from the biblical revelation led only to idolatry. In Scripture, God provided the correcting lenses that rescued reason from its fallen state. Among New England theologians, this conclusion was axiomatic."[5] Daniels notes that during the struggles of the Revolutionary period, even Samuel and John Adams thought that "Republican virtue might not survive . . . unless the spirit of self-denial was re-invigorated. . . . Puritan asceticism found a voice in the guise of republican simplicity."[6]

Puritanism and Theater

When it came to theater, Puritans on both sides of the Atlantic thought theater was evil. It was not accepted or legitimatized in the colonies until the end of the eighteenth century, after the American Revolution. According to Daniels,

> Politics and circumstance mixed with theology to produce this unremitting hatred. At the same time as Puritanism emerged as an alternative to the Church of England, theater emerged as the center of Elizabethan entertainment. Because the stage lay at the heart of elite English culture and literary life, Puritans associated it closely with the monarchy and Anglicanism. Thus, political and historical associations rendered theater odious to religious reformers.[7]

I do not consider it a stretch to observe here that the colonial Puritan reaction to the extravagance of the Church of England, the religion of a government from which they fled in pursuit of religious freedom and later revolted against for civil freedom, paralleled another tension within the Puritan between what Daniels calls "self-denial and self-gratification." He believes that to a certain extent all societies struggle with this dilemma.[8]

Theater created social problems in Elizabethan England, which is why the Old Globe (built in 1598), the Rose (1587–1605) and the Swan (1594–ca. 1637) were situated outside the city of London. They were often closed by officials when plays were banned for moral reasons or during civil unrest or outbreaks of the plague. Theatrical companies also charged large sums, and sexual immorality (this meant homosexuality since actors were male) among their members was well known by the public. The Puritans burned down the Old Globe in 1644, while the Rose was demolished during a time when interest in the theater briefly waned.

But theater throughout the colonies was proscribed in the seventeenth century. It was not until the mid-1700s when *The Merchant of Venice* was performed in Virginia, staged by an Englishman named William Hallem,[9] that colonists, then consisting of people from different faiths, began to accept theater. It was not easy going, however. New England passed a law banning theater in 1767. It was repealed in 1792 by the Massachusetts General Assembly when a delegate named John Gardiner published a pamphlet that "challenged the beliefs, icons, and traditions that had survived unquestioned in public discourse since the founding generation." The opposition relied upon the old, outdated Puritan ascetic, but Gardiner noted that Yale and Harvard were teaching Greek civilization, the origin of drama. He pointed out that "the rest of the nation . . . regarded New England's ban on theater absurd." Most important, Daniels says, "Gardiner forced New England to confront its Puritan past."[10] Gardiner's

Making Better Use of Our Theological Traditions

efforts resulted in the repeal of the law in Massachusetts, and though the critics remained, the dominance of Puritanism as a public influence in direct government was over.

The Puritan hegemony in American politics may have ended in 1792, but its religious and cultural heritage lives on here, as C. S. Lewis believed it did in England. In a 1961 essay titled *An Experiment in Criticism*, he wrote about the influence of Puritanism in British education, specifically literature. In it he describes the moral heritage of Puritanism on literature students in a way that may shed light on how Christians in America may respond not only to literature but also by extension to cinema and other forms of entertainment:

> One sad result of making English literature a "subject" at schools and universities is the reading of great authors, from early years, stamped upon the minds of conscientious and submissive young people as something meritorious. When the young person in question is an agnostic whose ancestors were Puritans, you get a very regrettable state of mind. The Puritan conscience works on without the Puritan theology—like millstones grinding nothing; like digestive juices working on an empty stomach and producing ulcers. The unhappy youth applies to literature all the scruples, the rigorism, the self-examination, the distrust of pleasure, which his forebears applied to the spiritual life; and perhaps soon all the intolerance and self-righteousness. . . . This is where the literary Puritans may fail most lamentably. They are too serious as men to be seriously receptive as readers.[11]

Catholics and Jansenism

> I like Pascal but I don't think the Jansenist influence is healthy in the Church. The Irish are notably infected with it because all the Jansenist priests were chased out of France at the time of the Revolution and ended up in Ireland. It was a bad day if you ask me. I read a novel by Sean O'Faolain about the demise of the Irish novel. Apparently someone had suggested that there wasn't enough sin in Ireland to supply the need. O'Faolain said no, the Irish sinned constantly but with no great emotion except fear. Jansenism doesn't seem to breed so much a love of God as a love of asceticism.
>
> Flannery O'Connor[12]

Reinforcing O'Connor's point, first- and second-generation Irish missionaries, in addition to the French, Spanish, and to a lesser extent Germans and Italians, made up a dominant percentage of the Catholic hierarchy and parish priests that influenced American Catholic life from the colonial era through the present.[13]

If it can be said that primitive Puritanism continues to influence morality in America regardless of whether a person belongs to a faith community or not (I contend that it does), it can just as easily be said that European Jansenism as an aesthetic movement among Catholics continues to influence Catholic attitudes toward morality, leisure, and entertainment because of the connection to our spiritual roots through Irish (and French) missionaries.[14]

There is a curious link between Puritanism or Calvinism and Jansen in the teachings of Augustine of Hippo regarding justification: when and how a person turns from sin to God and grace.[15] Anthony Fisher, OP, now auxiliary bishop of Sydney, Australia, parallels Jansenism and the Tridentine Movement[16] theologically and historically in a 1990 article "Lefebvrism—Jansenism Revisited?"[17] Jansenism, he says, "held the neo-Calvinist position that as a result of the fall, human beings are irremediably corrupt and only a few can be saved, and these only by irresistible grace." I think it is important to connect Puritanism and its influence on leisure and morality, and the influence of Jansenism on Catholic aestheticism and morality because both have helped shape the public culture that gave rise to the Hays Production Code, which I will address in the next section.

Cornelius Jansen (1585–1638) was a Flemish theologian, the bishop of Ypres, and an expert on St. Augustine. His great work, *Augustinius*, was not published until after his death. It became controversial because it was deemed to be more Protestant than Catholic regarding free will and grace. The five propositions (two articulated and three extrapolated from the work) were interpreted as emphasizing "the absolute necessity and irresistible character of grace, leading critics to conclude that the book was denying free will, promoting moral rigorism, and generating pessimism about the possibility of salvation."[18] The actual text was condemned by the Inquisition in 1641, and the propositions were condemned in 1653 by Pope Innocent X. These gave rise to a movement that would be called Jansenism. This movement became a basis of piety in France, most notably through the influence of the nuns of Port-Royal, especially their abbess Mere Angelique and the confessor to the nuns, Abbé Saint-Cyran. Blaise Pascal (1623–62), the French mathematician, physicist, philosopher, and erstwhile theologian, had a sister who was a nun of Port-Royal, and his own conversion and religious practices and writings were heavily influenced by the movement. Always in poor health, he came to believe that "sickness was the natural state of Christians." Jansenism emphasized the moral depravity of human beings, intense piety, and rigid moral rectitude

Making Better Use of Our Theological Traditions

as well as the person's unworthiness to receive the Eucharist unless he or she had pure love and disdained the world—thus only a few would ever be worthy. This created spiritual elitism and also gave rise to an emphasis on external expressions of piety over one's inner dispositions. The treatise *De la fréquente communion* in 1643 by the theologian and philosopher Antoine Arnauld (1612–94) propagated Saint-Cyran's penitential doctrine to France and from there to Europe and beyond.[19]

In an interview, Robert Welch, SJ, emeritus professor of political science at Loyola Marymount University,[20] traced the roots of Jansenism (and Calvinism) to second- and third-century Gnosticism, a philosophical movement that has influenced Christianity ever since. Gnosticism reduced the explanation for the world to a dualistic concept of good and evil forces battling for world dominance. A good force contained a true, elite knowledge (gnosis) that was purely spiritual, symbolized by light and limited to a few. The evil force contained the world of matter and darkness. This view resulted in the Christian sect of Manichaeism, which held that there were two gods, one good, one evil. St. Augustine first learned his Christianity as a Manichaean, converting to orthodox Christianity in AD 387. Gnosticism-Manichaeism reemerged, as their descendant or reinvention, in the eleventh through thirteenth centuries as Albigensianism in France. This belief reiterated the dualism and elitism of its ancestors and held that God, who was omnipotent, was the epitome of cruelty.[21]

The Second Vatican Council (1962–65) attempted to cleanse the church of the remaining influences of Jansenism, especially in documents such as *Lumen gentium* (1964; *Dogmatic Constitution on the Church*), which speaks against the elitism perpetuated by Jansenism:

> At all times and in every race God has given welcome to whosoever fears Him and does what is right. God, however, does not make men holy and save them merely as individuals, without bond or link between one another. Rather has it pleased Him to bring men together as one people, a people which acknowledges Him in truth and serves Him in holiness.[22]

Gaudium et spes (1965; *Pastoral Constitution on the Church in the Modern World*) gave the church a pastoral framework to interact with the modern world, and *Dignitatis humanae* (1965; *Declaration on Religious Freedom*) stated that each human being, because of his or her essential dignity, is free to seek religious truth without coercion by any person or state. *Inter mirifica* (1963; *Decree on the Instruments of Social Communication*) praised the media, and like the church's previous documents on cinema, television, and radio, and early Puritan attitudes toward leisure, added a familiar-sounding caution at the same time:

> The Church recognizes that these media, if properly utilized, can be of great service to mankind, since they greatly contribute to men's entertainment and instruction as well as to the spread and support of the Kingdom of God. The Church recognizes, too, that men can employ these media contrary to the plan of the Creator and to their own loss. Indeed, the Church experiences maternal grief at the harm all too often done to society by their evil use.[23]

The efforts of Vatican II, however, did not forestall the reemergence of Jansenism through traditionalist movements such as the one led by Archbishop Marcel Lefebvre (1905–91) of Paris (and Econe, Switzerland). In an article comparing Jansenists and modern traditionalists in the Catholic Church, Anthony Fisher, OP, states:

> At the heart of the Jansenist position was a profound pessimism about the world and the power of the human will to resist evil. . . . Thus, in continuity with several other strands in Christian history, these two groups responded to pessimism about human nature, the Church and the world by embracing a severe moral and disciplinary regime which (for all the Jansenists' talk about grace) was intended to mark out the true believers and help ensure their salvation.[24]

Fisher illustrates this return to moral rigorism by the excommunicated Lefebvre[25] and his Society of Saint Pius X by quoting an exhortation attributed to Lefebvre by one of the members:

> We should know how to do without television and break with the desires of the flesh, the lusts of the eyes, the pride of life and honors. We must know how to do penances, abstaining from all that is too much of this world, all that panders to the flesh and indecent dress. All such things should be wholly forbidden to true Christians or we shall be bereft of God's grace, the grace needful now to our salvation. We should go from one disaster to another.[26]

The kind of Irish-Catholic–influenced (or European-immigrant-Jansenist–influenced) asceticism that American novelist Flannery O'Connor refers to in the quote that begins this section endures today within some expressions of Catholic culture, for example, in books, journals, and prayer books that favor and reflect a pre–Vatican Council II approach to morality and spirituality or asceticism. I have a theory that the polarized response to the Harry

Potter books and films is an example of a reaction stemming from ascetically induced fear that obscures judgment of the actual merits of the books and films.[27] This helps explain, I believe, the unintegrated approach and lack of understanding of storytelling in the way many Catholics judge cinema. Note, however, that people often try to be more Catholic than the official church ever taught them to be—as demonstrated by the scene in Alan Parker's *Angela's Ashes* (1999), when the young Frank McCourt gets sick and possibly upchucks the consecrated host in the backyard after partaking of his first Holy Communion, and his grandmother drags him to the parish church to go to confession, to the great irritation of the priest. (I remember that as novices we intuitively grasped the depressing approach to asceticism expressed in older books in the library as "worm theology"—see Ps. 22:6.)

Tom Shadyac's *Bruce Almighty* (2003) shows how a perception of God as a "mighty smiter" looks in everyday life in the United States. "Why do you hate me?" Bruce (Jim Carrey) yells at God when he's late for work. He expresses his view of God as "a mean kid sitting on an anthill with a magnifying glass, and I'm the ant. He could fix my life in five minutes if He wanted to, but he'd rather burn off my feelers and watch me squirm." Bruce's story illustrates the human battle between good and evil, light and dark, and a negative and positive image of God. Happily, Bruce's image of God grows and changes, and he moves beyond his own little world of frustration to being the miracle that God (Morgan Freeman) tells him he has the power to be. But where did Bruce get his ingrained image of God? The film does not tell us but seems to assume that Bruce's view is a common one. According to the Internet Movie Database,[28] about 70 million people saw the film, and it grossed just under $250 million in the United States alone, not counting DVD sales. So we can safely assume that it made sense to a great many people. The films of Martin Scorsese written by Paul Schrader (e.g., *Taxi Driver*, 1976; *Raging Bull*, 1980; *The Last Temptation of Christ*, 1988; and *Bringing Out the Dead*, 1999) are a curious mix of Catholic guilt expressed visually and Protestant guilt expressed verbally. Scorsese's recent film, *The Departed* (2006; written by William Monahan), moved on from the burden of Catholic guilt to the conflict of conscience. It might have been a very different film, and no less compelling, if it had been penned by Schrader.

Jansenism and Puritanism Revisited

Thus, the discussion about justification and grace actually boils down to one's theology and the image of God and the image of the human person one has formed through the process of doing theology—that is, "faith seeking understanding,"[29] or how a person relates to and processes someone else's theology, such as one heard in church while growing up or through religion and Bible teachers or from parents and grandparents. Is the human person worthy of God's love and salvation from sin? Does a person possess free will and the belief, or not, in the possibility that God forgives sin and can transform a person by grace? The narrow path to Jansenist justification is reserved for only a few, almost as if the person is more acceptable to God the more one condemns human nature. This has often led to superficial asceticism such as that illustrated in Lasse Hallström's film *Chocolat* (2000). This cinematic fable, judged O, morally objectionable, by the USCCB/OFB,[30] highlights what happens when Lenten asceticism is empty and merely practiced for all to see rather than for spiritual conversion and growth in one's relationship to God. The movie is an imaginative tale drawn straight from the Gospel (see Matt. 23:1–5). But interpreting it literally rather than as a fable (or according to how some Catholics might interpret it as a criticism of the church) resulted in this unnecessary condemnation.

In addition to *Chocolat*, other recent films that illustrate both a Puritanical and Jansenist approach to teaching, living, and controlling the content and spirituality of Christianity include Lars von Trier's *Breaking the Waves* (1996), Gillian Armstrong's *Oscar and Lucinda* (1997), Stephen Frear's *Liam* (2000), Mark Stephen Johnson's *Simon Birch* (1998), and, again, Alan Parker's *Angela's Ashes* (1999).

Flannery O'Connor wrote to a friend and fellow novelist:

> About the novel of religious conversion: . . . I think you are wrong that heroes have to be stable. If they were stable there wouldn't be any story. It seems to me that all good stories are about conversion, about a character's changing. . . . The action of grace changes a character. . . . Part of the difficulty of all this is that you write for an audience who doesn't know what grace is and don't recognize it when they see it.[31]

Although he admits to haste in his characterizations of readers, C. S. Lewis continues his lament and comparison about the influence of Puritanism on how people read literature:

> A young woman most penitently confessed to a friend of mine that an unholy desire to read women's magazines was her besetting "temptation."

It is the existence of these literary Puritans that has deterred me from applying the word *serious* to the right sort of readers and reading. It suggests itself at first as just the sort of word we want. But it is fatally equivocal. . . .

This is where literary Puritans may fail most lamentably. They are too serious as men to be seriously receptive as readers. I have listened to an undergraduate's paper on Jane Austin from which, if I had not read them, I should never have discovered that there was the first hint of comedy in her novels. . . . We are breeding up a race of young people who are as solemn as brutes ("smiles from reason flow"); as solemn as a nineteen-year-old Scottish son of the manse at an English sherry party who takes all the compliments for declarations and all the banter for insult. Solemn men, but not serious readers; they have not fairly and squarely laid their minds open, without preconception, to the works they have read.[32]

The Hays Production Code

Pornography and violence and anything else in excess are all sins against form, and I think they ought to be approached as sins against art rather than sins against morality.

Flannery O'Connor[33]

In 1911 Pennsylvania became the first state in the United States to pass a law permitting the censorship of films. However, towns and cities began as early as 1907 (Chicago) to censor movies and refuse to issue a license for them to be shown. The criteria for censoring films consisted of "indecent," "immoral," "sacrilegious," or otherwise objectionable, and such censorship depended on the community's sensibilities and differed from place to place (e.g., which part of a woman's body could be shown or how long a kiss could last; "Moral reformers were outraged at sexual content. . . . The film *Carmen* was condemned in Ohio because girls smoked cigarettes in public. . . . Southern states banned anything that even remotely questioned racial segregation"[34]). By 1922, following the Roscoe "Fatty" Arbuckle affair,[35] local censorship boards were cropping up around the country.[36] "The Progressive Era's anti-vice crusade, which included a fair representation of clergy, attacked this new, popular medium as a threat to public peace and morality."[37] Although concern for what children would watch was voiced, censorship for the sake of children over adults did not seem to be at issue. Either the film was censored or banned for everyone, or it was permitted. This resulted in cinematic reductionism since all content had to be acceptable for children. Certainly this has had an enduring twofold impact on the film industry in the United States: one, it seems to have created a polarization in the audience ("G" movies are good and "R" movies are bad, regardless of the story); and two, the multiplication of bland stories that pass for "family" films.

In an effort to stave off government control of film content and to centralize the arbitrary criteria applied to censorship, the industry decided to oversee itself by founding the Motion Picture Producers and Distributors of America (MPPDA) to monitor and clean up the film industry. The MPPDA hired Will Hays, the former postmaster general and head of the Republican National Committee, to head the organization and set standards for movies. Although he issued a list of guidelines for a Production Code, Hollywood was not happy with Hays's control.

In 1930 a Catholic layman in Chicago persuaded Cardinal George Mundelein that movies should be vetted by the church before production. The cardinal enlisted Father Daniel Lord, SJ, to write a Catholic code for movies. It was a detailed list of prohibitions and rules that Hays, with some minor changes, adopted as the Motion Picture Production Code of 1930 (known as the Hays Code).[38]

In 1934 the Production Code Administration (PCA) was established. It required studios to obtain a certificate of approval for each film before release, or pay a $25,000 fine. The MPPDA appointed Joseph Breen as the director of the PCA under Hays to enforce the Motion Picture Production Code.[39] Thus began the era of separate beds. The Production Code stayed in effect until 1968 when Jack Valenti, then the new president of the Motion Picture Association of America (MPAA; it succeeded the MPPDA), in collaboration with organizations of theater owners and film importers, issued a voluntary film rating system.[40]

This new system was a sea change in how the film industry would monitor itself and still avoid control by local and state governments to censor what they thought was inappropriate, because the system redefined its purpose. Jack Valenti wrote:

> So the emergence of the voluntary rating system filled the vacuum provided by my dismantling of the Hays Production Code. The movie industry would no longer "approve or disapprove" the content of a film, but we would now see our primary task as giving advance cautionary warnings to parents so that parents could make the decision about the moviegoing of their young children.[41]

Making Better Use of Our Theological Traditions

The Legion of Decency

The Catholic Legion of Decency was founded in New York in 1933 (or 1934; sources vary on the date) at the urging of the papal delegate to the United States, (later Cardinal) Amleto Cicognani (1883–1973). The purpose of the legion was to identify and combat objectionable material in movies. He spoke of the "massacre of innocence of youth" and pushed for a campaign for "the purification of the cinema."[42] The Legion of Decency office was established by the United States Catholic Bishops and a classification code developed. The office was renamed the National Catholic Office for Motion Pictures in 1966, and in 2001 it was renamed again as the United States Conference of Catholic Bishops' Office for Film and Broadcast.[43] In the beginning, many Protestants and Jews belonged to the Legion of Decency (originally the National Legion of Decency) until it was made into an office of the Bishops' Conference and became a strictly Catholic concern.

The Academy of Motion Picture Arts and Sciences (AMPAS) has a National Legion of Decency Collection in its archives consisting of various lists and ratings books that date from 1941 to 1951. AMPAS describes the Legion of Decency thus:

> The National Legion of Decency was formed in 1934 by the Catholic Bishops of the United States. The legion published rating lists designed to provide "a moral estimate of current entertainment feature motion pictures" and prepared under the direction of the New York Archdiocesan Council of the Legion of Decency with the cooperation of the Motion Picture Department of the International Federation of Catholic Alumnae. Films were rated as unobjectionable (Class A), objectionable (Class B), or condemned (Class C). Reasons for deeming a film objectionable include suggestive dialogue, lack of moral compensation, lustful kissing, and acceptance of divorce.

The Legion of Decency's Code[44] was said to be stricter than the Hays Code, and Catholics were urged to take a pledge that read:

> I condemn all indecent and immoral motion pictures, and those which glorify crime or criminals. I promise to do all that I can to strengthen public opinion against the production of indecent and immoral films, and to unite with all who protest against them. I acknowledge my obligation to form a right conscience about pictures that are dangerous to my moral life. I pledge myself to remain away from them. I promise, further, to stay away altogether from places of amusement which show them as a matter of policy. (1934)

In 1938 all Catholics were urged to renew their pledge annually at Mass on December 8, the Feast of the Immaculate Conception, which commemorates the teaching that the Blessed Virgin Mary was conceived without original sin.

It is interesting that as part of a five-year campaign (2000–2004) called *Renewing the Mind of the Media*,[45] dioceses were invited to voluntarily take part by having their parishes urge churchgoing Catholics to sign a media (not just movies) pledge card that was inserted in the bulletin, checking off what they would do or avoid.

In a 2006 interview with Ellen McCloskey of the Catholic Communications Campaign (CCC) of the USCCB, I asked her to describe the goal of signing the pledge cards. She said that it was hoped that the number of cards returned would be so impressive as to create a news photo opportunity and a way to inform the public and media makers about the kind of entertainment the Catholic audience wanted. However, the concurrent clergy sex abuse headlines obscured any meaningful message the campaign might have voiced to media industries because the church's moral credibility was severely compromised. Also, McCloskey admitted, the educational dimension of the *Renewing the Mind of the Media* campaign was not clear. Overall, the results of the five-year program were underwhelming. McCloskey hopes that a Web-based media literacy project will be developed in the near future that will motivate audiences to engage critically with the media.

Harry Forbes, who has headed the USCCB/OFB since 2004, stated in a telephone interview that reviews and subsequent ratings are "recommendations." He also said that the office's ratings have never carried the weight of sin, should a person decide to see a film it condemned (i.e., a C rating before 1966) or found morally offensive (the current O rating).[46]

Church, State, and the Movies

In 1915 the Supreme Court ruled that in the case of *Mutual Film Corp. v. Industrial* the exhibition of moving pictures was a business pure and simple, conducted for profit, like other spectacles, and was not to be regarded as part of the press of the country or as organs of public opinion.

In a lucid article titled "Controversy Has Probably Destroyed Forever the Context: The Miracle and Movie Censorship in America in the 1950's,"[47] Ellen Draper discusses the 1950 Italian film *The Miracle* and the controversy surrounding its US release and the subsequent US Supreme Court decisions.

Making Better Use of Our Theological Traditions

Noteworthy are four court decisions, three regarding film and one regarding books. The first case, *United States v. Paramount* in 1948, guaranteed movies the protection of the First Amendment (although this ruling was on an antitrust case that effectively ended the Hollywood studio system): "We have no doubt that moving pictures, like newspapers and radio, are included in the press whose freedom is guaranteed by the First Amendment."[48] The second was *RD-DR Corp. v. Smith* in 1950, a case dealing with the city of Atlanta's banning of *Lost Boundaries* (1949) on the ground that it would "adversely affect the peace, morals, and good order" of the city. The court declined to judge the case, perhaps because, according to Draper, "the Supreme Court would have had to confront the movie's potential effect upon its audiences, and impose a legal definition on the nature of film upon the city of Atlanta."[49] In the third case, *Burstyn v. Wilson* in 1952, regarding New York's attempt to ban *The Miracle*, the Supreme Court recognized the state's right to "establish a system for the licensing of motion pictures," but it upheld First Amendment protection for movies, stating that "motion pictures are a significant medium for the communication of ideas" and that films could not be banned on the grounds that they are deemed "sacrilegious." Finally, in *Roth v. United States* in 1957, "the Court accepted as the test for obscenity a book's 'impact upon the average person in the community' on the assumption that the 'present day standards of the community' could be objectively known, and could differ from community to community."[50]

On June 26, 2006, a television industry newsletter read:

> The cost of saying *&$@!# or doing anything remotely similar, just went up by about a gazillion percent. Yesterday President Bush made it official—the FCC now has the authority to levy fines of $325,000 per violation of the broadcast indecency rules. And how does the FCC define indecent? If "in context [it] depicts or describes sexual or excretory activities or organs in a patently offensive manner as measured by contemporary community standards for the broadcast medium." As far as indecent speech—it has [to] be when the little ones are in bed, determined by the FCC as after 10p and before 6a.[51]

Do Ratings Influence How We See the Movies?

Judging Only Its Content

I think Ellen Draper said it best when, at the conclusion of her review of Supreme Court cases, she observed the following about storytelling and by extension, art:

The theory that was lacking [as precedent for the Supreme Court] was an understanding of film as a medium of fiction. It was not merely judicial confusion [over the decades]; in fact, the Supreme Court's rulings on movie censorship in the 1950's reflect the public's confusion directly.[52]

Is the public still confused or is what Draper describes the descendant of the moral and societal ambivalence expressed by Daniels in *Puritans at Play?* One thing is for sure: as Draper affirms, there are immense differences in the way people see films, and as Valenti implies, the audience's sensibilities and social standards as to what is acceptable change over time.

When Jack Valenti changed the MPAA's code to a ratings or classification system, he noted that

> our primary task [is] giving advance cautionary warnings to parents so that parents could make the decision about the moviegoing of their young children.
>
> The movie ratings system is a voluntary system operated by the MPAA and the National Association of Theater Owners (NATO). The ratings are given by a board of parents who comprise the Classification and Rating Administration (CARA). CARA's Board members view each film and, after a group discussion, vote on its rating. The ratings are intended to provide parents with advance information so they can decide for themselves which films are appropriate for viewing by their own children. The Board uses the same criteria as any parent making a judgment—theme, language, violence, nudity, sex and drug use are among content areas considered in the decision-making process.

Henry Herx, former head of the USCCB/OFB, wrote in 1995 that the purpose of the Catholic rating system was "information for guidance"[53] for anyone who was seeking such information. At present two laypersons run this office, and there are no stated or objective criteria at this time on which classifications or ratings are based. "It's a judgment call," said Harry Forbes in a telephone interview.[54] Detailed notations are made for every film reviewed by the USCCB/OFB. This one appeared the week of June 18, 2006, for the film *Click,* at the end of the review:

> Unneeded vulgar humor including flatulence, innuendo, and sexual sight gags, crude language and expressions, profanity, promiscuity, ethnic stereotyping, transgender character and drug references. A-III—adults. (PG-13)

The MPAA analysis of the same film reads:

> Rated PG-13 for language, crude and sex-related humor, and some drug references.[55]

I would argue that the kind of rating/classification and content analysis provided by the MPAA and the USCCB/OFB reflect the American public's continuing confusion and ambivalence about what constitutes obscenity and how specific the details need to be. This, then, seems to reflect the audience's confusion between the film's "content" and its "context," between the external "data" it uses and the "meaning" it enfleshes when interpreting a film. This tension describes the confusion that the mother watching *Millions* had in the example with which I began the chapter.

Further, the disparity of purpose between the MPAA and USCCB/OFB classifications adds to the confusion. While people and theaters are legally obligated regarding their response to MPAA classifications or ratings, the USCCB/OFB ratings implicitly appeal to conscience even though they are the results of the interpretation of one, two, or even three people (who may or may not have any theological training), who are following unpublished, that is, unarticulated criteria.[56] While this lack of criteria may leave open the possibility for judging films according to changing sensibilities and standards of the Catholic population (which puts the moral objectivity of a film into question even though this seems to be the premise of the USCCB/OFB classifications), I believe the cumulative result leads to moral ambiguity and ambivalence regarding cinema, which sometimes splinters members of the Catholic audience even before they see a given film.

What Accounts for This?

This brings my topic full circle. Our culture in America is in tension within and between personal, religious, cultural, and judicial realms. While the MPAA issues ratings as guidance for parents, it leaves adults, or those aged eighteen and above, to inform and decide for themselves. The USCCB/OFB, without stated criteria, seems to rate films according to an objective standard, yet one that is ambivalent and shifting.

In 2003 the USCCB/OFB replaced one of its classifications, the A-IV, which was positioned just before its condemnatory O rating (morally objectionable), with that of L (limited adult audience, films whose problematic content many adults would find troubling). Once again, according to Harry Forbes, this change was an attempt to address the issue of a film's context. Some members of the Catholic faithful, however, have told me that they find this a sellout. Yet I believe this L rating, accompanied by an informed review, may assist Catholic viewers in appreciating cinema stories in greater depth, even as films shed light on the human condition by showing the darkness of sin. At the same time, this rating accentuates the tension between objective moral standards and shifting moral sensibilities even more.

From "Content" to "Context"

But do these ratings or classifications influence how we see a film? On the one hand, earlier this year I asked this question of the more than one hundred members, predominantly Catholic, of the Cine&Media online group, which I moderate.[57] The few responses I received all said they rarely refer to the USCCB/OFB's ratings and prefer to check various reviews. On the other hand, I give presentations across the country and speak with hundreds of people every year, and from them I often hear opinions similar to those expressed in the two letters at the beginning of this chapter about the film *Millions*. I receive very heated letters about my film reviews if I do not note even implicit sexual activity. Parents express fear about the media, not only for their children but also for themselves. They often sheepishly admit to me that they never go to the movies, or that they never go to an R-rated movie because, well, that means it's bad (as if G, PG, and PG-13 movies were good). I freely admit to people who attend my catechetical or media literacy workshops that I do not wear my religious habit when I go to movies to review them, or when I serve on juries at film festivals, so as not to give other members of the audience whiplash, especially if it is an R-rated film. To do so would be a distraction for me, and for them, because of the implicit understanding that R-rated means bad, or at least inappropriate for children and nuns.

Parents and educators often refer to media "impact" rather than "influence," and when this attitude toward media prevails, it is difficult to talk about how to read a film or ways of storytelling. "Impact" reflects a perception of having no control over the media in our lives, which is not the case because, as research has demonstrated, no one is mentally passive regarding media experiences,[58] and everyone has some level of control except for very young children or people who are mentally impaired. However, that cinema "influences" how we negotiate meaning about life and decide who and what are important certainly is the reality. Media values are in the cultural air we breathe; they reflect and can simultaneously grant a false sense of transcendence to material things and behaviors that seek immediate gratification or reinforce the sense of entitlement that profit-driven media create. At the same time I believe that the majority of concerned adults and parents do not know how to read a film so as

Making Better Use of Our Theological Traditions

to discover "seeds of the gospel," and that sin on the screen scares them. Flannery O'Connor wrote about storytelling as art:

> I'm not one to pit myself against St. Paul but when he said, "Let it not so much be named among you" I presume he was talking about society and what goes on there and not about art. Art is not anything that goes on "among" people, not the art of the novel [storytelling] anyway. It is something that one experiences alone and for the purpose of realizing in a fresh way, through the senses, the mystery of existence. Part of the mystery of existence is sin. When we think about the Crucifixion, we miss the point of it if we don't think about sin.[59]

"Information for guidance," especially regarding age appropriateness for children, while essential and helpful for parents in a media age, does not take the place of parental involvement in children's media consumption, or responsible and critical acceptance of film classifications. One Catholic told me recently that to see Ang Lee's *Brokeback Mountain* (2006) was a sin because the USCCB/OFB gave it an O rating. This is a complex matter because it involves conscience. I, for one, found nothing morally objectionable about the film, but I was sensitive to how some Catholics would perceive the homosexual relationship in the film to be immoral (and yes, the Catholic Church teaches that homosexual activity is objectively wrong). However, the film did not glorify the homosexuality, but accentuated the loneliness of the characters and society's intolerance for people born with a homosexual orientation. If indeed Christ died for everyone, then how do people with a homosexual orientation make sense of Christ, whom they do not see, and the people who judge and even kill them (physically or spiritually) in Christ's name, whom they do see? In the last analysis, the USCCB/OFB did not deal with the greater social context of the human/ humane dimension of the film but seemed to respond to a narrow social context (what some Catholics might think of the office for the rating it gave) rather than to the inner context created by the film itself.

Web sites such as ScreenIt (www.screenit.com) appeal to busy parents who want to know every possible objectionable aspect of a film, that is, a detailed and exhaustive content analysis of the movie, before deciding to permit their children to see it or not. What is missing from such sites, however, is any effort to assist parents and the audience in general to understand how to read a film—to develop skills for critical engagement, on the one hand (that includes assessing a film for age appropriateness, how the film represents the human person, resolution to conflict, and so forth), and for understanding storytelling in its various forms (print, cinema, television, video games, and genres), on the other hand. Lacking, as well, is any help in understanding a way to integrate cinema as a form of leisure with Christian behavior and spirituality. Has content analysis (i.e., the focus on the film's representations of sexuality, violence, and language, as well as drugs, alcohol, and smoking) resulted in the loss of the soul (i.e., the context of the story) and blunted our ability to engage in parables—stories and storytelling—the very way Jesus communicated meaningfully with the people of his times? I think so.

In 2002 the Pontifical Council for Social Communication began the process of preparing a document on cinema and spirituality as it had about the Internet, pornography and violence, advertising, and so forth. The intention was to issue a document that would be accessible for the ordinary filmgoer in the multiplex, to relate cinema and spirituality to their movie experiences. Reverend Peter Malone, MSC, then president of SIGNIS and former president of the International Catholic Organization for Cinema (OCIC), was asked to be the architect of the document; an American layman, Russell Shaw, who had drafted the previous documents for the council, was the writer. However, after reviewing and discussing the draft at the council's meeting in March 2004, it was decided not to go forward. Archbishop John P. Foley, president of the council, told the plenary session that the document was shelved. There was no explanation given and nothing further has eventuated.[60]

One of the key concepts of media literacy education is that no one sees a movie, reads a book, or hears a song in the same way. The film *Priest* was released in 1995, when I was in graduate school in London. I attended a screening with Catholic heads of seminaries, spiritual directors, and leaders of religious communities. A question-and-answer session with screenwriter Jimmy McGovern and one of the producers followed, as did thoughtful reflections by the Catholic press in Britain and the OCIC. While not urging people to see the film, the Catholic Media Office of the United Kingdom said that "while there is indeed much to criticize in the film, there is also much that is praiseworthy."[61] Almost simultaneously, the Catholic Church in the United States, represented by Cardinal O'Connor of New York (who admitted he had not seen the film), the Catholic League, and the majority of the Catholic press, called for a boycott of the "cheap," "ludicrous," "viciously anti-Catholic" film, saying that it was "little more than what kids used to scrawl on bathroom walls." The UK government rating was 15, that is, children age fifteen and up were permitted to view the film in theaters without a parent. The MPAA rating was R and the

USCCB/OFB rating was A-IV, for adults with reservations (this rating has been replaced with an L rating now). What accounts for the difference in these ratings, in how *Priest* was judged by the UK government, the MPAA industry, and the Catholic hierarchy vis-à-vis the US Catholic rating? It proves that audiences do not see the same film the same way, but also that there is a larger context at work outside the film (the world in which the film exists and is experienced, the diegesis) when judging a film's social and moral value and age-appropriateness.

Perhaps the problem of how we, as Protestant and Catholic Christians, see movies is really about the dynamic of the human person in conflict with him or herself (what Bruce Daniels referred to in his *Puritans at Play*), between what we know, the cognitive/religious teaching (objective morality or literal reading of the film), and what we feel, the emotional/ spiritual response to the film (what C. S. Lewis calls the surrender of ourselves and our imagination to let the film or work of art reach us: "Look. Listen. Receive. Get yourself out of the way. There is no good asking first whether the work before you deserves such a surrender, for until you have surrendered you cannot possibly find out"[62]). Finally, there is the behavioral/moral dimension of the person in decision making, the choices involved in deciding to see and experience a film and to let it speak to us so as to find seeds of the gospel in the context of the story.

Many Christian viewers continue to find it difficult to watch depictions of what film reviewer Peter Malone calls "de profundis" elements of a film,[63] when the main character falls so low that the dramatic redemption makes the film worth experiencing. Malone, whose style of reviewing has been described as "mediation rather than objective critique,"[64] also says that people of faith ought not to be afraid of wilting before depictions of sin and redemption. The film becomes a "moral laboratory" into which our moral and ethical imaginations can enter, find seeds of the gospel, and figure out life. In the last analysis, however, what we may be dealing with is a preponderance of guilt produced by centuries and generations of pessimistic religious teaching—teaching, that is, as Flannery O'Connor says above, more about asceticism for its own sake, than redemption.

Notes

1. Sally Fitzgerald, ed., *The Habit of Being: Letters of Flannery O'Connor* (New York: Farrar, Straus, Giroux, 1976), 172; letter to John Lynch, September 2, 1956.

2. Bruce C. Daniels, *Puritans at Play: Leisure and Recreation in Colonial New England* (New York: St. Martin's Press, 1995), 16.

3. Ibid., 18. Daniels's source is "The Government and Improvement of Mirth, According to the Laws of Christianity in Three Sermons."

4. Ibid., 20.

5. E. Brooks Holifield, *Theology in America: Christian Thought from the Age of the Puritans to the Civil War* (New Haven: Yale University Press, 2003), 29.

6. Daniels, *Puritans at Play*, 23.

7. Ibid., 66. Daniels refers to Winton V. Solberg, *Redeem the Time: The Puritan Sabbath in Early America* (Cambridge: Harvard University Press, 1977), 52–53.

8. Daniels, *Puritans at Play*, 23.

9. Ibid., 68.

10. Ibid., 71.

11. C. S. Lewis, *An Experiment in Criticism* (Cambridge: Cambridge University Press, 1961), 10–12.

12. Fitzgerald, *Habit of Being*, 304; letter to Dr. T. R. Spivey.

13. Sister Claudia Leopold, "The Greening of America," *Extension Magazine*, March 1993 (page numbers not available; article sent to me in an e-mail).

14. For more information, see Jay Donlan, *The American Catholic Experience* (New York: Doubleday, 1985), 143–44, as well as his bibliographical references.

15. Cf. Ra McLaughlin, "Is Calvinism a Catholic Invention?" Third Millennium Ministries Web site, www.thirdmill.org/answers/answer.asp/file/99981.qna/category/ch/page/questions/site/iiim.

16. Includes Catholics who explicitly reject Vatican II as well as those who prefer pre-Vatican II liturgy, catechetics, forms of piety, narrow attitude toward salvation and religious freedom, and moral rigidity but remaining within the church.

17. Anthony Fisher, OP, "Lefebvrism—Jansenism Revisited?" *New Blackfriars* 71 (June 1990): 274–85.

18. Richard P. McBrien, ed., *Encyclopedia of Catholicism* (San Francisco: HarperCollins, 1995), 686, s.v. "Cornelius Jansen."

19. For example, the Sulpicians, known to be an orthodox and morally strict French order founded in 1641 to educate priests, staffed the first seminary in the United States, St. Mary's in Baltimore. A Sulpician, Louis William Valentine Dubourg, was the first president of Georgetown University, the first Catholic university in America.

20. Culver City, CA, July 16, 2006.

21. Thus Jansenism and Puritanism, as the embodiment of this dualistic and elitist world-view, continues, said Welch, in the religiosity of contemporary US politics. He noted especially George W. Bush's naming of the "axis of evil" and the "evildoers" after the 9/11, 2001, attacks on the World Trade Center in New York so as to provide a rationale for the preemptive war with Iraq: good vs. evil. He went on to say that this outlook was demonstrated in Westerns, with the good white hats and evil black hats, in cinema's first hundred years and continues in films such as George Lucas's *Star Wars* trilogies. Another aspect of gnostic influence on both Puritan and Jansenist theology is how it sees the body (material) as bad and the spiritual as good. The rigid alignment of good vs. evil and light vs. dark leaves little room for the exercise of the moral imagination in the gray area that stories often generate.

22. Paragraph 9.

23. Paragraph 2; in particular for the praise and caution approach toward cinema, see *Vigilanti Cura* (1939), www.vatican.va/holy_father/pius_xi/encyclicals/documents/hf_p-xi_enc_29061936_vigilanti-cura_en.html; and *Miranda Prorsus* (1957), www.vatican.va/holy_father/pius_xii/encyclicals/documents/hf_p-xii_enc_08091957_miranda-prorsus_en.html.

24. Fisher, "Lefebvrism," 274–85.

25. Lefebvre was excommunicated July 2, 1988 by Pope John Paul II in the apostolic letter *Ecclesia Dei*.

26. Fisher, "Lefebvrism" 274–85.

Making Better Use of Our Theological Traditions

27. A simple search for "Catholic response to Harry Potter" on the Internet confirms this (a search for Protestant responses yields similar results).

28. Internet Movie Database, www.imdb.com/title/++0315327/business.

29. St. Anselm of Canterbury, 1033–1109, in the *Proslogion* written in 1077–78.

30. The USCCB's Office for Film and Broadcast condemned the film by giving it an O rating (morally objectionable), interpreting it as a disingenuous fable attacking Catholicism.

31. Fitzgerald, *Habit of Being*, 275; letter to "A."

32. Lewis, *Experiment in Criticism*, 10–13.

33. Fitzgerald, *Habit of Being*, 134; letter to Father J. H. McCown.

34. Marjorie Heins, "The Bishops Go to the Movies: The Miracle: Film Censorship and the Entanglement of Church and State," *Conscience*, March 22, 2003.

35. He was a great comedian, falsely accused of rape and murder at a party, but even after he was exonerated, he never made another film. The incident associated Hollywood and bad behavior in the minds of people, even though this was not a movie, but instead an incident about a film star.

36. David Gill and Kevin Brownlow, "Single Beds and Double Standards," 1980, video, Thames Video Collection.

37. Heins, "Bishops Go to the Movies."

38. See the Motion Picture Production Code of 1930 (Hays Code), www.artsreformation .com/a001/hays-code.html.

39. See www.artsreformation.com/a001/hays-code.html.

40. Jack Valenti, Motion Picture Association of America, "Ratings History," www.mpaa .org/Ratings_history1.asp.

41. Ibid.

42. Gregory Black, *The Catholic Crusade against the Movies, 1940–1975* (Cambridge: Cambridge University Press, 1997), 20.

43. For current classification system, see United States Conference of Catholic Bishops, www .usccb.org/movies/weekly/shtml.

44. Unfortunately I was unable to find a statement of this code.

45. "Renewing the Mind of the Media" is a phrase taken from the writings of John Paul II; the campaign was approved by the USCCB in 1998 and sponsored by the U.S. Conference of Catholic Bishops' Media Office and funded by the Catholic Communications Campaign—the CCC—of the USCCB.

46. According to Harry Forbes (December 13, 2006), who heads the USCCB/OFB, this is the statement his office sends to people who question whether seeing a film designated as an O, morally offensive, is sinful: "The classifications of the U.S. Conference of Catholic Bishops' Office for Film and Broadcasting have always been intended to be a guide for parents to aid in what films are most appropriate for their children. How an individual applies the classifications to their own viewing is strictly the choice of the individual. The classifications reflect the moral suitability of the films reviewed, while the reviews also take in the movies' aesthetic qualities. This serves to prevent movie patrons from getting unwanted surprises when they see a film either at the cinema or rent or purchase one at a store. Just as parents are the best judges of their children's emotional, spiritual, and moral development, you are the best judge of your own moral, spiritual, and emotional development, and what you do with the movies in question will undoubtedly best reflect your values."

47. Ellen Draper, " 'Controversy Has Probably Destroyed Forever the Context': *The Miracle* and Movie Censorship in America in the 1950s," *The Velvet Light Trap* 25 (1990): 69–79, republished in *Controlling Hollywood: Censorship and Regulation in the Hollywood Era*, ed. Matthew Berstein (New Brunswick, NJ: Rutgers University Press, 1999), 186–205.

48. Documents from the *Paramount* Antitrust Case, 1938–1949, found at www.cobbles .com/simpp_archive/1film_antitrust.htm.

49. Draper, "'Controversy.'"

50. Ibid., 189.

51. Cynthia Turner, Cynopsis Media online newsletter, June 16, 2006, www.cynopsis.com/content/view/410/53/; also see Jim Puzzanghera, "FCC Backtracks on 2 Charges of Indecency, *Los Angeles Times*, November 8, 2006, p. C1, which shows the continued difficulty, and hence limited credibility, the Federal Communications Commission has in determining what kind of language and when it is admissible in television broadcasts and thus what fines are to be levied for infractions.

52. Draper, "'Controversy,'" 191.

53. Henry Herx, *The Family Guide to Movies and Videos* (Washington, DC: United States Catholic Conference, Office for Publishing and Promotion Services, 1995).

54. Harry Forbes, who has headed the USCCB/OFB since 2004, stated in a telephone interview on December 11, 2006, that there has been recent discussion within the office about formulating the USCCB/OFB criteria for their in-house reference.

55. Ironically, the MPAA's mission is for parents while the USCCB/OFB is for everyone, yet the MPAA is much less detailed about objectionable material. Our culture in America is in tension over an objective standard, yet ambivalent or shifting at the same time.

56. Harry Forbes stated in the December 11, 2006, telephone interview that reviews and subsequent ratings are "recommendations" and that the office's ratings have never carried the weight of sin should a person decide to see a film it condemned (C rating before 1966) or found morally offensive (the current O rating).

57. Cine&Media, cineandmedia@yahoogroups.com, started in 2000.

58. Robert Hodge and David Tripp, *Children and Television: A Semiotic Approach* (Cambridge: Polity, 1986).

59. Fitzgerald, *Habit of Being*, 142; letter to Eileen Hall, March 10, 1956.

60. From a phone interview with Peter Malone, December 13, 2006.

61. Statement issued by the Catholic Media Office of the Catholic Bishops of England and Wales, February 24, 1995; for a collection of articles from both the secular and Catholic press from the United Kingdom and the United States, see Rose Pacatte, "Media Education within Initial Formation Programmes of Women's Religious Communities of the Catholic Church" (master's thesis, Institute of Education, University of London, UK, 1995).

62. Lewis, *Experiment in Criticism*, 19.

63. Peter Malone and Rose Pacatte, *Lights, Camera . . . Faith! The Ten Commandments* (Boston: Pauline Books & Media, 2006), xxvi.

64. Robert Molhant, former Secretary General of SIGNIS, at a talk in Rome, December 5, 2006.

14

Within the Image

Film as Icon

GERARD LOUGHLIN

Vachel Lindsay (1879–1931) was one of the first writers to analyze narrative cinema as art and as a medium for religious ideas and spiritual sentiments. For Lindsay—writing in 1915—the silent "photoplay" offered a universal language of hieroglyphic images that viewers could discuss while watching the film; the auditorium filled with the low hum of the "conversing audience." Film, for Lindsay, was sculpture and painting in motion, produced by artists whom the church could embrace as once it had embraced the great painters and sculptors of the past. "The kinescope in the hands of artists is a higher form of picture-writing. In the hands of prophet-wizards it will be a higher form of vision-seeing."[1] But while the film industry saw a market in religious stories from the first—passion plays were being filmed in France and the United States from as early as 1897 and 1898 respectively—the churches were often less convinced by arguments such as Lindsay's.[2]

Masha (Margarita Terekhova) on the fence in *The Mirror*.

However, while the ability of film to tell religious stories with power and sometimes subtlety is not in question, its ability to be a spiritual medium is more doubtful. In part this is because the dominant forms of cinema are irreducibly commercial, concerned with entertaining mass audiences. There is still a market for biblical dramas, as Mel Gibson's *The Passion of the Christ* (US 2004) has shown. Many mainstream directors (e.g., David Fincher, Ken Russell, Martin Scorsese) have explored religious themes in thoughtful and surprising ways, while others—such as the Wachowski brothers in their *Matrix* trilogy (US 1999/2003)—have dressed up their fantasies with religious ideas, winning popular acclaim and commercial success. Religion and pseudospirituality still sell. But whether film can attain to the power of religious parable, to the austerity of the great icons, and itself become the occasion of hierophany is another matter.

Paul Schrader provides a clear and accessible analysis of how certain film directors—Yasujiro Ozu, Robert Bresson, and Carl Dreyer—have achieved a "transcendental style" that evokes a sense of the transcendent, of a spiritual reality beyond what is seen.[3] Schrader claims that the style is universal, apparent in both East and West, in Ozu's Japanese Zen sensibility and Bresson's French Catholicism. The style consists in both the way a story is told and in the narrative arc of its telling. The film affects an apparently artless detachment from what it yet carefully observes, while the story moves from the mundane, through a moment of disparity or crisis, to

Making Better Use of Our Theological Traditions

a final stasis or quietude, in which the transcendent is revealed: whether as the unity of nature, the ground of being, or as the salvific grace of God.

Schrader defines a form of film that "induces" a sense of the transcendent, suggesting a spiritual cinematic machine that seems to deny the working of a freely bestowed grace; but perhaps the transcendental style is the form that grace takes in the cinema, since in Catholic thought the supernatural is but the natural restored to its original beatitude, as when we share our food, or extend a hand in forgiveness. Certain forms of life reveal their createdness (for those given to see). Thus, irrespective of the director's intentions, one can identify aspects of the transcendental style in the work of avowed atheists, such as Pier Paolo Pasolini's *The Gospel according to St. Matthew* (Italy 1964) or Alain Cavalier's *Thérèse* (France 1986), a study of Saint Teresa (Martin) of Lisieux. Indeed, Nicholas Philibert's small-scale documentary about a small French country school, *Être et avoir* (France 2002), can be read as a spiritual film, since it finds the disparities involved in human socialization and their comforting in the everyday work of a dedicated schoolteacher, exceptional only in the compassion of his daily labor.

The great Russian "prophet-wizard," Andrei Tarkovsky (1932–86), worked for most of his career under the scrutiny of the atheistic Soviet state, and so could not have made explicitly religious films. He had to show religion as something past, a matter of defeated relics in the modern world. But it is unlikely that he would have made "religious films," even if he could have done so. Tarkovsky's carefully crafted vocabulary of natural motifs and meditative camera movements (slow zooms and lengthy panning and dolly shots) enables a form of transcendent "vision-seeing" that is as much about the loss of spirituality as about its necessity.[4] And yet at the same time it opens to the possibility of a truly spiritual cinema—a *via positiva* that is at the same time a *via negativa*—a way into the light that resides in the dark; a glimpse of the invisible in the visible, in the depths of the seen. This essay is an exploration of this possibility—a reading of the Tarkovskian image, an exercise in cinematic theology.[5]

Moving Air

The coming of the god is announced with the stirring of the air, with the bending of grasses in the field, the movement of leaves on the tree. We cannot see air, except as it moves things, though we can feel it on our skin, blowing against our face, ruffling our hair. Perhaps we can smell air, or is it only the lightest of things moving, perfumes and pollens, tickling the nose? Perhaps we can taste it, a clear or sultry air, or again is it only the tasting of things, sea spray and fine earth? We certainly feel and hear air, as it brushes past us, rustling leaves and swaying grasses, announcing the coming of the god, and then, when the wind drops down, and the day becomes still and tranquil, the god's passing, or resting, very quietly close by.

One may recall those moments in the films of Andrei Tarkovsky, where natural elements—falling rain or windblown grasses undulating in waves—seem to presage a reality or significance beyond the articulation of either the films' characters or their viewers. One may recall the early scene in *The Mirror* (USSR 1974), where the narrator's mother, Masha (Margarita Terekhova), is sitting on a fence, smoking a cigarette, with the soft light of the setting sun coppering the leaves of the trees behind her. She is looking out across the field that is the very field below the house in which Tarkovsky spent his childhood summers, the house which had been destroyed but was rebuilt for the film.[6] The scene is the second in the film, the first after the main titles. From her seat on the "springy bar of the fence," Masha can look down the slope of the field to where people can be seen walking along the road from Ignatievo to Tomshino, though the road itself cannot be seen. Travelers can be recognized only when they have passed the bush in the middle of the field. "Somebody walking along the road vanished behind the bush. If he now came out on the left of the bush, then it was HE. If it was on the right, then it was not he, and now he would never come back."[7] But it is not he; it is not the narrator's longed-for father, who is away at the war. It is a passerby (Anatoly Solonitsyn), a doctor who has lost his way.

The film's encounter between the stranger and the mother, waiting for her husband, closely follows Tarkovsky's novelized script for the film, *A White, White Day* (or *Bright, Bright Day*). But the film's meeting is lighter in mood while yet more resonant with unspoken possibilities and feared losses. In the script the doctor sits down on the grass before musing on the sentience of nature, but in the film he first sits on the "springy bar" of the fence, beside Masha, causing it to break and landing both of them on their backs, almost lying together like lovers. Masha jumps up and brushes down her clothes, but the doctor remains where he is, listening to the buzzing of insects that has suddenly grown loud on the soundtrack. Then he takes his leave and starts back down the path, across the field toward the bush. "For a long time, mother followed him with her eyes. Then she slid off the fence and walked slowly home. A breath of wind

Making Better Use of Our Theological Traditions

sprang up and bowed the alder bush that grew by the fence."[8] But in the film, Masha is already off the fence when the doctor leaves, and as he goes she notices a speck of blood behind his ear and calls after him. And the breath of wind that springs up is more than a breath, more than a sudden flurry. It springs up out of the stillness of the late afternoon and races across the field, from the distant bush, past the doctor, to break in the foreground, bending the alder and brushwood at the edge of the film frame. It springs up and races toward us, toward Masha, as she stands in the protection of the wood, at the edge of the field. The wind is both natural and unnatural, and a viewer cannot but feel that it invests the meeting of the waiting woman and traveling man with an import beyond its seeming inconsequence. It marks their encounter with some significance and fills the late afternoon with either blessing or foreboding. It is surely the sign of a presence, a symbol for something metaphysical. Yet Tarkovsky insisted that nature appears in his films as simply nature, as rain falling, fire burning, and wind blowing.

> Rain, fire, water, snow, dew, the driving ground wind—all are part of the material setting in which we dwell; I would even say of the truth of our lives. I am therefore puzzled when I am told that people cannot simply enjoy watching nature, when it is lovingly reproduced on the screen, but have to look for some hidden meaning they feel it must contain.[9]

Natural Symbols

Tarkovsky simply wants to bring the "real world" to the screen, "so that it can be seen in depth and from all sides, evoking its very 'smell,' allowing audiences to feel on their skin its moisture or its dryness." He doesn't want them to be asking "Why? What for? What's the point?" He wants them to surrender to the "immediate, emotional aesthetic impression," to nature as it is in itself, brought into the cinema and placed upon the screen. We should trust what we see.[10]

> Nature exists in cinema in the naturalistic fidelity with which it is recorded; the greater the fidelity, the more we trust nature as we see it in the frame, and at the same time, the finer is the created image: in its authentically natural likeness, the inspiration of nature itself is brought into cinema.[11]

Tarkovsky records, perhaps with amusement, that audiences reacted with incredulity when he insisted that there are no "symbols or metaphors" in his films. "They persist in asking again and again, for instance, what rain signifies in my films; why does it figure in film after film; and why the repeated images of wind, fire, water?" Why indeed, for it is somewhat disingenuous of Tarkovsky to complain that he does not "know how to deal with such questions."[12] For while it may take some time before a poetic filmmaker can or will say why a particular shot or camera movement was required, the filmmaker had from the first an unspoken, intuitive knowledge—a deeper discernment—that made it seem necessary to produce the image, to undertake the arduous setting up of lights and camera, of the machines and technicians that produced the illusion of wind, rain, or fog. For rarely can a film director afford to wait upon the elements to disport themselves as required. Tarkovsky's nature is always premeditated because always constructed. The strange wind that disturbs the stillness of the evening is utterly real because of the real effect of a helicopter, flying toward the camera, just out of shot. Like the words of a poet, Tarkovsky's nature has been carefully honed for its purpose.

Honing nature in *The Mirror*.

And when pressed—pressing himself—Tarkovsky will admit that there are some metaphorical or symbolic moments in his films. He cites the

Making Better Use of Our Theological Traditions

last shot of *Nostalgia* (Italy/USSR 1983), when he brings the "Russian house inside the Italian cathedral."[13] Just after the collapse and presumed death of the film's protagonist, the Russian poet Andrei Gorchakov (Oleg Yankovsky)—perhaps in the "moment" of his death—we see him seated on the ground outside his dacha, his country house in Russia, the lost home that appears in so many of Tarkovsky's films. The poet rests his weight on one arm, and a dog sits to his left, and both look straight ahead at us the viewers, while the camera slowly tracks back to reveal that this strange and impressive setting—which we already recognize from the poet's dreams earlier in the film—is now situated within the ruined nave of an abbey church, its glassless windows reflected in a foreground pool.[14] Today this doubled landscape—the Russian inside the Italian— would be computer generated, and all the poorer for it. Like the wind and rain, Tarkovsky's dreamscape is utterly real, a constructed miniature landscape, with a scaled-down model house, creating a false perspective. As the camera pulls back to show the full setting, snow begins to fall "as though in a dream,"[15] both in the middle and far distance, throughout the nave, which now harbors the Russian countryside.

Doubled landscape: Andrei Gorchakov (Oleg Yankovsky) in *Nostalgia*.

This scene, as Tarkovsky puts it, is a "constructed image which smacks of literariness"; a depiction of the dying Gorchakov's state of mind, caught by the past in the ruins of the present. Tarkovsky offered two contradictory readings of the scene. On the one hand it may figure the poet's dirempted world, torn between past and present life—as was Tarkovsky, filming in Italy while yearning for Russia and the life to which he did and did not wish to return.[16] Or it might figure not diremption but its mending, a "new wholeness in which the Tuscan hills and the Russian countryside come together indissolubly," merged into the being and blood of the poet, even as he feels that he must return to Russia. Tarkovsky worries that the scene may lack "cinematic purity," but feels that it is free from "vulgar symbolism," for it refers not to something outside of the scene, to something other than Gorchakov, but to the writer himself, who is in the scene.[17] The shot refers to itself. It is its own world.

Within the Image

Tarkovsky seeks to show the truth itself, rather than something else that stands in for the truth. When Tarkovsky rejects symbolic readings of his work it is because he is thinking of the symbol as a stand-in, a substitute, and Tarkovsky wants something more immediate, something that does not point away from itself, but into which we are led. He wants something that is, as it were, a symbol of itself, and so not a symbol as we might ordinarily understand the term. Tarkovsky admits that when it rains in his films it is not just a case of bad weather, but nor is it a symbol of something other than rain. We should resist the temptation—strong though it is—to take Tarkovsky's gentle downpours as signs of God's grace, symbols of a more metaphysical event. The wind that blows across the fields and through the trees in *The Mirror* is not mere happenstance, but nor is it a symbol, a stand-in, for the "pervasive Holy Ghost, in Christian belief the third person of the Trinity alongside Jesus and God," as Mark Cousins is too quick to tell us in his history of film.[18] How then should we understand it?

Rain—or snow or wind or fire—appears in Tarkovsky's films in order to produce what he calls an "aesthetic setting in which to steep the action of the film." It appears in order to show us a world.[19] Tarkovsky tells us that he wants to put his own world on the screen, as he feels and sees it, "in its ideal and most perfect form." "I am re-creating my world in those details which seem to me most fully and exactly to express the elusive meaning of its existence."[20] As Tarkovsky (with Aleksandr Misharin) puts it, he hopes to answer—to *show* the answer to—a fundamental question, the question of *The Mirror* and of all Tarkovsky's films: "What did Man live for, what does he live for and what will he live for; by what great, secret powers, *invisible to our gaze* . . ."[21]

Tarkovsky—as he himself admits—is not consistent in his discussion of symbols. "However, it is for the artist both to devise principles and to break them."[22] When asked about the dogs that appear in his films—in *Solaris*, *Stalker*, and *Nostalgia*—he could retort that they were just dogs.[23] But on other occasions he does not hesitate to inform us about his intended symbols. Thus he tells us that the watering of the withered tree in the closing scene of *The Sacrifice* (Sweden/France 1986) is a "symbol of faith."[24] However, the fact that Tarkovsky can offer us two contradictory readings of the final shot in *Nostalgia* suggests how his images escape any symbolic straitjacket, and not least the intentions of their maker, so that even he is uncertain of their import. Elsewhere Tarkovsky is led to affirm what we might think of as open symbols, images with no single meaning, reference, or resonance, but suggestive of a multitude, intimating what cannot be put into words. "Symbols cannot be stated or explained, and, confronted by their secret meaning in its totality, we are powerless."[25] Whether we call them images or symbols, it is clear that Tarkovsky wants to produce pictures that are not mere transcriptions, but material visions, and so we are led back to his claim to have produced images that are neither symbolic nor mere verisimilitude, neither stand-ins nor mere "bad weather."[26]

Material Vision

At one level, of course, many of Tarkovsky's images are just of weather, of the elements by which we are buffeted. The reverse side of Tarkovsky's transcendentalism is a concern to show us the materiality of life, saturated with substance.

> Rain is after all typical of the landscape in which I grew up; in Russia you have those long, dreary, persistent rains. And I can say that I love nature—I don't like big cities and feel perfectly happy when I'm away from the paraphernalia of modern civilization, just as I felt wonderful in Russia when I was in my country house [Myasnoye], with three hundred kilometers between Moscow and myself. Rain, fire, water, snow, dew, the driving ground wind—all are part of the material setting in which we dwell; I would even say of the truth of our lives.[27]

But even as Tarkovsky affirms life's materiality, he ascribes to it a meaning that goes beyond mere facticity. Rain, fire, water, snow, dew, and the driving ground wind are part, but not the entirety, of truth. They appear in Tarkovsky's films as "reality effects," but not as that term is normally used, as fabricated markers of contingency, apparent accidentals. Tarkovsky's images are their own reality, intensifiers of the world, productive of what he calls its elusive meaning. And so, if we choose to take Tarkovsky seriously when he tells us that there are no symbols or metaphors in his films, and in spite of his statements to the contrary, we have to think of his images not as symbols but as icons. For icons—though perhaps deploying a symbolic language—are in no sense stand-ins or substitutes. They are just themselves but disclose more than themselves. And because they are disclosive—disclosive when venerated—they are venerable. Tarkovsky's *Andrei Rublev* (USSR 1971) famously ends with a color sequence of the great fifteenth-century painter's icons, and it is the theology of the icon that best helps us understand Tarkovsky's attempt to produce nonsymbolic "symbols," images that resonate with what cannot be seen while yet fully in view. "Icon painting," Sergius Bulgakov writes, "testifies to the beyond and its aspects; it does not attempt to prove, it simply presents."[28]

In Tarkovsky's world the wind moving the grass is not symbolic of the god passing by, of a spirit drawing near, or of anything at all. It is simply the movement of the wind. But that is the movement of the god, for the religious imagination; not a sign of the god, but the god passing. The rain in Tarkovsky's films is not a sign of God's grace; it is God's grace falling, gently from heaven.[29] Perhaps we can say that when we enter Tarkovsky's world we have passed over to what in our world must still be symbolized. We are within the symbol, so that everything is as it appears, but what appears is just out of reach of what can be named, at least by us. And isn't this always the case with the appearance of the gods?

Tarkovsky's nonsymbolic symbols—showing only what is to be seen— are like representations without originals, like icons. For icons are images that have no model, in the sense that what they show cannot be seen except in the image itself. Thus an icon of Christ is not a portrait of the man Jesus, since the icon does not show us the man, but the incarnation of *deity* in the man, and deity is not visible. The icon is not just a picture of Jesus as he was, as he might have been if caught by a camera, but Jesus as he is, sitting on the right hand of the Father. He is the Christ who lives now, a mystical reality that is yet utterly concrete, mystical in its materiality, both in the consecrated elements of the Eucharist and in the receiving church, which is Christ's body, as well as in the stranger who comes unbidden. Thus the icon that pictures divinity cannot refer us to anything else, to a yet more lifelike image beyond itself; just as Jesus, in whom God is to be seen, does not refer us to anyone else other than himself. Thomas wants to know the way to God, to the Father, as if it might be somewhere else, when in fact it is before him already. "I am the way, and the truth, and the life," says Jesus. "No one comes to the Father except through me.

If you know me, you will know my Father also. From now on you do know him *and have seen him*" (John 14:6–7 New Revised Standard Version, emphasis added). Jesus is the icon of the Father, but all we can see is Jesus himself.

When watching one of Tarkovsky's films, we might almost say that we are within the film as icon, within a series of images that are not metaphoric of some other, unseen images, but are rather a series of images in which the unseeable is shown. As already suggested, Tarkovsky's transcendent is utterly material, his beyond entirely immanent, up close and so invisible, and this answers to the materiality of the icon, to the board and paint, which catch the viewer's gaze and make him or her look. The icon's claim to immanent transcendence is authorized by, and follows from, the logic of divine incarnation, by which matter is given to display its transcendent cause the more it is itself. To touch Jesus was to be touched by God.[30] The authorizing logic for daring to paint the divine was finely caught by Thomas Aquinas when puzzling over the corporeality of Gabriel, when appearing to the Virgin: a veritable icon of the divine blessing (Luke 1:26). For Thomas did not doubt the record of the evangelist, that the angel appeared to the corporeal eye, and not to the eye of the intellect, as might have been expected, when the tradition agreed that intellectual vision was superior to both spiritual and physical sight.[31] Thomas found the answer to his dilemma in the fittingness of corporeal vision for the announcement of the incarnation. For it "fitted in first with the message itself," since Gabriel "came to tell of the incarnation of the invisible God. It was appropriate then that an invisible being assume a visible form."[32] If God was to appear in flesh, his angel could do no less.

Time-Pressure

Famously, Tarkovsky thought that film, and his films in particular, could incarnate time. Film gives us time that we would not otherwise have. As we watch the unfolding drama of a shot or series of shots, a "sculpture in time," as Tarkovsky—like Vachel Lindsay—called it, we are watching a temporal structure that has come from elsewhere, from nowhere, and been manifested before us. And this manifestation has its own time or times; a rhythm of temporalities, of differently pressured movements. "The consistency of the time that runs through the shot, its intensity or 'sloppiness,' could be called time-pressure: then editing can be seen as the assembly of the pieces on the basis of the time-pressure within them."[33] And the structure of edited time-pressures in Tarkovsky's films is rarely simple, even in his simplest scenes. It is often a folded, multilayered dynamic, with several interrelated times within the same duration; a temporal palimpsest. In the scene where the mother and doctor meet, at least three times are folded upon one another. First, there is the present of the meeting, visible on the screen—the time it takes the doctor to approach across the field, talk with Masha, and depart, and for the wind to come across the field, twice over. Tarkovsky wanted us to notice the time of his films—the time that it takes to watch them—and risked ever longer shots in order to alert us to their passing, pushing us beyond the point at which we might become bored, to one where the time itself becomes freshly present: the falling rain really falling in the cinematic icon; the wind really blowing across the field of the image.

The scene of the meeting runs for about six minutes. But this diegetic time—which fills the viewer's present—is cast into the past by the narrator's recalling of the meeting even as we watch it, so that it is both past and present at the same time. Admittedly the narrator, Alexei (Innokenti Smoktunovsky), only introduces the scene. And it concludes, not with the narrator, but with Tarkovsky's own father—the poet Arseni Tarkovsky (1907–89)—reading one of his own poems in voice-over. But these unseen speakers—the real father and his fictionalized son, who never appears as an adult in the film—are enough to cast the scene into the past, to present it as a memory, and to let us know that the mother is herself given over to memory, to waiting for the return of her husband, the narrator's father. But this also complicates the scene, for whose memory does it show? The narrator's, who awaited his father? His mother's, who awaited her lover? The scene brings their past into the present. But as it runs on, its authorship is unsettled by subtle hairline cracks in the time line, as if the memories of different people, or of different immediacies—those directly recalled and those appropriated from others, or imagined on the basis of photographs or other mementos—have been interlaced, almost seamlessly. (And of course the screen image is constructed by Tarkovsky from his own memories and photographs of his parents and of himself as a child, when living in the home he has so lovingly rebuilt for the film.[34])

When the doctor asks Masha for a light for his cigarette, he seems to notice something behind her, and she, as he bends to light his cigarette from hers, turns around to look in our direction. The film cuts to a midshot of the young narrator, the five-year-old Alexei (Filip Yankovsky), asleep with his sister in a net hammock, strung between the trees. It is an image

Making Better Use of Our Theological Traditions

of utter tranquillity, of energy spent at the end of a summer's day. But the framing of the shot, together with the children's obliviousness to the adults' interchange, suggests that it cannot quite be what Masha sees on turning around to look into the camera. The shot has a slightly different time-pressure from the others in the scene. It is as if she has looked into the past, into another memory—whether her own or someone else's—of the summer days spent at the house among the trees. It also signals, somewhat slyly, that even if Alexei, the narrator, could have remembered this scene from his childhood, he was asleep when it happened.[35] It is a dreamed memory.

Dreamed memory: Alexi (Filip Yankovsky) and his sister in *The Mirror*.

When the doctor departs, he leaves screen left—or more nearly bottom—and continues to talk with Masha from off camera. She calls to him about the blood behind his ear, and we cut to a shot of him in the field, and he seems to be farther away than he could have walked in the time since his exit of the previous frame. Of course it may be accidental, but this slight, almost unnoticeable elision of time—a speeding of its flow—further serves to unsettle, however subtly, the simplicity of an otherwise purely linear scene.

Veneration

Yet we may say that not everyone is given to see what the icon has to show, that the prototype appears in the type only for the eyes of faith, when illumined by the light that comes from the icon itself, the emanating, circulating light of the Spirit, which shines forth in order to catch those eyes, to make her viewers look into the light, to lead them back to the effulgence of the divine glory. Finally that which is seen and the light by which it is seen are one and the same.[36] The divine appearing is dependent, codependent, on those who look; but their looking is called forth by that which they are seeking to see. And this circulating gaze finds its parallel in the compelled look of the cinema audience, each individual of which will see the film differently. Tarkovsky records that he once thought film presented an unambiguous, "total" image, "a total effect, identical for every audience," but that he was forced to admit that he was wrong, that the vision appears in the relationship between the screened image and the viewers by whom it is seen. One might say that the film appears not on the screen but in the space between viewers and viewed, in the reflected light of the screen, which permits the screen image to be seen. Moreover, this relationship, which is neither screen nor eye, but the space between, is a movement of mediation, an interpretative flow which the cinematic iconographer excites by refusing or hiding sight.

> The basic principle—as it were, the mainspring—is, I think, that as little as possible has actually to be shown, and from that little the audience has to build up an idea of the rest, of the whole. In my view that has to be the basis for constructing the cinematographic image. And if one looks at it from the point of view of symbols, then the symbol in cinema is a symbol of nature, of reality. Of course it isn't a question of details, but of what is hidden.[37]

In the sense that Tarkovsky wished to exclude them, there are no symbols in his films because his images do not point away to something else, but only *into* themselves, into the *time* of their viewing, the duration where viewed and viewer meet and another "reality" appears. And this art of the "hidden"—which shows what is beyond or, better, *within* what is seen—works by withholding, by limiting its vision to a discrete range of repeated images. And this also is the practice of icon painting, which works with an "exceedingly limited scale of artistic means."[38] Moreover, by withholding images from the audience, Tarkovsky obliges his view-

Making Better Use of Our Theological Traditions

ers to become coproducers of the film image, the cinematic vision, "on a par with the artist in their perception of the film." This is a cinema of "reciprocity" in which the audience comes to share with the author in the "misery and joy of bringing an image into being."[39]

An audience has to want to see what Tarkovsky has to show in order for it to come into view, just as the devout must pray before the icon if they are to see its wonders, if they are to catch sight of its showing. The devout must look with love—*in* love—and Tarkovsky desired nothing so much as that his films should have a loving audience. "I do nothing in particular to please an audience, and yet hope fervently that my picture will be accepted and loved by those who see it."[40] Tarkovsky would not seek to humor his audience, because he desired not adulation but devotion to his showings, just as the prophets, faithful to their visions, come to tell us not what we want but what we need to see.[41] "An image is an impression of the Truth, which God has allowed us to glimpse with our sightless eyes."[42]

Notes

1. Vachel Lindsay, *The Art of the Moving Picture* (1915; New York: Modern Library, 2000), 176–77.

2. See further Terry Lindvall, *The Silents of God: Selected Issues and Documents in Silent American Film and Religion, 1908–1925* (Lanham, MD: Scarecrow, 2001).

3. Paul Schrader, *Transcendental Style in Film: Ozu, Bresson, Dreyer* (New York: Da Capo, 1972); see also Schrader, *Schrader on Schrader*, ed. Kevin Jackson, rev. ed. (London: Faber & Faber, 2004).

4. "Devoid of spirituality, art carries its own tragedy within it. For even to recognize the spiritual vacuum of the times in which he lives, the artist must have specific qualities of wisdom and understanding. The true artist always serves immortality, striving to immortalize the world and man within the world." Andrei Tarkovsky in Giovanni Chiaramonte and Andrei A. Tarkovsky, ed., *Instant Light: Tarkovsky Polaroids*, foreword by Tonino Guerra (London: Thames & Hudson, 2004), 98.

5. On cinematic theology see further Gerard Loughlin, *Alien Sex: The Body and Desire in Cinema and Theology* (Oxford: Blackwell, 2004); and Gerard Loughlin, "Cinéma Divinité: A Theological Introduction," in *Cinéma Divinité: Religion, Theology and the Bible in Film*, ed. Eric S. Christianson, Peter Francis, and William R. Telford (London: SCM, 2005), 1–12.

6. Vida T. Johnson and Graham Petrie, *Andrei Tarkovsky: A Visual Fugue* (Bloomington and Indianapolis: Indiana University Press, 1994), 115; Andrei Tarkovsky, *Sculpting in Time*, trans. Kitty Hunter-Blair (1986; Austin: University of Texas Press, 1996), 132.

7. Andrei Tarkovsky and Aleksandr Misharin, "A White, White Day" (1968/1984), in Andrei Tarkovsky, *Collected Screenplays*, trans. William Powell and Natasha Synessios (London: Faber & Faber, 1999), 263–321, esp. 268.

8. Ibid., 269.

9. Tarkovsky, *Sculpting in Time*, 212.

10. Ibid., 213.

11. Ibid., 212.

12. Ibid.

13. Ibid., 213–14.

14. The church is the twelfth-century Abbey of San Galgano in Tuscany.

15. Tonino Guerra and Andrei Tarkovsky, "Nostalgia" (1978–82), in Tarkovsky, *Collected Screenplays*, 471–503, esp. 503.

16. "I have to say that when I first saw all the material shot for the film I was startled to find it was a spectacle of unrelieved gloom. . . . This was not something I had set out to achieve; what was symptomatic and unique about the phenomenon before me was the fact that, irrespective of my own specific theoretical intentions, the camera was obeying first and foremost my inner state during filming: I had been worn down by my separation from my family and from the way of life I was used to, by working under quite unfamiliar conditions, even by using a foreign language. . . . I was startled to find how accurately my own mood while making the film was transferred onto the screen: a profound and increasingly wearing sense of bereavement, away from home and loved ones, filling every moment of existence. To this inexorable, insidious awareness of your own dependence on your past, like an illness that grows ever harder to bear, I gave the name 'Nostalgia.'" Tarkovsky, *Sculpting in Time*, 203–4, 206.

17. Ibid., 216.

18. Mark Cousins, *The Story of Film* (London: Pavilion Books, 2004), 307. Cousins is also too quick in his theological note on the Trinity, since the Son and Spirit are the same "substance" as the Father and so also God, and thus not "alongside" but *in* one another.

19. Tarkovsky, *Sculpting in Time*, 212–13.

20. Ibid., 213.

21. Andrei Tarkovsky and Aleksandr Misharin, "Proposal for the film 'Confession'" (1968), in Tarkovsky, *Collected Screenplays*, 257–61, esp. 261; emphasis added.

22. Tarkovsky, *Sculpting in Time*, 216. Here one might also think of those more recent dogmaticians, the Danish confessors of Dogme 95, the filmmakers Lars von Trier and Thomas Vinterberg. See Richard Kelly, *The Name of This Book Is Dogme 95* (London: Faber & Faber, 2000).

23. Johnson and Petrie, *Andrei Tarkovsky*, 38.

24. Tarkovsky, *Sculpting in Time*, 224.

25. Vyacheslav Ivanov quoted approvingly in ibid., 47.

26. Natasha Synessios also argues that reducing the natural elements in Tarkovsky's films to symbols and metaphors "demeans his vision." Rather, we should understand them as inviting us to "enter, ponder and observe the world unfolding on the screen; a world whose elements and matter are familiar, yet made strange." Natasha Synessios, *The Mirror*, KINOfiles Film Companions 6 (London: Tauris, 2001), 70.

27. Tarkovsky, *Sculpting in Time*, 212.

28. Sergius Bulgakov, *The Orthodox Church*, trans. Lydia Kesich (1935; Crestwood, NY: St. Vladimir's Seminary Press, 1988), 143.

29. As Antoine de Baecque notes, Tarkovsky's earth is never without water, and its watering announces the "essential," that which is to be seen *in* the seen. "La terre de Tarkovski n'est cependant rien sans eau, l'eau lourde, bornée, bordée, où croupissent les nostalgies, comme l'eau du ciel, lueur de pluie qui annonce l'essentiel." Antoine de Baecque, *Andrei Tarkovski* (Paris: Editions d l'Etoile / Cahiers du cinéma, 1989), 21.

30. "We declare to you what was from the beginning, what we have heard, what we have seen with our eyes, what we have looked at and touched with our hands, concerning the word of life" (1 John 1:1 NRSV).

31. See Augustine, *The Literal Meaning of Genesis*, in *On Genesis*, trans. Edmund Hill, OP (New York: New City, 2002), 464–506 (bk. 12).

Making Better Use of Our Theological Traditions

32. Thomas Aquinas, *Summa Theologiae*, Blackfriars translation (London: Eyre & Spottiswoode, 1969), *prima pars* 3a.30.3; see Janet Martin Soskice, "Sight and Vision in Medieval Christian Thought," in *Vision in Context: Historical and Contemporary Perspectives on Sight*, ed. Teresa Brennan and Martin Jay (London: Routledge, 1996), 29–43, esp. 31.

33. Tarkovsky, *Sculpting in Time*, 117.

34. See Giovanni Chiaramonte, "The Image as Remembrance," in Chiaramonte and Tarkovsky, *Instant Light*, 119–30, esp. 119–21; Andrei Tarkovsky, *Journal, 1970–1986*, traduit de russe par Anne Kichilov avec Charles H. de Brantes (Paris: Cahiers du cinéma, 2004), 106–11.

35. Johnson and Petrie, *Andrei Tarkovsky*, 116. It is entirely appropriate that many of the first Russian viewers of the film—of Tarkovsky's own generation—saw not so much his or his characters' memories, but their own. See Tarkovsky, *Sculpting in Time*, 10–11; Johnson and Petrie, *Andrei Tarkovsky*, 133.

36. See Vladimir Lossky, *The Mystical Theology of the Eastern Church* (1944; London: James Clarke, 1957), 218; Loughlin, *Alien Sex*, 90–95.

37. Andrei Tarkovsky, *Time Within Time: The Diaries, 1970–1986*, trans. Kitty Hunter-Blair (1991; London: Faber & Faber, 1994), 65 (January 24, 1973).

38. Bulgakov, *Orthodox Church*, 142, 144.

39. Tarkovsky, *Sculpting in Time*, 20–21; Johnson and Petrie, *Andrei Tarkovsky*, 39–40. For similar coproduction in the films of Nicholas Roeg, see Loughlin, *Alien Sex*, 230–31.

40. Tarkovsky, *Sculpting in Time*, 170.

41. "As soon as one begins to cater expressly for the auditorium, then we're talking of the entertainment industry, show business, the masses, or what have you, but certainly not of art which necessarily obeys its own immanent laws of development whether we like it or not." Tarkovsky, *Sculpting in Time*, 170.

42. Andrei Tarkovsky in Chiaramonte and Tarkovsky, *Instant Light*, 16. Earlier versions of this essay were presented at conferences, seminars, and symposia in Durham, Glasgow, Lancaster, and Oxford in the United Kingdom, and in Los Angeles and San Antonio in the United States, and I would like to thank all who responded so generously on those occasions. In particular I would like to thank Catherine Barsotti, Craig Detweiler, Paul Fletcher, Robert Johnston, Terry Lindvall, George Pattison, James K. A. Smith, Elaine Storkey, Norman Stone, and Barry Taylor.

15

Transformative Viewing

Penetrating the Story's Surface

ROBERT K. JOHNSTON

> One's theological method in large part determines one's theological outcomes.
>
> Pamela Dickey Young

Theologians and film critics often find in movies a depth that penetrates beneath the surface of the story. Perhaps such thick descriptions are, in fact, definitional of our enterprise. For example, in her book *Finding Meaning at the Movies*, Sarah Vaux writes: "All of the films in this book have been chosen because they take life from the search for the deeper meanings that lie behind life's surface events and seemingly chance encounters."[1] Roy Anker echoes: "But most movies have a lot more going on than mere diversion or distraction. Like all the arts, traditional and avant-garde, elite and popular, hip and kitsch, movies sometimes offer a way of exploring life's larger riddles and testing out possible solutions to them."[2]

Vaux and Anker are Protestants interested in exploring the dialogical possibilities between theology and film. Andrei Tarkovsky, the Russian Orthodox filmmaker, is less dialogical and more sacramental in expressing his belief that such explorations in film may be "spiritual" in nature. In his book *Sculpting in Time*, his discussion of the film image begins with a quotation from Thomas Mann's *Magic Mountain*: "Let us put it like this: a spiritual—that is, significant—phenomenon is 'significant' precisely because it exceeds its own limits, serves as expression and symbol of something spiritually wider and more universal, an entire world of feelings and thoughts, embodied within it with great or less felicity—that is the measure of its significance."[3] So, too, is the Catholic critic Richard Blake. Criticizing those in the church who want to use film educationally or ethically to make their messages more "relevant and palatable," Blake argues that film can be seen as a "form of divine revelation."[4] Two of my recent books—*Finding God in the Movies* (with Catherine Barsotti) and *Reel Spirituality*[5]—similarly suggest by their very titles that movies have a spiritual capacity inviting exploration. Some can even prove transformative, as the movie *Becket* was in my life and *The Year of Living Dangerously* in Cathy's.[6]

Ed McNulty, a Presbyterian minister and one of the pioneers in the field of theology and film, expresses well these common assumptions of the discipline:

> I believe that *some* filmmakers are . . . attempting to explore the world beneath the surface appearances of life. As genuine artists, they invite us to explore the pain and the joy of being human, to look deeply into ethical issues and dilemmas, and at times to enter into worlds far different from our everyday experience. . . . Such films help us to understand a little better what it is to be a human being and, in a few cases, even to see a little more clearly the emerging kingdom of God.[7]

Multiple examples exist. But though it is easy to find critics who note the depth and breadth of meaning in film—a spiritual center—it is more difficult to describe or delimit what this depth is, let alone define how we might unpack it. Are there guidelines that can be offered? Are there types of criticism that can be recognized? Are there theological precedents that can be mined? Is it possible that recognized methods of theological interpretation could be used to inform film criticism?

Medieval Interpretation: An Unlikely Resource

For some time it has seemed to me that help for the theology and film critic might come from a most unlikely source. Could the medieval method of biblical interpretation, in which multiple levels of meaning are uncovered from the text, help chart a way forward? Could Origen and Cassian, Gregory the Great and Thomas Aquinas, Bernard of Clairvaux and Nicholas of Lyra provide us a hermeneutical key? For these premodern Christian scholars, the "text" in their purview was sacred Scripture—God's "special revelation" to the people of God. Can this strategy for unpacking revelatory text be reapplied to general revelation, to experiencing the sacred in literature and even Hollywood film? I believe the answer is yes.

For over a thousand years, scholars in the Christian church used a fourfold interpretive strategy to help unpack the meaning of the Bible. The text was to first be understood historically (*literally*), before it could be opened up "in faith" producing greater spiritual understanding (*allegorically*), "in love" leading to moral insight and action (*tropologically*), and ultimately "in hope" providing a transcendent experience that was a foretaste of heaven (*anagogically*). Here was a comprehensive method of interpretation, one that discovered through a literal reading of the text a threefold spiritual sense as the reader received instruction in faith from the *past* (allegory) and insight for action toward our neighbors for the *present* (tropology), while contemplating the mystery of divine love in which God's *future* was experienced mystically.

John Cassian (360–465) provided an early example of the use of this *quadriga*, or fourfold sense, by contemplating the city of Jerusalem. On the literal level of history, Jerusalem was a Jewish city set high on a hill in Palestine. According to allegory, it was the church of Christ, proclaiming through word and sacrament its message of salvation. On the tropological level, it was the soul focused on works of love. Finally, on the anagogical level, it was Jerusalem, the heavenly city of gold, our ultimate abode.[8] A mnemonic couplet widely used in medieval schools summarized well this fourfold method:

The letter teaches of deeds,	*Litera gesta docet,*
allegory of what is believed;	*quid credas allegoria;*
morality of what is done,	*moralis quid agas,*
anagoge of things to come.	*quo tendas anagogia.*[9]

Medieval biblical exegetes sought to "know" God—literally, faithfully, lovingly, hopefully. Their goal was to experience the sacred text "from the inside out," receiving God's revelation "formatively within us."[10] To facilitate their inquiry, they developed this fourfold method of interpreting the Scriptures.[11] Harkening back to such church fathers as Origen and Augustine, who recognized the need to approach Scripture with a "double vision—at one and the same time literal and spiritual," their concern was not only with what a text said, but with what it meant.[12] Their contribution over the next thousand years was to delineate more fully how such a spiritual interpretation played itself out in the threefold manner of the theological virtues (in faith, love, and hope; and thus with reference to past, present, and future; or again, in a way that spiritually engaged the interpreter intellectually, socially, and spiritually). There was fluidity in their approach. The progression was not tightly linear, though there was a recognizable logic to its unfolding. Nor was it necessary to always uncover all four senses. Definitions even varied somewhat. Moreover, these medieval church leaders did not believe that it was necessary to interpret every passage of Scripture allegorically. Many texts were plainly stated. John 3:16, for example, nurtured the spiritual life without further allegorization and thus did not need to be interpreted according to some deeper meaning that lay behind or beneath the surface of the text. But other texts demanded a deeper gaze if their spiritual reality was to be known.

Even in their spiritualizing, these theologians did not believe they were "importing meaning into a biblical text." Instead, they were "discerning meanings already present."[13] In the twelfth century Hugh of St. Victor, in his prologue to Ecclesiastes, wrote:

> All Scripture, if expounded according to its own proper meaning [the literal], will gain in clarity and present itself to the reader's intelligence more easily. Many exegetes, who do not understand the virtue of Scripture, cloud over its seemly beauty by irrelevant comments. When they ought to disclose what is hidden, they obscure even that which is plain. I personally blame those who strive superstitiously to find a mystical [anagogical] sense and a deep allegory where none is, as much as those who obstinately deny it, when it is there.[14]

A century later, Thomas Aquinas was even more adamant about grounding all interpretation of the Bible in the literal sense of the text, though for Aquinas the "literal" should allow not only for history but also for metaphor: "The literal sense is not the figure itself, but the thing which is figured."[15] But having made all such qualifiers, what is readily apparent to the student of the Middle Ages is that for the medieval interpreter of Scripture, the text not only has a surface meaning but also embedded within that is a spiritual sense that invites our deepening gaze.

Medieval Biblical Criticism Reapplied

As I have explored how this ancient hermeneutical strategy might be applied more broadly to theology and film criticism, three modern theorists, Mark Burrows, Northrop Frye, and C. S. Lewis, have helped me. All three reapplied the medievalist's insights on reading Scripture to a poetic reading of a text more generally. In the premodern insights of medieval interpreters, they sought a way for the arts to move beyond the sterility of the modern critical enterprise.

Mark S. Burrows

Although Burrows is first of all a historian of Christianity, the focus of his scholarship for some time has been on uncovering a theological poetics for today. The prospect for such, he believes, "has a long precedent in the actual writing of the pre-modern West." He writes, "We find it in the monastic tradition of *allegoresis*, . . . a method of reading 'inscribed in the very logic of the imagination.'"[16] Burrows's concern in particular is with the rediscovery of a manner of listening—or attention—that engages a text holistically. As Burrows portrays it, the monastic reader was interested not merely in the informative, or in extracting the useful or exciting, but in a transformative encounter with the text. Coming expectantly to the Bible, the reader sought to create a living conversation with it. In this sense, an allegorical/spiritual reading of a text was as much a mentality as a method. The allegorical reader believed that "no text—and no life—speaks with a single voice, that every act like every text contains, as Bernard [of Clairvaux] suggests, 'different meanings under one shell.'" Burrows continues:

> As an essentially poetic practice, allegorical reading makes meaning from the material lying readily at hand, precisely in its givenness. It stays rooted in the specificity of what is already visible by rereading images with figurative playfulness as these arise in narrative.[17]

When, for example, Bernard read the Song of Songs, which on the surface was a passionate interchange between two lovers, he "assumed that the poetic narrative meant this but also something more." The literal sense thus became "the basis for interpreting the spiritual life." There was "a resonance of meaning hidden beneath the surfaces of the ordinary and familiar." Contrastingly, argues Burrows, our modern distrust of allegory often means that though we welcome the meaning accessible on the surface, we remain uneasy with what lies hidden beneath the text. We have lost confidence "that meaning may be present even when it is not obvious to us."[18]

Burrows would have us recover the practice of a twofold reading of the text—not merely the literal, but also the allegorical. "For the letter [alone] kills, but the Spirit gives life" (2 Cor. 3:6). He suggests that our vocation as readers, like the poet's, is the art of imagining, where we have a sense of tenderness toward the text, an attentiveness toward the work before us as well as our own experience. The title of one of Burrows's articles captures his intention: "To Taste with the Heart." Burrows concludes this particular reflection on the importance of allegorical interpretation by quoting Emily Dickinson:

> Not "Revelation"—'tis—that waits,
> But our unfurnished eyes—.[19]

Here is our necessary beginning point for any deep engagement with the arts: the "furnishing" of eyes.

Northrop Frye

Where Burrows dealt more generally with the sense of the allegorical as an aid to theological poetics, Northrop Frye used his encyclopedic literary knowledge to help reenvision the medievalist's fourfold method so as to be useful for the reader of literature today (and by extension, those engaged in the arts more widely). I have found two of Frye's lectures, unpublished until recently, to be of particular help. Given at Emory and Henry College in March of 1979, they use Dante's ladder of meaning to present Frye's own theory of literature's "levels of meaning."[20]

Dante, as is well known, took the typical reading of the Bible in his era as his model for the interpretation of all significant secular literature, working out a hermeneutic that progressed through the same four levels of interpretation as the church's reading of the biblical text. Frye notes, for example, how Dante (in his letter to Can Grande) commented on the "polysemous" meaning of one of the Psalms: "When Israel went out from Egypt, the house of Jacob from a people of strange language, Judah became God's sanctuary, Israel his dominion" (Ps. 114:1–2).[21] According to Dante, when Christians first read that sentence, they look at it *literally*. It refers to history, to those events when Israel walked out of Egypt. But Dante realizes, because it is in the Bible in the context of the Psalms, the text means more than this. Dante is led, therefore, to a second level of interpretation, the *allegorical*, which devotes itself to *credenda*, to matters of belief. In his recollection of the Exodus, for example, the whole drama of the gospel is prefigured. When Christians read in the Psalms that Israel came out of Egypt, their larger belief in the biblical story culminating in the Christ event is referenced and made alive. Yet, for Dante, this wider allegorical vision is still incomplete, for this understanding of the Christian faith remains "only an understanding." It has yet to become part of one's full experience, one's life.

What Dante (and Frye!) are interested in is not simply the reader's knowledge of the text but our "possession of it and the incorporation of it into our own experience." "What you really believe is what your actions show you believe," writes Frye.[22] We must move, that is, beyond the *credenda* (from what we believe) to the *agenda* (to what we are to do, to the moral duties incumbent upon the reader). We must act out in love the faith of the past. Here is the *tropological* level of interpretation. Yet even here, the interpreter is not finished, for the moral life ends with death. Thus, we are compelled, in hope, to recognize the *anagogical* sense of the text. There is a spiritual world beyond the finite, the world of eternity, that mysteriously meets us in the here and now. In short, for Frye, as for Dante, "there is a whole universe of significance of which we get glimpses in the arts but which our ordinary experience misses."[23]

C. S. Lewis

As Burrows explored the poetic meaning of a work, he recognized in the medieval mystics a hermeneutical key—an attitude of attentiveness before the text that is required before its power can be experienced. In a similar way, Frye recognized the possibilities of applying Dante's polysemous method of interpretation to secular literature today. There is much in both of their reflections on the written word that is applicable to the arts in general, and to film in particular. That is, there is value in the medieval church's suggestion that a thickness in interpretation should be attended to—that a spiritual depth can be discerned, but only as the literal is opened up to the spiritual. As Emily Dickinson suggests, the problem is not the absence of "general revelation," but the blindness of the filmgoer to see it.

Before turning to several film examples to test our hypothesis, it will be illumining to pause yet again to consider the aesthetic theory of C. S. Lewis. For Lewis, like Burrows and Frye, was at heart a medievalist. Holding the Chair of Medieval and Renaissance English at Cambridge University and having published *The Oxford History of English Literature*, volume 3, *English Literature in the Sixteenth Century, Excluding Drama*, Lewis had a

Making Better Use of Our Theological Traditions

neomedieval understanding of story, one that privileged the subject to which the story might draw us.[24] In approaching a story, he argued, we must surrender ourselves to it. "Look. Listen. Receive," says Lewis. "Get yourself out of the way. (There is no good asking first whether the work before you deserves such a surrender for until you have surrendered you cannot possibly find out.)"[25] Here, again, is the necessary first stage of criticism, the need to receive the story as presented.[26] However, this is only the first stage.

For Lewis, a story is, or should be, more than the succession of events we call plot—more, even, than any excitement felt. A story is the embodiment or mediation of the "more," that is, that which lies beyond the perception of the reader, the horizon or atmosphere that frames our conscious critical day-to-day existence. Plot is important, but only as "a net whereby to catch something else," says Lewis. "The real theme may be and perhaps usually is something that has no sequence in it, something other than a process and much more like a state or quality." For Lewis this something more is not an escape from reality, though it is a reality baffling to the intellect. "It may not be 'like real life' in the superficial sense, but it sets before us an image of what reality may well be like at some more central region."[27] When children, for example, read of enchanted woods, they do not begin to despise the real woods. Rather, "the reading makes all real woods a little enchanted."[28]

According to Lewis, a good story has a mythic quality:

It arouses in us sensations we have never had before, never anticipated having, as though we had broken out of our normal mode of consciousness and "possessed joys not promised to our birth." It gets under our skin, hits us at a level deeper than our thoughts or even our passions, troubles oldest certainties till all questions are reopened, and in general shocks us more fully awake than we are for most of our lives.[29]

Lewis realized that there is no guarantee that a given story will cause a given reader to come alive, to respond in this way. But as the story is encountered openly, its mythmaking potential can best be actualized. For Lewis, his experience with Macdonald's *Phantastes* had been such a mythic event:

It was as though the voice which had called to me from the world's end were now speaking at my side. It was with me in the room or in my body, or behind me. If it had once eluded me by its distance, it now eluded me by its proximity—something too near to see, on this side of knowledge.[30]

Lewis's critical model is perhaps closer to Origen's more general concern with the literal and the spiritual than with Dante's fourfold method. But the air they breathe is similar. In both cases there is a concern that the inner meaning of the story and the reading "self" are grasped together in faith, love, and hope. Lewis writes, for example, of his own experience of longing that story elicited: "I still cannot help thinking . . . that the experiences themselves contained, from the very first, a wholly good element."[31] Or again, Lewis suggests there is almost a mystical contemplation as the "more" is evoked. Here was for Lewis his experience of *Sehnsucht*, what he called "spilled religion." "The unconverted man who licks [these drops] up . . . begins to search for the cup whence they were spilled."[32]

The Medieval Method Reapplied

How then might we proceed concretely in making use of this fourfold method of interpretation with regard to theology and film criticism? A consideration of two widely differing movies can aid our discussion, suggesting how this premodern hermeneutic, so long considered "classic and unquestioned," might once again prove useful, this time for our postmodern age. The first is a small documentary, *March of the Penguins*, filmed by the French and then rescripted for American audiences. It proved to be the surprise hit of the summer of 2005. The other, *Titanic*, which came out in 1997, is the highest grossing blockbuster of all time worldwide. What is it about these movies that captured the viewing public? Could it be that a "thick" viewing of these movies is not only appropriate but has also been the experience of millions of viewers? After testing whether a fourfold method of interpretation does, in fact, illumine the power and meaning of these movies for viewers, we will turn in conclusion to offer several final observations.

March of the Penguins

During the summer of 2005, *March of the Penguins* was a surprise hit with general audiences.[33] Perhaps even more surprisingly, it proved to be at the time the second most blogged movie by Christians (after *The Passion of the Christ*), chiefly because some religious conservatives, both Christian and Jewish, turned its "story" into social propaganda. According to both the *New York Times* and the *Chicago Tribune*, this documentary about the mating ritual and rearing process of emperor penguins was considered by some pundits to be "nothing short of a miraculous allegory about the universality of family values, the value of monogamy, the perversity of gay marriage and the wisdom of intelligent design"![34] Lennard Davis, in his commentary about Jewish and Christian responses to the movie, belittled such "theologizing," questioning how intelligent a design it is to leave penguins no pouch in which to put their egg, or what kind of statement it is regarding monogamy when these birds choose a new mate each year. For him, this "religious" response to the film was yet another example of Judeo-Christian heavy-handedness with regard to culture. And surely it is. Such allegorization brings to mind the words of the Reformer William Tyndale, who reacted to the misuse of the allegorical method in the sixteenth century: "Of what text thou provest hell, will another prove purgatory; another *limbo patrum* . . . and another shall prove of the same text that an ape hath a tail."[35]

Yet though such gnostic misviewings of the movie have mercifully passed into oblivion, the question remains: Is there not a legitimate spiritual viewing of this movie, one that would take seriously what so many Christians and non-Christians alike reported as they engaged the images, music, and words of this film? Was their response simply sentimental manipulation? Might there not legitimately be multiple levels to our experience of the film? What might a Christian response to the movie that followed the leads of medieval interpreters look like?

On the literal level (in this case, the historical/documentary meaning of the text), *March of the Penguins* is a journey into a world most of us will never see or experience—the world of the emperor penguin of Antarctica. In an environment where the average temperature is fifty degrees below zero and gale-force winds blow, the emperors have survived for centuries. While the film is a visual feast from the opening scenes of ice floes to the textured close-ups of the penguins' coats, it is also the poignant story of their survival (wonderfully narrated by Morgan Freeman). We watch the emperors march single file from the sea to their mating area up to seventy miles away (actually it's more of a waddle—when they aren't belly sliding on the ice) followed by elaborate courtship dances and songs and the laying of one egg. Then while the females make the arduous journey back to the sea for food, the males huddle in mass for warmth, each with an egg safely cradled on top of his feet and under his coat. When the mothers return to feed the newly hatched babies, the fathers similarly return to the sea. And so it goes until the summer comes and with it the melting of the ice floes so that the young penguins can enter the ocean and begin their life in the sea. Four years later, they too will return to the place where they were born and continue the cycle of life.

March of the Penguins is, however, more than simply eighty minutes of penguin "sex," though it is also that. For many viewers, it also brings with it a heightened understanding about life, all life. As we experience these penguins, the film opens us out to our own struggles for survival, our own need to protect and care for our "family" and children. Somehow in the penguin's dance of survival, where timing is everything, we comprehend something about ourselves. We too have our struggles for survival; we too need to give and receive protection; we too must respond at the right time. What might otherwise be theoretical is made visceral.[36] The amazing truth of the movie is this: in my vicarious identification with these penguins, my understanding is enlarged. *March of the Penguins* is not simply about the lives of some birds that waddle; it also sheds light on our lives—all creatures big and small. Despite its brutal hardships and unforgiving ways, even life in the Antarctic is precious. There is a resonance, the particular opening out onto a larger meaning.

As the wonder of creation is portrayed, however, more than the broadening of our understanding can take place for some. *March of the Penguins* invites viewers to respond holistically to the images they encounter. Our responsibility must be somehow to work as hard as these penguins do to preserve life. In his critique of conservative Christian reactions to the movie, Davis says that when he went to see the film, he was left thinking: "How could there be a god that would subject the poor penguin to such horrendously difficult reproductive technology?" And as to the notion of loving families, it seemed strange to him that "the mothers and fathers abandon their chick to return to the sea when the chicks seem knee-high to a grasshopper, never to see them again."[37] But surely this is not the point of view of the film. It is wonder, not cynicism, that sets the tone for this movie (helped, of course, by the photography, the music, and the majestic voice of Morgan Freeman). Though a few females are portrayed trying to steal the eggs of others after the loss of their own due to the clumsiness of their mates, this only reinforces the movie's larger perspective of the sanctity of life—all life. Given the winter, everyone must do her or his part to help their world survive. Seeing these birds huddle together for survival, the perspective of the Preacher comes to mind: "If two lie together, they keep warm; but how can one keep warm alone?" (Eccles. 4:11). Here is the film's unspoken but enacted *agenda* (something that goes beyond simple *credenda*). We have a moral duty to act out in love our commitment to life, all life.

And finally, as viewers, some of us will marvel not only at creation and creature, but also at the choreography of the Creator. Mystery and ambiguity remain, but so too does wonder. The ancient sage wrote:

For everything there is a season, and a time for every matter under heaven: a time to be born and a time to die. . . . He has put a sense of past and future [i.e., "eternity"] into their minds, yet they cannot find out what God has done from the beginning to the end. I know there is nothing better for them than to be happy and enjoy themselves as long as they live; moreover, it is God's gift that all should eat and drink and take pleasure in all their toil." (Eccles. 3:1–2a, 11b–13).

Even if our "times" remain shrouded in mystery, their sacred center can be discerned. The filmmakers imbue *March of the Penguins* with such humor, fear, pain, suffering, joy, and love that for many viewers, the reality of the Creator is not in doubt. *Penguins* might not be an argument for intelligent design, or propaganda for the perversity of gay marriage, but it has provided many viewers an experience of transcendence.

In this way one can take note of particular moments, or critical aspects, of our viewing of *Penguins*. There is, or can be, literal, allegorical, tropological, and anagogical viewings of the movie. But it is also the case that the receptive process for the filmgoer is a much more organic, interactive conversation between the film's story and our stories than this schematic might seem to suggest. During the summer of 2005, my wife and I saw this movie (it was our second time) with two friends who were in the midst of a vocational crisis as the husband finished his schooling. They were struggling with whether they could risk their future by having the young father take the job he felt prepared (even "called") to do, even though it would not provide a livable salary. Though the mother could continue to work part-time, the new job most likely would mean struggle and insecurity for both of them, and daycare for their baby. A more secure, yet less compelling, position was also available. We went to the movie not thinking about such life circumstances, but only to enjoy the experience, which we all did. In fact, the movie proved so overpowering that at coffee afterward, no one could really say much. But the next day our friends told us that, after reflecting together on their experience in the theater, they had decided to risk the unknown with regard to his job: "If God can take care of these 'stupid' penguins, surely God can take care of us as well." The movie had engaged our friends holistically, providing them greater understanding of life's adventure, concrete guidance as to their appropriate action, and energizing hope as they trusted the Creator for their future. None of this could have been predicted ahead of time, and certainly not manipulated. Their response was simply the result of the living conversation they had with a movie about emperor penguins and their survival. There was a re-viewing of the images with a spiritual "playfulness" that arose out of the film itself. Our friends had had a transformative encounter with the movie.[38]

Titanic

Many dismiss the movie *Titanic* (1997) as "popcorn" fare, and it is for some, perhaps most. But for millions of others, the viewing experience proved to be more. To give one example: Michael Flaherty—the founder of Walden Media, which has brought to the screen such best-selling books for children as *Holes, Because of Winn-Dixie, The Chronicles of Narnia: The Lion, the Witch and the Wardrobe, Bridge to Terabithia*, and *Charlotte's Web*—tells of the time in 1998 when he was still teaching junior high in the public schools in urban Dorchester, near Boston. Trying to connect with his uninterested and nonreading students, he asked them what they had done over the weekend. Most of them had the same answer: "We saw *Titanic*." The following Monday he asked the same question, and to his surprise he got the same answer. They had gone again to see *Titanic*. The next Monday, several shared that over the weekend they had gone to a ship museum in Boston, fascinated with what they had first seen in the movie. And the next weekend, others talked about going to the library to check out books on the *Titanic*. And thus the "reverse" mission for his company was born—one that translates classic children's books onto the giant screen in the hope of interesting kids in reading the books!

The film story for *Titanic* functions simultaneously on several levels. It is, of course, a *disaster* movie "about" the sinking of a seemingly invincible ocean liner on its maiden voyage (the third-most-written-about historical event in the twentieth century). The filmmakers, particularly the artistic directors and set designers, were meticulous in creating an exact replica of the ship, right down to the wallpaper and china in the ship's dining room. And director James Cameron's use of documentary footage of the ship's wreckage, now two and a half miles below the surface of the sea, opens the movie and fast-forwards that history into our present. The movie is also a love story between Jack and Rose. It is an old-fashioned *romance*, in which the commoner sweeps the society girl off her feet, helping her escape from her privileged but narrowly constricted world into a life of adventure and fulfillment. Many critics feel that the chemistry between Kate Winslet (Rose) and Leonardo DiCaprio (Jack) makes the movie work.

Yet *Titanic* is also a *message* movie portraying how two people overcome class differentiation. It depicts an ethically better way in which the upstairs-downstairs dichotomy of British society is rejected. We as viewers are appalled as those in the third-class cabins are allowed to drown, while those in first class are helped into lifeboats. And finally, the movie's story is *mythically* shaped around a Christ figure, an "innocent" Jack sacrificing his life so that Rose might live. As the movie closes, Rose finishes her telling of the story by saying, "He saved me in every way that a person can be saved." Here is the perspective through which the entire story is presented. Together, these four interwoven stories provide the *literal* foundation for the movie.

But viewers also respond spiritually. As we watch the movie, Rose's story also becomes our own story (this is why so many viewers returned for multiple viewings, for they found themselves in the movie). The compelling power of her story allows us to understand in a new way the importance of trust and to recognize that it is in community that we find our true humanity. Her retelling also brings to reality a new sense of possibility to women, who understand, in ways that words alone cannot convey, the freedom and wholeness that was Jack's gift to Rose. Here is an *allegorical* take on the movie's meaning, one that sheds new light on our own existence.

On still another level the film encourages us ethically to fight prejudice, to oppose materialism, and to recognize hubris. *Titanic* challenges our deep-seated trust in technology and brings to light our own sense of class, whether that be in regard to the immigrant debate going on at present in Congress or the continuation of third-world sweatshops that allow our clothing to remain inexpensive. Although Rose has a place in the lifeboat because of her station, she relinquishes her privilege in order to try to help Jack survive. Here is a *tropological* viewing.[39] And ultimately, in the sacrificial love of Jack, we experience something of the shape of our own salvation, as well. As the movie ends, we see Rose drop the large diamond, which she had long ago been given, into the ocean where Jack lies below. Through his life and death, Jack provided Rose meaning and fullness; she needs no additional crutch or guarantee. Jack's is a love that has transcended all limitation, even a watery grave. Here is the *anagogical*.

The real success of the movie *Titanic* derives from its ability to open up organically to such a thick, spiritual viewing—one that points outward in faith, love, and hope beyond the movie's story line to the reality of something that transcends our finitude. It has allowed many to journey on what Michel de Certeau calls "an itinerary . . . that is the meaning of experience."[40] Or to quote Emily Dickinson once again:

> Not "Revelation"—'tis—that waits,
> But our unfurnished eyes—.[41]

Film Viewers: Mystics of the Quotidian

Some movies invite viewers not only to be entertained, but also to be transformed.[42] They offer their audience not just another set of disclosures, but a means of being disclosed. In this sense film is like other art. It provides its viewers "not a version of the facts, but an entirely different way of seeing."[43] Kafka's challenge to readers in his day is to the point for all who engage the arts, even in its hyperbole: "If the book you are reading [movie you are watching, music you are hearing] does not wake us, as with a fist hammering on our skull, why then do we read it? . . . A book must be like an ice-axe to break the frozen sea within us."[44] At their best, movies engage with their viewers in ways that can productively transform our attitudes, actions, and horizons, even our interpersonal, communal, and spiritual possibilities. Here is the experience of many who saw *March of the Penguins* and *Titanic.*

Of course, not all movies allow this deeper gaze. *Mission: Impossible III* (2006) and *Basic Instinct 2* (2006) exhaust their interpretive possibilities at the surface level of their narrative. They are expendable, like paperback murder mysteries that one buys to be distracted on an airplane and then discards. But other movies invite something akin to the medievalist's contemplation, a contemplation that cannot be contained. These films tend to endure. The Internet Movie Database (IMDb) ranks the favorite movies of all time, based on responses from its massive readership.[45] There is the occasional "mere entertainment" movie that shows up: *Raiders of the Lost Ark* (1981) comes in sixteenth and *The Sting* (1973), eighty-second. But the overwhelming majority of movies listed have demonstrated the power to shape and transform their viewers (could there be a causal connection?). Here are the top twelve listed: *The Godfather* (1972), *The Shawshank Redemption* (1994), *The Godfather, Part II* (1974), *The Lord of the Rings: The Return of the King* (2003), *The Good, the Bad and the Ugly* (1966), *Casablanca* (1942), *Schindler's List* (1993), *Pulp Fiction* (1994), *The Seven Samurai* (1954), *Star Wars Episode V—The Empire Strikes Back* (1980), *Star Wars* (1977), and *One Flew over the Cuckoo's Nest* (1975). As in all art, movie pulp and the sentimental fade, but that which invites viewers to linger tends to endure.

Notes

1. Sarah Vaux, *Finding Meaning at the Movies* (Nashville: Abingdon, 1999), xiv.
2. G. Roy Anker, *Catching Light* (Grand Rapids: Eerdmans, 2004), 217.

Making Better Use of Our Theological Traditions

3. Andrei Tarkovsky, *Sculpting in Time*, rev. ed., trans. Kitty Hunter-Blair (Austin: University of Texas Press, 1989), 104.

4. Richard Blake, "Secular Prophecy in an Age of Film," *Journal of Religious Thought* 27, no. 1 (Spring–Summer 1970): 63, 69; cf. Richard Blake, "From Peepshow to Prayer: Toward a Spirituality of the Movies," *Journal of Religion and Film* 6, no. 2 (October 2002), www .unomaha.edu/wwwjrf/peepshow.htm, where Blake asks, "Is it possible that film viewing may lead the imagination down a path that approaches prayer?"

5. Catherine Barsotti and Robert K. Johnston, *Finding God in the Movies: 33 Films of Reel Faith* (Grand Rapids: Baker Books, 2004); Robert K. Johnston, *Reel Spirituality: Theology and Film in Dialogue*, 2nd ed. (Grand Rapids: Baker Academic, 2006).

6. See Johnston, *Reel Spirituality,* 287–89.

7. Edward McNulty, *Praying the Movies* (Louisville: Geneva, 2001), ix.

8. Cf. David Steinmetz, "Calvin and the Irrepressible Spirit," *Ex Auditu* 12 (1996): 94–107; Beryl Smalley, *The Study of the Bible in the Middle Ages* (New York: Philosophical Library, 1952), 28; Henri de Lubac, *Medieval Exegesis,* vol. 2, *The Four Senses of Scripture* (Grand Rapids: Eerdmans, 2000), 199.

9. Quoted in Richard A. Muller, *Dictionary of Latin and Greek Theological Terms* (Grand Rapids: Baker Academic, 1985), 255, s.v. "Quadriga."

10. Eugene Peterson, *Eat This Book: A Conversation in the Art of Spiritual Reading* (Grand Rapids: Eerdmans, 2006), 59.

11. This fourfold method was fluid, with countless variations in practice, and was more often implicit than explicit. The publication of Henri de Lubac's magisterial study, *The Four Senses of Scripture*, points out the wide variations. Yet as Kevin Hughes states, "de Lubac . . . argues that ancient and medieval Christians carried out an interpretive practice, or, even more, a reality of the relationship between Scripture and the life of faith, that they may not fully have comprehended," ("The 'Fourfold Sense': De Lubac, Blondel and Contemporary Theology," *Heythrop Journal* 42 [2001]: 451–62).

12. This was based on Paul's use of allegory (cf. his discussion of Sarah and Hagar in Gal. 4:21–5:1) and his comment that "the letter kills, but the Spirit gives life," 2 Cor. 3:6). For much of this paragraph, I am indebted to the careful scholarship of David Steinmetz, "Calvin and the Irrepressible Spirit," 94–107, and "The Superiority of Pre-Critical Exegesis," *Theology Today* 37, no. 1 (April 1980): 27–38.

13. Such spiritual discernment was not easy. Its practice required a mature disciple of Christ. Moreover, it required the believing community, the church. "Biblical interpretation was . . . by its very nature a communal activity conducted by people who participate in the reality of which the biblical text speaks." Steinmetz, "Calvin," 96.

14. Hugh of St. Victor, quoted in Smalley, *Bible in the Middle Ages*, 100.

15. Thomas Aquinas, *Summa Theologiae* (part 1, quest. 1, art. 10).

16. Mark S. Burrows, "'Raiding the Inarticulate': Mysticism, Poetics, and the Unlanguage-able," in *Minding the Spirit: The Study of Christian Spirituality*, ed. Elizabeth A. Dreyer and Mark S. Burrows (Baltimore: Johns Hopkins University Press, 2005), 346.

17. Mark S. Burrows, "'To Taste with the Heart': Allegory, Poetics and the Deep Reading of Scripture," *Interpretation* (April 2002): 175.

18. Ibid., 173–77.

19. Poem 685, in *Complete Poems of Emily Dickinson* (Boston: Little, Brown, 1960), 228, quoted in ibid., 180.

20. Northrop Frye, "Reconsidering Levels of Meaning," *Christianity and Literature* 54, no. 3 (Spring 2005): 397–421. Frye later incorporated these ideas into the final chapter of his *The Great Code* (1982), and again in the opening chapter of *Words with Power* (1990). Cf. Northrop Frye, *The Great Code: The Bible and Literature* (New York: Harcourt Brace Jovanovich, 1982) and Frye, *Words with Power* (San Diego: Harcourt Brace Jovanovich, 1990).

21. The text reads, "For the elucidation, therefore of what we have to say, it must be understood that the meaning of this work is not of one kind only; rather the work may be described as 'polysemous,' that is, having several meanings; for the first meaning is that which is conveyed by the letter, and the next is that which is conveyed by what the letter signifies; the former of which is called literal, while the latter is called allegorical, or mystical. And for the better illustration of this method of exposition we may apply it to the following verse: 'When Israel went out of Egypt, the house of Jacob from a people of strange language; Judah was his sanctuary, and Israel his dominion.' For if we consider the letter alone, the thing signified to us is the going out of the children of Israel from Egypt in the time of Moses; if the allegory, our redemption through Christ is signified; if the moral sense, the conversion of the soul from the sorrow and misery of sin to a state of grace is signified; and if the anagogical, the passing of the sanctified soul from the bondage of the corruption of this world to the liberty of everlasting glory is signified." Quoted in Joseph Anthony Mazzeo, *Structure and Thought in the "Paradiso"* (Ithaca, NY: Cornell University Press, 1958), 31–32.

22. Frye, "Levels of Meaning," 417.

23. Ibid., 419. Living as he did within Christendom, Dante might have understood this truth more narrowly than we can today, certainly more narrowly than Northrop Frye did. Nonetheless, Frye recognized the possibilities of using this schema, which Dante had applied to his own *Commedia*, as a methodology for interpreting secular literature today.

24. Cf. William Dyrness, "Art" (unpublished manuscript). For a fuller description of Lewis's understanding of story, see my discussion in "Image and Content: The Tension in C. S. Lewis' Chronicles of Narnia," *Journal of the Evangelical Theological Society* 20 (September 1977): 253–64.

25. C. S. Lewis, *An Experiment in Criticism* (Cambridge: Cambridge University Press, 1961), 19.

26. In his *Experiment in Criticism*, Lewis draws an analogy with sculpture: "An 'appreciation' of sculpture which ignored the statue's shape in favour of the sculptor's 'view of life' would be self-deception. It is by the shape that it is a statue. Only because it is a statue do we come to be mentioning the sculptor's view of life at all" (p. 84).

27. C. S. Lewis, "On Stories," *Essays Presented to Charles Williams*, ed. C. S. Lewis (Grand Rapids: Eerdmans, 1966), 103, 101.

28. C. S. Lewis, "On Three Ways of Writing for Children," reprinted in C. S. Lewis, *Of Other Worlds* (London: Geoffrey Bles, 1968), 30.

29. C. S. Lewis, "Introduction," *George MacDonald: An Anthology*, ed. C. S. Lewis (New York: Macmillan, 1954), 16–17.

30. C. S. Lewis, *Surprised by Joy* (New York: Harcourt, Brace & World, 1955), 180.

31. C. S. Lewis, "Christianity and Culture," in *Christian Reflections*, ed. Walter Hooper (Grand Rapids: Eerdmans, 1967), 23, quoted in Dyrness, "Art."

32. Lewis, "Christianity and Culture," footnote to the above passage, quoted in Dyrness, "Art."

33. *March of the Penguins* was produced for $8 million and grossed close to $100 million worldwide (over $77 million in the United States alone). The movie spawned a plethora of spin-offs: illustrated books both for adults ($30, 160 pages) and for children ($5.95, 32 pages), boxer shorts with penguins on them at the Gap, travel opportunities to penguin habitats. The *Los Angeles Times* ("Where Penguins Rule the Roost," December 4, 2005, L9), e.g., had a full-page feature on penguins in their travel section! Wrote Tony Wheeler, "So if you've seen 'March of the Penguins' and now want to see those fabulous fowl, it's easier (and cheaper) than it has ever been."

34. Lennard J. Davis, "Penguins: A Poor Case for Intelligent Design, Family Values," *Chicago Tribune*, November 6, 2005, sec. 2, p. 3; e.g., Michael Medved is quoted as praising the movie because it "passionately affirms traditional norms like monogamy, sacrifice and child rearing."

Making Better Use of Our Theological Traditions

Medved continued, "This is 'The Passion of the Penguins,'" comparing this documentary to *The Passion of the Christ*.

35. William Tyndale, *The Obedience of a Christian Man* (1528), quoted in Anthony Thiselton, *New Horizons in Hermeneutics* (Grand Rapids: Zondervan, 1992), 190.

36. *March of the Penguins* provides no political agenda about human life as intended by the Creator (here is the mistake that Lennard Davis ridicules regarding the response of the conservative right). But it does offer insight concerning "life," all life—particularly my own life.

37. Davis, "Penguins," sec. 2, p. 3.

38. Perhaps a comparison can further clarify this "thick description." *Winged Migration* (2001) was another French-produced nature documentary, also with spectacular photography and portrayals of survival. It too was about birds, though this time those that soared effortlessly. However, lacking a compelling narrative structure—a story—it failed to transport most viewers beyond the surface beauty of the images (though the surface beauty is no small feat in itself). The analogical, the moral, and the transcendent dimensions of this movie remained largely absent, despite the stunning visuals. And the box office receipts reflected this lack: $11 million for birds that flew, verses $77 million for birds that waddled but a film that soared!

39. Denny Wayman and Hal Conklin, on their Internet site Cinema in Focus, write: "The lessons of the 'Titanic' are of such a human nature that it speaks directly to the soul. Though we may be able to survive we will never thrive as a people or as individuals until we learn how to love with a commitment that is able to sacrifice ourselves for the sake of others"; "Titanic," www.cinemainfocus.com/Titanic_4.htm. Wayman and Conklin's response remains to a certain degree theoretical, given the fact they are writing to a generic Web site audience. David Dark provides a more vivid example of the ethical possibility of film as he reflects on the effect of his seeing *The Mission* as a teenager: "The preview had gotten my attention with a crucified Jesuit being sent over a waterfall in South America. And as Jeremy Irons' Father Gabriel next went back up it, extending and embodying good news to the Guardini tribe, . . . I was pummeled by one scene after another of lived Christian witness. As I tried to recover myself from the devastating final scenes (in tears, exiting the theater. . .) . . . I wanted to be a part of it. I wanted to try to be an envoy of God's mercy as well as a recipient." David Dark, "God with Us (and Them)," *Books and Culture* 12, no. 3 (May/June 2006): 26.

40. Michel de Certeau, quoted in Mark S. Burrows, "Raiding the Inarticulate," 354.

41. Dickinson, quoted in ibid.

42. Kathleen Norris, herself one who has been deeply influenced by the life and thought of the monastics, writes: "I have come to believe that the true mystics of the quotidian are not those who contemplate holiness in isolation, reaching godlike illumination in serene silence, but those who manage to find God in a life filled with noise, the demands of other people and relentless daily duties that can consume the self." Quoted in Peterson, *Eat This Book*, 111.

43. Jeanette Winterson, *Art Objects, Essays on Ecstasy and Effrontery* (New York: Alfred A. Knopf, 1997), 28, quoted in Burrows, "Raiding the Inarticulate," 349.

44. Quoted by George Steiner, *Language and Silence* (New York: Atheneum, 1970), 67, as quoted in Peterson, *Eat This Book*, 8.

45. As of December 30, 2006.

Movies Cited

Usual Suspects (d. Bryan Singer, 1995) 174

Vagabond (d. Agnés Varda, 1985) 104n8, 106n17
Vampyr (d. Carl Theodor Dreyer, 1931) 93, 95, 106n17
Vera Drake (d. Mike Leigh, 2005) 104n8, 104n17
Vertigo (d. Alfred Hitchcock, 1958) 57, 90, 98, 105n17, 141
Volver (d. Pedro Almodóvar, 2006) 90, 105n17

Walk in the Clouds, A (d. Alfonso Arau, 1995) 195
Wend Kuuni (d. Gaston Kaboré, 1982) 82
Werckmeister Harmonies (d. Béla Tarr, 2000) 101, 105n17
What Dreams May Come (d. Vincent Ward, 1998) 88, 106n17
White, White Day, A (d. Andrei Tarkovsky, 1975) 290, 301n7
Who Framed Roger Rabbit? (d. Robert Zemeckis, 1988) 235

Willy Wonka and the Chocolate Factory (d. Mel Stuart, 1971) 183
Wind That Shakes the Barley, The (d. Ken Loach, 2006) 104n8, 104n17
Wind Will Carry Us, The (d. Abbas Kiarostami, 1999) 47, 99, 100, 105n17
Winged Migration (d. Jacques Perrin, 2001) 321n38
Wings of Desire (d. Wim Wenders, 1987) 92, 106n17
Winter Light (d. Ingmar Bergman, 1962) 92, 106n17
Witness (d. Peter Weir, 1985) 131
World, The (d. Zhang Ke Jia, 2004) 104n17

X-Men (d. Bryan Singer, 2000) 25n5

Year of Living Dangerously, The (d. Peter Weir, 1982) 131, 244, 256n26, 305
Yi-Yi (d. Edward Yang, 2000) 105n17
Y Tu Mama También (d. Alfonso Cuarón, 2001) 196

General Index

abilities, cognitive, 227–28
abstraction, visual, 41
academia, film in, 33–36
accommodation, phase of, 170–72
action, coping, 226–27
action, film. *See* movement, film
affect. *See* emotion
affective intentionality, fiction-directive, 221
Affect Program Theory, 227–29
African film, 82
Albigensianism, 269
allegorical level, interpretive, 26n18, 306–9
anagogical level, interpretive, 26n18, 306–7
anatomy, emotional, 228
anthropomorphic thinking, 171
appraisal/reappraisal model, 225–27
Aristotle, 231
art, film as, 175–77
assimilation, phase of, 170–72
atmosphere, 55–56
attendance, movie theater, 181, 183
attentiveness, viewer's, 158
audience. *See* experience, viewer's
avoidance, coping by, 226–27
awards, film, 73–74, 78–79
awareness, levels of, 165, 170

basic emotions, 227
Bazin, André, 40
behavioral circumscription, 221
beliefs. *See* ideologies, cultural; normative
    analysis
biblical literacy, 127, 132
Blaxploitation films, 63
Block, Bruce, 37–38
body, human, 32
Bonhoeffer, Dietrich, 243–47
boundary maintenance, 84
Braudy, Leo, 39–40, 43

breaking out, discovery and, 169–70
Bultmann, Rudolf, 248–53
Burrows, Mark S., 308–9
Burstyn v. Wilson, 277

Calvinism. *See* Puritanism
capabilities, affective, 227–28
Catholicism
    film festivals and, 73–74, 77–79
    Jansenism, 267–73
    Latinas and, 190–91
    Legion of Decency, 275–76
    rating systems and, 274, 278–80, 282–83,
        285n46
    Vigilanti cura, 86n24
causation, sense of, 171
character, music and, 60–62, 63–64
childhood development, 170–72, 228
Christ, mind of, 232–33
church history. *See* historical studies
circumscription, behavioral, 221
closed films, 40–44
codes, meaning and, 65–66
cognitive development, 170–72, 228
cognitive theory, 222–30
colonialism, film and, 82–83
color, musical, 55–56
colorscript, 37–38
comedy, 150–51
community, religious. *See* religion,
    institutional
concrete thinking, 171
congregations. *See* religion, institutional
connections. *See* discovery, knowledge and
consumerism, religious, 115–16, 118–19. *See*
    also subjectivity, spiritual
content, film, 277–83
context, cultural, 132–33, 238–41, 280–83
cool, concept of, 64–65

coping mechanisms, emotional, 226–27
courts, film ratings and, 276–78
Cox, Harvey, 256n41
criteria, emotional, 224–25
cues, emotional, 225, 229–30
cultural codes, 66
cultural ideologies. *See* ideologies, cultural
cultural isolation. *See* isolation, cultural
culture, popular, 59–65, 150
Cupitt, Don, 242

Decency, Legion of, 275–76
DeLancey, Craig, 225, 227–29
demographics, US, 180–81
demythologization, 23, 248–53
development, cognitive, 170–72, 228
development, personal. *See* subjectivity,
  spiritual
Deweyian-Sartarin view, 223
dialectical materialism, 220
dialogue
  film, 57
  interdisciplinary, 21–22, 109–23, 127–41,
    206–9
  interreligious, 73–74, 205–6, 209–17
didacticism, 153–56, 157
diegetic emotion, 230
difference. *See* racism
differentiation. *See* boundary maintenance
directors, film, 37–43
discovery, knowledge and, 163–65, 169–70
displacement, discipline of, 157–58. *See also*
  escapism
displacement, emotional, 228
doctrine. *See* didacticism
documentary films, 79–80
dramatic codes, 66
dwelling, discovery and, 169–70
dwelling, spirituality of, 114

editing, film, 39
Eisenstein, Sergei, 39
electronic music, 69n26
emotion
  music and, 54, 56–57, 58–59, 65–66
  in normative analysis, 221–22, 233–36
  theories of, 23, 222–30
entertainment. *See* escapism; leisure
epistemology, 163–78
equilibration, phase of, 170–72
escapism, 147–50, 153–56, 157–59

ethnography. *See* racism
exclusion, cultural. *See* racism
existentialism, Heideggerean, 257n52
experience, viewer's
  cultural ideology and, 111–12, 179–96
  emotional, 23, 219–36
  epistemology of, 162–78
  film selection and, 95–97
  music and, 58–59
  studies of, 22, 137–38, 145–60

Feijoada, 200n59
festivals, film, 73–74, 78–79
fiction, paradox of, 221–22, 229
film history. *See* historical studies
filmmaking, 37–38
film studies. *See* academia, film in
foreign films. *See* world cinema
foreignness, concept of, 74–76
form, human, 32
formalism, cinematic, 39–43
formalism, ideological, 220
fourfold interpretation. *See* interpretation,
  levels of
freedom, intellectual. *See* didacticism
free will, human, 40–41
Frye, Northrop, 309–10
fun. *See* escapism

gender. *See* women, film and
Gnosticism, 269, 284n21
goodness, question of, 96

habits, meaning-making, 152
Hays Production Code, 273–74
heart, language of, 231–32
Heidegger, Martin, 257n52
Hendershot, Heather, 140–41
Hermann, Bernard, 55
hierarchy, cognitive, 227–29
Hispanic culture. *See* Latinas
historical studies, 21, 127–41
Hollywoodcentrism, 20, 76. *See also* world
  cinema
Homer Project, 136
hope, filmic, 216–17

iconoclasm, 31–33
icons, 24, 32, 44–46, 296–97, 300–301. *See
  also* imagery, film
identity. *See* racism

ideologies, cultural, 110–13, 179–96,
    205–17, 219–22. *See also* normative
    analysis
idolatry, imagery and, 31–33
imagery, film, 19, 24, 29–48, 294–97,
    300–301
imagination, theological, 184
immanence, 35, 39–43
immediacy, experiential, 41
impact, media, 280
indexes, semiotic, 44
individual, cult of the, 117
individualization, spiritual. *See* subjectivity,
    spiritual
influence, media, 280–81
institutions, religious. *See* religion,
    institutional
intentionality, emotional, 221, 223, 228–29
interdisciplinary dialogue. *See* dialogue,
    interdisciplinary
interiority, religious. *See* subjectivity, spiritual
international films. *See* world cinema
interpretation, levels of, 24–25, 26n18,
    305–18, 320`n21
interreligious dialogue. *See* dialogue,
    interreligious
introspection, personal, 116
intuition, knowledge and, 164
isolation, cultural, 20, 74–76, 79–84, 152.
    See also world cinema

Jansenism, 267–73, 284n21
journalism, religious origins of, 139
juries, film. *See* awards, film

Kieślowski, Krzysztof, 41
knowing, tacit, 22, 167. *See also* epistemol-
    ogy; experience, viewer's
Kuleshov effect, 39

Latinas, 22, 179–96
Lefebvre, Marcel, 270
Legion of Decency, 275–76
leisure, 264–65
levels, awareness, 165, 170
levels, interpretive. *See* interpretation, levels of
Lewis, C. S., 310–12
liminality, imagery of, 41
literacy, biblical, 127, 132
literal level, interpretive, 306–7
literature, film and. *See* narrative, film

Manichaeism, 269
map, visual, 37–38
markers, emotion, 230
Marxist critique, 220
materialism, dialectical, 220
materiality, filmic, 295–97
meaning, making of. *See also* experience,
    viewer's
    epistemology and, 163–78
    with images, 39
    music and, 56, 65–66
    studies of, 22, 137–38, 150–56
mechanisms, coping, 226–27
Medieval interpretation. *See* interpretation,
    levels of
mimesis, 221–22
modularity, cognitive, 227–29
Mood-Cue Approach, 225, 229–30
morality. *See* normative analysis
moral level, interpretive, 26n18, 306–7
Motion Picture Production Code of 1930.
    See Hays Production Code
movement, film, 57–58, 68n6
multitasking, 158
music, film, 19–20, 51–67
Mutual Film Corp. v. Industrial, 276
myth, 23, 248–53, 311

narrative, film. *See also* story, nature of
    emotion and, 224–25, 230
    music and, 55–56, 62–64, 66–67
    textuality of, 19, 36–44
    world cinema and, 83
nature, symbolic, 291–97
New Audience Research, 137. *See also*
    experience, viewer's
nonfictive affect, 221
normative analysis. *See also* ideologies,
    cultural
    film selection and, 95–97
    as interreligious dialogue, 23, 205–17
    modern theologies and, 238–55
    ratings systems and, 261–83
    viewer experience and, 153, 158–59,
    219–22, 230–36
novel, eighteenth-century, 116, 119–20

objectivity, 163–65, 169, 223
OCIC, 77–79. *See also* Catholicism
open films, 40–44
orientational pluralism, 218n5
Other, the, 81–82. *See also* racism

transformation, viewer, 95–97. *See also* experience, viewer's
tropological level, interpretive, 26n18, 306–7
turn, subjective. *See* subjectivity, spiritual
two-stage model, emotional, 225–27

United States v. Paramount, 277
uses and gratification (U&G) studies, 137

values. *See* ideologies, cultural; normative analysis
veneration, iconic, 300–301
viewer, effects on. *See* experience, viewer's

viewing practices. *See* selection, viewing
Vigilanti cura, 86n24
violence, filmic, 214–16
virtue, Aristotelian, 231
visual elements, film. *See* imagery, film
Volf, Miroslav, 81–82

will, human, 40–41
women, film and, 179–96
Woolen, Peter, 44–45
word-based faith, 31–33
world cinema, 20–21, 73–85, 152
worship, entertainment and, 156

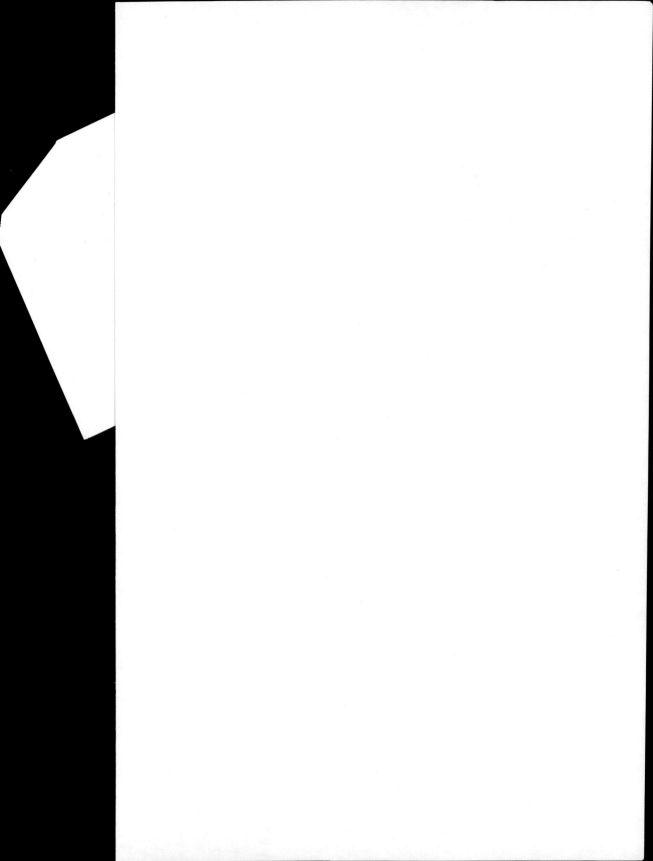